Alvan Stewart, Luther Rawson Marsh

Writings and Speeches of Alvan Stewart on Slavery

Alvan Stewart, Luther Rawson Marsh

Writings and Speeches of Alvan Stewart on Slavery

ISBN/EAN: 9783337412777

Printed in Europe, USA, Canada, Australia, Japan

Cover: Foto ©Suzi / pixelio.de

More available books at **www.hansebooks.com**

WRITINGS AND SPEECHES

OF

ALVAN STEWART,

ON SLAVERY.

A. B. BURDICK, 145 NASSAU STREET.
1860.

GENERAL CONTENTS.

PREFACE.

It was originally the design of the compiler to have appended the writings and speeches of Mr. Stewart, as well on slavery as other topics, to a memoir of his life, now in preparation. But the variety and length of these anti-slavery productions, and the peculiar interest with which these questions are now debated, have induced me to publish, some entire and some in part, selections of his speeches and writings relating to that tangled problem, whose present is so fraught with difficulty and danger, and whose future hangs portentously in cloud. We may hope, I think, that if there can be any solution, by mortals, of this great and complicated subject, it will be discovered by the earnest gaze of millions of men, now directed to it. And when an original thinker like Mr. Stewart, moved by disinterested impulse, and an ardent love of truth, has for years applied the powers of his mind to a consideration of the problem, in all its ramifications, it may aid the national discussion of it—employing, or destined soon to employ, the tongues and pens of the whole country—if the opinions and arguments, thus wrought out in the first stage of the controversy, shall be gathered and given to the public—if right, to triumph, if wrong, to suffer overthrow.

Among the earliest and most persistent of those who enlisted to resist the aggression of the slave power, and to combat the injustice of the slave system, a full history of his labors and coöperation, would reveal the thorny path which these reformers were obliged to tread, and the mode by which the mighty question, from being generally ignored and buried in forgetfulness, has, amid the stormiest opposition and the fiercest threats, now at last, in the space of twenty-seven years, loomed up in its gigantic proportions, before the anxious gaze of the Republic and the world. But as my object here is to let the arguments of Mr. Stewart stand or fall by themselves, I have only space to give, independent of what may be obtained from the writings themselves, a cursory view of a few of the prominent events of his career, as connected with this topic.

Those who may read these addresses will be surprised, I doubt not, that the author, in the very opening of the discussion, should have so fully surveyed the subject in its length and breadth, with a glance at once so comprehensive and minute, and have preoccupied, so thoroughly, the whole field now filled by the advancing debate; as if, with his fearless associates, bearing the standard of the army of Freedom, he marched, twenty-seven years ago, as "a *moral recruiting sergeant*" (for so he styled himself) into the wilderness, and firmly planted the ensign upon a summit, around which the van are now assembling, but not yet reached by the on-ward hosts.

In anticipation, therefore, of a biography, not yet complete, hereafter to appear, to consist of autobiographical sketches, professional speeches and anecdotes, addresses on Internal Improvements, Tariffs, Education, and other topics of public interest, extracts from journals and correspondence, temperance orations, and the current narrative of his life—I have arranged and now give to Humanity the following thoughts of Alvan Stewart, in its behalf, the promulgation of which, in his day, though restricted by prejudice from an extensive circulation, yet cost him the sacrifice of popularity, and many friends.

This statement is due to those who, yet holding the author in remembrance, are often inquiring for his Life, and who might else suppose this to be the memoir they knew to be in progress, instead of, as it is, a single phase of a character, broad, catholic and interesting.

LUTHER R. MARSH.

NEW YORK, *May*, 1860.

ALVAN STEWART.

—•••—

PRELIMINARY CHAPTER,

BY THE EDITOR.

ALVAN STEWART AS AN ANTI-SLAVERY MAN.

In a great moral contest, the man who, in his life-time, has fought bravely for what he deemed the right, does not cease to battle when he is dead. The thoughts he forged—his moral and intellectual weapons—still lay on the field of action, inviting the grasp of those who may succeed him in the contest. Eleven years have gone their rounds since Alvan Stewart was removed from his warfare in the cause of human rights, but we shall find, I think, that no arms since wrought, have a keener edge, a heartier stroke, or a more ponderous weight, than those his hands let drop, when he could lift them no longer.

Mr. Stewart was, early in life, impressed with the evil of slavery, and, in October, 1816—nearly half a century ago—while detained at Charlottesville, Virginia, by a personal injury, he wrote to his friend, Judge Morse, of Cherry Valley:

1*

The blacks have corrupted the whites beyond conception. Virginia may bid farewell to slavery, in time, if the blacks improve by mixture for a hundred years, as they have for the last century. Curses on the Dutchman who sold the first cargo of slaves at Jamestown, in 1620.

And when the subject began to be agitated at the North, about 1833, and the anti-slavery sentiment to assume an organized form, Mr. Stewart became convinced that slavery was a crime, and that duty demanded the exercise of all legitimate and constitutional efforts to restore the slave to his rights and to himself.

Yielding to the requisition of conscience, he consecrated himself to the cause. He organized societies, delivered addresses, wrote reports and essays, collected and expended money, and travelled far and wide. He was of the most active and efficient of those men of the dawn-light, who enlisted in the morning of the enterprise. He founded an anti-slavery society at Utica, of which he was elected president. But from the beginning, he, and they who acted with him, encountered the most determined and vindictive opposition. The doctrines they enunciated were covered with odium. Every advance was in the face of ridicule and reproach. Threats of personal violence were lavishly outpoured. Public feeling was so excited that it was scarcely safe for a man to repeat the very words of the fathers of the Republic on the subject. But neither he, nor those with whom he acted—the very heroes of reform—were to be deterred, by any personal considerations, from pursuing what seemed to them the path of duty; and, until the close of his life, in 1849, we find him constant to his first convictions, and strenuous in his labor to advance them, equally diligent and bold, whether amidst applause or menaces, whether in the kindred and sympathetic circle—small though it was—that approved him, or ostracized by society and party; whether health gave vigor to his voice and action, or his pen was feebly held from the illness that assailed him.

"You must know," he says, in a letter to his sister, "that in six months I have travelled not less than 6,000 miles in running to and fro on the earth, pleading for the slave. I have done four times more labor for him this year, than in any previous one. God be praised, our cause is doing nobly in Maine, Massachusetts, Ohio, Michigan and New York."

Again he writes:

UTICA, *November* 2, 1842.

DEAR BAILEY:

SIR; I ought to be extremely thankful to the Giver of all good, to be enabled to say, that the month of October just past, in point of labor, has been the most favorable of my life, as I have been enabled to do more than in any other month of my existence, to aid the cause of man-hood struggling to throw off its *thing-hood.* October, with its wild winds, howling tempests, descending rains and falling snow, disrobing the bygone summer of its queenly attire, to put on the solemn dress for the winter solstice, seems more than any other month, in this latitude, to warn us of the value of time, its fleetness, the brevity of the summer of human life, how soon all that is bright and beautiful must lie covered with the shroud, and how truly, with most of us, it may be said, that in the cares and sorrows of each single day, we lose sight of the chief object of existence, until the great harvest is past, and at the end of our journey, learn that we have entirely mistaken the right road. The Anti-slavery Liberty men of this State have made September and October the campaign months, in which the war against slavery has raged with more than its accustomed vigor.

THE SLAVERY MOB OF 1835.

Upon the announcement that a meeting of the Utica Anti-slavery Society would be held on the evening of the 11th August, 1835, placards were posted around the city, requiring all good citizens, who were opposed to interfering with the concerns of the South in the rights and privileges guaranteed to them by the Constitution, to attend. The rumor of an expected riot spread through the town.

Fear of a serious disturbance kept some of the members of the society away. The house was crowded to suffocation, above and below. Mr. Stewart, the president, delivered an address. But the public had not yet quite reached the conclusion, that, in this country, free discussion should be interdicted, and the evening passed without any attempt at violence.

Mr. Stewart then drafted a call for a State Convention, to be held at Utica, on the 21st of October, 1835, for the purpose of forming a New York State Anti-slavery Society. This call was signed by himself and others, to the number of 438, in different portions of the State. Upon its announcement, the people were in arms. Prominent and influential men rushed to the attack. Streams of indignant calumny, from a hundred presses, were poured upon the writer of the call and his associates.

In the county of Oneida, and particularly in Utica, the excitement was vehement, and deepened in intensity as the time approached. For days and weeks before the Conven tion, it was the subject of exasperated conversation and threatening denunciation at every corner. The most violent passions were aroused against it, and its projectors.

On the 16th of October, the Common Council of the City of Utica, by a vote of 7 to 4, granted permission to the proposed Convention, to hold its session in the court-rooms at the Academy. On the next day a large concourse of many of the most respectable citizens of Utica gathered, in indignation, at the court-rooms, to repudiate the action of the Council. Resolutions were adopted, charging the vote to be a flagrant usurpation of power—a direct indignity to the good citizens of Utica—that the meeting would not submit to the disgrace of an abolition assemblage in a public building of the city, reared by the contribution of its citizens, and designed to be used for salutary public objects, and not as a receptacle for deluded fanatics, or reckless incendiaries, and that it was the incumbent duty of every citizen to use all lawful and proper means to avert the disgrace which would rest on the city if the Convention were suffered to assemble.

As the time approached, great preparations were made by the opponents of the Convention to prevent it. Bullies from the Sixth Ward in New York were imported for the occasion. Orders were given to grocers to distribute liquors gratuitously to the mob. A bloody collision seemed inevitable. But there were men in this reform who knew not fear. Lewis Tappan, of New York, who did not intend to be present, on hearing that, if he did, he was to be the recipient of a coat of tar and feathers, put himself to much personal inconvenience, that he might be there to witness the performance. Notwithstanding the threatening storm, the Convention met, pursuant to the call, at the Second Presbyterian Church.

Promptly, as the clock struck the hour of meeting, it was called to order by Mr. Stewart, who addressed the assemblage. He had the entire programme arranged and prepared so as to perfect, speedily, the organization of a State Anti-Slavery Society, and accomplish the business portion of the meeting, before any disturbance should overtake them: for it was well known that an excited and angry meeting, led by some of the most influential politicians of the city of Utica, indeed of the State, was then in session a block or two off, at the Court House, and it was every moment expected that that assembly would come, *en masse*, to the church, to prevent, by force, the organization of the Convention. Through Mr. Stewart's generalship and promptness the Convention was organized, the Constitution he had prepared was read and adopted, the officers appointed, and the new society launched, as an organized body, before the clumsy, but furious mob arrived. While Mr. Lewis Tappan was reading a declaration of the sentiments of the Convention, the force, in the form of a numerous committee of the citizens of Utica who had been appointed at the Court House meeting, entered the church, followed by an enraged mob which crowded the building. The committee demanded to be heard. The multitude shouted. It was impossible even for a Stentor to lift his voice above the terrific din. Alderman Kellogg,—a man of great personal strength—was seized, struck, and his coat torn to pieces. The proceedings of the Convention were drowned in the yells, oaths, tread, and rush of the frantic throng. Mr. Stewart vainly attempted to be heard. Angry menaces at intervals, as the crowd paused for breath, rang through the church. The aged secretary, a clergyman and a Revolutionary soldier, was rudely handled and his papers seized. The brave old man would not surrender them, but scattered them defiantly in the air. The Convention, unable to proceed in this deafening uproar, adjourned, and the delegates left the house amid a shower of threats and imprecations.

"I was standing near Mr. Stewart," says Mr. Storms, "at the height of the excitement, and saw a porter, named Matthews, a canal runner, and a powerful man, take hold of him. Stewart had been long enfeebled by poor health, but his dormant muscles waked up at the touch of his assailant; his whole soul seemed in his arms, as he lifted the stout porter from his feet and tossed him off, like a fly.

It was always a mystery to Matthews how his strong new coat was rent in twain (unnoticed at the time) as he was flung from Stewart's giant grasp."

After the adjournment, the hotels were visited by sections of the mob, and the foreign delegates ejected. The excitement did not abate. In the evening the mob demolished the Anti-Slavery printing office—destroyed its furniture, and strewed the street with the offending types. Mysterious rumors indicated that a night attack was contemplated upon Mr. Stewart's house.

Mr. Stewart, becoming convinced that the mob was in earnest in its designs to assail his mansion, went about the necessary preparations for defence. Carpenters were immediately employed; hasty barricades, consisting of large timbers, were put up at the doors and windows. A number of friends were assembled, who were of the right stuff, and fifty muskets obtained and loaded, and all was ready for action. Stewart directed the defences deliberately, but with earnestness and decision. One of the members of the convention, from abroad, who was present, said, "Mr. Stewart, I can't stay with you, I am a peace man." "So am I," replied he, "but this house is my castle. It is my duty to defend this household, and I shall do it. I am captain of this fort, and if they come, I'll mow down fifty of them, in the name of the Lord." It became rumored in the town that a cordial reception at Stewart's house might be anticipated. Scouts were sent forth to spy out the position of affairs. Their reports were not favorable to the safety of the enterprise, and the contemplated assault was totally abandoned.

The members of the Convention, the next day, accepted the invitation of Gerrit Smith, Esq., and proceeded some forty miles to Peterboro', to continue their deliberations. They were pelted on the way with stones, mud, and eggs not of the freshest, as they marched, as it were, through an enemy's country.

Such were some of the difficulties which the pioneers in

this movement had to meet and overcome, and such the excited state of that public mind on which they wished to make an impression. What a change has come over the sentiment of the North, since that period!

I give, in this volume, the speech of Mr. Stewart at this Convention, as reported; for, though the subject had not fully ripened in his mind, it is yet interesting as one of the very leaders of that great discussion, by tongue and pen, which has since ensued.

In a libel suit, brought by a lawyer, for being charged with inciting the mob to assault the Convention, on its way to Peterboro', Mr. Stewart, in summing up for the defence, said:

No *opinion* is matter of visitation by a mob. There is no evil so great, but a mob is greater. It overthrows our social system. In monarchies, the armed soldiery *defend* liberty.

This advocate who complains that the defendant charged him with inciting the mob to attack the Abolitionists, would destroy northern liberty to support slavery. Liberty, it seems, is to be preserved by putting a town in uproar, by banishing 600 people, by driving men from their beds, by taking life.

It was all done to advance liberty, by this second Cincinnatus—this lawyer, and his professional coadjutor, *sitting up nights* to take care of the liberty of their country. Rather were they trying to pull the rope of the curfew bell of American freedom.

These Abolitionists were fleeing from a mob at Utica; but they ran from Scylla to Charybdis—they ran from the giant of mobs, and were brought up by the squadrons of these two captains of rotten eggs— these egg-and-mud marshals. Instead of the deep learning and pens of these two *promising props* of the country being employed, to show that the Abolitionists were wrong, mud and eggs were used, as a safer kind of logic in their hands, than the artillery of the mind.

These men thought that they were a portion of that salutary public opinion of the United States, which governors have told you was the medicine to bring the friends of liberty to their senses.

George Thompson, then in this country, writes him from

Boston, *October 2, 1835.*

Dear Sir:

Your favor of the 22d ult., inviting me to the New York Convention to be held on the 21st, is before me. I hope, God willing, to be present. It will indeed be delightful to meet the friends of the glorious cause in such a meeting, for such a purpose. May He who rules the elements in the moral as in the physical world grant us his presence, and make the Convention, however it may be assailed, the means of promoting his glory and the interests of the oppressed.

The call is nobly signed. The pro-slavery prints may well be disconcerted. It is ludicrous to hear the "Journal of Commerce" talk of a *death* struggle. Had the sapient prognosticators who manage that paper judged rightly, they would have read that document as the annunciation of the approaching advent of an infant Hercules—ordained to seize the monster by the throat.

The State Society, when formed, will be a weighty link in the chain of causes.

My kind regards to all around.

Very truly yours,

Geo. Thompson.

The Abolitionists had grown into such formidable proportions, that Governor Marcy, in his annual message for 1836, thought fit to administer to them a severe rebuke. This called out a reply from Mr. Stewart, hereafter given, of which he thus speaks in a letter to Mr. Tappan:

Utica, 11*th February*, 1836.

Lewis Tappan, Esq.

Dear Sir: I venture to introduce to your consideration a rather surly child of mine. You will find the child in the "Standard and

Democrat," printed in this city, and I intend to send it to Governor Marcy to *nurse*.

To drop a figure, a communication of seven or eight columns directed to Marcy, and signed by my name, exhibiting my views of the Abolition part of his turgid message, especially on the Constitution of this State and of the Union, which two Constitutions furnish the highest defence against all assaults, if we can have the benefit of them. I trust that I have been so fortunate as to present some few views on the Constitutions which are neither threadbare nor hack-neyed, which will not impede, if they do not hasten, the cause we love. The production is intended to prevent legislation by this State. I have no means of multiplying copies beyond the single edition of a newspaper; perhaps it is well I have not.

But if our Executive Committee should think it might aid us in preventing legislation in this State, or anywhere else, they are welcome to use it in any shape or form they please.

I think it our duty to express our notions on Constitutional Law, as well as our adversaries; it is all on our side.

Theodore Weld is lecturing, and has been for four nights, in the Mob-Convention-Church, in Utica, to the admiration of hundreds. The house is strained every night. He will stay here till March. Not a dog wags his tongue, mob-like, against us. The days of mobs are gone by. Mr. Weld is one of the most astonishing men of the age. He is logic and eloquence.

We are gaining; our cause goes forward with great success.

Mr. Weld will go, in March, and lecture two or three weeks in Rochester, and then, after that, two or three weeks in Buffalo, and then return to this county and make this county the head-quarters of his efforts for some time.

New Jersey and this State will be the two States, if any, which will pass laws abridging our rights. I feel it, therefore, our duty to throw every obstruction before their despotic wheels in our power.

Please lay this before your Executive Committee. Accept of the assurances of my most affectionate esteem and Christian respect for yourself and coadjutors in the cause of humanity.

Your friend,
ALVAN STEWART.

Alvan Stewart was an undoubted abolitionist—that is
to say, in favor not only of the non-extension of slavery, but
of its abolition.   Yet great misapprehension prevails on this
subject.   It will not be found, I think, that he ever advocated any infringement on the rights of the South—that he
was of those (as all *abolitionists* seem to be supposed to be)
who would endeavor, by force, to interfere with the condition of affairs at the South—that he desired to violate any
syllable of the Constitution.   He stood by the Constitution
of the Union—by the Union itself—with all his might.   He
considered that instrument as a document of liberty, and
held that slavery was contrary to its benign provisions.   His
arguments, to prove this, are now given to the public; and
it might not be hazardous to prophesy, that, though
delivered in their time, in the face of party rancor, and
amidst the sneers of the body of the people, saved from
extinction only by the genius with which he invested them,
they will, if not by the present, yet by some future generation, come to be regarded as displaying the clearest
insight, and giving the loftiest interpretation to that great
compact of the people of the States.

He lent no countenance to that radicalism which lifts its
sword against the government of the country.

What the Constitution *does* mean, how its various provisions are to be construed, are, surely, legitimate subjects
of debate.   Men have not always agreed, do not now
agree, as to this construction.   Chief Justice Marshall owes
his renown to his judicial construction of portions of this

instrument, and Daniel Webster, in its discussion, added new laurels to his brow as a great forensic orator. Those of its provisions, which, on the one side, are supposed to prove that that document acknowledged slavery, and, on the other, were claimed to make it a document of liberty, it was the desire of Mr. Stewart to discuss, to bring up for fair and full consideration before the minds of the American people, and that they should render their honest verdict thereon, at the ballot-box.

It was not always the fortune of Mr. Stewart to agree, on every point, with all those who have associated with him in onslaught upon slavery. Small as was this little band, and hopeless as seemed the enterprise to their united strength, yet it was disturbed by factions, and its efforts distracted and weakened; disagreements occurred as to the best modes of prosecuting the object they had at heart.

The question of political action was a fire-brand in the camp; thrown there by the fearless hand of Mr. Stewart. This question, fruitful of discord, was, whether this little knot of men, with voice so weak as to be scarcely audible amidst the din of contending political parties, should attempt to stand up alone, and assert its independence? Was the basis broad enough? Would they not be crushed between the two great parties of Whigs and Democrats, into which the nation, North and South, was nearly equally divided? With many, the ties of party were so old and strong, and the association so dear and enduring, that they could not be broken. Others believed that the true policy was to keep aloof from all party action and association, and so awaken opposition from neither, but woo the affections of both.   But Mr. Stewart, early in the history of this movement, became convinced that the Anti-Slavery cause could make itself *felt*, only when its advocates should arise and stand up between the two great political parties, distinct and independent, and seizing, with a controlling hand, the balance of power, should direct it to the achievement of the great object at which they aimed.   But, before putting forth these views, he was compelled to wait for the time to ripen.   When he did advance them, he met with opposition, even in his own ranks.   Independent of the world's antagonism, he had much to strive with in his struggles for conscience sake.   He was the great originator and champion of the doctrine of political action.   He did not despair, but continued to portray the great good that would result from bringing the subject of emancipation into the political arena.

Some, in the Anti-Slavery party, set up a creed of nineteen propositions, and sought to make a compliance with them all a test of communion.   But Mr. Stewart strenuously opposed this.   He thought it calculated to divide, weaken and destroy.

"I believe," said he, "that we have quite enough, in the enforcement of our one idea, to employ all the moral and political capital we possess—that those who are anxious to consume time, in the consideration of other topics, as a part of the abolition crusade, and feel especially bound to place free trade or tariff, as a good or an evil to be obtained or rejected, in the same catalogue with the liberty or slavery of three millions of men, will do well to secure another room where they can amuse those who sympathize with them, rather than pain and distract those who have no taste for nineteen undertakings until they have some evidence of their power to accomplish ONE.

"If you have attempted to tear out one stump from your field, by your oxen, lever and screw, and could not raise it, will you not put on more oxen and thus increase the power? Oh, no, say these gentlemen, if you cannot uproot the stump with the strength you possess, then, by all means, hitch on to eighteen other great oak and hemlock stumps, at the same time, and it will be sure to come. Apply your ciphers to this *rule of three*, and let us know—if ten yoke of oxen cannot cause the roots of this sturdy stump to forsake their ancient bed, how many yoke will it require to upheave this and eighteen others, at the same time?

"Men differ in their belief, when they attempt to make a creed, in proportion as they multiply the number and elements of discord. And it has always been found a great achievement in a reformation, to reduce the undertaking to a single object; for, as subordinate subjects are increased, the best friends fall out by the way, as to the means of prosecuting the main design.

"Irish Emancipation was carried alone, about 1825, after the labor of a quarter of a century. The English Reform Bill was carried in 1832-3, after the nation had struggled for it for more than a century. West Indian Emancipation triumphed in 1833, after a terrible combat in the public mind. The reduction of British postage was achieved about 1840, and the abolition of the corn laws effected in 1846, after an unparalleled commotion. Now, had these five questions been yoked together—embodied in a creed—men withholding their vote for candidates, unless, like a jury, they were unanimous upon all these topics, all would have failed. Our friends in England have only accomplished these glorious objects, by doing one thing at a time. It is here, as there, the only key to success."

Mr. Stewart did not believe it to be the duty of the citizens of the free States to pursue and surrender fugitive slaves. In a letter relating to this subject, he says:

"The jury trial law is not repealed; and if it were, I defy the slaveholder to obtain a slave from central New York. I defy him, thou dost defy him, he, she or it defies him, we defy him, ye or you defy him, they and all defy him. We defy him in every mood and tense of the English language."

The Rev. John Pierpont writes to him:

BOSTON, MASS., 24 *March*, 1840.

MY DEAR SIR:

I have long owed you a letter of acknowledgment and thanks for your very kind, gratifying, complimentary, sympathizing, amusing, honest and flattering letter of 14th November last. I did, when I first received it, as I do now, most heartily thank you for it. It was so encouraging—it expressed such a downright, hearty sympathy in my poor efforts and my pretty hard trials, that it was like sunshine to me after a long northeaster. Thank you, my dear sir. It was good *per se*, and it was, and is, especially good, considered in relation to the strifes and struggles that both the writer and *the written to* have to pass through in these stirring and sifting times.

And now, my dear sir, allow me to return you my thanks, also, for the speech you made before the Young Men's Anti-Slavery Society, etc., at Albany, last month. The first sentence in the report of that speech is a volume. The events of every day that has passed over us since the moral reforms—temperance and anti-slavery—have been started in this country, go to confirm not only the truth of the remark that "a nation may lose its liberty in a day, and not miss it in a hundred years"—but the application of that truth to our own abused and blinded country. Was there ever a country so blessed, and, at the same time, so cursed, as is ours?—so blessed of God—so cursed by the avarice and servility of man? What Samsonian strength the young giant must have in his back and muscle, that he can stand up as he does with slavery—that "old man of the sea "— upon his shoulders, and that he can get along as he does with such a sea of rum to wade through—and keep himself alive even, covered over as the poor fellow is with leeches of office from the crown of his head to the soles of his feet. My dear sir, can he stand up much

longer, think ye? I do not ask can he stand up a *free* young giant
—that is out of the question. Free he is not. Free he has not been
for years. But can he stand at all, and bear much longer the weight
of his own chains? From all his curses, from rum and slavery, and
what is equivalent to both and the cause and father of both—his own
avarice and immorality—may the Ruler of the nations ere long send
him a good deliverence!

I know, my friend, that I need not exhort you to go on in the
course that you have marked out for yourself. "Fight the good
fight of faith," in your own most ·excellent way. Give no quarter.
Let your good old broadsword split 'em down from chin to chine;
spare 'em not till they cry for quarter. I suppose that *then* the
tenderness of your nature will not allow you "thrice to slay the
slain." I thank the God whom you serve, that you have so much
of this world's goods that the foes of freedom, of God, and of cold
water, cannot starve you by thrusting you out of your stewardship,
upon the cold world, to dig or beg, as they are trying to, me.

Believe me truly,
Your friend,
Jno. Pierpont.

Whittier writes:

Amesbury, 18th 1st Mo., 1842.

My dear Friend:
Thou hast doubtless already seen by the " Emancipator & Free
American " that we have declared our determination to secure, if
possible, thy attendance at our Convention of Liberty at Boston, on
the 16th of next month; and I now, in behalf of the Liberty party
of Massachusetts, and in accordance with my own feelings, earnestly
invite thee to be with us on that occasion.

The legislature of the State will be in session, and our evening
meetings will be held in the State House. We *must* have thee with
us. We shall have a mighty gathering from all parts of the State—
and we want thy voice among us uplifted in the name of God and
humanity. Do not disappoint us. Thy attendance at the Worcester
Convention was of immense service to us. I do not say this by way
of flattery; all of us know it here. There is an intense desire to hear

2

thee, and thou wilt have such an audience as could not be gathered elsewhere in the Union.

Please write me a line on receipt of this, informing me whether thou shalt be able to come. Once more let me adjure thee to let no small matter prevent thee from complying with our request. In the language of Chinese diplomacy—I hope thou wilt consider this—" a special edict! and obey accordingly."

With kind regards for thy family, I am, as ever, thy friend,

JOHN G. WHITTIER.

A correspondent of the " Press " writes :

In an Anti-Slavery Convention, held at Port Byron, New York, in 1842, in the midst of a speech of Mr. Bradley, the door of the church in which the convention was held was opened noislessly, and there appeared the tall, straight figure, and pale, grave face of the slave's friend, Alvan Stewart. The spontaneous and universal burst of applause, from the entire audience, well indicated the impression left by his eloquence upon their hearts during his visit among us last winter. Upon being called upon, he arose and made one of his best speeches. What a wonderful faculty he has to hold a subject up before his audience—what quaint sayings and unparalled comparisons! At one instant his audience would be rolling with laughter, which would soon give place to sobs and grief. Never did I witness a greater manifestation of his honest, holy feeling, than when he alluded to his large meeting, at Fort Defiance, on the Maumee, in Ohio, but a few weeks since, under the " Old Council Oak." This venerable monarch of the forest had, he said, from time immemorial, been the shelter of the various Indian tribes, who for centuries had met under its spreading branches, for council, in peace or war. While alluding to the fact that, in that honored place, the citizens of Fort Defiance were assembled to listen to his stories of the poor slave's wrongs, his whole soul was stirred within him, and a flow of tears burst from his eyes, producing a corresponding feeling throughout the audience.

William Goodell, than whom no one is more familiarly

acquainted with the progress of the Anti-Slavery movement, writes :

If you will permit me, I will take the liberty to suggest two or three things wherein Mr. Stewart was of most essential service to the cause of freedom.

1. He was *the first* to insist, earnestly, in our consultations, in committees and elsewhere, on the necessity of forming a distinct political party to promote the abolition of slavery. You will find notice of this on page 469 of my history of "Slavery and Anti-Slavery." At this time, Mr. Stewart stood alone on the Executive Committee of the New York State Anti-Slavery Society, at Utica, in advocating the measure. Gerrit Smith, as president of the society, and member of our Executive Committee, was at that time (Feb., 1839) opposed to it, nor was I, myself, as one of the committee, and as editor of the "Friend of Man," the society's organ, prepared to advocate the measure. President Beriah Green shared also in the hesitancy of the rest of the committee. Myron Holley, at a convention in September of the same year, introduced a resolution and address in favor of a distinct party (Hist. p. 470); but Mr. Stewart had previously done much to prepare abolitionists for that movement. So that the Liberty party, the Free-soil party, the Free Democracy, and the Republican party—whatever may be said of their varying platforms and policy—*all* owe their origin to *Alvan Stewart*, in the first place, and to Myron Holley afterward, more than to any other men. Mr. Stewart presided at the Albany Convention, 1st April, 1840, at which the Liberty party was organized. Gerrit Smith by that time had become ready to coöperate in the measure.

2. Alvan Stewart was the first to elaborate a compact argument in defence of the doctrine that the Federal Government had constitutional power to abolish slavery in the slave States. Though Mr. Stewart based his argument solely upon one single clause of the Constitution (Amendments, Art. V.), yet his argument was extensively regarded a triumphant one, and the debate it elicited among abolitionists gave rise to a number of elaborate discussions of the subject in pamphlet form afterward. The great change of senti-

ment already perceptible, and still in progress, concerning the bearing of the federal Constitution on slavery—a change destined, perhaps, to revolutionize the national policy—is largely attributable to the labors of Alvan Stewart in 1837–8.

To *you*, sir, I may add my conviction, that, in pioneering these two measures—(1) a distinct political party; (2) a national policy directly and positively *against* slavery—to the extent of its utter extirpation, Mr. Stewart has laid a foundation for a reputation as enduring as the cause of freedom in America. Whether his measures are ever adopted or not, his *proposal* of them belongs not less to the history of the country than to his own biography, and should be made prominent in both.

8. I ought to add, that Alvan Stewart, as chairman of the Executive Committee of the New York State 'Anti-Slavery Society, at Utica, rendered quite as effective services in devising plans, ways, means·and appliances, for propogating anti-slavery sentiments, and initiating anti-slavery organizations, and rendering them effective, as he ever did in his public speeches, debates, and writings. No one *out* of the Executive Committee could have any adequate knowledge of his labors in this department, nor due appreciation of their importance in the promotion of our cause. In 1836, he threw up his extensive and lucrative law practice, to devote himself to the *one great* cause, of which he regarded the then three and a half millions of slaves his *direct* clients, and the entire American people, their liberties and their national prosperity, as indirectly, and yet in reality involved.

Not all the plans and projects of Mr. Stewart were accepted and adopted by the Executive Committee. Perhaps *some* of them may have been chargeable with the "eccentricity" with which his brilliant genius was marked. Not all of them that were adopted worked as happily as might have been desired. But enough of them, either *modified* or *unmodified*, in committee, *did so far* succeed, as to entitle him to the credit I have given him, and to the gratitude of the country.

No part of my life do I remember with more pleasure than my social intercourse and public labors with Alvan Stewart. Some-

times we have earnestly differed from each other as earnest men
will, intent on a common cause. But none of those differences ever
lessened my esteem for him, and admiration of him.

Much as I enjoyed, at the time, those brilliant scintillations of wit,
eloquence, pathos, humor, and eccentric thought for which he was
so very remarkable, and which so enlivened the social conversation
and the public speeches of Mr. Stewart, my *memory* is not as retentive of them, *in detail*, as of the more serious points of argument, opinion, sentiment, plans and measures which it was my
privilege to discuss with him, in consultations, in committees and
otherwise, for the promotion of the objects we were intent upon
promoting. Nor am I as well qualified to relate, effectively, his
sallies of wit and humor, which I do partly remember, as I ought to
be, to give them their full force. I will endeavor, however, to
recall and to sketch a very few of them.

Sometime in 1836 or '7, Mr. Stewart earnestly defended a couple
of colored boys, arrested at Utica as fugitives from slavery in Virginia. The boys in some way got free, and made good their escape
to Canada. Much excitement was occasioned, and the pro-slavery
presses of the North exerted themselves to throw odium upon Mr.
Stewart for his participancy in the affair. The southern papers
copied the inflammatory statements and comments of their northern
allies, and the name of Alvan Stewart was execrated by the slave-
ocrats from Maine to Georgia. In the midst of all this, Mr. Stewart
received a letter from the old lady in Virginia, to whom, according
to the statutes of Virginia, the boys belonged. She thanked Mr.
Stewart for his kindness to her boys, who, she said, had escaped
from Virginia, with her approbation. They had been pursued
by her nephews, her presumptive heirs, who were intending to
sell them to the far South, as soon as the old lady should die. This
statement accorded precisely with the story Mr. Stewart had
received from the colored boys.

It was in reference to the same or a similar effort of Mr. Stewart,
that he received a letter of hearty commendation from another lady
in Virginia, whose husband was a slaveholder, and a strong pro-
slavery man. She informed Mr. Stewart, that soon after the recent
birth of her eldest son, she had ordered her carriage and had driven

a considerable distance with her babe, to a neighboring parish, and had him christened by the name of *Alvan Stewart*, much to the astonishment of the parson, the audience, and, afterward, of her husband, when he learned what had been done! That Virginian *Alvan Stewart*, if now living, is nearly old enough to vote as his mother would doubtless counsel him. In conventions Mr. Stewart sometimes told the story in answer to the question—"Why don't you go to the South to preach your abolition?" He thought he *was* going to the South, most effectually, by working at home.

In Alvan Stewart's day, it was thought a knock-down argument against an Abolitionist to ask whether he would be willing to have a white man marry a "nigger." One day, in a large convention, while Alvan Stewart was speaking on some resolution, he was interrupted by a pert young gentleman, neatly attired, with the stereotyped question. Mr. Stewart replied, in a polite and dignified manner, explaining that Abolitionists only asked that colored persons should enjoy the protection of law like other persons, and be secured in the exercise of their inalienable rights. Abolitionists had never set themselves up to be matchmakers, had never undertaken to determine who people should marry. With this explanation he attempted to resume the thread of his discourse. But the questioner was not satisfied. He repeated the question again, and, with an air of triumph, demanded an explicit answer. Stewart straightened himself, and stood, as in an attitude of deliberation. "Well," said he, "since the gentleman is so anxious to have the question distinctly answered, although, as I have said, it does not belong to the Abolition question, I will frankly state my own position on the subject. Let me then say to the gentleman that if he should fall in love with a colored girl, and should find that he could not be happy without her, *I should interpose no objections to the marriage.*" This was said with a sober and innocent look, as if the speaker really supposed the questioner was anxious to get his consent to such a connection. The house roared with laughter, at the expense of the pert young gentleman, who seemed annihilated. But there Alvan Stewart stood, as sober as a judge, without relaxing a muscle. After the tumult had subsided, he turned to the young man, with the same innocent, sober countenance, saying: "Is my young friend relieved of his anxiety?" Another roar, louder and more prolonged than the first, used up what there was left of the interrogator.

Alvan Stewart was never more in his element than when, on the platform of a large and enthusiastic anti-slavery convention, he pleaded for contributions and subscriptions of funds for the Executive Committee, to carry on the cause. This advocacy was always assigned to him, and he executed his office in a manner peculiarly his own. After stating the principles, measures and objects of the Society, and the uses it had for funds to sustain lecturers and presses, and to print and circulate tracts, etc., he would begin to call for subscriptions and donations in a style resembling that of an auctioneer, calling for bids. "Who will be the first to subscribe $100?" If a lower sum was offered, he would say: "Wait, we must have the $100 men first." Collectors, in the mean time, would be passing around the room to take names and moneys. One after another in the assembly would rise and announce their names and the sums they would give; Alvan Stewart, at the same time continuing his appeals, interrupted constantly by the announcement of names, residences, and sums in process of being reëchoed on the platform, noted down by the secretaries, and handed up, in bills or pencilled pledges, by the receivers. Alvan Stewart's ear caught every name, and his lips returned thanks to each donor by name—all commingling with his imploring appeals, witty conceits and original remarks. Such a medley of pathos and puns, of demonstration and drollery, mortal ears never before heard. The attempt, by any other man, would have seemed a satire—a broad farce. But in the hands of Alvan Stewart, all went to make up a symmetrical whole—sympathy and assistance for the slave. "Thank you, Mr. A., in the name of all that is abominable in slavery." "Twenty dollars from Mr. C." "Thank you, Mr. C., in the name of all that is precious in humanity." "Ten dollars from Mr. D." "Thank you, Mr. D., in the name of all that is sacred in holy justice." "Thirty dollars from friends in Tonawanda." "Thanks, kind friends, in the name of all that is dismal in the Tonawanda swamp." And so he would go on, by the half hour or hour. Nobody was tired. The footing up of the subscriptions and the counting of the bills convinced every one that none but Alvan Stewart could have raised one half the amount. On one occasion a liberal donation coming from Mr. Hill—"The Lord bless Mr. Hill," said Stewart, "may he grow to be a large mountain."

"Abolitionists," said Mr. Stewart, "are the most grateful people in the world. They make more account of small favors than any other people living. They are like country shopkeepers who wind up their advertisements with, 'The smallest favors gratefully acknowledged.'" This he said in gentle reproof of the too easy credulity of Abolitionists, in giving credit to the half-way concessions and professions of political men who sought anti-slavery suffrages on the ground of compliances, of little or doubtful practical value, and who thus submitted to compromises, incompatible, as he believed, with their principles as Abolitionists, and fatal, in the end, to their success. To some who said, "Half a loaf is better than no bread," he would reply: "That depends on whether you get the half-loaf or *lose* it, and whether what you *do* get be wholesome nutriment or poison." To opposers who called Abolitionists "*men of one idea*," he would say, it was more creditable to have *one such* idea, than to have *all* the ideas that ever floated upon the brain of a pro-slavery man.

I was riding with Stewart, to attend an anti-slavery convention. Our road led through a thriving village, in which was a large manufacturing establishment, upon which, besides the principal sign, was the inscription "*Power to let*," meaning water or steam power. "*Power to let!*" exclaimed Stewart; "yes, Abolitionists have got power to let—surplusage of argument to spare—*motive power* enough—moral, political, religious, economical, and philanthropic—to abolish all the slavery in creation, and all the other curses and abominations of which the human mind ever conceived. Yes, if every planet in the solar system were inhabited, and disgraced with slavery; if every fixed star in the firmament were the centre of a planetary system, and every planet thereof inhabited with slaveholders and slaves, Abolitionists have got motive power to spare sufficient to break the fetters of every slave in the universe. Yes, Abolitionists may advertise '*Power to let!*' And yet," he added after a pause, "it remains to be seen whether pro-slavery priests and politicians haven't got stupidity and selfishness enough to resist it all." In the Convention the next day the audience had the benefit of the idea.

During the log-cabin furore that carried the election in favor of

Gen. Harrison, Mr. Stewart said he expected that our next Presidential canvass would produce a candidate to be supported on the ground of his not living in any house at all, but burrowing, like a woodchuck, in a hole on the hill-side.

It is difficult to repeat effectively Mr. Stewart's peculiar sayings. The manner, the tone, the air, the expression of countenance, are all wanting. And so, for the most part, are the *occasions* and the *design* of his saying them. In respect to the *publication* of many of them, *he* might say if living—as the clergyman did to a committee who applied to him for a copy, for the press, of an eloquent sermon he had just preached, during a *thunder-storm*—"If," said he, "you will agree to print the thunder and lightning along with it, I will give you a copy."

Says Gerrit Smith, in a letter of May 2d, 1857, to the writer:

"Mr. Stewart was emphatically a man of genius. I never knew one more so. He was a man of great thoughts. I never knew one of greater. He was a man, too, of very tender heart. His pity for the poor and oppressed was very deep. Above all he was a Christian.

"I knew Mr. Stewart well. We were friends for many years. I admired him and loved him."

It may be thought that Mr. Stewart sometimes dealt in language too harsh and uncourteous; that he should have denounced slavery in a more delicate and silken phrase. But it will be remembered in palliation, if palliation be needed, that *he* was roughly used by the advocates of the system he was opposing; that all the vituperation of our vocabulary was hurled against him; the shafts of ridicule, the bolts of anger, the arrows of fierce denunciation, all the slanders that malice could invoke—nay, that words were not the only weapons that rattled on his shield—that his popularity was sapped, persecution was started on his track, ostracism attempted, and infuriated mobs yelled around his house. A man under such circumstances may not be held to the strict civilities of debate. Strange would it be if some strong expressions, not domiciled in boudoirs, should at times escape him.

Besides, it was no poetical or dainty task he had in hand. He was not to describe a landscape or paint a rose. He saw this monster evil lifting high its awful form and shadowing the land. He felt it to be his duty, however great the disproportion in the power of the antagonists, to fight to the utmost. Such a conflict was one of earnestness, in which there was no time to weigh sentences, or balance courtesies, or bring forth his argument with "By your leave." If the slave trade on the high seas was justly denounced as a "*piracy*" by the international laws of Christendom, justifying a yard-arm punishment; if the pages of our own federal statutes confirmed in this respect the opinions of the civilized world, he saw no reason why the same language was not equally applicable, in principle, to the same trade *between* the States or *in* the States. I have not softened the language he has chosen in the speeches and writings I have compiled ; for it is only by preserving his exact phraseology that a just and truthful idea can be obtained of the man *as he was.*

That, in his years of labor on the questions of peace, of temperance and slavery, he was impelled by the purest and most earnest convictions, by the liveliest sympathy, and by a devout religion, those who saw him daily, who heard his familiar conversation from morn till eve, who never observed the slightest evidence of apathy or insincerity, who witnessed the heroic and concentrated energy with which he sacrificed health and wealth and fame upon the altar of philanthropy, are surely well qualified to judge and most sacredly believe.

The change in the conduct of the world toward him, upon the announcement of his temperance and anti-slavery sentiments, was marked and striking. Before that time he had been much courted, feted, admired. But such was the extreme odium attached to the causes his convictions compelled him to espouse, that even *his* great general popularity fell before it; and he became the target, for many years, for all the poisoned arrows of intemperance and slavery. And it was in sustaining himself under this great reverse of public sentiment toward him, and, for many years, to the day of his death, breasting the tide of public ridicule, vituperation, and, in many instances, malignity, and perseveringly, laboriously, doing what he thought to be his duty with unflinching firmness and untiring energy, that his character stands out in boldest relief, and limns itself upon the canvas in colors most enduring.

One of the greetings which have come to me during my work will, I am sure, be gladly read by those who remember how the writer of it—Theodore D. Weld—held increasing audiences at fever pitch, with his flashing eye, his clarion tones and marvellous eloquence, without manuscript or note, for sixteen successive evenings, in the very church from which the Anti-Slavery Convention had been, but a few months before, forcibly expelled.

"Right heartily glad am I," says Mr. Weld, "that a memoir of Alvan Stewart is to be published, and that you are to write it. The world would be cheated out of its own, if the good and great in Alvan Stewart were to be left in the custody of tradition, subject to all its distortions and dilutions. . . .

"I never saw him in private life, except once at his own table, a part of an evening, at his house when it was full of company; and now and then as we shook hands, and spoke a word of cheer to each other, in our hurryings up and down, driving the brunt of the anti-slavery conflict.

"Personally I knew him less than I knew any other of the most prominent anti-slavery men of New York city, and State. Yet I knew enough of him to impress me profoundly with the conviction of his rare powers, exhaustless versatility; that marvel of humor, ever fresh, ever at flood tide, and ever *his own*—those batteries of wit, irony and sarcasm always in play, every shot telling, and never leaving one the less in the locker—that power with the '*reductio ad absurdum*' in argument, in which he had no peer; but better far than all, that depth of pathos, those outwelling sympathies, never at ebb: that ever yearning heart-ache for the wronged, that moral courage that always dared yet never knew it dared; all these, with a kindred host come thronging around me at the thought of *Alvan Stewart*. Blessings on his memory. His works do follow him."

And when Mr. Stewart was removed, by death, from his labors in this cause, the following evidence of the estimation in which he was held, by the friends of reform, appeared as his obituary:

It is with pain that we learn that Alvan Stewart is no more among the living throng of mankind. His death took place in New York city, May 1, 1849, at his home with his family in the 59th year of his age. This is an event we have been contemplating for months, and always contemplated it with feelings of sadness.

Mr. Stewart was a native of New York, and though of respectable family, emphatically the artificer of his own fortune. He commenced his professional life at Cherry Valley, Otsego county, where he acquired eminence as a lawyer, and for several years had a large lucrative practice. In 1832 Mr. Stewart made this city (Utica) his home, and until falling health demanded a change of climate.

Alvan Stewart was a man—an original man—copying nobody, imitating nobody, and inimitable in himself, both as to genius, modes of expression and the character of his mind and manners. He was well read, and had a mind well stored with varied learning; but his borrowed thoughts and vast information derived from books, received by passing through his mind and finding utterance through his peculiar genius, an originality and freshness which added to their power. But it was not merely books or stereotyped ideas that distinguished Mr. Stewart and elevated him to a post in society, and gave him an honorable name among the distinguished men of the age. It was his originality as a thinker and actor, and his independent self-directed course on the questions of the times in which he lived. As a man of humor and wit, mingled with gravity and profound good sense, he stood forth as peculiar to his day and age. These gave him a power at the bar and force as an orator. But it is of Alvan Stewart as a philanthropist we desire to speak.

Perhaps no living man in America, certainly no one in the State of New York, has done more signal service for the cause of human freedom than Alvan Stewart; and it is almost equally true of the Temperance Reform. Mr. Stewart was among the earliest, and certainly among the ablest supporters of the temperance cause. He espoused these enterprises when it cost something to make the sacrifice. With no earthly or time-serving motive to gratify—while to " entirely refrain " from the agitation of unpopular subjects would have saved him from a world of odium and malignant misrepresentation—he obeyed the convictions of his inner man, threw himself into the breach, giving to persecuted reform the support of his superior talent and personal influence. His name became synonymous with " abolition," and " teetotalism," at a time when men's souls were tried. Nor did he shrink from the worst opprobrium which such an identification of himself with reform, brought on his head; but the power of his conviction of the truth and uprightness of his cause enabled him rather to *prefer* the bad opinion of the world to the applause of a time-serving age. It is not strange that those who can see no virtue in efforts to relieve mankind of the untold evils of drunkenness—to upturn and overthrow the despotism of American slavery—should be at a loss to estimate Mr. Stewart's motives; nor is it strange, that, when he in his zealous support of the truth should rebuke religious and political delinquency and frustrate the designs of the politicians, on his head should fall vile slander, and that he should be pointed out as a fanatic. Those who have sought to convict the leaders of the abolitionists of being *ambitious* have had the most hopeless cause ever brought before the bar of public opinion. Alvan Stewart was a lawyer of the first class. His talent, varied and extensive information, education and wealth, naturally placed him in the upper circle of society; and for him to descend from motives of ambition to take the drunkard by the hand and recognize the despised African as a man and a brother, would have been a freak in human character unaccounted for in the philosophy of human nature. The truth was, Mr. Stewart was highly *conscientious*, and gave to reform, his thoughts, his time and his money, from a sincere love of it, and lived and labored to better mankind, trusting to the future to vindicate his name, and the Judge of all the earth to mete to him his reward. For some five years we were privileged with an intimacy and constant intercourse with Mr. Stewart, and we know that with him the religious sentiment was predominant and that a clear conviction of duty governed his actions. That he was not without faults, we are duly sensible; but his imperfections were not of a character to seriously detract from a life devoted to the good of his race, and of signal service to mankind. He gave himself *heartily* to the cause of reform, and that too when reform, feeble and neglected, most needed his wise counsels and strong and vigorous support. From the moment of his consecration, his devotion was untiring and unremitted, until reluctantly forced from active service by disease and a broken constitution. In his retirement, his reflections were those of a good man in view of duties done and responsibilities honorably met, and the faith which bringeth salvation was his stay and support in his failing years. Alvan Stewart has lived to some purpose. The world has been made better by his living in it, and the example of his life will shed blessings on ages to come. If a slave now lifts to heaven his manacled limbs, or a drunkard reels through the streets, neither that slave nor that drunkard can reproach Alvan Stewart, for duties left undone in his behalf. To them he gave the better portion of his life—to their deliverance he consecrated his powerful mind and the best portion of his days—and the blessings of the poor and oppressed will rest on his name. We mourn the death of Mr. Stewart and sympathize in the sorrowful feelings the news of his death will impart. To us he was a friend, forbearing and sympathizing. To us he was a counsellor whose advice was imparted with almost parental tenderness. His friend-ship we shall ever hold in grateful remembrance, and we hope to profit by the lessons of wisdom which have fallen from his lips.

THE SCOPE OF THIS BOOK.

Let us move, in the solid column, upon the ranks of slavery! Let us lock our arms, by the power of united political action. Let every man's name be enrolled who has fired the bullet of his ballot against slavery. Let every name be registered by the middle of September. Sixty-five thousand men were found on the Ides of November, 1844, inscribed on the muster roll of human freedom.

THE ARMY OF LIBERATION.

You are the moral army of liberation. It is not an enlistment for one year, but during the war. This army, with its additions, fights for glory in its most exalted sense. To deliver three millions of slaves to self-ownership, and give them the right to do everything which is not wrong, are the pass-words of the army of deliverance. The army of liberation will remove the fetters from mind and body of enslaver and enslaved of fifteen States, and double the agricultural and treble the manufacturing and mechanical products. Another part of their mission is to establish 36,000 common schools, those nurseries of truth and knowledge, the elements of self-government, in those fifteen States. This army of liberation will carry 500 printing presses, and one million of Bibles, and 20,000 school-masters and mistresses, as free-will offering, in the day of a most glorious emancipation, to these States. This army is charged with the high duty of blotting out Mason & Dixon's line, the line of eternal discord. This army is to collect the bowie-knives and revolving, hair-triggered pistols of these States, and place them in the bottom of the fathomless sea. This army is to make labor honorable in these fifteen States. This army is to remove all northern jealousies, and unite North and South, East and West, in eternal bonds of fraternity. This army is charged with the modification of southern and northern opinions as to the constitutional powers of the Federal Government, on the subject of tariffs for revenue or tariffs for protection, or free trade, and direct taxation, believing the extremes, left and right, will see eye to eye, and will walk hand in hand when a common interest *controls*, and common instrumentalities are employed to obtain subsistence. This army is also charged with the purification and exaltation of American character, by creating a bond of union between the abstractions of human freedom and the living practicalities—by bridging that hitherto yawning gulf; and this army is charged with the utter extirpation of that desolating hypocrisy, which so long, in Church and State, destroyed the use of language, in suffering a holy abstraction, in religion or politics standing as our creed, to be a license practically, to act out all manner of abominations; the purity of the creed making atonement for the profligacy of the conduct under it. This army of freedom is charged with rescuing the character of this great nation from the burning sneers and unanswerable sarcasms of old Europe, which declared that as hope for man ascended high, reality dug dungeons deep and low in which to hide our shame.

THE DECLARATION OF INDEPENDENCE.

This army is charged with the faithful execution of the Declaration of Independence; the *great unperformed*, the

greatly admired, but *unavailable*. For seventy years the
nation has been so overwhelmed with the truthfulness and
grandeur of its conceptions, that they have been content to
stand all of this time and shout their admiration before an
astonished world, and annually arrest the very wheels of
human affairs, while on the 4th of July, we stretched the
utmost power of human genius for the strongest conceptions
of intellect, and for the most consuming thoughts, to be
delivered in the most beautiful robes of language, to stamp
that impression of veneration on the mind of others as deeply
as it had sunk in our own.

THE SHIP OF STATE.

We stand looking at this splendid ship of state, yet on
the stocks, her masts raised, yards trimmed, canvas spread,
and ballast in, and provisioned for a circumnavigation of the
whole circle of human necessities, with orders to call at
every port, island and country in her course; carrying justice, law, equal rights to all men, furnishing them with a
remedy for the wrongs inflicted for ages, possessing the sure
and certain power of striking fetters and bonds from the legs
and arms of men, with the power of opening prison doors
and of placing the victims on the great platform of equal
and eternal rights, and giving them power to make the laws
they are required to honor, and in future, the obligations
they are bound to obey.

The Liberty party is charged with the high duty of
launching and navigating the old ship of American Independence, which has stood ready for a launch from the 4th
of July, 1776, while the seas have swarmed with pirates and
buccaniers, who have even come upon her deck and sworn
by her stripes and colors, that she never shall be launched
as long as wood grows and water runs. These pirates and

freebooters have sucked the free blood of the nation from its veins, and now threaten the lives of those who may endeavor to launch this ship, and declare that she was never made to go to sea; she was only made to stand eternally on the stocks as an object of unexplainable admiration, as an abstract ship, to be deified on the stocks on the fourth of July, and point the orations of Juniors and Sophomores, at a college commencement; and in fact, they say, if you do launch her, they will bore holes in her bottom and sink her and all her glorious freight, as she was meant to be a ship only on land and not on the water; and these pirates are ready to prove that one of the old ship carpenters who built her at Philadelphia, was heard by one of the pirates to say, that the ship was not made to go on the water, but was intended solely for the *land*. And many say, who are not pirates, that we must search for the intention of the old ship-builders and hands who framed and made this ship; if some of them did say it was their intention that this ship should sail on the land, then we, their posterity, are bound to sail on the land, though the ship itself would contradict it, even if every builder should swear that the land was her destined element.

Will the army of liberation put themselves in position to launch this ship, and go on board of her as her navigators?

POLITICAL PARTIES.

There have stood two great parties at the North, who have often pretended they were willing to launch the ship, but the pirates and buccaniers made such an outcry about the story of one of their number having heard one of the old carpenters of Philadelphia say, that she was made to sail on the land, they have not dared to do it. These two parties at the North have been so anxious to carry out the *intention* of the FRAMERS that they have waited seventy years for the pirates to bring forward their proof that such was the original understanding; the pirates have made arguments through several thousand days, while their witness was coming, who never came, trying to prove by arguments most profound, that it could never have been the intention of sailing the ship except upon the land; for, say they, sailing upon the sea, would be at war with our piratical business on the sea, which is older than the framing of the ship, and was in existence on the 4th of July, 1776; therefore the ship must be intended to sail on the *land*, or stand upon the *stocks*. The northern two great parties have been overwhelmed with the *good sense* as well as absoluteness of this *prodigious argument*, and have been staggered, for seventy years, by its weight, and have not yet made up their mind as to the character of the reply, or even of its possibility. The argument is so consuming, and wherewithal so reasonable, they fear it is unanswerable.

THE REVOLUTION SUCCESSFUL THROUGH THE PRINCIPLES

OF THE DECLARATION.

Now the Liberty party Abolitionists hold the Declaration of Independence to be an elementary law, the law of laws, the rock of first principles, to which the nation descended, and on which it built *in the honest hour of its agony;* and that every other institution or constitution contravening its great essentials is null and void; for without that declaration asserting that "all men were created free and equal," our independence could not have been achieved, and but for that we should this hour have been revolving, as colonial satellites, around the Sea-girt Isle. Had our Declaration of Independence contained what many say the Constitution of the United States does, a proposition to support slavery (which

I deny), and had the great Declaration contained, what I admit is found in the Constitution and laws of several States in the South, to wit, slavery, or had the great Declaration contained the converse of its own mighty proposition, and asserted that some men were created to be free and some were created to be slaves, then the battles of Trenton, Saratoga and Yorktown had never been fought; the British "Court Gazette" would on the 1st of January, 1777, have published an obituary of our Revolution, in these words : " Order reigns in the Colonies. Trans-Atlantic freemen refused to pour out their blood to sustain the abhorred proposition that some men were created to be slaves." To attempt to ingraft slavery into our system, is a direct fraud upon every drop of blood spilled in the Revolution, every sacrifice endured, every dollar spent, or misery suffered.

THE ABJECT NORTH.

The North has been periodically humbled, kicked and trampled under foot, by the South. The just punishment of heaven has been poured upon the North, for fortifying and propping slavery. The North in Church and State, has emasculated the Christian religion, and constitutional law, to uphold slavery. The North, for its tameness, and hunting up arguments to quiet slaveholding consciences, and basely making briefs to aid slaveholding lawyers to undermine justice and overthrow liberty, is treated with a supercilious contempt, by the South, the real wages of meanness. In Congress, the northern man does not rise to the position of a privileged serf. This is just; that men who go round the country soliciting posts in Congress and on the bench of the Supreme Court of the United States, foreign Ambassadorships, and seats in Presidential cabinets, should be obliged to earn their positions by crushing slaves and slandering the Declaration of Independence, and the venerable dead who fought for its adoption; also by sneering at men who contend for freedom, justice and law, misnaming them fanatics and enthusiasts. The South have inflicted on the grovelling North pains and penalties, as the instruments of heaven's vengeance. Yes, tenfold more of real judgments, than everything done, thought, or attempted, by England, which lit the torch of the Revolutionary war.

The slaveholders are tantalized, by the sight of the prosperity of free labor. 20,000 voting slaveholders regard the free North and its institutions with malevolence and hatred, and God, for just and holy reasons, has used those slaveholders as a whip of scorpions, to punish the base bowing North, in property, character and life, by war, taxation, and debasing humility, as a just retribution for upholding slavery and slaveholders; and for having forsaken the Scriptures of truth, and having perverted, by base interpretation, the Constitution of the United States, from its high freedom-protecting sense to a low and degrading piratical covenant, to be employed for the destruction of human rights, rather than their support. The North bowed in the college, pulpit and Congress, to the dominion of the man-stealer, and employed its brains in the destruction of human liberty, by a servile yielding, to slaveholding construction of religion and law. The southern slaveholding merchants sought and obtained credit in the North, and $500,000,000 would not meet the losses of the North, in sixty years which were cancelled by southern bankruptcy. Thus the North was justly, and in part, made slaves to work for the South, as a just punishment on us, who would not see injustice in the position of the slave. The slaveholders envied us, and hypocritically became the advocates of the rights of impressed seamen; yes, men whose own fields were worked by impressed and stolen black men.

THE WAR OF 1812.

The war of 1812 the South decreed, and 137 millions were wasted by government in its prosecution, and 200 millions more were lost on the sea and land, by our merchants and farmers. The South placed Major General Smyth, at Buffalo, a slaveholding lawyer of Virginia; Major General Winder, a slaveholding lawyer of Maryland, at Forty Mile Creek, on the side of Lake Ontario; Major General Wilkinson, a Louisiana slaveholder, at the Cedars and Rapids of the St. Lawrence; and Major General Wade Hampton, the great sugar-boiler of Louisiana, and the largest slaveholder in the United States (having over 5000 crushed human beings bowing to this tyrant), was located at Burlington, Vermont: four slaveholding generals, with their four armies, were stretched out on our northern frontier, not to *take* Canada, but to prevent its being taken, by the men of New England and New York, in 1812, '13 and '14; lest we should make some six or eight free States from Canada, if conquered. This was treason against northern interests, northern blood, and northern honor. But the South furnished the officers, the President and the cabinet. This revelation could have been proved by General John Armstrong, then Secretary of War, after he and Mr. Madison quarrelled. But these slaveholders could add Louisiana, Florida, Texas, and perhaps half of Mexico, at the expense and disgrace of the nation, to extend the area of slavery; and the North with two votes to the South one, professing to be opposed, yield at last to the wish of this unprincipled greediness and inordinate robbery. Forty millions are paid to establish slavery in Florida and murder the Indians. How many hundred millions have the North lost, after erecting the most expensive manufactories, and filling them with machinery to have them all brought to nothing by a prostration of the tariff, as at this time, in order to ruin the North, without benefiting the South! But will the North still present her back for the rod, will she still vote for a slaveholder as President of the United States? The North can never deliver herself and the nation from this thralldom, until a majority declare they will vote for those men only, who, if elected, will do all in their power for the constitutional abolition of slavery.

THE RECOIL OF SLAVERY.

If this nation had never undertaken to hold up the hands of the slaveholder and crush the colored man, there would have been double the amount of wealth there now is in the United States. All of the disgraceful wars and the three hundred millions of expense thereby, would have been saved, and one thousand millions lost by southern bankruptcy and change of northern pursuits, lifting up and dashing to the ground tariffs for revenue and protection, and that everlasting *whirl* of inconstancy, breaking up the sober and adjusted calculations of men, by throwing interests most momentous against the rocks, leaving nothing but ingenuity to collect the fragments and form another nucleus, and as it grew to importance, malevolence would again undermine it, and the barbarity of slavery raze it to the ground. But for slavery we should have ascended the Mount of Civilization, to a point never before attained; the land would have been filled, even through the present regions of guilt, pauperism and destruction in the South, by industrious, prosperous and cultivated dwellers of the land, rejoicing under their own vines and the results of economical industry, the social system advancing, minds refined, education universal, with peace in all our borders. In making the slave suffer, how we have been punished therefor!

ONE IDEA.

Since things are so, let the Liberty party take possession
of the ship, launch it, and put *out to sea*, as soon as their
strength will permit. Let the Liberty party be united.
The great one idea, that a man is a man, the world over, and
is entitled to freedom, and that slavery is a sin against God
and a crime against man everywhere, and that it is your duty
to vote, and you will only *vote* for those who will do all in
their power to crush the crime of slavery, is that on which
you must and will succeed. There never was a great one
idea, founded in eternal truth and the nature of things, which
did not succeed; and there never will be, as long as the
promises of eternal truth stand good.

ALVAN STEWART'S FIRST PUBLISHED SPEECH

AGAINST SLAVERY,

A QUARTER OF A CENTURY AGO, 1835.

ALVAN STEWART, Esq., of Utica, rose and said, that with the consent of the Convention, he would trespass a few minutes on the time of this numerous and honorable body.

He said this was the first Convention which had ever assembled in the United States under such a remarkable state of facts as now existed, and which seem to distinguish this from all public bodies of men who have ever met in this land before. For the last forty days, at least three hundred of the public presses have daily poured a continual shower of abuse upon the callers and the call for this Convention, characterized by a spirit-of vengeance and violence, knowing and proposing nothing but the bitterness of invective, and the cruelty of bloody persecution. Our enemies have sent their slanders against us, whispering across the diameter of the globe, telling the haughty and sneering minions of Absolutism, on the other side of the world, that the sons of the Pilgrims had proved recreant to their lofty lineage, unfaithful to their high destiny, untrue to the last hopes of man. ·

Said Mr. S., Is it true that the philanthropy which warms our hearts into action, for the suffering slave, can exile our patriotism, and prepare our souls for the most heaven-daring guilt? Is it true, because we feel for bleeding humanity, that it makes us cruel? Can pity produce it? Can love beget hate? Can an affectionate respect and kind feeling for all the human beings whom Providence has cast in these twenty-four States, be evidence that we wish to cut the throats of two millions and a half of our white neighbors, friends, brethren and countrymen ? Does a generous regard for the injured slave imply hatred for the master ? If so, the converse of the proposition must be true, that to love the master implies hatred to the slave. Neither proposition is true ; yet the enemies of this Convention have acted toward us as though these propositions had the assurance of certainty, as we have on a clear day at twelve o'clock at noon that the sun shines on the world.

MISREPRESENTATIONS.

We have been proclaimed traitors to our own dear native land, because we love its inhabitants. Our humanity is treason, our philanthropy is incendiarism, our pity for the convulsive yearnings of down-trodden man is fanaticism. Our treason is the treason of Franklin and Jay ; our incendiarism is that of Clarkson and Wilberforce ; our fanaticism is the fanaticism of Earl Grey and Lord Brougham, and the majority of the wisest heads in proud Old England ; our sentiments are those expressed by William Wirt, Patrick Henry, and Thomas Jefferson.

Our creed is to be found in the two great witnesses of God's revealed will to man—the Old and New Testaments. The Declaration of Independence, the Constitutions of our country, and the laws passed under them, we make the rule of our conduct, in imparting our sentiments to others on the subject of slavery.

The enemies of our noble sentiments and elevated intentions, have resorted to the old beaten track of misrepresentation, and by adding to our code views never promulgated, by charging us with intentions never harbored, with expectations never cherished, and as remote from the mind of an abolitionist as infidelity is from the conscience of piety, as meanness is from generosity, as bigotry is from charity, as truth from falsehood, as freedom from slavery, they would fain make us unfit for this world.

We are not judged by evidence, by our own declarations, by either what we have said or done, but by acts which our wily adversaries prophesy we will do, or commit, in some future period of time; and thus they lift the curtain which shuts from all mortal eyes (but prophets') the great unbounded future, and by looking down the vale of time, they behold us engaged in the diabolical and blood-thirsty work of getting laws passed to abolish slavery in the District of Columbia, and the slave Territories, and in this way knocking the fetters from the bondman, which our adversaries call treason calculated to dissolve the Union.

UNIONISTS.

What Union? I doubt not you may see some of these Union patriots here to-day, who would take your life and mine, and that of every member of this Convention, and in so doing think they had done their master a service, and lift up their hands for eternal and unmitigated slavery to every colored man, woman and child in the United States, and throw into the same pile all who differed with them in sentiment, to promote the interest of their master. *These are the patriotic Unionists,* who secretly wish to dissolve the Union, by letting the great cancer grow on the neck of the Union, without attempting its cure or removal. These are the friends of the Union, who are willing to see 2,500,000 men, women and children sacrificed to the demon of Slavery. Those Unionists are willing to destroy you and me, Mr. Chairman, because we are not terrified at the roaring of the slaveholders, and because we feel for two millions and a half of men, women and children who are now being offered at the shrine of cruelty, lust and avarice. These lovers of the Union refuse to hear the loud lamentations of bitter sorrow and hopeless grief, which, like the voice of a mighty flood, ascend day and night from every plantation, every factory, every corn-field, every rice-field, every tobacco-field, every cotton-field, and every kitchen of eleven States, and penetrate the ear of God.

Mr. S. said, The *slaves* never held a convention on the subject of their wrongs; they never met to petition for a redress of grievances, or remonstrate against the manifold injuries by which they are broken down. No! their petition was never read within the walls of legislation! Solemn thought even to us, who for a moment have become his mouthpiece, to tell his wrongs to the world, and demand redress. We, even we, white-skinned Republicans, appear to be on the eve of losing our rights as white men, for having, from the deepest impulses of humanity, become the slave's organ, to explain to an unfeeling world the wrongs inflicted upon him. If white men in non-slaveholding States, encounter so much noisy violence and injury, in barely pleading the cause of the slave before those who have no interest in the slave's body, and whose only interest is to cringe and flatter the master of the slave, what must be the condition of the poor slave, left to plead his own cause against his own master— that master who is fed sumptuously every day, and clothed in purple and fine linen by the *unpaid labor* of the *slave?* When will the glutton, the wine-bibber, the adulterous, the avaricious, and the cruel, listen to the voice of the unaided slave? But some say, "The slaves can be set free twenty or thirty years hence." Ah! will men have less wants then? more justice and humanity then than now? No. Again, if it is right to liberate slaves fifty years hence, the right is the same now, for there will be human beings in the world then, who will claim the slaves by a long line of descent, who will have as many wants to supply with slave labor as men have now. The sun will shine as hot, the rice-lands will be as unhealthy as now.

ABSTRACT SLAVERY.

But we are told by our enemies they love the slaves as well as we do ; and then, with the next word, insult and . abuse us for telling the world his wrongs, or attempting any redress. Mr. S. said he confessed that this was a new mode of manifesting an equality of love. But perhaps we do not understand our opponents ; they may mean that they hate slavery in the abstract, but love it in detail. Or perhaps they mean that they hate the abstract slavery and mean to destroy abstract slavery, by hating all white men who are in favor of its abolition. Perhaps they hate slavery in the abstract, but love the man who causes it in detail so well, that abstract hatred for one purpose is pure love for another. A man might as well say that, abstractly, he hated murder, adultery, swearing and stealing, but that he loved the murderer, adulterer, swearer and thief. Away with northern Jesuitism, which is opposed to abstract slavery, but in favor of its continuance, and ready to kill any one who wishes to change the present posture of slavery, as it practically exists. Oh, shame ! hast thou not a new blush for such conscience-ruining sophistry ?

The same ingenious and fatal distinction has been taken by the wretched metaphysicians, who were willing to barter American liberty to get gold and power, on the subject of free discussion the summer past.

Anti-abolitionists at the North say they believe in free discussion in the abstract, and will not allow it to be drawn in question. But this means, as we find it interpreted and translated in the Dictionary of Daily Experience, that each man may discuss slavery, or anything else, in the silent chamber of his own heart, but must not discuss it in public, as it may then provoke a syllogism of feathers, or a deduction of tar. An abolitionist may have the abstract right of discussion, but it must be disconnected with time and place;— if a majority of his neighbors differ with him, there is no place *where*, or time *when*, he may discuss. This abstract discussion requires an abstract place and abstract time; the abstract place must mean the solitude of the wilderness, or loneliness of the ocean; and the abstract time must mean some portion of the *past* or *future*, as it is never the *present*.

The liberty of an abolition press is to be silent; the liberty of conscience for an Abolitionist is to think to himself; or else to think like his slavery-loving neighbor, or stop *thinking*.

DISSOLUTION OF THE UNION.

The threat of dissolving the Union is the universal medicine for every political difficulty at the South. One day Georgia threatens the dissolution, on account of her Indian territory, gold mines, and State jurisdiction, and the missionaries; then again the poor Union was to be dissolved by the post-office robbing State of South Carolina, to vindicate the beauties of nullification.

Then again, this Union was to have been dissolved in 1828, 1830, 1831, 1832, at four distinct periods within a short space, because the tariff laws were not made to suit certain slave States; but the noble Union held together; we did not hear of a single rafter or brace flinching, in 1835. The Union is to be again dissolved and charged in account current to abolition. The joke of it all is, that northern men profess to be frightened to death every time a negro-driver cries " dissolve the Union—dissolve the *Union*." As well might a man who lived in a powder-house, every time he became angry call for firebrands!

Let southern men dissolve this Union if they *dare ; slavery* would *then* take care of itself, and its masters too ;—in one *little month* both would become extinct. No ! oh, deceived northerner! the southern man will be the last to dissolve this Union ; by it he expects to enjoy his slaves, without it he cannot, one day. But the wily politician of the South has discovered the ghost that never fails to frighten the North, and the North has been kept in a political sweat for the last ten or twelve years, for fear the men, who could not exist as slaveholders without this Union, would dissolve it.

It seems dissolution is threatened by the South, unless thirteen free States disfigure and disgrace their statute books with bloody laws to protect slavery, forbidding Abolitionists to speak, write or publish anything against slavery, or petition for its abolition in the District of Columbia, under heavy penalties; the despotism of which laws would so far exceed any in Russia or Turkey, that Nicholas, and the Grand Seignior, would recoil with instinctive abhorrence, from so foul an insult to our common humanity. So it is not enough that eleven States must bend their backs under the shameful load of slavery, with statute books blushing for the wrongs done by man to man, which all the unfathomed waters of the great deep could not wash away ; but the tongues of northern men, on the subject of slavery, must cleave to the roofs of their mouths, and the indicting hand be palsied in giving the world a history of the negro's woes. MY COUNTRYMEN, YE SONS OF THE PILGRIMS, THE TYRANT IS AT YOUR DOORS, LIBERTY IS BLEEDING, LIBERTY IS DYING, slavery has robbed you of the liberty of discussion, of conscience and the press. Armed mobs are to do the work of the slaveholder, till the legislature obeys his mandate.

Then read from your own statute books your doom ; you are a slave without his privilege ! Had the six hundred delegates, freemen, now before me, been deterred from meeting this day, from fear, IT WOULD HAVE BEEN WORSE THAN IN VAIN, THAT A WARREN FELL, A MONTGOMERY BLED, AND A LAWRENCE EXPIRED.

You, for this moment, are the representatives of American liberty ; if you are driven from this sacred temple dedicated to God, by an infuriated mob, then, my brethren, wherever you go, liberty will go ; where you abide, liberty will abide ; when you are speechless, LIBERTY IS DEAD.

RESPONSE TO THE MESSAGE OF GOV. MARCY,

FEBRUARY, 1836.

I venture to introduce to your consideration a rather *surly* child of mine, which I intend to send to Governor Marcy to nurse.

A. S.

To William L. Marcy, Esq.,

Governor of the State of New York:

What you have written for the public eye in your late message on the subject of abolition, will be answered. The state of mind under which you labored, in this part of your message, it is to be hoped is rather its official state than its private and individual. For it is hardly to be believed that an individual, moving under such a weight of error and sustaining such a burden, would be equal to the discharge of the common duties of life, where truth and tranquillity of mind are so often required. But how much error, prejudice and misrepresentation you are enabled to carry before an abused public, it shall, in part, be the business of this communication to show. Your duty, as far as the Constitution may be your rule, is to communicate to the legislature, the condition of the State, and recommend such matters as you deem expedient.

The Constitution contemplates that you should submit facts to the legislature, or your conclusion from them. You write like most men who have a given conclusion prepared before they know the facts from which it should come, or without regard to fact. No matter, with this class of writers, what may be the distance between fact and assertion, for they appeal to their imagination for their facts, and to their prejudices for their conclusion. You seem not to be aware that you were born and live in an abolition age; that in the last 30 years more has been done for the abolition of slavery than before, in the long and eventful existence of this world. But one would suppose, from your message, some new combination in crime, some hideous monster had arisen, so wonderful in its character, so powerful in its operations, that it will require in its extermination the loss of the liberty of the press, of conscience, discussion, and of the inviolability of the mail. One darling object of the abolition part of your message is, to create a body of public odium against a portion of your fellow citizens, and from your official height to hurl the missiles of insult and abuse, till your virulence ceased from the labor more tired than satisfied.

THE CRIME OF ABOLITIONISTS.

You have charged your fellow citizens with high crimes and misdemeanors; crimes which have made the gibbet their homes, the guillotine their companion, the gallows their elevation.

The crime of these abolitionists, as you know, in its length and breadth, height and depth, is a belief that slavery is wrong, and ought immediately to come to an end, and that they take the liberty of telling the world so; and endeavor to make others think like themselves. You know, as disconnected with the present Presidential question, that every ninety-nine men out of one hundred, at the North, if put on their oaths, would swear that they considered slavery a wrong or a sin, and that they believed it ought immediately to terminate.

This is the feeling of thirteen of the twenty-four States and is the essence of abolition. There are a few aristocrats at the

North, whose consciences are unaffected by the unspeakable
wrongs done the slave, who would, with yourself and Governor McDuffie, agree that domestic slavery is the true foundation of the social edifice. As much as you may affect to be
surprised to find your sentiments so fully known, it will be
proved from your late message before this communication is
finished. If ever a society should be formed in South Carolina or Louisiana to perpetuate slavery, you may expect, at
their first meeting, a resolution will be passed conferring on
you an honorary membership in the most flattering language.
I believe it would pain you from your inmost soul if you
believed the efforts of the Abolitionists should be rewarded,
in the next five years, with universal emancipation.

VOICE OF THE FATHERS.

You profess with many of the slaveholders to admire
Thomas Jefferson as a sort of Moses who led the people of
this land out of the wilderness ; he said he trembled for his
country, when he remembered that God was just, and in a
servile war that no attribute of the Almighty could be found
to aid the white man. In sentiment, Thomas Jefferson was
an Abolitionist.

Patrick Henry, Luther Martin, and William Wirt were
believers in abolition doctrines and proclaimed them to the
world. Such men could not exist with their sentiments suppressed, where the happiness of millions was concerned.
The late John Jay, one of the triumvirate of the Federalist,
and governor of this State, was an Abolitionist, in the largest
sense of the word. Benjamin Franklin, not unknown to fame,
was an Abolitionist. The men who composed the first Congress which ever met, in 1774, recommended that the slave-
trade should cease in the December after; were not these
men Abolitionists ?

ENGLAND'S GLORY

Clarkson, Wilberforce, Huskinson, Canning, Lord Brougham, O'Connell, and Earl Grey were *Abolitionists ;* those intellectual giants who led glorious England, at the cost of one million dollars, to destroy slavery in her dominions ; yes, the year 1833 shows you England expending by a single act of legislation, in behalf of suffering humanity, more than all the other legislatures in the world have done. England, proud and noble old England, on whose dominions the sun never sets, whose rule one hundred and fifty millions obey, one-fifth of the human race, is a mighty nation of Abolitionists ; and if every page of the works of England's great *dead* were torn from the libraries of the world, and every monument of her glory in arts and arms forever destroyed, save, oh ! save her the act of legislation of 1833, by which 820,000 slaves were emancipated at the cost of $100,000,000. She would then stand alone in that sun of glory which would never set.

Were Jefferson, Henry, Martin, Wirt, Jay, Franklin, Clarkson, Wilberforce, Huskinson, Canning, Brougham, Grey, O'Connell, and England's millions, all fanatics, and reckless incendiaries ? For these English Abolitionists are as much like American, as truth is verity.

THE ABOLITION AGE.

But, sir, I will give you more abolition, and show you that you are so far behind, as to be out of sight of the march of events, if you do not discover this to be the abolition age ; and if there is one thing more than any other, on which the Americans and Europe, with the different governments of which they are made up, have acted in the last twenty years in harmony, it has been in the abolition of slavery and in expressing the universal abhorrence of the trade. Bonaparte, in 1815, on his return from Elba, declared himself an Abolitionist, and by decree forbid Frenchmen being engaged in the slave trade.

In 1817, Louis XVIII. became an Abolitionist and ratified the act of Bonaparte. Spain, in December, 1817, declared the slave trade should cease after May, 1820; and thus Ferdinand VII. became affected with abolitionism. Portugal, in 1818, abolished this trade north of the Equator.

Holland, Prussia, Denmark, and Russia, expressed their abhorrence about the same time. These several decrees of abolition by the several countries of Europe, were hastened, and probably accomplished, in obedience to a general resolution, passed by the holy alliance, which Congress of Sovereigns met at Vienna in 1815, and from the irrepressible feelings of common humanity, and with a view to the drawing an odious comparison between their monarchical sentiments, without negro slavery, and our republican government with it, declared that the voice of the civilized world demanded the universal abolition of African slavery, in all its connections with that ill-fated continent.

Abolition has an abiding home, from the pillars of Hercules to the regions of eternal ice : in the nobleman's bosom, in the palace of kings, in the Congress of sovereigns. The empire of Mexico, with as many slaves of negro and Indian as this nation contains, abolished slavery, in the last twenty years; this is an empire of Abolitionists. Hayti is a volcano of abolitionism, warning the world, when men have come from slavery to freedom, to never attempt their reduction a second time. What are all those mighty republics on both sides of the Andes and Equator but empires of pure abolitionism? Brazil, it is believed, stands alone, in the crime of slavery; excepting which, through the vast plains of the tropics, no slave is seen working in the light of the sun, where nature, attired in her grandest costume, looks down from Chimborazo, the throne of her majesty, while the voice of liberty commanded the slaves of mammon's slaves to come from the bowels of the mountains, the deep mines of the earth, from misery's home, from three hundred years of bondage, to equality, liberty and law. These, also, are the empires of abolitionism. The Abolitionists of the United States have, in the Empire of Mexico, South America, Hayti, and the countries of Europe, which in the last thirty years have manifested their disposition to be Abolitionists, no less than two hundred and fifty millions, or one-third of the human family, being the whole of the civilized and Christianized world, except a part of my own dishonored and disgraced country. But this is not all the capital with which we, insulted Abolitionists, have to set up business. We think we have a large amount of abolition stock garnered up in the hearts of thirteen free States of this republic; yes, we believe we have magazines of this explosive substance, in the sad regions of slavery, treasured in the trembling hearts of Christian masters, who remember that God is just. We have five hundred abolition societies, one hundred and fifty of which have been added since the outrage of Utica. This is abolitionism dwindling! so you try to deceive the South till after the ides of December, 1836. The voice of these five hundred societies will ring in your ear and the slaveholder's till there is not a slave in America. It is the voice of Mexico, the voice of South America, the voice of Hayti, the voice of all Europe, the voice of the age, the voice of the world, the voice of Almighty God.

Yet, sir, you have had the weakness to echo back the tyrant's yell, and call that voice when it has been sounded by your constituents, the voice of recklesness, the voice of fanaticism, the voice of the incendiary. We find you meditating a stab at the Constitution you have sworn to protect. We find you telling the legislature in that message, that you have no doubt they possess *that* attribute of State sovereignty, which has the power to silence this voice of abolitionism forever.

SURRENDERED POWERS.

You say, with great cunning in your logic, that the legislature must possess it, because this State has not surrendered the power to the General Government. A strange argument to fall from the lips or pen of a man bred a lawyer, once a judge and now a governor. Upon that principle the legislature might appoint a king to rule the State of New York; because the people of the State never delegated the power to the General Government of making a king, therefore it must be reserved to the legislature, who, if they have not power to make a king, it would prove the State was not a sovereign and independent State, and was destitute of the attributes of sovereignty. The people of this State have never surrendered the trial by jury to the control of the General Government, therefore, according to your reasoning, the legislature have a right to abolish it in all cases. For if they could not abolish it, there would be a want of sovereignty. The right to take private property for public purposes, without compensation, has never been surrendered to the General Government, therefore the legislature of *this* State have the right. If the Roman Catholic religion should be found disagreeable to the eleven slave States, and they should make a great outcry against their ceremonies and ritual, and threaten to split the Union, unless the State of New York passed laws to banish or punish with death, all professors of the Roman faith, you would say with the same propriety you have now done in relation to the abolitionists, that this State had never delegated to the General Government the power of suppressing or regulating religion, therefore the legislature has the power of abolishing the Roman Catholic religion, with a penalty of death for disobedience; for if the legislature has not this power, the State lacks an attribute of sovereignty, which cannot be, when that attribute is necessary for preserving peace with our neighbors.

Into such unfathomable depths of absurdity your zeal to serve the slaveholder has precipitated you. You forgot the very Constitution from which you derived your authority to make your message. You forgot that, whether powers are delegated to the General Government or not, we have a Constitution restraining you, the judiciary and the legislature, from the exercise of certain powers forbidden to be used under any circumstances whatever.

There is a class of rights of the most personal and sacred character to the citizen, which are a portion of individual sovereignty, never surrendered by the citizen, in coming into the compact of civil society, either to the State or General Government, and the constitutions of the States and Union have told the world, after enumerating them, that there is a class of unsurrendered rights, which the citizen refused, in making the compact, to throw into the mass or common stock of surrendered rights for legislative discretion; and the legislatures of the States and Union are forbidden by the constitutions of the States and Union from touching those unsurrendered rights; no matter in what distress or exigency a State may find itself, the legislature can never touch those unsurrendered rights as objects of legislation. We may suppose the citizens of this State saying at the time the Constitution was formed, as we learn from the Constitution itself, "we will not submit all the rights we possess in a state of nature to the discussion of legislative action; they are too sacred, too liable to abuse, they are a part of our personal sovereignty, which we will never submit to the will of another, and we here mark these personal reserved rights of individual sovereignty in the constitution of the State of New York.

"We will never surrender the free exercise and enjoyment of religious profession and worship; without discrimination and preference, it shall be allowed in this State to all mankind."

2d. And the following are the words of our State constitution which you had forgotten, or hoped the Abolitionists had: "Every citizen may freely speak, write and publish his sentiments on all subjects, being responsible for the abuse of that right; and no law shall be passed to restrain or abridge the liberty of speech or of the press."

The 8th section of the 7th article of our constitution shows you and the world that the people of this State never surrendered the liberty of speech, discussion, or the press to the legislature. Oh, what scenes of abuse would have been played off before this world, if licensed presses, gagged discussion, and mail inquisitors had been tolerated! And we should have seen such laws passed in this State by a party who had the ascendency, if the constitution had not forbidden it, by which one half of the community could neither speak, write nor publish anything of their adversaries, under the pain of indictments, fine and imprisonment. We infer this from the nature of man, for those arguments which reason cannot answer, force has often attempted. We see you willing (in case Abolitionism continues to hold up its head), in subserviency to slave dictation, to leap the barriers of the constitution, and advise the legislature to do the same act, and seize upon the liberties of speech, discussion and the press. Yes, you profess your willingness to make slaves of the Abolitionists, load them with chains and cover them with disgrace, trample on the ruined Constitution of your country, to purchase the haughty smile that may play over the features of that despot who owns five hundred slaves, as he sees the Empire State wallowing in the mire of tyranny, and bowing down its head in fearful trepidation before the unrelenting cruelties of slavery and the boisterous howls of despotism. You may lay the axe to the root of the tree of liberty, you may cut it down, so that liberty of speech, discussion, and the press shall be laid in one common grave; this is the course adopted by mobs, in anticipation of your legislative recommendation; by those mobs which have dishonored your administration, and have nearly overwhelmed the republic; let them cheer you and the makers of those laws; but be assured those laws when passed will be treated with scorn and contempt, and their execution, when attempted, will be written in blood.

ABOLITIONISTS ABOVE-BOARD.

Abolitionists have nothing to conceal; their actions are done on the house-top, their progress is under the eye of the world, their march is in the face of the sun, they have no community to abuse and mislead, they have no mobs to inebriate and flatter, they have no support but religion and humanity, they have no power but the opinion of the civilized world and the voice of eternal truth; they have no auxiliaries, but everlasting justice, and enlightened conscience; they have no prospect of success, but in the inability of eleven slave States to resist their own good, and brave the withering scorn of an insulted world.

You seem to sneer at " the potency of abolition arguments to instruct a slaveholder in his duty." You assert that the slaveholders understand and practise the *rights* and duties growing out of civil and political liberty, as well as the citizen of the North. Is it so, governor? Then you approve of Governor McDuffie's message, who asserts slavery to be right, and the pillar of the social edifice; and what would incline one to have no doubt, that at heart you love slavery like a southerner, you do nowhere in your turgid message, even insinuate that slavery is wrong, or express the feeblest desire it should come to an end. The fair interpretation, in the judgment of charity, is, that your message was intended as an artful indorsement of all the bold and horrible doctrines of McDuffie's message, by which two and one-fourth millions of human beings are to toil under the mercies of the lash, from the cradle to the grave. And you, sir, educated in the sunshine of New England's morality and abhorrence of slavery, have for a mess of slaveholding presidental pottage, proved traitor to the rights of man, and in defiance of reason and conscience, thrown yourself into the putrid and cancerous embraces of slavery.

You have published the bans of your marriage to slavery, in a message to the legislature of this State—what will be the fruits of your elevated alliance it requires neither second sight nor a prophet to tell; it will be dishonor and unmeasured regret.

MOBS, THE PANACEA FOR ERRORS OF OPINION.

You say, "I rely on the influence of public opinion to restrain the misconduct of citizens of a free government, especially when directed with such unexampled energy and unanimity to the evils under consideration, and perceiving that its operations have thus far been *salutary*, I entertain the best hopes that this remedy itself will entirely remove the evils or render them comparatively harmless."

Thus we have your solemn indorsement of all the mobs which have, or may hereafter, disgrace your administration; all the mobs which by violence may drive the freemen of this State from their own houses and churches, while discussing the questions as to the evils of slavery, and the best manner of terminating those evils—yes, these mobs are what you call a "sound and enlightened public opinion," headed by some half-a-dozen minions of slavery, your friends, leading them on with clubs, stones, brick-bats, the dregs of community under the influence of liquor, maddened by your street orators, at sentiments charged on Abolitionists they never entertained, opinions they never advanced, projects they never harbored. Then the mob will advance upon the house of silence, order, sobriety, philanthropy and prayer, and with all sorts of screams and yells, throw missiles and break doors and windows, with oaths, blasphemies, swearing vengeance while they rush into the house like famished tigers, and drive with violence and blood the inmates therefrom, while they tear the Bibles and psalm-books in tatters, threatening instant death to some, and violence to all; the whole night after being spent in drunkenness and debauchery, while the village or city is horror-struck by the violence, misrule and uproar.

This is your enlightened public opinion, which you and the minions of slavery have brought to bear on Abolitionists the past year, which you so highly approve—and hope will still be employed.   Is this the governor of the State of New York, who is the leader of mobs by a public approval in his message of 1836 to the·legislature of this State?   A mob, which all men but yourself, who have dared to write on the subject, have considered a greater evil than any possible one they could be invoked to remedy, you have selected as one of the most efficient and salutary means of correcting errors of opinion.   The mobs of 1835 have done more to destroy the confidence of the friends of liberty, in a republican form of government, than all the untoward events which have happened since the settlement of America.

· But I need not pause to inform a statesman of the operations of a machine, which he has selected as the leading executive organ of his administration, a remedy so salutary

in its nature, so healthy and vigorous in its effects, in dis-
lodging error from the human mind, being especially calculated for this end from its moderation in action, its wisdom in
the selection of its arguments, the urbanity with which they
are enforced—being only equalled by the conclusiveness of
the logic employed to illuminate a mind lost in the labyrinths
of *fanatical incendiary recklessness*, which means, to wish a
slave a freeman, and instead of a brute for a master, that he
may have the law.

You suppose your new discovery to be a universal panacea
in government. If men are wrong in their notions on the
subject of religion, or do not think like a majority of their
neighbors, let a mob go and burn their houses or barns;
that will make them think like the majority; or if the minority
should discuss their opinions in their own houses or churches,
let the mob in upon them with a flood of brick-bats; they
will see the errors of liberty of speech and free discussion,
and repent of it in the awfulness of silence.

A stone sent against a man's head by a mob, is the short
and improved mode of introduciug truth in the place of falsehood. Do I need an authority to sustain this position? I
will cite to you the governor of New York's message to the
legislature of New York, in January, 1836. If a man is
affected with philanthropy, or love to his fellow man, let a
mob of tigers lead him by a rope around his neck, and choke
him till he is black—he will see his mistake. If a man has
seen that passage of Holy Writ, by which we are commanded, " Whatsoever things ye would that men should do
unto you, do the same thing to them," let the individual be
taken by a mob, tarred, feathered, and then be carried two
miles on a sharp rail with a string of cow-bells hanging round
his neck. This is Governor Marcy's medicine for a mind so
obstinately diseased—and he hopes that, by such a course,
this fanatic will read his Bible in this way, " Whatsoever

you *would not* that men should do unto you, *do that unto them.*" The grand benefit of this scheme, when carried out in its fullest extent, is to save a community from the trouble or distraction of having two or more opinions on one subject. By applying mob law, we need have but one opinion, on any subject from an oyster to a fixed star.

It may become useful to have a military mob at the Capitol, to cut short protracted discussion ; let the government originate whatsoever laws the public welfare may require, and if Congress were taught a few wholesome rules of military mobism, they too have nothing to do but to think like the government ; and if any man is refractory, and wishes to discuss, let him be shot through the head with an ounce ball, and he will never think different from the government again, or discuss. Thus Congress might do all the business of the nation in the afternoon, and save the country much expense in sitting from December to July, employed in noisy discussions and clamorous debate.

ABOLITIONISM DYING.

But, sir, in stating the fact that abolition is hastening to an end in this State, you are greatly mistaken, for since the Convention was broken up in Utica, by your mob-regulation, in administering one of their salutary lessons of rebuke, one hundred and fifty societies have been added to the Abolitionists.

Governor, you are like some other men who state their wishes for facts, and are not able to distinguish between their meditations by day, and their dreams by night.

But am I mistaken in supposing this part of your message was made to order, for transportation south of the Potomac, and was not intended for domestic use, but was intended as a New Year's present to your southern friends, therefore is not subject to the common laws of criticism, which require certainty enough to make it a relative to a probability ? Permit me to assure you, that the attempt of the mob at Utica, to suppress free discussion by a convention of more than five hundred men, as respectable as any body of persons who ever met for the public good, on this continent, has been the direct means of adding thousands to the Abolitionists.

Let me assure you further that your leading political friends in this vicinity, many of them, one year ago signed a petition to abolish slavery in the District of Columbia ; I mention this to prove, as conclusive evidence, the general abhorrence society, uninfluenced by extraneous causes, feels against the crime of slavery. I think he must be an unapt scholar in human affairs, who can draw any distinction between the crime of slavery, in the District of Columbia, or in the State of South Carolina.

THE CONSTITUTION AND SLAVERY.

You seem to assert that some section, article, or, if neither, the spirit of the Constitution of the Union, is violated in the crusade of Abolitionists against slavery. To redeem that instrument from the imputation thrown on it as perpetually upholding slavery has been the main cause of this communication. What is there in our federal Constitution since the expiration of the 9th section of the 1st article in 1808, on the subject of slavery ? For I admit that all the horrors of slavery were wrapped up in the 9th section of the 1st article which expired in 1808. Its words are these : " The migration or importation of such persons as the States now existing shall think proper to admit shall not be prohibited before 1808," which section, strange to relate, is made irrepealable by the Constitution-making power itself, by a clause in the 5th article. Sir, the Constitution itself, in providing for the short life of the 9th section, thereby impliedly admits the wrong which might be done under it, in taking the slave trade into its arms for nineteen years, and covering it under its sanctions. Do you not know that under the soft and mild phraseology, "The migration or importation of such persons as the States now existing think proper to admit, etc., from 1789 to 1808," for the space of nineteen long years, not less than one million of the fathers and mothers of the present generation of slaves were stolen and kidnapped from Africa by virtue of the irrepealable 9th section of the 1st article? Yes, the South refused the benefit of this Constitution, and of the confederacy, and were willing to forego all the blessings it confers, rather than surrender the bloody advantages of the slave trade for nineteen years. This reveals the secret, and shows which at that time they would have preferred, the atrocity of the slave trade, or the Union without it. And to bring the South into the measure of the Union and adoption of the Constitution, the North were constrained, in their *then* distressed condition, to accept the Constitution, on such bloody and cruel terms. What an instrument to hold up in the face of the sun in the presence of the civilized world!

The bonus or premium given by the North to the South for the adoption of the Constitution, as the *sine quâ non* on the part of the South, was that the slave States for nineteen years should have the unforbidden right to crimson every river of Africa with the blood of her children, the right for nineteen years to make her valleys and mountains echo with groans of her kidnapped sons and daughters, the constitutional right for nineteen years to pillage, rob, ravish and murder her inhabitants, and by the light of their blazing homes, make midnight like noon, to pursue and overtake the affrighted and horror-struck inhabitants and load them with fetters, in a ship of the middle passage, many of whose bodies fattened the wake-pursuing · sharks, while the men of the Carolinas stood upon the shore, to purchase the survivors under the irrepealable ninth section.

This expired ninth section of our Constitution, to our eternal dishonor, was the most solemn and deliberate insult ever offered to our common humanity, and is without a parallel in the long annals of human atrocity; but thank God—in 1808 it came to an end.

Since 1808, that instrument is free from the imputation of sustaining slavery, directly or indirectly; and the man who should offer it as an authority to prove the perpetuity of slavery, ought to blush for his temerity. Its silence in the use of the word *slave* is a rebuke louder than a thunder peal, telling the world slavery should never exist by its authority, that if the offence was committed, for the first nineteen years of its existence, yet the absence of the word "*slavery*" was a protest against the offence, and an everlasting acknowledgment of the shame the instrument would have felt by its insertion.

The Congress of the United States, in May 1820, to manifest the horror they felt, for the crimes committed under the 9th section of the first article of the Constitution, then expired, declared by a public law, that any American citizen, who should be guilty of kidnapping, or taking a negro from Africa (being the precise act tolerated by the Constitution from 1789 to 1808), should be declared a *pirate* and punished with death. Sir, is not the act of Congress of 1820, the most solemn rebuke ever found in the records of legislation, of the evils tolerated in the 9th section of the first article?

The 3d section of the 1st article of the Constitution, for the purpose of fixing the basis of a representation in Congress, says that "to the whole number of free persons, including those bound to service for a term of years, and excluding Indians not taxed, three-fifths of all other persons are to be added." This section, the friends of slavery contend is a constitutional compact, to uphold and maintain slavery; I contend it proves the reverse of the proposition, and is a section which expresses, in spirit if not in words, the abhorrence this Constitution has for slavery. The free States, in fixing a basis for a ratio of representation, include every man, woman, child, pauper, idiot, alien, criminal or malefactor, in those States, under the word "free persons," in the first line quoted from the section. What is the argument or fact insisted on by the slave States?   Why, that under the word, "persons," their slaves shall be counted in fixing the ratio or basis of representation, as a counterpoise to the women, children, idiots, paupers, aliens and criminals, included under the words "free persons, in Massachusetts." The non-slaveholding States, or those who had but few slaves and were in a course of emancipation, saw their opportunity, which they did not fail to improve, to wit, that if slaves were to be counted as persons, in fixing the ratio or basis of representation, five slaves should count no more, in the enumeration, than three free persons ; which would be a continual encouragement, and, in fact, a premium to be paid in *political power* for the emancipation of the slaves, who would then swell in the count from three to five-fifths. If all the slaves were made free, in the slave States, those States would be entitled to twelve more members of Congress than they now have. This is the amount of political power offered by the Constitution to the slave States, in case those States will emancipate their slaves. The language of this section of the Constitution is, slavery is wrong, and you of the slave States are to be punished in the loss of political power, as long as you uphold it; by abating the amount of your representation in Congress two-fifths upon this class of persons, it is intended to express the abhorrence the Constitution has against slavery, by an abatement of your political power, until you set your slaves free.

This is a constitutional premium in favor of human liberty. Suppose the Constitution had on its face forbidden the slaves to be taken into the account, in fixing a basis of representation. Would not this have been the strongest expression possible against slavery? If that would be the effect of a total rejection of the slave enumeration, is not the argument the same in kind, if not in degree, which rejects two-fifths of the slave census?

Thus the Constitution shows itself inimical to slavery, in that way which would most strongly tend to its abolition. If the slave had not been taken into the enumeration upon any principle, the bounty offered by the Constitution, for their emancipation, would have been forty representatives, in Congress, to which their numbers, when emancipated, would entitle them. The tone of political power would have been too strong for slavery itself, and would have burst its bonds.

If this argument is sound when applied to a rejection of the whole number of slaves, it must be when applied to the rejection of two-fifths; the difference is only in degree; in the supposed case, the bounty paid for emancipation would be forty seats in Congress, whereas it now offers twelve or thirteen. The principle is the same. The Constitution is neutral; it leans many degrees in favor of liberty, and against slavery as a system; not barely in cold advice, but in holding up motives of political power for its abandonment.

The apologists for slavery at the North and South, who wish to hang upon the skirts of the Constitution, and convert the temple of liberty into a cave of slavery, claim to find a constitutional compact for slavery in the 2d section of the 4th article of the Constitution, by which persons held to service under the laws of one State, escaping into another, shall be delivered up, on claim of the persons to whom the service is due. Though slaves may have been delivered up, who were even fugitives from one State to another, by virtue of this provision, yet, it does not follow, that this section was necessarily created for such an object.

No, sir, a man who should contract to work for another two years, or any other given time, an apprentice bound to his master, a principal fleeing from his bail, or a child from his parent, or a wife from her husband, would all fairly come within the scope of this provision of the Constitution, and fulfill its spirit and letter, without necessarily including or excluding fugitive slaves.   And this section of the 4th article of the Constitution would be equally necessary as now, if there were not a slave in this land.   The Constitution would be clearly defective, without such section, were there no slaves, for the surrender of the apprentice, the principal in case of bail, the wife, the child, etc., fleeing from those persons to whom their services were due.   Suppose there was a treaty between England and the United States, that England would surrender up all fugitive slaves fleeing to her dominions from the United States, to their owner, would that treaty be a bar to England's expositions to obtain from us the abolition of slavery?   No!   Strange would be the reply of the United States if she should say, "Ah! England, by agreeing to surrender our fugitive slaves, you have covenanted slavery is right; you therefore have barred yourself from censuring the practice; you have adopted it and made it your own; the agreement to surrender is an agreement that slavery is an institution of Heaven and a pillar of the social system.   You have no business to intermeddle, expostulate, or even to endeavor to convince, by arguments, that it is wrong."

This would be called strange morality, and still stranger logic.   The Constitution in many of its parts is nothing but a treaty between the then thirteen, now twenty-four States, doing that by a perpetual Constitution, which independent nations do by treaty.   The second section of the 4th article is of this character, and does by no means sustain slavery, on its face or by necessity, but without the clause, if there was not a slave in the land, the States would be involved in continual difficulties, in relation to those persons fleeing from one State to another.

AMERICAN SENTIMENT AND LEGISLATION.

It shall be my business to show that, as far as this nation has acted on the subject of slavery, the nation is anti-slavery in its character, and abolitionist, as it concerns the great crime against man. So far as its opinions and sentiments are deducible from its laws, a brief review of national legislation may be instructive in its deductions. For it is said the character of a people may be learned in their laws. This is a political axiom.

The first Continental Congress which met in Philadelphia in 1774, expressed its deep abhorrence of slavery, and manifested its principles in a resolution of loud condemnation of the slave trade, by a resolution not to import or purchase any slave imported after December, in that year, and thus abolish the trade.

2d. The Constitution of the United States refused to countenance the slave trade after the first of January, 1808.

3d. By the acts of Congress passed March 22, 1794, and May 10, 1800, citizens and residents of the United States were forbidden, under penalties, from engaging in the transportation of slaves from the United States to any other country; or from one foreign country to another foreign country, for the purpose of traffic. In fact, these States presented the moral absurd, on account of the 9th section of the 1st article of the Constitution of the United States. These two acts of Congress forbid the American citizen from being concerned in the slave trade everywhere, except he brought the slave to *his own land.*

4th. By an act of Congress, passed 2d March, 1807, the slave trade was prohibited after the 1st of January, 1808, under a severe penalty, being the day the 9th section of the 1st article expired.

5th. On the 26th April, 1818, Congress passed a law, by which the penalties were increased for importing slaves.

6th. By an act of Congress, passed in 1819, armed vessels were authorized to go to the African coast and stop the trade, as far as our citizens were concerned, and seize the vessels of those who had slaves.

7th. By an act of Congress, passed 15th May, 1820, it was declared that if any American citizen, or any person for him, should land in Africa, and import a person therefrom, with the intent of making him a slave, or forcibly bring said person on board said ship, such citizen or person should be adjudged a pirate, and on conviction, suffer death.

Thus we have no less than seven solemn expressions of the nation; one a resolution of the old Congress, and six acts of Congress since the adoption of the Constitution.

Thus we see public opinion, as the law, marching forward in a steady progress, from the simple resolve that it was wrong, through all the grades of ascending penalty, till the crime became piracy, and its punishment death.

The principle on which these laws of the nation rest, is that slavery is a crime, perpetrated by him who deprives another of his liberty by dispossessing him of all right to the fruit of his own labor, or the benefit of his own powers, mental or corporeal. Can the wit of man show me any difference in the extent or amount of injury done to a slave, in being stripped of all the rights which make him a man, whether it be done north or south of the equator, in this parallel of longitude or that degree of latitude, on this side of the world or the other, in Africa, on the ocean, in Carolina or Vermont?

The injury done to him is one and indivisible, the same in all times and all places. To him all forms of government are alike, he can claim nothing from any; the despotism of Turkey, the monarchy of France, the republic of the United States, find him nothing but a *thing* bereaved of every natural or acquired right. No change changes his destiny. The slave is the same anywhere, everywhere, in all times, the same yesterday, to-day and forever. If so, how powerfully do these acts of Congress upbraid and reproach every slaveholder in this nation, and you, his apologist, with injustice.

Those statutes are a moral indictment in which every slaveholder in this nation may find his name, with that of his apologists included. If the lowest moan of the oppressed is heard and remembered in heaven against the oppressor, what must be the size of your offence against poor miserable humanity, to throw the weight of your official temporary consequence against the slave, by which he may be sunk lower in the mire, and be made an exile from the land of his fathers no less than from your cold bosom.

Have not the northern States, in consenting to the 9th section of the 1st article for nineteen years, become " particeps criminis " against those, or the children of those, who were brought here by it? Have we not a right to repent and remonstrate with our partners in guilt, who are now rolling in wealth on the unpaid labor of those beings, or their children, brought here under the 9th section? But you still point to the Constitution of the United States to uphold this offence—you would fain make it confess itself the citadel of slavery. Is this Constitution that nondescript, in political science, with the words of liberty on its tongue, and republicanism in its mouth; is it that hag, "which palters in a double sense, and keeps the word of promise to the ear, to break it to the hope?" Does it veil beneath its folds an eternal engagement to keep millions in the most hopeless bondage?

A rule of great benignity in the construction of a statute,

for which we are indebted to that great legacy of wisdom bequeathed us by the common law, is, that where words in a statute admit of a double construction, that which is in favor of human liberty and justice is always to be adopted. Another rule derived from the same source is, that when there is doubt in the construction of a statute, the preamble of that statute may be resorted to as a key to unlock the mind and true intent of the legislature in the enactment of the law. Let us apply these principles to the Constitution of the Union.

Is it to be believed or endured that a Constitution whose preamble proclaims to the world that it was made " for a more perfect union, to establish *justice*, promote the *general welfare* and secure the blessings of *liberty* to *ourselves* and our *posterity* forever," is only a covenant of eternal injustice, with everduring misery to millions of our population? If your construction of this Constitution, with that of the slave-holder's be right, the preamble should have been in these words: " We, the people of the United States, in order to establish successful injustice and eternal tyranny over the millions of our black population, and to secure our own independence, welfare and prosperity as far as white men are concerned, do establish," etc.

We have the direct authority of the framers of the Constitution, that their object in the Constitution was to promote liberty and justice; you and your southern friends by your construction say it was made to promote eternal injustice, and hopeless slavery to millions. Which shall prevail, your opinion or that of the men who made it?

Could a stranger to our institutions find the time or section where slavery is sustained in the Constitution?

Would he find it in the 4th section of the 4th article, which guarantees to every State in the Union a republican form of government?

Would he select Louisiana, a State in which a majority of the inhabitants are slaves, and some of them with chains on their legs, with iron bands belting their waists and necks, with iron horns four feet in length fastened to those iron collars, to prevent the wearer's escape, in the cane-brakes, while others have a chain twenty feet long fastened to the belt of the waist, at one end, while the other is united to a sixty pound weight of iron, which the slave lifts and carries in advance, the length of his chain, and then returns and works up to it with his hoe, and thus repeats the operation as often as necessary, and when night comes, amidst rattling chains, cracking whips, and gory backs, they are marched into pounds, and again chained to staples in the wall, till the coming morn? Yes, the 4th section of the 4th article is a standing covenant against slavery.

And it is impossible to fulfill that guaranty of a republican form of government while one half of the persons in a State are slaves to another. For, could Louisiana with 100,000 white men and 200,000 slaves be said to have a republican form of government, which regards all persons as equal in the eye of the law?

This section of the Constitution is violated by every slave State, and will never be honored or respected till universal emancipation takes place.

For the very idea of a republican form of government holds all persons under it equal in the eye of the law. Can a State tolerating slavery be said to have a republican form of government? If so, the most stupid tyranny which ever governed the dolts of India may be called a republican form of government. An aristocracy might be called a republican form of government, for in that form the grandees are equal; but the common people are not the equals of the grandees, in the eye of the law, any more than the slaves of Carolina are the equals of Gov. McDuffie in the eye of the law.

OMISSIONS IN THE MESSAGE.

The time may not be far distant, when the ghost of this message will haunt your dreams of popularity by day and by night, and show its spectral form astride every path of your future advancement. The time may not be far distant, when your repentance may be too late, for lending your official message as an indorsement of all the mobs by which your administration has been sullied, by which the dignity of the State has been dishonored, which will draw down upon you the reproaches of an insulted people; while you have barely firmness to resist the myrmidons thirsting for William's blood in Alabama, while in effect you beg pardon of Governor Gale for your refusal to deliver him up. You might as well have sent an apology for not selling the sovereignty of the State, as you had conveyed that to the mobs. You can overlook the insult done to the sovereignty of New York by slave States in offering $50,000 to kidnap one of our principal citizens, and carry him from his home to be sacrificed to the orgies of slavery, in a foreign land. Such insults on sovereignty as these, cannot draw forth a line of reprehension from your pen.

Neither did you know the State was insulted in her sovereignty, when you saw 50,000 of your fellow-citizens indicted under general presentments of southern juries, charging your citizens to the amount of four hundred societies of abolitionists, with the crimes of murder, robbery, arson, and holding them up as objects of odium to the civilized world. All this you bear with tameness, permitting the world to believe that the State over which you preside has hundreds of organized societies who are incendiaries, and whose object is to burn houses, cities and towns; men who have made themselves obnoxious to the vengeance of the human race.

Do you vindicate them, and point the world to the Constitution and laws of their country, which they have never violated? No; but you are torturing your invention to find how an act of an Abolitionist, which is right and constitutional in the State of New York, because people in other States do not like it, for that cause, may be punished as criminal here.

Before you can render that criminal in Abolitionists, in foreign States, which is innocent at home, you must destroy your Constitution. What an insult to New York for Virginia to demand that New York shall violate her constitution, and turn the constitutional acts of her citizens into crimes, because, forsooth, Virginia fears her own citizens in time may, by the force of reason and discussion, entertain the same opinion as New York, to wit, that slavery is wrong. Hunt the pages of legislation through the civilized world for your precedent, and your search will be as hopeless as your object is iniquitous.

FREE SPEECH.

Farewell to liberty, law and unsurrendered individual sovereignty, fenced by the most solemn constitutions, when the citizens of New York may not discuss, or print and circulate their sentiments on any moral problem, or any question of right and wrong, of liberty or slavery. As well might France call on the United States to apologize for the President's message, as for Virginia to call on New York to bow down to slavery in apologetic laws, in overthrowing the constitutional barriers erected for the defence of our citizens. If we obey one State, we ought in civility to obey every State's request, so that we may have not less than twenty-three distinct tracks marked out for this State to pursue, or twenty-three masters. The State of New York says, I know my citizens have violated no duty and are acting within their constitutional limit; but the acts of my citizens are not approved by other States, and on the principle of intermediate or international law, to preserve peace and friendship with my neighbors, I must take away their constitutional rights, and instead of my being their master, my neighbors are to be their future governors, lords and judges. Virginia might as well ask for the title deeds to our sovereignty, and that our citizens should sign a perpetual indenture of apprenticeship to her haughty State. The North have, in paying tribute to the word *Union*, consented to the insertion of the 9th section of the 1st article, by which all Africa for nineteen years was made a slaughter-yard for southern cupidity; the North yielded the three-fifth slave representation ratio to the threat of severance by southern dictation; the North admitted Missouri into the Union as a slave State, from the boisterous clamor of southern tyranny, that if the North did not yield, the Union should be rent; the North, in 1832 and 1833, to the terrific cry of nullification and dissolution, sacrificed one thousand millions of northern industry, capital and property, in the destruction of the American system, to propitiate the slaveholder and save the Union.

The last demand now made is under the stereotype threat of dissolving the Union, unless the northern States legislate by express direction of the South, and destroy liberty of speech, discussion, the press, and thirteen constitutions of thirteen States, in obedience to her surly despotism.

Let the non-slaveholding States beware that they do not insult the spirit of the age, dishonor the memory of the valiant dead, and make their posterity blush for the craven spirit of their ancestors.

The time, sir, is at hand when the non-slaveholding States must act in a crisis of all that is dear to our citizens, and will prepare for the annals of the historian, a page of glory or disgrace; and as that page shall be written, so will the destiny of the Republic be settled: if Slavery is in the ascendant, that page will be the Epitaph of Liberty.

ADDRESS TO THE ABOLITIONISTS

OF THE STATE OF NEW YORK.

As reported by a Committee appointed by the first Annual Meeting of the New York State Anti-Slavery Society, of which Committee Alvan Stewart, Esq., was Chairman, and which was unanimously adopted, October, 1836.

To rescue the helpless, to resist oppression, to elevate the despised, to combat despotism, to instruct and soften the conscience of the master, to make free, exalt, enlighten and invigorate the faculties of the slave, stand before the world, as the objects of prominent pursuit by the New York State Anti-Slavery Society.

What object so sublime, as that which abates the sufferings of man as a physical being, while it amplifies the undying powers, makes the individual conscious of the greatness of his origin, the superiority of his heaven-descended lineage, and his ultimate destiny beyond the oppressions of time, and the cruelties of a transitory world?

What is worthy the pursuit of a tenant of immortality, except that which may place his own body, and that of his neighbor, in the best attitude to have the soul illuminated with the knowledge of itself, of its Author, its obligations to itself, to man, and to God?

But the question is asked every day, who is my neighbor? Every human being, on whom the sun rises or sets, who feels the cold of winter, or the heat of summer, whether he is seated on the throne of power or languishes in the damps of the dungeon; whether he is fed from the table of abundance, or eats his moldy crust under the shadow of a wall; whether he be the owner of the rice, cotton and sugar fields of the sultry South, or the naked, scar-marked, chain-loaded, whip-beaten, under-fed, and unpaid slave who cultivates them.

No matter where he received his birth; whether idolatry has forged its wretched chains for his mind, whether he be educated to lift his hand on the solitudes of Africa, to strip others of what they have; no matter how great the debasement of mind, even if lost in the mazes of Confucius' infidelity; no matter how that mind has been defiled by the rust of superstition, in a succession of ages; no matter with what fearful orgies of the midnight blaze and flowing blood, the sons of Christendom have robbed the black man of himself; no matter how solemn the form by which the planter of the South, by bargain and sale, by written instruments drawn in conformity to the highwayman's code, may make out his title (yes, let him show his bond for human flesh) ; no matter how bloody legislation may attempt to create title deeds, by which man may be sold to man ; no matter how solemn the form of the last will of the dotard, trembling on the confines of the grave, who endeavors to bind to another the slave who has served him through life's brief course; no matter how often he may begin his will, "In the name of God, amen "—(Solemn mockery! God-insulting adjuration! Yes, let southern lawyers bring their 40,000 recorded wills, let us behold these scoffers now, in their noiseless graves, binding 500,000 human beings, to eternal slavery, calling on God with an "amen"—"so might it be," to ratify what might raise a blush on a ruined archangel's cheek;) no matter for all this casuistry, this network of fraud, this inversion of truth ; no matter for all these things, the slave is still a man, our brother, and an inheritor of Eternity—he is still the man who went down from Jerusalem to Jericho, and fell among thieves; and this Society is the Samaritan, who will take him up, bind his wounds, and restore him to himself. Yes, if anything makes one nearer, and dearer, and more of a neighbor than another, it is because his helplessness and misery demand it, and we must obey the heavenly mandate. To enlarge the compass of action beyond the efforts of individual benevolence, in behalf of the poor American slave, and form this Society, one year ago, brought together 600 of the choice spirits of this State, the sons of humanity, from the borders of Lake Erie, the hills of Montauk, the mountains of Delaware, the waters of Champlain, the banks of the Hudson, and the shores of Ontario.

American Slavery is a pyramid of crime—a death shade thrown over this guilty land. Though we were driven from this temple of the Most High, dedicated to Him "who is no respecter of persons," by a mob of native Americans—whose principles on that occasion, were the same as those taught in the school of Danton, Marat, and Robespierre, yet we have reason to thank the Source of all good, that while these enemies of God and man intended it for our harm, it resulted in our good, in adding many thousands to our numbers. Under the sanction of the principles, embodied in the constitution of our Society, we are assembled in the same house, a second time, to publish to our countrymen, the secrets and movements of our Society, with our future intentions. These principles and intentions are inscribed on the hearts of the benevolent, and make their home in the temple of eternal Justice. They are principles which are not depending upon the ebullitions of a floating, unthinking mob, who will shout hosannas to-day, and crucifixion to-morrow; whose minds are unfixed as the whirlwind, one day insulting Heaven and dishonoring earth with fiendish shouts over prostrate humanity, while the next, they build temples to canonize the ashes of the victims they have immolated, and then place in the highest niche of human remembrance, that man as philanthropist, when dead, who, when living, was loaded with obloquy, and covered with reproach. These principles bind in holy harmony a band of philanthropists, who deride the scorn of the haughty, who love the lowest being invested with a never-dying mind, who move forward and upward against the descending stream of popular violence, carrying consolation and deliverance to the prisoner—unawed by the bold front of defiance, but upheld and cheered by the rewards of the final judgment; when the master and slave, the scorner and the scorned, the oppressor and the oppressed, shall stand up for a final analysis of character, before the Judge, at whose presence the heavens and earth will flee away.

To lend energy to truth, to give confidence to virtue, to be numbered with the feeble, to take seats with the humble, to divide our substance with the hungry, never to forsake the dumb, never to cease displaying the slave's wrongs to this guilty age, always to continue haunting the imagination of this slave-grinding nation, with the crimes of the past, the wickedness of the present, and the accountability in the future; while at the same time we implore the Parent of the Universe to hear the cries of the millions of his helpless children, which are ascending day and night from the slave-cursed fields of southern despotism; are objects lying near our hearts.

VIEW OF SLAVERY.

Let us take a view of slavery, as it appears in masses, either for the purpose of seeing the amount of robbery committed on slaves of this land, as a question of money; or the amount of brutal chastisement inflicted to obtain the labor performed; and then let us examine briefly the constitutional power of Congress, to abolish the internal American slave trade, now prosecuted with most of the horrors which accompanied the old African slave trade.

There are at least 500,000 slaves in the slave States, each of whom, at the present prices of produce, earns, over and above his wretched subsistence, $200 per annum, or one hundred millions of dollars. The other 2,000,000 of slaves we put down as earning no more than their miserable subsistence, which is, beyond a doubt, greatly undervaluing their labors. This calculation leaves the slaveholders in the receipt of a net income of one hundred millions of dollars, not one dollar of which belongs to the slaveholder, but every dollar ought to be the slaves'. To-obtain this one hundred millions of dollars from the poor slave, there are inflicted at least, on an average, twenty lashes or blows on the person of each slave, which would not be inflicted were they not slaves, amounting to fifty millions of lashes on the two and a half millions of slaves, or, in other words, a blow is struck for every two dollars earned by the slaves. The fifty millions of lashes is the return the slaveholder makes as a compensation for the $100,000,000 earned for the masters by the poor slaves.

The united robberies, piracies, forgeries, counterfeit-money-passing, and thefts of the whole world for one year, will not equal the sum of which the American slaves are robbed annually. The American slave has been robbed every day for 200 years gone by, by a people whose chivalry consists in the generosity of *that act.* The fifty millions of lashes struck on the American slaves (which would not be if they were free) exceed all the acts of cruelty of the civilized and barbarian world beside. Yes, the twelve slave States of America are the head-quarters of cruelty for the world; the residence of duelling, the native land of Lynch law, where its professors reside and its scholars practise. These States are the asylum of piracy, made respectable by the sanctions of law, where immortal minds are ruined, *in the wholesale,* by constitutional edicts; where the marriage contract is exchanged for wandering adultery. This is the land dedicated to amalgamation, where 500,000 mulattoes testify the affection and *honorable love* existing between the *master* and the *female slave*. This is the land where fathers sell children, and brothers and sisters sell brothers and sisters. This is the same land whose clergy have found a curious edition of the Bible, sustaining these acts upon the authority of Divine commands. These are the lands where the instinct of the bloodhound is improved by pursuing, overtaking and revelling in human flesh. This is the chivalrous land, the inhabitants of which, for fear of insurrection, are pillowed on guns, pistols and swords! Here are the great man, woman and child flesh markets of the world. Immortal souls are the merchandise of the auction room. This is the land where Abolitionists are threatened, defamed, and put to death; this is the land which threatens the dissolution of the confederacy; this is the land of SLAVES.

WHAT HAVE ABOLITIONISTS DONE?

But it is sometimes asked what have Abolitionists done to terminate abuses so shocking, and outrages so insupportable? If any cause could excite self-congratulation, and stimulate to noble and expanded exertions in behalf of the future, it is the cause of Abolition. What cause ever before in less than three years, in the face of obloquy, and a nation's opposition, was found able to organize between six and seven hundred societies, comprising the most elevated piety, the warmest philanthropy, the most distinguished talents, with untiring industry?

In the space of three years the attention of several State legislatures have been awakened. Almost a fifth of the time of the last Congress of the nation was consumed in the discussion of the lost rights of the slave; and the gaze of the world has been fixed on this great struggle of suffering humanity.

If the cause of Abolition had secured nothing more than

such universal attention, and such formidable combinations
for its suppression, it would have been ground for the most
devout thankfulness. But this is not all. The Abolitionists
have measured swords with the slaveholder on several great
questions, in their infancy, with entire success.

SLAVEHOLDERS FOILED.

The slaveholders of 1835 and 1836, demanded,

1st. An expression of Congress, that it was unconstitutional to abolish slavery in the District of Columbia, and the
Territories of the nation. But the slaveholders were *foiled:*
—Congress refused to utter that wicked sentiment ; and that
refusal is equivalent to a verdict, exactly the reverse of what
the slaveholders insolently demanded ; and it is an acknowledgment that Congress has the power to abolish slavery
in the District and Territories.

2d. That slaveholders demanded that Congress should not
receive the petitions of Abolitionists ; but Congress decided
they would receive them.

3d. The South asked Congress by law to gag the press, by
a system of espionage to confer on the 10,000 deputy post-
masters a power to *peep* and *pry* into every secret that passed
through the mails, so as to exclude all anti-slavery written or
printed communications, from a passage into the slave States.
But this bill Congress, after solemn deliberation and long
discussion, *refused* to pass, but passed, in favor of Abolitionists, a law, which is the converse of the slaveholders' defeated bill. In the 32d section of the new post-office law of
last winter, Congress has made it a penalty not exceeding
$500, and imprisonment not more than six months, and a
removal from office, together with a disqualification to hold,
forever thereafter, the office of post-master, to delay any
letter, newspaper or package, on its passage to its destina-
tion, or to refuse to transmit or deliver said letter, paper or

package to its proprietor. This is all Abolitionists could ask, in order to redress such outrages as those at Charleston and New York last year. In fact, this law is powerful in its consequences, and no postmaster will dare delay the passage or delivery of the most "violent" anti-slavery pamphlet or newspaper a single minute, short of forfeiting his office, and subjecting himself to the penalty of a dungeon.

No Abolitionist could have asked for a sterner law for his protection than Congress made in reply to the slaveholders' insolent demand.

4th. The governors of many of the slave States loudly demanded, by messages and special communications, directed to the free States of the North, that the legislatures of these States should violate their own constitutions, and set at naught their Magna Chartas, and pass laws forbidding the existence of Anti-Slavery Societies, suppress speeches or writings against slavery. But the free States refused to comply with one iota of these demands.

5th. Southern legislatures have, by resolutions, made the same request as their governors, and met with no better success.

6th. The South have done homage to the Abolition sentiment at the North, by keeping their slaves at home and not insulting our feelings by their presence the summer past, in such numbers as formerly. Two reasons have operated on them to do this: 1st. They felt ashamed to acknowledge themselves slaveholders by such palpable evidence. 2d. The fears of the slave's escape, or that the slave having been brought here by his master, would become free the moment he touched our soil. For the law for delivering up slaves applies to fugitives, and not to slaves brought here by their masters; all of whom are free the moment their feet rest upon the soil of any free State, unless the slave is registered according to law.

7th. The decision of the Supreme Court of Massachusetts, one of the most distinguished courts for legal talent to be found in this or any other civilized land, has decided, the past summer, that all slaves brought into that State by their masters become instantly free: which proposition or decision is equally true of all the other free States. If this decision is not correct, a slaveholder might bring a gang of slaves with him here for six months at a time, and thus trample on the laws of the free States, as well as insult the feelings of all good men. This he cannot do without permission of the State given him by law.

The decision of the court of Massachusetts will be found to be, with the argument which supports it, an important bulwark of American liberty. If this decision be not sound law, this monstrous consequence must follow, that a free State would allow a foreigner or a citizen of another State, privileges denied to its own citizens.

It has always been considered in the law of nations, that great comity was shown the citizen of another State, if he was put on an equal footing with the citizens of the country whose hospitality he enjoyed; but to allow a Virginian to be followed by a train of trembling slaves, to this State, would be not only to place that individual above our own citizens, but also above the laws and institutions of the State itself. But as self-evident as this proposition seems, its assertion at this time, from so high a source, cannot but be regarded as one of the most cheering evidences in favor of the principles of abolition and humanity; and, in fact, as one of the great landmarks in the career of *universal emancipation.*

The year 1836 will ever be remembered as a year in which Christian philanthropists in Great Britain extended their noble hands to our aid, in the most dignified expressions of kindness and sympathy. We cannot but regard the friendship of the great, the good, and the powerful in

England, at this time, as one of the most cheering circumstances to arouse the desponding, and sustain the true-hearted, amidst the persecutions of slaveholders, or the insults of their apologists. Nothing has more employed the attention of good men in England, the summer past, than in learning the nature and horrors of American slavery. To such a point of detestation has the slaveholder sunk in English estimation, that it is believed none of the first men of the southern States, who are slaveholders, would be admitted into good English society, where the fact was known, any sooner than persons who were smugglers, or engaged in the African slave trade.

We should be much surprised, if the same course of treatment in coming years should not be pursued by the best class of society in the free States toward the slaveholders.

It may be laid down, as indisputable, from the foregoing statements, that the slaveholders have been driven from every position they endeavored to occupy, and routed most disgracefully, on their own chosen field of battle. Yes, they have been beaten at all points, from their high-handed and wicked attempts to cut off the slave's chance of escape from his chains.

SOUTHERN CHIVALRY.

Perhaps it is wrong not to award what is even due to a chivalrous slaveholder. It must not be denied, and justice compels us to admit, that sixty slaveholders in Tennessee, in the summer of 1835, did surround, take, and arrest Amos Dresser, an Abolitionist—a harmless, talented young man, travelling through that State—and whipped him twenty lashes on the naked back, because he was a member of an Abolition Society in Ohio, and then banished him from the State. The chivalrous citizens of the State of Georgia, in the year 1836, surrounded, waylaid, and took a Mr. Kitchell, a citizen of New Jersey, a pious youth, a recent graduate of the Theological Seminary at Princeton, travelling in the South, on account of infirm health, upon the suspicion of being an Abolitionist (which it is since understood he was not) and tarred, feathered, and violently beat him, and expelled him from the State. Thus we see how glorious the laurels of chivalry appear in the victories won on the fields of Tennessee in 1835, and the no less auspicious campaign which filled the cup of Georgia's renown in 1836.

The slaveholder the summer past, has been following his usual chivalrous pursuits—the recapturing of fugitive slaves in the free States—and in some instances has been successful in reducing to a second bondage, those who had been beyond chains and whips ten and fifteen years, by the aid of those supple instruments of tyranny—the well paid constable and justice of peace, whose consciences are more alive to an obedience to the requisition of the act of Congress for retaking fugitive slaves, than they are to the loudest calls of humanity. Yes, had the slave the same sum of money to pay the magistrate and constable for his escape, which the master pays for his judicial kidnapping, few fugitive slaves would ever cross Mason & Dixon's line a second time.

Let the finger of this world's scorn be pointed to that officer, judicial or ministerial, who shall lend himself to the slaveholder to reduce a man a second time to bondage, who will for the slaveholder's gold basely convert the writ of *habeas corpus*, the slave's passport to freedom, into a writ of eternal imprisonment, by which a slave is taken from the custody of himself and equal laws, and delivered to an enraged and lawless master, from whom death can only discharge him.

COLOR IN A QUANDARY.

The amalgamation compound of the Anglo-Saxon and African blood adds annually 15,000 human beings to the slave population, in the shape of mulattoes, as a triumph on the part of the slaveholder over the supposed dignity of the white man, by making an intermediate landmark between the extreme castes.

The slaveholder talks of sending the manumitted slave to Africa as the land of his origin. What will he do with the mulattoes?　Upon that principle, the poor mulatto must spend one year in Africa, and then one year in England, Ireland, Scotland, France, Germany, or whereever, in Europe, the ancestor of his white American father came from; so this compound of Europe and Africa must spend his life in a perpetual pilgrimage, in going from one continent to another, dividing and spending the remainder of his existence in the pursuit of the countries of his ancestor's origin. In fact, if the friends of the argument of hunting up the countries of remote origin of one's race, should think it too inconvenient for the mulatto, perhaps their humanity might be induced to allow them some intermediate island, as a half-way house, where they might rest themselves equidistant from ancestral origin.

But what mulatto in the United States, who has come to the years of discretion, but has pitied the mother slave, who bore him, and cursed his white father. Yes, *cursed him* for his or her existence; cursed him for giving him a body to ruin a soul; cursed him for this body in which the immortal soul withers!　Oh! might the mulatto slave cry out, " what! can I thank my white father for a body, which is not my own, which is but a thing! thank him for that body which is exposed to every indignity, blows and abuse. Thank him for that body which my father, my brothers or my sisters, my nephews, nieces and even my grandfather, may sell under the auction hammer to pay the debts or buy bread-stuffs for members of the church, in the land of chivalry. Shall my father eat me indirectly by consuming what is given for me in exchange on a sale of my body? Strange Christianity! which can uphold such practices as these!"

SLAVEHOLDERS UNMASKED.

The Abolitionists of the year 1836 have compelled the slaveholder to unmask himself and show the world his insincere heart, while heretofore he professed to regard slavery as an evil, and wished it might come to an end. This, they admit now to be *false*, and that they regard slavery as a blessing, and the substratum of the social edifice; as desirable for its own sake, and the best state of things of which the nature of human institutions admit, and they intend to perpetuate these blessings to future generations, securing their continuance to the end of the world.

THE UNION DISSOLVED.

The slaveholders have dissolved the Union so far as the 100,000 Abolitionists are concerned. No Abolitionist, however distinguished he may be in the circles of learning, piety, talents, or philanthropy, can place his foot on slavery's soil. If he does, he sinks below the slave, into the grave, by the hands of lawless violence. All law is powerless in his defence. The Abolitionist stands alone. The federal compact yields no relief. The slaveholders rush upon him with the ferocity of savage demons, and lynch him into eternity. This is the natural fruit of slavery.

CONTINUED PIRACY.

The same brute force, which the forefathers of the present proprietors of slaves employed in the forests of Africa, at the dread hour of midnight, to reduce the slave to possession, is now used by their chivalrous descendants to maintain their jurisdiction over the descendants of the kidnapped African.

The abolition of the old African slave trade was accomplished by the passage of six different acts of Congress, from

1807 to 1824, by which every succeeding act increased the penalty for bringing a person into this country to make him a slave, until the punishment was death—the pirate's doom. The internal slave trade between the several States in this country violates the same principles of justice and humanity which were violated by the old African slave trade, now abolished under the penalty of death.

What is more plain than the remedy for this glaring atrocity?

POWERS OF CONGRESS—INTERNAL SLAVE TRADE.

The same words, clauses and sections of the Constitution, which gave Congress the power to abolish the African slave trade, give Congress the ability to pass a law to abolish the internal slave trade now carried on between the slave States, in defiance of the loudest cries of humanity.

Congress has power given it by the Constitution to regulate the commerce between the several States. What commerce can be of so high a character, or so important in its consequences, as a traffic in human beings to the amount of more than 120,000 persons annually? More than double the amount ever imported from Africa before the abolition of the slave trade, amounting, in value, from fifty to sixty millions of dollars annually.

Maryland, Virginia, Kentucky, Tennessee, and the western parts of North and South Carolina, grow negroes as an article of traffic for the more southern States.

In fact, these States are supposed to receive as much money from abroad for their negroes sold to go out of their States, as for all other products exported besides.

FOREIGN SLAVE TRADE.

Let that same principle of humanity be the guiding genius of American councils, and abolish the slave trade between the States, which smote with uplifted and powerful hand, the slave trade with Africa, and slavery itself would die a natural death from its own oppressive weight in the slave-selling States, while the abounding soils of the far South must, two-thirds of them, be cultivated by freemen or lie waste.

FOREIGN SLAVE TRADE COMPARED WITH THE DOMESTIC.

Did the South vote to abolish the slave trade with Africa for the meretricious purpose of monopolizing the slave market of the world, and creating one on the American soil, transcending in the annals of its cruelty, all that Clarkson or Wilberforce has told of Africa's desolations? Is it so! Were northern statesmen and philanthropists sleeping at their posts in allowing the southern States for twenty years after the adoption of the Constitution to ransack the coasts and interior of Africa, and tear from her her affrighted and screaming sons and daughters, to turn them into slaves, merely as seed, to lay and spread a broad foundation for a future slave trade on the shores of America? Is all this seeming repentance for the wrongs done ill-fated Africa, by which our laws inhibit the importation of slaves under the penalty of death and the pirate's fate, a mere bubble, a device of trade, amounting to prohibition from abroad, to increase the value of a trade of the same description at home? Has the slave trade of Africa been banished under a scale of ascending penalties, terminating in a pirate's death, barely to introduce a slave trade into America, the victims of which, in part, are the sons and daughters of white men, and thus make white blood and black blood share the terrors of the American domestic slave trade, vastly exceeding in point of numbers, annually, those imported from Africa, in any one year, from 1789 to 1808? And inasmuch as the slaves of Maryland, Virginia, Kentucky, Tennessee, and the mountain parts of the two Carolinas, are better informed and cultivated in their knowledge of right and wrong, than the nations of Africa, by so much the more are their sufferings increased, in being torn from their natal soil and the relatives they have, than the less informed children of Africa.

HORRORS OF THIS TRAFFIC.

The slave has no interest in property or things, or in the soil. His whole earthly interest is in the love and sympathy of his relations, and in the beings for whom he has formed strong attachments in his youthful days. Therefore he is by a removal from those places where he was raised, and in severing all the bonds that make life supportable, doubly robbed—always of himself, and lastly of his friends and relations. The only objects that rendered him able to bear the burden of life, are taken from him by this awful traffic. Hundreds commit suicide every year, and rush into the next world, being stripped of everything in this by which life might be sustained. The slave has nothing but what exists in the social affections; strip him of those objects, and his misery must be perfect—his agony helpless. No man can tell the story of such bereavement, who has not been torn as a slave from the soil where he was born, to bid an eternal farewell to all his friends and relations—the only property or interest he possesses (if so it may be called) on this earth. He is never permitted to revisit those friends to whom he can never write. An impassable gulf separates them ! No. He parts with all he loves at once, forever, never to be renewed on the shores of time; not for his own interest, not for a noble act of benevolence. No. He goes to wear out his life for another, as a slave under the whip, for that man who never thanks him for his labor, but rewards him with hunger, nakedness, stripes, sorrow and contempt, till the grave, pitying him, takes and forever shelters in its bosom the son of toil, misery, insult and pain.　It is said, not less than 120,000 are taken annually from the northern slave States to the far South.

EFFECTS OF COLONIZING.

Every attempt by the South to aid the Colonization Society, to send free colored people to Africa, enhances the value of the slave left on the soil.　By sending off free colored people to Africa, there is no competition with the slave on the soil, for the purpose of labor.　The slaveholder controls the entire sinews of labor by his own will, and can fix his own price.　If there were free colored persons to hire themselves out on the plantations of Louisiana, Alabama, Mississippi and Arkansas, the slaveholders of Virginia, and the other slave-growers, would find a competitor in those sugar and cotton States, in the free laborer, whom the slaveholders are desirous of removing, that they may sell their slaves.

·　IMPORTANCE OF ABOLISHING THIS TRAFFIC.

But let the internal slave trade be abolished, and slavery would come to an end by its own weight, in Virginia, Maryland, Kentucky, Tennessee, and the western parts of North and South Carolina.　These countries, in which Americans are grown for the internal slave trade (shameless trade!), if these slave-growers could not send their surplus Americans abroad, and sell them at great prices, would sink under the weight of a population whom their old exhausted slave soil could never support.　And they would be compelled to manumit their colored people from necessity, if they were forbidden under penalties, such as are inflicted on those in the slave trade with Africa, from sending them out of the State, or Territory, or district where the slaves happened to be.　The far South would be compelled to abandon slave labor and employ free colored people, in a great degree, if they could no longer import slaves from abroad to supply the havoc created by overworking, underfeeding, and an unhealthy climate.

Again, slavery never can be abolished in the District of Columbia or the Territories, with any expectation of advantage, until the internal slave trade is abolished between the States. For the moment the slaveholder in the District of Columbia, or in the Territories, perceived that a law was about to be passed for the abolition of slavery in the District or Territories, before such a law could be passed, the District of Columbia or the Territories would be stripped of their slaves, who would be sent off in coffles and sold at auction in some of the slave States. Thus it becomes every way important that Congress should exercise its unquestionable constitutional power, and restrain the " migration " of slaves from one State, one district, or one Territory, to another, under the heaviest penalties, such as would be obeyed.

THE CONSTITUTION.

The fourth clause of the eighth section of the first article of the Constitution of the United States says, that Congress shall have power " to regulate commerce with foreign nations, and among the several States, and with the Indian Tribes."

The first clause of the ninth section of the first article of the Constitution says that " the migration or importation of such persons as any of the States now existing shall think proper to admit, shall not be prohibited by the Congress prior to the year 1808, but a tax or duty may be imposed on such importation, not exceeding $10 for each person."

The authority to abolish the domestic slave trade between the States, is derived from the fourth clause of the eighth section above cited; and the prohibition of the exercise of the power of Congress, by the Constitution, until 1808, by the ninth section of the same article (which alludes to the question of slavery alone), is conclusive evidence that the framers of the Constitution itself, understood the power to be conferred by the fourth clause of the eighth section, or else the prohibition of the exercise of this power, in the ninth section, until 1808, would have been useless. For it is a principle of construction admitted, that a power to do an act cannot be raised by implication, from any clause of the Constitution, unless it become necessary to exert that power by legislation to carry into effect some acknowledged power of the Constitution. Therefore, the Constitution construes the eighth section "to regulate commerce with foreign nations, and among the several States," as being a source of authority by which Congress might abolish the foreign slave trade, and also the internal slave trade amongst the States. But it may be urged that a power to regulate commerce, does not carry with it a power to destroy it. This objection has often been raised, but always overruled by the decision, that a power to regulate commerce is the same as a power to create and destroy, to make or unmake, and therefore Congress, under the power to regulate commerce with foreign nations or among the States, has power to abolish any particular traffic or commerce, which Congress believes to be unprofitable to the nation, or disgraceful to its humanity. Congress, in six distinct acts, from 1808 to 1824, passed for the abolition and utter extinction of the African slave trade, has acknowledged the construction now contended for, that a power to regulate is a power to alter, change, modify, abolish or annihilate. Unless this proposition be true, these acts abolishing the African slave trade would be unconstitutional and void, as well as a host of other statutes deriving their power from the same source. Congress has power, under the word " regulate," utterly to annihilate commerce with a particular nation, by embargoes, acts of perpetual non-intercourse, and, finally, by open war, which is the end of all commercial relations.

It may be inquired, how can the traffic, or commerce amongst the States, or between one State and another in relation to slaves, be regulated? In the first place, the *States* as between two or more of them have no power by treaty or legislation, to regulate this matter, as long as slavery is permitted in those States; for Virginia cannot pass a law that a man from Maryland importing a slave from Maryland, shall be subject to a penalty of $500, or three years imprisonment, or that the slave *ipso facto*, by having been brought from Maryland to Virginia should be free. Because the citizens of Maryland might cite the 2d section of the 4th article of the Constitution of the United States, in which it is declared " that the citizens of each State shall be entitled to all the privileges and immunities of citizens in the several States," which the State of Virginia cannot overthrow.

In subjecting a Marylander to forfeiture, loss of liberty, or any other penalty in Virginia, for importing his slaves with himself, would be a course of treatment shown to the Marylander, not recognized by Virginia toward her own citizens, for having slaves in their possession; the law would be unconstitutional and void, *as the law of a State.* If the individual States have not power to prevent the slave's migrating by command of the master from one State to another, it would follow, unless Congress has jurisdiction of the subject matter, that the internal slave trade among the States must be beyond the reach of the individual States or the power of Congress. This is an absurdity, which we are not prepared to believe or adopt, that a subject so fraught with abuses, at the horrors of which the civilized world might grow pale—should have placed itself beyond federal or State legislation. The motives which appeared to influence the passage of the six different laws to abolish the African slave trade, were the irrepressible gushings of our common humanity in favor of the suffering slave, torn from his native land and sold into hopeless captivity. No interest but general humanity, prompted the legislation which forever shut down the hatchway on that bloody trade. Humanity now cries aloud—she goes in our streets—she weeps and howls on our highways—she knocks at the door of public feeling till her locks are wet with the cold dews of night—she goes across the ocean—she pleads not in vain for friends to fly to the rescue—she, through England, has sent back her indignant voice like the sound of many waters, to fall on the guilty slaveholder's ear in America.

Motives and reasons for abolishing the slave trade between the States are greater, as far as the question of humanity is concerned, than in the old slave trade. No doubt there are twice as many groans, sighs and agonies felt, suffered and endured from the American slave trade among the States, as were felt by the slaves brought from Africa to the United States in any one year, between 1789 and 1808.

Yes, two persons, at least, suffer the horrors of migration from one State to another, where one suffered by importation, from the coasts of Africa to the United States. The word " migration " employed in the first clause of the ninth section of the first article, is significant indeed, and means nothing more nor less than going from one State to another, not from one part of a State to another ; not coming from a foreign country beyond sea, that would be met by the other word "importation" which the abolition of the African slave trade undertook to prevent, in the six statutes passed for its abolition.

CONCLUSION.

It is firmly believed, that, were a rigorous law passed by Congress, forbidding the internal slave trade between the States, it would be equivalent to the manumission on the soil of two-thirds of the slaves in the United States in less than ten years.

It is therefore earnestly desired, that every anti-slavery society, or individual who may petition Congress on the subject, may make the annihilation of the domestic, or internal slave trade between the States, a point of the most prominent importance, and pray for its entire ABOLITION.

EXTRACTS.

SLAVERY ARRAIGNED.

THE slave still groans, humanity weeps, the helpless yet implore. We are in the midst of the greatest moral battle ever fought by Mercy, pleading against intelligent and vigilant villainy. The Abolitionists are the organ of national compassion, and are making up the dreadful issue between criminality enthroned upon laws, and justice beleagured by the myrmidons of robbery. We have arraigned the greatest criminal ever summoned to the bar of Divine and human reason, the triers of whom are the good and the just of *this* and all ages, and the verdict is written and pronounced by the Saviour of the world, who is the Foreman of this grand inquest, and brings in the verdict of *guilty*, while the Universe cries, "Amen." It has been the undertaking of Anti-Slavery men, for many years past, to make the men of this generation understand and believe that *such is* the rendered verdict of Divine as well as human wisdom. One half of this besotted nation denied the existence of such a verdict, while a vast portion of the other half folded their arms, and said, "If there was such a verdict, the criminal had the power to nullify it; and if the criminal saw fit to call the verdict of ' guilty ' an *acquital*, by a *law* of *his* own, *why that made it so !*"

REFORMERS MALIGNED.

We, perhaps, have encountered more obstacles than have often been presented to a band of Reformers. The political power of the country having been claimed and wielded by two great parties, nearly balanced, we might have reasoned, in ordinary cases, that if one party persecuted us, the other would have protected us; but, no, the party to which we might flee, felt that it had more to lose, in the estimation of slaveholders, than they could gain by our votes, and each party run a race, to the top of their speed, against us, and the one which could shout our condemnation the loudest was supposed to be nearest the goal of its ambition. In fact, the weight of our vote was nothing, as compared with the disgrace of our alliance. Both parties scouted us; the mobs howled around our conventions, and pursued us to our homes; the churches, in their aggregate capacity, refused to acknowledge that we had found truth; but all parties, religious or political, in power or out, the women-whippers, the *man owners*, and their *apologists*, the mobs, the Pharisee and Saducee, the sinner and publican, the drunkard and debauchee, formed one grand line, standing shoulder to shoulder, deriding our arguments, jeering at our philan-thropy, traducing the slave, mocking his sorrow, defaming truth and libelling Omnipotence, until the civilized world was shocked by the impurity of our sentiments, and the violence of our actions.

LIBERTY'S IMPERIAL GUARD.

Good men will be willing to spend and be spent, and work in our conventions, prepare resolutions, advocate them, write tracts and scatter them, notify meetings and attend them, print votes and distribute them, give money and time, and stand up for the slave on the bridge or in the boat, in the car or the stage, in the pulpit or the press, at the fire-side or the ballot box. These men will carry your reforma-tion through; they will not lead you in sight of the promised land, and at last advise you that the Constitution is in the way, and that you had better go back into Egypt and acknowledge Pharaoh's jurisdiction, and go to making bricks, raising onions, and weeding garlics; nor would they advise you to die in the wilderness for fear of those *huge Anakims*, and for the sake of saving the expense of a grave-yard.

DOUGH-FACES.

We shall conquer; we shall perform the mighty work. The world is coming to our side. Let those who are discouraged be sent home on an everlasting furlough to the Whigs and Democrats, and there let them *live* and *die*, contemplating the beautiful mysteries of *cowardice*, and the essential attributes of the *meanest position* ever occupied by man.

SYCOPHANCY INVADES THE COLLEGE.

The professor in our northern college respectfully approaches the young heir of a hundred negroes, and with his hat under his arm, and humble genuflections, timidly inquires, *when it will be convenient for him to receive an idea?*

THE GREEN MOUNTAIN STATE.

We slept at Manchester, and passed over the Green Mountains near this place, through one of those notches the Great Creator left for a passage of his creatures from one side to the other. It would be strange if Vermont, the rocks of whose eternal mountains are yet red with the blood of the war of independence, the war for *human rights*, should have been found throwing her weight into the slaveholders' scale, from expediency, fear of new measures, ultraism, or any other ghost, kept in the pay of the devil, to scare men out of their duty. But it is not so. Vermont will do her duty in the great struggle between slavery and liberty.

DESERTION FROM THE RANKS.

I will not accuse Mr. J—— of having deserted the glorious

cause of human rights for the sake of the *distinguished office of a justice of the peace.* I wish *merely* to say, that his election as justice by the Democrats, and his desertion from the friends of liberty, were *contemporaneous events* in that gentleman's history.

A PERVERTED EDUCATION.

If you begin early enough, you may teach a boy to worship a jackass, and every time he neighs and shakes his reverend head, the boy will take it for a divine communication.

DUTY TO REFUTE SLANDER.

I should have thought that Mr. —— would have hired a sick horse, or come on foot, or on crutches, from the Lower Saginaw to Pontiac, or Flint River, or any other spot on this terraqueous globe, to have made his honor shine through the interstices of the ribs of those gibbeted villains.

NEGLECTING THE TRUE ISSUE.

Our party committed a great mistake in Michigan, in turning their attention temporarily from the great question on which our organization was founded, to the consideration of a "local and minor point." It was as if, on coming to see John Rogers suffer, at Smithfield's burning stake, your attention was to be entirely consumed during the martyrdom, in beholding a *dog fight!*

JOHN BOWDOWN.

"I vote," says one, "for the Bold John Faithful!" On his ballot is virtually inscribed his sentiments, his legislation in the grand committee of the whole. The other casts his pro-slavery vote, saying, "*I go for John Bowdown to the South!*"

A BANDED POWER.

The *town power* is the *power of powers.* Let a dozen men

say, in December, "We will elect our ticket next town-meeting," the very fact that they have a given object before them will three-fold every man's exertion, and lend him new power, feeling and energy. But if a man works without a stint before him, he says, "I cannot see the length and breadth of the undertaking," and he will work as solemn and as stupid as the man who attempts to empty the mill-pond with his quart cup.

ECCLESIASTICAL RECREANCY.

The Church has been standing on the *north side* of the Hill of Expediency, slipping down its cold and icy surface, from height to depth, until her vernacular tongue, her shibboleth, became that of the mixed multitude in the vale below, whose idiom and pronunciation were taught in that classic man-chattel school.

MAHOMET'S COFFIN.

This year will settle the minds of the slaveholders and their apologists, and those timid neutrals who are existing at the *centre of gravity*, and are as likely to go one way as another; or, from an equality of attraction, to be held half way between a *well-balanced doubt and a thriving conjecture*, until they putrify for want of motion, and pass down to coming times as the *victims of position*.

DUTY TO VOTE.

When a man is summoned, as a spirit, from the unknown and indefinable surrounding eternity, he comes to take possession of a body which, at twenty-one years of age, is a sovereign, a law-maker in the land, and his Creator commands him to exercise his power for the benefit of his race, to remember those in bonds as bound with them, to love his neighbor as himself, and to do the greatest good to the greatest number. When he votes, he legislates through his agents and representatives; for, as a nation, we are always in a committee of the Whole.

FREESOIL.

I am rejoiced to see how good a *freesoil* man you have become. I rejoice at the movement, and if I had health, I would *roar* like a lion in the wilderness, from Montauk to Chatauque, publishing free speech, free men and free soil. Yes, I would make a furrow in the Free Soil so deep and so wide, that slavery would never dare look into it.

MODE OF LABOR.

We must not keep hanging round our favorite *deer-licks*, but scatter abroad, and carry our principles to the farmer at the plough, and to the mechanic in his shop, and the laborer at his toil, wherever he may be found. The time is gone by for us to sustain troops of paid lecturers, and now every man of us must be a lecturer, not heralded by a flourish of trumpets, but sustained and urged on by the sweet consciousness that he is doing his duty and pleasing his God.

GAGGERS.

Look at the three worthy gaggers—Pinckney, Patton and Atherton—a triumvirate of poor creatures, whose names will pollute every page of history, where their ineffaceable actions shall be recorded.

NAT TURNER.

In the Nat Turner insurrection, was the excitement confined to the three or four counties where the rising took place? No, by no means. The whole South was converted into a guard-house? Every master slept on his pistols, while the nightly patrols went up and down in every direction. An individual of the humblest station had struck a spark which well-nigh ignited the whole mass of volcanic material on which the South reposes.

ULTIMATE SUCCESS.

Do not be disheartened. Everything wears a new and glorious aspect. The matter is absolutely settled, that we must abolish slavery; and as sure as the sun rises, we shall, in a few years, ride over slavery at full gallop, unless she picks herself up and gets out of the way of Liberty's cavalry.

THE ANTI-SLAVERY WAR-STEED.

Our anti-slavery horse is a little restive, and will carry no other load in the first instance, except emancipation of every slave in the land. He will kick up and throw off the load, if you put on him a Presbyterian pack, or a Methodist bag, or a Quaker blanket, or a Democratic sack of queer matters, or a Whig harness; and he will even bite if you attempt to put a bridle of non-resistant bits in his mouth; he will not wear an abstract martingale. If you mean to have him thrive, feed him largely on *ballot-box oats*. He desires no manger but the ballot-box. As long as we fed him on the best oats we could get of either of the great parties, or those miserable wild ones called infinite scatteration oats, he throve like a certain steed fed on Connecticut long oats—to wit, whip-lashes—and under these scant feedings, in connection with his non-resistant provender, the poor fellow grew poor and mangy, until you could count his ribs as easy as you could the hoops of a flour-barrel. But since we have fed him on *concentrated ballot-box oats,* he has shed his old coat, begins to lift his head and tail, and runs round the field, and even *snorts* with exultation at his new and delightful sensations, and the fine prospect ahead.

THRIFT PALSIED BY SLAVERY.

Slavery has been one of the main causes of the deranged condition of our currency. History and philosophy teach that every system of unpaid, coerced labor, is intrinsically unprofitable and ruinous. When the city of New York struck her balance-sheet after the crash of 1837, she found the South her debtor in more than $75,000,000—little of which is yet discharged. Slavery has *leeched* the industrious North. The truthful philosophy of the *nine digits* teaches, that we can never regulate the currency, while the great Disturber has his hands on the monetary heart-strings of the country.

DO THE SLAVES DESIRE LIBERTY?

In Georgia, said Mr. S., about three years ago, there lived a man, black but noble, a giant in strength, and in form an Apollo Belvidere, about thirty-five years of age, a slave, with a wife and four children also slaves. The love of liberty burned irrepressibly in his bosom, and he determined to escape, and free his wife and children at all hazards. He had heard of Canada, as a place where the laws made every man free, and protected him in his freedom. But of its situation or the road thither, or the geography of the intermediate country, he knew nothing. A Quaker who resided near him, being privy to his design, resolved to aid him in its accomplishment; and accordingly carried the slave and his family fifty miles in a wagon by night. In the daytime they lay concealed in the woods, and on the second night the same man carried them fifty miles further. At the end of the second night, he told the black man that he could do no more for him, having already endangered both his life and property. He told the slave that he must not travel on the highway, nor attempt to cross a ferry, but, taking him by the hand, he committed him to God and the north star. This star he was to take as his guide, and it would lead him at length to the land of British freedom. The poor slave bade adieu to his benefactor, and after skulking in the day and travelling by night, he at length came to an unexpected obstacle. It was a broad river (the Savannah), of whose existence he had not the least knowledge. But as nothing remained but to cross it, he tied his two young children on his back, and between swimming where it was deep, and wading where it was shallow, his two elder sons swimming by his side, he at length made out to reach the opposite bank; then returning, he brought over his wife in the same manner. In this way he passed undiscovered through the States of South and North Carolina and Virginia, crossed Pennsylvania without even knowing that it was the land of Quakers; and finally, after six weeks of toil and hardship, he reached Buffalo. Here he placed his wife and children in the custody of a tribe of Indians in the neighborhood, for the poor man will always be the poor man's friend, and the oppressed will stand by the oppressed. The man proceeded to town, and as he was passing through the streets, he attracted the notice of a colored barber, also a man of great bodily power. The barber stepped up to him, and put his hand on his shoulder and said, " I know you are a runaway slave; but never fear, I am your friend." The man confessed he was from Georgia, when the barber said, " Your master inquired about you to-day, in my shop, but do not fear, I have a friend who keeps a livery stable, and will give us a carriage as soon as night comes, to carry your family beyond the reach of a master."

As the ferry boat does not run across the Niagara in the night, by day-break they were at the ferry house, and rallied the ferryman to carry them to the Canada shore. They hastened to the boat, and just as they were to be let go, the master was seen, on his foaming horse, with pistol in hand, calling out to the ferryman to stop and set those people ashore, or he would blow his brains out. The stout barber, quick as thought said to the ferryman, "If you don't put off this instant, I'll be the death of you." The ferryman thus threatened on both sides, lifted up his hands and cried, "The Lord have mercy on me! It seems I am to be killed any how; but if I do die, I will die doing right," and CUT THE ROPE.

The powerful current of the Niagara swept the boat rapidly into deep water, beyond the reach of tyranny. The workmen at work on the steamboat Henry Clay, near by, almost involuntarily gave three cheers for liberty. As the boat darted into the deep and rapid stream, the people on the Canada side, who had seen the occurrence, cheered her course, and in a few moments the broad current was passed, and the man with his wife and children, were all safe on British soil, protected by British laws!!

SPEECH DELIVERED AT PENNSYLVANIA HALL,

ON A RESOLUTION RELATIVE TO THE RIGHT OF PETITION.

THE House of Representatives of the Congress of the United States, a body created by the breath of the nostrils of the freemen of this nation, has, by a palpable violation of the Constitution, denied the right of petition ; and if there is merit in having been the first body of men clothed with high legislative power, who in this world have exercised it by refusing to hear the petitions of their constituents, then the House of Representatives stands alone in its glory, pre-eminent, without rival—treading a path which Egyptian Pharaoh, and Russian Nicholas, and the turbaned Sultan, have never ventured upon. What was the prayer of these denied petitioners? They asked the abolition of slavery—AMERICAN, REPUBLICAN SLAVERY!

"Hear, O Heavens! and be astonished, O Earth!"—the representative of yesterday denies the right of his constituent of to-day, to ask him to give liberty to the bondman; denies the constituent the right of having his petition so much as read in the presence of their high mightinesses! The future historian of this land, when truth shall have triumphed over delusion, when the sober dictates of humanity shall have conquered the dark spirit of slaveholding fanaticism, when quadrennial President-making shall not be a draft on the heart's blood of our expiring liberties—astonishment shall make him drop his pen to weep over the degeneracy of his boasting ancestors, till the love of his country's fame shall make him doubt these dreadful scenes in the narrative of the

20th and 21st of December, 1837. He will visit the city bearing the name honored by the father of his country, and turning over volume after volume of ancient Congressional records, shall sigh in the search of the liberty-murdering Congress of December, 1837 ; till at last he finds on that ill-fated 21st of December, 1837, that Mr. Patton of Virginia asked the previous question to be put for the adoption of a resolution, by which " all petitions on the subject of slavery to that House should lie upon its table *unread, unprinted, unreferred, undebated*, and *unconsidered ;*" and that it passed, one hundred and twenty for, and seventy-four against it. " Ah !" says the future Tacitus of this land, as he muses over these dark and man-dishonoring pages—" What is here ? The ' previous question '—the tyrant's gag !—the petitions on slavery ' *unread, unprinted, unreferred, undebated* and *unconsidered.*' Oh ! what a rent hath slavery made in the Constitution's robe !"

DECEMBER 21ST, 1837.

On the shortest day of the year—of least light—of most darkness—the deed has been done by slaveholders and their wretched apologists. Oh, the 21st of December, 1837 ! why must that day rob my country of its glory, its good name, and steep it in infamy ? Let the 21st of December, 1837, perish from my country's calendar. Let that day be darkness forever after. "Let not God regard it from above, neither let the light shine upon it. Let darkness and the shadow of death stain it; let a cloud dwell upon it; let the blackness of the day terrify it; let it not be joined unto the days of the year ; let it not come into the number of the months. Let the night be solitary, and no joyful voice come therein. Let them curse it, that curse the day, who are ready to raise up their mourning. Let the stars of the twilight thereof be dark. Let it look for light, but have none; neither let it see the dawning of the day."

BURIED ARCHIVES.

But as he turns with mournful steps from this painful soliloquy, he goes to a room thirty by twenty, and twelve feet high, and beholds the mighty mausoleum of the embalmed remains of the Great Unread, the Great Unprinted, the Great Unreferred, the Great Unconsidered—the dead corpse of a nation's right of petition, laid out in solemn state in the wing of the Capitol! There is a library of two millions of authors on one subject—the unread library of a nation's humanity! Behold the manuscripts, three times the number of the Alexandrian library. There lies the collected majesty of entombed Philanthropy. Yes, to this pile of recorded glory, those who wish, in coming generations, to rank high for the nobility of their descent, will send the faithful examiner to see if their ancestor did not sign these unread petitions to Congress, on their father's or mother's, or grandfather's or grandmother's, or great grandfather's or great grandmother's side. And if they did, the man who searches for ancestral merit by which to raise his own, will believe it a happy day for him, when he shall find the name of the progenitors of his race written on these unread and unprinted petitions to Congress, for the abolition of slavery, in the 34th, 35th, 36th, 37th and 38th years of the nineteenth century.

RIGHT OF PETITION.

The right of petition is as old as human want. It is the language of the child to the parent. His every want, his every necessity, appeals to the parent by way of petition. His every gratified desire is but the fruit of some granted petition. The pupil in the school, the scholar in the university, comes to his superior every day with petitions. The schoolmaster, the trustees of a school, or the inspectors of schools, or the commissioners of schools—the commissioners of highways, and the path-master have their petitioners. The overseers of the poor, the keepers of the county poor-house, have their petitioners. The commissioners of excise, who grant *rum-diplomas*—the supervisor, town-clerk, and justices are petitioned. Town meetings are petitioned. The board of supervisors ·sit weeks in their counties listening to and deciding petitions. The justice courts, the common pleas, the supreme courts, and chancery are thronged with petitioners. The governors of States, and the President of the United States, overwhelmed as they are with petitions, have they ever dared, or the subordinate bodies referred to, to lay petitions presented to them on their tables, unread and unconsidered? No. Legislatures in twenty-six States, sitting, on an average, three months in the year, or about one-fourth of the time—the immediate representatives of the people—sit for the express purpose of deciding upon the petitions presented to them by the people. Who ever heard of a legislature in one of those States, except New York, in 1837, ever refusing to read, print, or consider the petitions of the people?

Congress sits to hear the various petitions of this nation, except those affecting human liberty, more than one-third of the year. The whole form of our government, family, school, town, county, State, nation—whether in the legislative, judicial, or executive, at every step and angle of proceeding in human affairs, whether in Church or State, whether in prosperity or adversity, sickness or health, moves forward on the wheels of petitions. Petitioning or requesting, whether written or verbal, is one side of affairs, while the other is to consider and weigh the application on its merits, and grant or refuse the petition asked.

No, the whole system of Divinity, the worship of God,

whether it be that of the Mohammedan or the Jew—Protestant or Catholic—whether it be idolatrous or spiritual, in whatever form religion has been shadowed forth to this world, its votaries hold communion with the Unseen Power, by petition. Man as man, the erring, the weak, the naked and trembling mortal of a day, goes to the Being who is infinitely his superior, by prayer and petition.

The Almighty's ear is not dull of hearing our petitions and complaints. Petition is the everlasting language in all countries and all climes, in all ages and conditions, of the subordinate, asking assistance from man, or deliverance from God. This is inseparable from the condition of man, man free, or man a slave.

What subject so proper, whether presented in person or by another, as a petition to deliver the slave from his cruel bondage, his pain, his stripes, his insults—to repeal laws taking away all his rights; to petition that a man may have his wife, a woman her husband, and both, their children—and that the daughter and son may not be taken from them and sent where the parents shall see them no more—that their own backs may feel stripes no more—that they may hunger no more, thirst no more, be insulted no more, kept ignorant no more, chained no more, and unpaid for labor no more.

The beings, of all others, requiring the intervention of supreme legislative power in their behalf, are the poor slaves, already bereaved of every political right in this world. Shocking to relate, these same audacious men, who have stolen the slave from Africa, by tempting the kidnapper, with their money, to go and catch him, or have held the slave as though the slave was under special obligation to the master, that he even permits and allows him to breathe and swallow God's fresh air, and look upon the same sun without striking him dead, and that he ought to be delighted to have an opportunity to serve a man, naked or in rags, who will suffer him to hoe cotton from daylight in his cotton field till dark, and have a peck of corn a week, or four cents per day to buy food—ah! yes, these southern slaveholding members of Congress deny the right of petition in behalf of these most forlorn beings, who are made wretched by being made the victims of pilfering, by having their masters meanly rob them, and steal from them, and whip them, to get more out of them, and then say to them, " We have abused you so badly that we shall not allow you to state your wrongs to the world or to Congress, as we do not intend our *meanness* shall be known."

SLAVEHOLDERS' SHAME.

The truth may as well be known to the world first as last. The reason why the slaveholders rose up in the face of day and went out of the Hall of Representatives of this nation on the 20th December last, and concocted their successful scheme, which was put in execution the next day, to " lay all petitions on the subject of slavery, unread, unprinted, unreferred, unconsidered and undebated on the table," was from shame and conscious guilt, not having courage to face their deeds of cruelty, darkness, shame, crime, stealing, robbery, debauchery, and meanness, when held up to the glare of the world!   They withered in advance, before the coming storm. " Ah!" say they, " are we, the sons of chivalry, to be called thieves and sons of thieves—we, who are members of Congress, living in pomp on the unpaid labor of the helpless— are we to be called devourers of widows' houses, yea, of the widows themselves and their children ?   Shall it be told that we made the poor child motherless and fatherless, by selling, for money, the father from the children one year to a distant part of the country, never to return, the next year *that we have sold the mother whose sable breasts were the fountains of our infantile subsistence*—the next year that we have whipped and *sold our own children*, and, uninstructed, made them bondmen to the number of half a million, who have inherited from us, their white fathers, a bastard reputation, and all the wretched sorrows of a slave." Is this a father's legacy?

Deep, conscious guilt, on the part of the southern masters, has made them roar like the ocean's waves, to turn the eyes of the world in every direction except toward themselves— the ears of mankind to hear everything, except the thrice-told tale of slaveholding infamy. Fear, *fear*, shame, *shame*, yes, burning SHAME, laid those resolutions on the table.

REPORT ON SLAVERY.

What! could the slaveholder bear a reference of the two millions of petitions, to a select committee who felt deeply for the slave, with power to send for persons and papers, and with leave to said committee to sit in vacation, from the coming July till December after, to collect all the materials for a report, and draw the death warrant of slavery, as the very report itself would be?

This nation only requires the report of a select committee of seven persons, energetically employed a few months, to make out the indictment against slavery, to have a verdict of guilty pronounced by an injured and indignant nation.

What will be in that report? How will it be made up? What are the materials of such a report, and how are they to be obtained? Let us look at it a little.

1. This committee should send for all the codes of slave laws of the several States, and of the United States. Bring up, now, those statute books of blood and crime, and you will find them full of high treason against God and against humanity. Laws made by the very men who claim this property under those laws. And what do they establish? Why, power, irresponsible power, of man over man. This is

the beginning and the end—the pervading spirit of the whole code, from beginning to end. Name the civil right which these laws secure to the slave! There are none; there is no recognition of a single right in the slave.

2. What is the sustenance which these laws claim for the black man, as the only legal compensation for a life of compulsory toil? Read the words—" one peck of corn per week "—that is, two shillings a week, or about six mills for each meal. Our northern horses—pardon me, I do not intend to be low; it touches humanity, and cannot be low;—I was saying our northern horses must have at least twenty-five cents *per day* in oats—or fourteen shillings per week. The keeping of one northern horse is equal to that of fourteen southern slaves. There is no man in a laborious employment here, who does not pay a dollar and a half or two dollars a week for his board. Does a northern man eat fourteen times as much as one at the South ? No; but the saving is in the quality and cost of the food. Figures will tell you, that in the article of keeping alone, the master of 200 slaves will make a saving of $314 a week, barely by the deductions from the poor slave's stomach. This, in a year, would make the pretty sum of sixteen thousand dollars pinched out of these wretched men! The whole world would cry out. But until such an investigation can be made, I fear this nation will not believe the fact, although we show it in the very statute books of the South. Very probably there are numbers here to-day, who will set all this down as abolition slang, not worthy of belief or regard. But if they could see the evidence brought out in a Congressional report, the whole nation would shout in a voice that might almost rend the rocks, for the speedy abolition of this detestable system.

3. There is another thing which we should find in these statute books of the Slave States. No black man can, in any

circumstance, be a witness against a white man. Hang that
fact up before the nation and the world. Add to it, that by
the slave code no marriage can be binding between a slave
and his wife, but may be dissolved at any moment by the
arbitrary will of the master. Then, again, the parent has no
authority over the child, to train or govern him according to
the law of God. Hang that up to view. Go on, now, and
make a full synopsis of these laws. You will find, however,
that they have made provisions for hanging the man who
shall murder a slave. Now, then, let the committee summon
all the clerks of the counties throughout the slave region, to
bring their records, and certify whether there has ever been
a single instance of a master being hanged for the murder of
a slave. Yet, in North Carolina, not long since, two white
men were hung for merely coaxing a slave away from his
master. And, I suppose, a single sheet would contain a list
of all the cases on record, of punishments inflicted on masters
for cruelties or injuries inflicted on their slaves.

4. Next, I would have the committee of Congress call up
ten experienced planters from each of the slave States, to
testify what is the political economy of slavery. I would
require them to state, as honest men, whether the question
has not been often discussed among them, which is the most
profitable, to work slaves to death in five years, when cotton
is fourteen cents per pound, or to work them twenty years,
with cotton at ten cents. Inquire of them whether one-third
of the plantation slaves are not let out to tenants, whose only
interest is to get out of those poor creatures the greatest
possible amount of labor, with the least possible expense for
subsistence and comfort. And yet we have men among us,
who have rolled through the South in the public conveyances,
and seen the well-fed servants at the hotels, and who tell you
they know all about slavery, for they have been there, and
the slaves are the happiest class of beings in the world.

5. Next, I would send for some men of a class that I believe it is Patrick Henry describes, as the *feculum* of creation, the scrapings of humanity—the slave drivers, northern men, who have sold themselves, body and soul, to carry on this dreadful business in the detail. I would interrogate them as to the various modes of subduing a refractory spirit, of finding out whether a slave is sick or feigns sickness, and all the various expedients of cruelty, by which an overseer tries to build up the reputation of a great labor-getter.

6. Let our Congressional committee then send for a hundred free men from the slave States, who have never owned a slave themselves, nor their relations, and let them tell what they know about the cruelties and the pollutions incident to the system of slavery.

7. Then I would send for a hundred free colored men, who should be allowed for the first time, under the security of the strong arm of the nation, to testify of their wrongs. Let each one tell how often and by what hair-breadth escapes he has avoided being kidnapped into slavery. Let him turn to that law which allows the magistrate to exile a free colored man from his country, on ten days' notice, unheard, untried, without cause, without compensation, as passion or caprice may dictate, with confiscation of his estate; and if he refuses to go, to be sold as a slave, and his children after him forever.

8. Then I would have them call for a hundred of the ten thousand fugitive slaves, that have found a refuge in Canada, under the government of a hereditary monarch, from the tender mercies of our republican institutions. · Let them tell of hopes crushed and hearts broken, of what they endured in slavery, and of the sufferings and anxieties through which they have passed while in the pursuit of liberty.

9. Then I would have brought up before the committee a hundred slaves from the cotton-fields and the sugar-houses,

who should give ocular demonstration of what slavery is. I would have them freed, and protected by a strong force, and they should show their persons abused, their limbs mutilated, their brands and gashes, their backs cut from their shoulders to the heels with *republican stripes*.

When the committee have gathered all the information in their power, let it be embodied in a report. It would make a volume of a thousand pages. Then send that report through the land. Let the mails burst and the stages groan with the mighty load, telling the naked truth on this subject, in an official and authentic form ;—and I tell you, slavery never lifts its abominable head again. All that the nation wants is to have a case once made out to their conviction, that slavery *is what Abolitionists charge it to be*, and our work is done.

This mountain of iniquity would then stand before every honest mind in all its dreadful prominence. The people, horror-struck, would cry out against it. The foundations of the great deep of crime, as yet unfathomed, would be broken up. As yet who hath believed our report, as Abolitionists ? But this would be moral demonstration. It would be taken on the oath of the people of the dark and sullen regions of slavery.—Yes, with this report, the nation would pronounce their everlasting condemnation and overthrow of slavery, and all would Free.

SPEECH ON THE GREAT ISSUES

BETWEEN RIGHT AND WRONG.

DELIVERED AT PENNSYLVANIA HALL, MAY 16, 1838,

Before several Thousand People.

AMEN, and amen, have been shouted from the throats of the unthinking millions of this earth, as the mandates of tyranny were proclaimed, as the edicts of inhumanity were published to the world; while the lamentations of the oppressed have ascended night and day, as swift witnesses before the living God. These loud outcries of the injured against *unavenged* cruelty, have created epochs in the march of ages. At different periods of the world, there have been great *issues* formed between right and wrong, liberty and slavery, and on the determination of those issues have depended the stability or overthrow of empires, the rising and falling of nations.

The pages of history, divine or profane, are the recorded evidence, arguments, and facts of each generation as they have been summoned to share in the creation and decision of those issues. When the issue has been correctly framed, crime, ashamed of her own frightful progeny, has called in falsehood, with her open mouth, to deceive the weak and the thoughtless.

Truth has been insulted and clamored down by the roar of numbers, who have interrupted her narrative or insulted her for the humility of her dress, or derided her for want of those high-born relations which, in the shape of impudence,

6*

interest, superstition, obstinacy, and love of power, have confederated to impeach her, by sneering at the simplicity of her statements, by undervaluing the force of her arguments, while they have sung praises to the highest notes of Falsehood, sworn its deformity was beauty, and the harsh grindings in the prison-house of its oppression were the symphonies of sympathizing humanity; yea, more, they chanted praises of honor and glory to its deductions, and sung anthems to its sophistries, and cried amen to its conclusions.

Honest error has often been a powerful antagonist of truth, and the only enemy whom truth assailed with compassion, and before whom truth had reason to tremble. For when sincerity, one of the darling attributes of truth itself, varnishes error, the judges of the issue sometimes mistake the armor of Achilles for the mighty form which it was made to protect.

What is right or what is wrong? Where are the boundaries that separate?

How far human arrangements can change the abstract wrong into an expedient right, or the abstract right, if asserted, into a wrong, are mighty questions, settled in the early ages of the world, and thousands of times since; but they now seem to come forward as fresh questions, demanding a decision with all the eagerness of zeal, with all that gives weight to high pretension, and with an impatience that forbids delay, from the magnitude of the interests involved; so that our minds are compelled to become moral scales, to re-weigh and re-mark the mighty interests of humanity.

But these questions have been weighed and considered by Him who cannot err, who is the author of right, the enemy of wrong. His weights and measures are the enduring revelations of perfect wisdom. The delivered opinions of the Eternal came down to this world, while men were contending in the forum of philosophical definitions, groping in the twilight of their understandings, and wasting their lives in finding a standard of right in uninstructed conscience. The pity of Him whose home is immensity, who is from everlasting to everlasting, who placed the shining worlds on their great pathways, and gave them a momentum which flying ages do not weaken, who knows each rood and inch between all the self-balanced globes as they rush round the skies in their untired race of ages—of that God, who permits each one to travel its sublime and annual journey around the sun, was manifested in giving man a rule of action for time, eternity, forever, "LOVE THY NEIGHBOR AS THYSELF." The law of gravitation of the moral universe!

Every departure from this eternal landmark of duty, however small, has been the parent of crime and human agony.

FIRST ISSUE, CAIN AND ABEL.

The first issue ever made between right and wrong, the holy liberty of conscience, and the brutal violence of oppression, was between the two first of woman born. While the younger employed moral weapons to vindicate his sentiments, such as prayer and petition, and went to God for strength, wisdom, and direction; the elder used the modern club-logic; he preferred the bludgeon to manly debate; to silence investigation was better than to convince; to murder his opponent was easier than to answer his arguments. Cain was the founder of the brute-force system of logic, being the only method *then*, or *ever since* known by its admirers, of answering *unanswerable* arguments.

This mode of reasoning, like the extreme unction for the dying man, is not to be resorted to except in the distressing emergency of having no other mode by which to protect folly from contempt, obstinacy from rebuke, ignorance from pity, and crime from punishment. If Cain could have proved Abel in an error, then Abel might have died in his bed, at

nine hundred years of age, or more. But because he could
not, therefore he slew him. So we see the first witness called
to establish truth died a martyr; and the morning of the
new world was hung in black by the depravity of man.

NEXT ISSUE, NOAH AGAINST THE WORLD.

The next great issue made up for everlasting remembrance,
was between Noah and his family of eight souls, against the
world—of right against wrong. What, could eight persons
be the only ones right, and the whole world wrong beside?
It seems so. Truth is not always found keeping company
with the multitude, leading armies, or seeking the shout of
numbers.

But the last mountain top of the antediluvian world was
covered with water, truth then being on board the floating
ark, in the eight witnesses, on that ocean without shore or
island. These eight human beings were the connecting links
between two ·worlds; ånd lest their narrative should be
denied in the coming profane ages of philosophic skepticism,
the massive floors on which the ocean rolled, were torn up,
and piled away on the tops of mighty mountains, in monumental strata, on whose pages are written the history of a
drowned world—a record of God's judgment lithographed
on the primal formations of the enduring rock!

EGYPT AGAINST THE HEBREWS.

But the most sublime and grand issue ever framed between
guilty man and his Maker, on the trial of which such amazing
consequences depended, was WHETHER MAN SHOULD BE THE
PROPERTY OF MAN OR THE SERVANT OF GOD?—whether man
should lose his charter in himself and become incorporated in
another's self?—whether a man should cease to have use for
his mind and his body, so that another might take that mind
and body and appropriate it to himself, and extinguish all

claim of the individual in and to himself? This could not be permitted without denying God's interest and claim in each being whom he had created for His own will and pleasure. Therefore, as God had made man, he had a right to his own workmanship; and having conferred on man certain high powers, life, liberty, and the pursuit of happiness, which happiness consists in obeying his Creator's laws, this being could not abandon or surrender these rights to another human being, nor could another human being assume them—rights, which in their nature could neither be surrendered by one, or assumed by another, because of God's interest in man as his Maker. God had a claim on those unsurrenderable and unassumable rights—a mortgage on them which can never be extinguished in time or cancelled in eternity.

Egypt was the theatre of this momentous issue, in the event of which every question affecting human liberty was involved, considered and determined. Who were the parties? Haughty Egypt in the plenitude of her·power, with a population of twenty millions, the schoolmaster of the world, the granary of mankind, the home of civilization; whose proud cities opened and shut their hundred gates; whose imperishable structures of monumental marble must have equalled in expenditure the united energies of the generations of the nineteenth century; whose mountains for miles *inward* were penetrated and excavated with the silent palaces of the dead; whose power brought from the cataracts of the Nile to the Delta, the Monolith temple of solid rock—Egypt, with her acre-covering temples—with her artificial lakes, her giant sphinxes, her twenty pyramids, those piles of wonder where art seems to rival nature in her boldest work. And on the other hand, two and a half millions of *Hebrew slaves ;* a nation of tasked bondmen, brickmakers under their task-masters and drivers.

Egypt was the oppressor; two and a half millions of

Hebrews were the oppressed slaves, and God the judge, avenger and deliverer. Never was there such a display of Almighty power; never, since the creation of this world, has the Arm of Omnipotence been more signally revealed than in this manifestation of His utter abhorrence of slavery, and His love of human liberty. He caused the mighty river of Egypt to run with blood from its upper cataracts to its seven mouths, and as the Mediterranean received the tribute of the Nile, it blushed at Pharaoh's insult to Jehovah, in presuming to hold man as a slave. The hail and lightning, the ice and fire leaped from their chambers in the clouds to the slave-insulted soil, to avenge the quarrel of the abused. The locusts forsook their sullen solitudes of whirling sands, and in dark armies came riding on the winds to consume the products of the spoiler's fields. The murrain smote the cattle of the task-master; and on that last dreadful night uprose the death-wail along the reedy margin of the Nile, and from the heart of the mighty cities, as the Angel of Death passed silently and unseen from house to house and struck down two and a half millions of the first-born of Egypt. Pharaoh, in the pride of human glory, said to himself, "I will become the defender of Egypt's power against these slaves, my brick-makers, by whose unpaid labor I have reared those imperishable structures, which will stand to the last day of time, exciting astonishment and commanding admiration from generation to generation; I WILL NOT LET THE PEOPLE GO." The Almighty taught him the folly and crime of his presumption. To doubt the Deity's hatred of slavery, is to deny the truth of this astonishing account. It is to deny the Old and New Testament. It is to deny our own nature—the unwritten law of conscience. It is to deny and despise all the cries and pleadings of our humanity. It is to deny our very existence. It is to say there is no sin, that one thing is as right as another, stealing is as honest as labor lewdness is the same as modesty, cruelty as kindness, robbery as benevolence, piracy as a purchase. To deny the crime of slavery is to say there is no right, no wrong, no justice, no injustice.

Behold the flying fugitives! The Red Sea in their front, mountains on their right and left, and the uncounted hosts of Egypt in their rear. See the poor fugitives and their little ones in the pass of the mountains; overwhelmed with terror, they go to the banks of the sea, and it gathers its waters in walls—while the triumphant freedmen, with praises on their tongues, and in their hearts, turn round to behold the Almighty causing the Egyptian wheels to forsake their axletrees, and the wall of water to yield and cover up their task-masters forever!

A late traveller, of the last ten years, sent a pearl-diver down to examine the supposed path of the nation of fugitives, and discovered pieces of Egyptian armor and implements of war, attesting the truth of this highway in the deep, *never travelled over but once*.

These fugitive slaves had a cloud by day and a pillar of fire by night for their outstretched banner.

> " By day along the astonished lands
> The cloudy pillar glided slow,
> By night Arabia's crimson sands
> Returned the fiery column's glow."

They were fed with food direct from the Almighty's table for forty years in a land of emptiness and want, where the prowling hyena and gaunt wolf howled in the bitterness of hunger unappeased. The rock opened its flinty mouth, and sent its cooling waters after them. The Almighty, in scorn of human greatness, and to show himself no respecter of persons, made these despised, runaway slaves the honored recipients of the LAW of LAWS—the ten eternal orders of God inscribed with His fingers, and delivered to them, while the rocky heart of Sinai quaked and trembled with His thunders, and its summit shone with celestial brightness as the lightning blazed around its pinnacles, and, through the pauses of the storm, the voice of the great trumpet waxed louder and louder!

Thus these poor fugitives had the custodial care of the first Heaven-lent geography, which shows the pathway through which man must travel, in order to enter on the joys of that undiscovered country from which none return.

To them was intrusted God's revelation, the living fountain from whose waters of truth all of the civilized nations of the earth have drawn the fundamentals of jurisprudence. Yes, these fugitive slaves were God's librarians, and had the holy keeping of His laws, which have been the great moral light of this world.

IDUMEA'S BLIGHT.

But what was the treatment these oppressed and fleeing fugitives met with from the hands of the King of Edom—the land of Idumea?

Here we have an awful demonstration of God's detestation of a nation which could dare attempt to arrest or impede the progress of fleeing fugitive slaves, who sought a passage through a neutral country to the land of freedom. For that crime the malediction of the Most High has brooded over the land of Idumea!

Oh! what a solemn fulfillment of prophecy! Look at Petra, the city of the Rock in the mountains—the wonderful capital of this Heaven-doomed land—this nest of one of the world's great empires, girded about with everlasting mountain barriers. Behold her theatres, temples, and catacombs, vying with imperial Rome in the days of her Cæsars, cut from her granite mountains, with rocky roofs one thousand feet in thickness culminating above. Behold her mighty palaces without mortar, without joints, chiselled out of primeval rock—perfect after the long lapse of centuries, as when first opened!

Yet this ancient abode of polished life, which felt the movings of a mighty ambition, has, for twenty centuries, been abandoned of God and forsaken of man, only tenanted by the obscene bird and loathsome serpent—the sole inmates of the palaces of kings and lodgers in the chambers of departed greatness. No man abides in this lone land, no man says this is my home. A land once red with the blood of the grape, and thronged with populous life, it has become a sterile and majestic solitude—borne down by the withering curse of God, for the crime of opposing the escape of the fugitive Hebrew slaves from the land of the spoiler.

There stands, and will stand to the end of time, the witness, telling to each generation of the world, as they flow down the long stream of ages, " here was once a crime committed by man against man, by a nation of prosperity against a nation of fugitive slaves, flying in distress." The punishment was inflicted in the zenith of her glory, and she is the only country on the globe which has been depopulated from century to century, as an enduring testimonial of the Almighty's wrath. As the solitary traveller wanders over the ruins of Petra, he is alarmed as echo sends back her voice in answer to his footsteps from the lonely temple, the deserted palace, and silent catacombs; astonished, he lifts his eye, surrounded by everduring walls of rock, and beholds the only living being, an eagle, in the regions of the blue sky, revolving in his noontide gyrations over the doomed City of the Mountains.

The flight of the Hebrews from the house of bondage took place at a period when Egypt was the home of science—the Gamaliel at whose feet the learned and inquiring of other nations sat. She was at the head of the families of the earth, and within her borders were locked up those discoveries

which have since astonished mankind.   In the contest between
Israel and Egypt, therefore, it was enlightened strength contending against ignorant weakness.   There was too much
power to decide the question by reason and argument, on the
side of the Egyptians, and too much feebleness on the part of
the Hebrews.   But we are somewhat struck at the superior
refinement of the haughty slaveholders of Egypt, compared
with those of the United States.

Pharaoh, as the representative of supreme power, tolerated
Moses and Aaron with rights denied by an American Congress and southern slaveholders, to wit, the rights of PETITION
and FREE DISCUSSION.   For this matter was discussed no less
than seven or eight times in the palace of Egypt ; and Pharaoh
never denied the right of petition but once, and that was
when he told Moses not to come before him again.   But that
was at the time when Moses had ceased to petition, as the
business was lodged in the hands of the angel of death.

ADVENT OF THE REDEEMER.

The next great issue was the advent of our Redeemer.

The issue was between religion and its counterfeits; between religion and liberty on one side, and idolatry and
slavery on the other.

The Redeemer, the poorest man in Judea, and yet the very
God, took upon himself the form of a servant—the most
despised form of our common humanity.   The Redeemer
came to lift up large masses of mankind in the shape of the
poor, the imprisoned, the enslaved, the miserable, the ignorant, and place them on the summit level of our common
humanity, and vindicate their relationship to God.   And in
the course of three centuries after he preached his sermon on
the Mount, during which time ten generations came and
crossed the bridge of human life, the truths of that sermon
had grappled with principalities and powers, with prejudice,

and idolatry, and slavery, which had grown sturdy by their hold on mankind for a thousand years, and had filled the Roman world with chiselled gods of men's device, while the unpaid slave groaned from the Apennines to the banks of the Euphrates, from the Scamander to the Tweed, from the mountains of Mauritania to the dark-rolling Danube. At the end of three hundred years from the blessed Saviour's humanity, his holy principles had banished idolatry and slavery from the wide-spread Roman world, with its one hundred and twenty millions of inhabitants.

But, oh! how often did the fagot burn—did the martyr's blood flow, in defending the liberty of conscience and of person, before the world assented to these principles!

THE REFORMATION.

The next great issue to which the mind of Europe was summoned was the Reformation of the fourteenth century. Slavery and idolatry had come back to this world again. The contest again was between truth and falsehood.

The men of that generation made brick without straw; their substance was eaten out by ecclesiastical imposition; a midnight of despotism brooded over the faculties of the moral world. Slaves in a state of serfism or villanage, were groaning beneath the military pomp of the feudal system.

The human mind rose up from the sleep of a thousand years, and shook from itself the accumulated errors of ages, and broke those bandages in which the independence of the mind and body had been swathed.

From great issues and mighty trials like these, have been drawn all the truth, the religion, and liberty which have blessed this world.

But hypocrisy, with ruin and darkness rioting in its heart, entered the portals of the church, and put on the cast-off livery worn by ruined angels, when their guilty ambition expelled them from the realms of light; and, professing veneration for God's eternal witnesses, the Old and New Testaments, these impostors have declared, that these witnesses spake that which they did not—that these witnesses declared slavery was an institution of Heaven, sanctioned by the God of justice and mercy!

These baneful perversions of Divine truth have been employed for the most malignant purposes, so that southern professors of religion and professed ministers of Christ, pretend to get their authority to rob the slave of himself, his mind, his body, his wife and children, from the Bible!!

THE ISSUE OF 1776.

North America, in her political behavior, is a contradiction in terms. She was the land of refuge for the oppressed. Corrupt Europe, of the seventeenth century, drove from her bosom her most pious, noble, and independent sons, to search for liberty of conscience in the howling wilderness of the Occidental world. The Puritan of New England, the Catholic of Maryland, the Episcopalian of Virginia, and the Friends of Pennsylvania, claimed, like the Hebrews in Egypt, the right of making the wilderness their temple to worship God. Yes, they leaped the barriers of the ocean's solitudes, and nestled down amongst the wild aborigines, to enjoy the liberties of body and mind, and escape oppression. Oh, horrid solecism! that such a land should now become the grand rendezvous of slaves, outnumbering those of any other country in the civilized world.

The year 1776 astonished the world with a new issue, which reached up and down and all around the circle of humanity. This issue was tendered to the oppressors of mankind throughout the world, by the patriotic Congress of the United States, who threw in the teeth of tyrants, feudalists, monarchists, the inheritors of power, the primogeniturists, the kidnappers, slaveholders, man-despisers, and man-haters, these words of mighty import: "*All men are created equal, and are endowed by their Creator with certain inalienable rights, among which are life, liberty, and the pursuit of happiness;*" and to vindicate the truth of this proposition, the people of these United States poured out their blood like water, for seven years.

Philosophers, philanthropists, politicians and jurists had written tomes and folios of metaphysical musings and abstractions, to settle the starting point of man's existence—the rights of one as compared with those of another in coming into the compact of civil society.

But in going up to a remote antiquity, to learn what principles governed those lawgivers who laid the foundations of civil polity for those old nations in Europe, fable occupies the place of veritable history, and history teems with its thousand falsehoods, and bewilders the mind without instructing the judgment, and leaves the inquirer at the horizon's distance from certainty, if not from truth.

The feudal system, the doctrine of primogeniture—that executive, legislative and judicial powers, were matters of inheritance—may be considered the elementary doctrine of Europe.

That men are born equal is a great moral proposition, coming from God, and as old as man, and grows out of His own eternal benevolence, by which it is said that God is no respecter of persons.

The doctrine of primogeniture is that by which the oldest child, being male, is born to the inheritance of the whole landed estate of a father or relative, and the other children of no part; by which the oldest child of a king, or prince, or duke, earl, or noble, however weak, is born to the inheritance of executive, legislative and judicial power, while the son of the peasant, however cultivated by learning, or however superior by force of an exalted genius, is only born to obey.

Many of the members of the House of Lords, in England, inherit their seat to legislate for their countrymen, by the same law by which they hold their father's estates. They inherit both. They inherit judicial power, wise or foolish, as a court of *dernier ressort*, to reverse the decisions of the chancellor and twelve judges of England, on a statute which these members of the House of Lords inherited power to make. In England, nothing but idiocy, insanity or crime can deprive some four or five hundred Englishmen from being law-makers and judges in the last resort; and that, too, without the express consent of a living man in England manifested in their favor, but barely by inheritance.

The feudal system, primogeniture, and that certain persons inherited the executive, judiciary and legislative powers of their country, and also inherited the allegiance and obedience of the nation, have been the fundamental laws of most European countries from the downfall of the Roman Empire to this hour.

Look at England and her colonies of fifty millions of inhabitants, and her East India possessions of one hundred millions more, making one hundred and fifty millions of human beings, or one-fifth of the human race, at the head of which, by force of the above doctrine, as Queen, is a young boarding-school, piano-playing girl, eighteen years of age, with power to declare war and deluge the world in blood, make peace, veto the united legislation of Lords and Commons in Parliament assembled, to direct fleets and lead armies.

The doctrine of this world on the 3d of July, 1776, was, that some persons are created superior to others, inheriting the right to make, judge of, and execute laws, which the rest are created to obey.

But before the sun went down on the 4th of July, 1776, the mighty moral discovery was proclaimed from this very city, that " all men are created equal, and endowed by their

Creator with certain inalienable rights, among which are life, liberty, and the pursuit of happiness; that to secure these rights, governments are instituted among men, deriving their just power from the consent of the governed."

Such men as Milton, a Sydney, and a Russell, in their musings upon the rights of humanity, had caught glimpses of this truth—shadowy and undefined, like the vision which passed before the face of Eliphaz the Temanite—a spirit passed before them, " but the form thereof was not discerned."   They had prophet revelations of the dawning of a better day.   Looking down the vast future, they beheld on those plains in the land of the setting sun, beyond the wilderness of waters, where Hesperus trembles on the borders of the circling heavens, man in full possession of the great charter of his rights.

This mighty discovery is but a DEFINITION OF MAN, as considered in relation to every other man.   But no great politician or philosopher in the European world dared make this definition known, because it would have been high treason against the fundamental laws of European society.   This definition would have brought to the block the best man in Europe, as the reward of his temerity.

The three great truths, or political discoveries, are: 1st. Equality at birth.   2d. The universal endowment of the right to life, liberty, and the pursuit of happiness.   3d. That all governments should be made to secure these high interests.   Therefore, all governments must be made by those whose interests they are intended to secure.   Well might the politicians, philosophers, and philanthropists, believe the philosopher's stone had at last been discovered; and that the signers of the Declaration of Independence had been permitted to ascend, like Moses, into the Mount of God, to discover, from a loftier altitude, the relations of man to man. Good men cried out in ecstasy, from every corner of the earth where the human mind was not so degraded as to have *forgotten* the loftiness of its lineage.

The new and joyful era had arrived, in which the governed, to protect his liberty, his life, and pursuit of happiness, made and created the governor. THIS IS A REPUBLICAN FORM OF GOVERNMENT. The purchase money of this truth was paid in blood, which flowed from the free hearts of our fathers. Oh, costly definition of human liberty! The assertion of this great definition of man, in his social state, is, by force of its terms, the abolition of all slavery, wherever the definition is honored or respected.

But with us this definition of human rights is, practically, but an empty abstraction, instead of being the very life of our republicanism?

To tolerate slavery a single year in one of these States, after this Declaration of Independence, was a base hypocrisy, a violation of our engagements to mankind, and to God. "*And for the support of this Declaration*," said they, "with a firm reliance on the protection of Divine Providence, we mutually pledge to each other our lives, our fortunes, and our sacred honor."

This awful and solemn *promise*, made in behalf of liberty, to all persons in this land, in the presence of mankind and the great Jehovah, in that awful moment of a nation's agony and peril, stands *unredeemed, uncancelled,* and *unsatisfied ;* sixty-one years and three hundred and fifteen days have gone to join the years and days beyond the flood; every year, every month, yea, every day and hour, have gone to the Judge of all the earth, clamoring, long and loud, for the execution of this *vow.*

The issue of 1776 was not alone between the governments of the old world, and their children, the colonies of the new. This issue, tendered by the framers of the Declaration of 1776, was done not only for the United States; but as the representatives of human nature oppressed, their document was the property of both Americas, and of the New World. Liberty for all is demanded; labor in all is honorable; tyranny is everywhere odious; kidnapping and stealing men and their labor is the essence of sin and meanness. Look at the products of their issue. Behold thirteen of the United States free from slavery!

Six empires on this continent have pronounced that the color of a man's skin and his liberty have no relation to each other, and that all men are created equal and free, to wit— Mexico, New Granada, Central America, Venezuela, Chili and Peru. These blood-bought countries have started the great journey of liberty and independence, with slavery abolished throughout their great domains. In fact, the continent is an abolition continent; the Catholic countries, in the march of liberty, have gone beyond this land of boasting Protestantism.

Under the glorious issue, framed by the fathers of independence, that all men are created equal, the bondmen of Massachusetts, of Connecticut, of New York, of Pennsylvania, and of New Jersey, have thrown down their broken yokes, as the trophies of the great definition, and the shout of freedom which burst forth and rolled in thunders through the unmeasured prairies of the West, swept over the Rocky Mountains, and Mexico caught the joyful sound, and declared all men forever free in the land of Montezuma.

The white, the black, the red, joined in the chorus: ALL MEN ARE CREATED EQUAL. Yes, five empires more heard the thrilling sounds, and from the lonely mine-digger of the cavern-worlds beneath the bed of the Pacific, to the solitary shepherd on the snow-clad Cordilleras, and from the Mexican Gulf to the ever-blazing fires of the Andes, as the eternal truth went up the mountains and rolled over the pampas solitudes of the South, and flowed down the mighty rivers, all heard the words of resurrection and of life, and from the trance of ages stood up in the primeval sovereignty of MAN!

St. Domingo heard that man was born free and created equal, and, at the end of three centuries of slavery, stood erect—a nation of freemen, manufactured out of goods and chattels. England, in the days of George the Third, paid four hundred millions of dollars to destroy *our* definition of man, and in the reign of William the Fourth, the same nation, fifty-seven years after, paid one hundred millions of dollars to purchase it for eight hundred thousand slaves in the West Indies. Those new lexicographers who overturned the governments of the new world by the power of a *definition*, and cut the bands of transatlantic connection, and turned the world upside down, and unlocked suffering humanity and delivered it from its prison-house, if they could be summoned from the long dreamless sleep of their graves, would be overcome with astonishment to find thirteen States of this republic still clinging to slavery with a death-grasp ; and that their declaration, which had driven slavery from all other parts of the continent, was unable to deliver two and a half millions of the most wretched slaves the sun ever shone upon. These fathers, summoned from their graves, might well inquire what is the cost of this refusal by southern men to acknowledge our definition of man.

And what would be the answer? The derision and collected scorn of an insulted world—the loss of liberty of speech, and the freedom of the press, and of conscience—too cowardly to discuss slavery, and afraid of the truth,—a loss of character for bravery and moral courage—loss of the benefit of the personal industry of the whites, that being considered dishonorable ; while to rob, steal, commit adultery, and covet, are virtues—the South by slavery, making their wives, the white women, miserable—the slave losing the benefit of the Bible—the whites, by amalgamation with their slaves, obtaining the privilege of selling their own children, brothers and sisters of selling their own brothers and sisters —the fear of assassination and insurrection—large sections of exhausted slave-lands, with a curse of perpetual sterility upon them—a universal brutifying of the black man's mind —universal concubinage—reducing two and a half millions of equals to beasts and chattels—ferocity, murder, duelling, called " chivalry "—the countless murders committed by slavery during the lapse of two hundred years, yet unatonéd for and unavenged—the white masters living under the standing charge that all their wealth, their daily gains, the livings and subsistence of Congressmen, judges, governors, church-members, men and women, are made up and obtained by daily robberies and larcenies, stamped with the infinite meanness of inflicting assaults and batteries on the slaves, their natural equals, to compel them to give their masters an opportunity of stealing the fruits of another's industry—thirteen States living by petit larcenies. The acme of human glory, in relation to man's elevation, and the lowest depth of his guilty debasement, manifested in the same country !

In the old-world men inherited, as property, the three great departments of power—to wit, the Legislative, Judicial and Executive; while in the slave States of the new world two hundred and fifty thousand irresponsible despots inherit and own, not only all the political power of two million, five hundred thousand slaves, but inherit and own their bodies —the fearful and wonderful workmanship of God—immortal chattels, celestial merchandise.

The slaveholder's practice tells God He made an undue share of immortal mind, and it is his (the slaveholder's) business to *re-adjust* His highest work, by increasing the brute creation, in diminishing the immortal. The slaveholder, therefore, *un-mans*, and reduces to *things*, beings a little lower than angels. The same slaveholder would have laid his wicked hands on angels, and impressed them into his service, if he could.

Behold thirteen States of the American Republic, legislating for the division of stolen goods, enacting that stealing is a patriarchal institution, and adultery sanctioned by the Bible —passing the most formidable laws against any person who shall call them stealers of men, of women and of children. The brute force system surrounds and protects their awful larcenies upon *mankind*.

I will present another rather unamiable view of slavery.

A South Carolina slaveholder has a son by his slave, in his own likeness. That son must be deprived of the Bible. The father employs the brutal lash upon his son's body, to make him work harder and earn more, that his father may steal those earnings, and with them send a missionary across the diameter of the globe, to tell the heathen, if they do not repent, they will be lost. We will suppose a heathen in India repents, and out of gratitude becomes a missionary himself to South Carolina to warn the people of their sins, heathenism and slavery. But the Indian missionary would be murdered, by lynch law, for teaching the slave and master the same doctrines, on their own soil, which the master at the expense of making his son a slave and a heathen at home, scourged and imbruted, had obtained means to send this very heathen in the old world. What would East Indian Christians think of South Carolina ethics, morality, or religion?

THE NO-TONGUE MEN.

But the adversaries of the great truth of man's equality at birth, have made new discoveries in behalf of falsehood and against liberty, viz., that slavery is too powerful and sensitive to be assailed with the tongue or the pen of free discussion. There are two divisions of the no-tongue, no-pen, no-discussion men. One party admits slavery an evil, but its constitutional intrenchments are so deep and wide, and it is so awfully dangerous to speak or write against the institution of slavery, that they are willing to make an assignment of the liberty of speech, the right of petition, the power of the pen, the liberty of conscience, to the slaveholders, as a standing tribute, to be paid by the men of the north division of the confederacy, for the privilege of not being made field slaves for the present; for the privilege of looking on the same sun at the same time; of beholding the same waxing and waning moon ; although the fruit of this assignment has been wet with the blood of ten thousand annual murders, or twenty-seven daily ones, for each of the sixty years gone by, from malignant passion, by violence and over-working and under-feeding.

HOD-CARRIERS.

The other division contends it is a Bible institution, a State institution, and a corner-stone of the Federal Union ; and further, that no man, woman or child, shall deny these propositions, but with the penalty of death, with or without law.

This last division of men are the head men and master builders in the Bastile of slavery, while those of the first division are the mere HOD-CARRIERS OF SLAVERY—the docile creatures at the North, who are willing to forego their humanity, their intellectual liberty in themselves ; and if they, as northern men, are willing to forego so much, they can see no reason why the slaves, for the benefit of our blessed Union, ought not, *as good republicans*, to be willing to forego life, liberty, wife, children, and endure stripes, hunger, nakedness, ignominy, and reproach, from generation to generation. Ay, these good patriots of the North can see no reason why two million five hundred thousand slaves ought not to be content to be stript of all things, and lashed over every mile of the journey of life, to furnish the cement, made of sweat, tears, and blood, which binds the North and South together !

THE TEMPLE OF LIBERTY.

To combat such weather-beaten heresies and time-honored presumptions of slavery, and rebuke the craven spirit of its apologists, is the reason we have come together to dedicate this temple to Liberty. In the thirty-eighth year of the nineteenth century, we find it necessary in America, the home of the oppressed, in both senses of the word, to erect a temple of Free Discussion, where the philanthropists of this generation may meet for high and holy communion with the God of Freedom, and beseech his aid in the emancipation of the slave!

Yes, in a land on whose door-posts and gates liberty is inscribed, and among a people in whose mouths liberty and equality find so permanent an abode—in such a land this edifice is necessary, in order to welcome humanity and liberty to a home *they may call their own.* What will the slaveholder think as he passes this temple built for the deliverance of his despised slaves, for whom he never built a school-house, nor scarce a church?

What an array of accusations shall throng the slaveholder's guilty memory as he looks upon this building, every brick of which is a bitter reproach to him! The mortar of the wall cries like an unappeased ghost against him. The foundation stones shall tell him they are softer than his heart.

To this spot the pilgrims of humanity will come to worship God, in the land of the setting sun.

As I entered your city, thought I, here is the peculiar home of the slave; here are the descendants of Penn, the place where all men were declared to be born equal. Methought, in a sort of reverie, I saw a band of fugitive slaves flying from Maryland, wet with the swimming of rivers, faint with hunger; their tattered clothing told me that they were the unpaid laborers of the wretched South. They sought the place where they might tell the history of their wrongs. But the doors of the noble Roman Catholic pile of architectural grandeur were shut against them ; they went to the Methodists' chapel, because their discipline was written by John Wesley, who loved the slave; but they were answered, " our bishops cannot listen to the tales of slaves ; it is a political question, we cannot unite church and state ;"—to the Baptists, but they could not think of giving offence to their Georgia brethren ; to the Episcopalians, but the man in canonicals said, " it was his pleasure and his pride to say, his church had never been affected by ultraism ;"—they turned to the Presbyterians, who would have opened their church, as they said, " but from fear of disobliging a majority of the next General Assembly, who might want their house in which to denounce the Abolitionists ;" but directed them to the Quakers, who had always been their friends, and to their sympathies they commended them. To the Friends they bent their faltering and wretched steps—but they were told " they had always been their friends, and neither ate nor wore the slave's productions, but hoped no stronger test would be required of them, for as to opening their meeting-houses to listen to the story of their wrongs, they did not feel free to do it."

Oh, miserable fugitives !—They have run the round of sectarian church-humanity ; none have bidden them welcome. " Let us," they say, " go to the Hall of Independence, and see if the ghosts of Hancock, and Rush, and Franklin still hover there !" But the door of that old hall was barred and bolted by a generation *who knew not Joseph.* They were told, " it will not do to talk about your scourged backs, broken hearts, unpaid labor, severed families, ravished wives, and murdered sons ; *that is a part of the compact ;* and if we of the North should listen to you, the two hundred and fifty thousand slaveholders would knock this Union into fragments, so there would not be enough left of our common country to make a school district. Get you gone, there is no place for you here."

They have turned away in despair. But what sudden change of joy is passing over their sad countenances? They have heard of this Hall—this Temple of Liberty built for the very purpose of giving a hearing to the wrongs of the afflicted, those who have none to help, those about to perish! And here we are, thank God! this day, in the first temple ever erected to the memory and redress of the slave's wrongs, since this world began! This is a new place under the sun. It is pity's home, the abode of enlightened humanity. ·

This is a temple dedicated to the insulted and outraged of our land. This will be their future court and senate house, where their hitherto untold wrongs shall come up in holy remembrance before God, while the means for their deliverance shall be considered in the ample range of free discussion, unfettered by priest, deacon, people, or trustees. No house was ever erected for a nobler or more glorious purpose— there is not one on whose roof the sun of Heaven shines, from the Chinese temple of a hundred bells to the pagoda of India, from the mosque of St. Sophia to St. Paul's, from the cathedral of Milan to that of Westminster, around which the sympathies of noble hearts and the prayers of the poor will gather, as around this Hall dedicated to the Rights of Man!

This is the home of the stranger, the resting-place of the fugitive, the slave's audience-chamber. Here the cause of the slave, the Seminole, and the Cherokee shall be heard. Here, on this rostrum, the advocates of holy justice, and Heaven-descended humanity, shall stand and plead for poor insulted man ; here with boldness shall they untwist the guilty texture of those laws which from generation to generation have bound men in the dungeons of despair. Here, too, shall criminal expediency be hung up to a nation's scorn

and the world's contempt; that expediency which adjusts
political balances with the tears and blood of slaves, or sees a
nation made homeless and exiled beyond the Mississippi for
the purpose of securing its golden mines. Here shall the
good cause come, though excluded from sectarian churches;
here the despised form of *shrunken humanity* swells beyond
the measure of its chains, as it ascends and seats itself
beneath this dome, and feels itself enlarged by surrounding
compassion.

This Temple of Liberty, I trust, will stand as a monument
of honor to its founders, a standing reproach to the generation of this country in the thirty-ninth year of the nineteenth
century—a generation, whose House of Representatives, in
Congress, could resolve that all petitions on the subject of
slavery should lie on its table, " unread, unprinted, unreferred,
undebated, and unconsidered"—a generation, who, in a fundamental act of constitutional and organic law, could strike
from its roll of voters, in the primary assemblies, forty thousand freemen, because of their complexion—a generation
whose moral cowardice, only exceeded by their treachery to
the rights of man, forced a necessity upon the true lovers of
man and worshippers of God to erect this building, as a house
where Truth might commune with her admirers, Patriotism
with her followers, and Humanity with her friends.

Let this Hall be like a moral furnace, in which the fires of
free discussion shall burn night and day, and purify public
opinion of the base alloy of expediency, and all those inver-
sions of truth, by which first principles are surrendered in
subserviency to popular prejudice, or crime!

Let the gratitude of every lover of his country be expressed
toward the gentlemen, who, in erecting this building, have
in the most solemn manner rebuked a guilty age. As brick
after brick shall molder away, may the coming generations
of mankind furnish men who shall restore the perished brick,

the time-worn stone, and wasted wood of this temple, until wrong and crime shall be banished from our country, and the eye of the Angel of Freedom, gazing over its vast extent of territory, from the St. Croix to the Mexican Gulf, and from the Atlantic to the Pacific, looks down upon no slave!

EXTRACTS FROM LETTERS TO SAMUEL WEBB,

OF PHILADELPHIA.

UTICA, 20th May, 1838.

DEAR WEBB:

The moment I was leaving home for Herkimer County, I went to the post-office, and what did I find? Your letter confirming what I had heard the night before. Alas, alas, for Philadelphia! Has she become the captive of slavery? Is this the gratitude shown to Philadelphia for harboring, protecting and defending 500 slaveholders in her bosom? Yes, the unpaid labor of the slave has been employed by the slaveholder to madden a ferocious populace to be guilty of Heaven-daring deeds, which only find a parallel in the atrocities of the French Revolution.

The home of piety and humanity, and the refuge of oppressed men—a home fit for the spirits of the blessed—has been burnt by the paid stipendiaries of brutal, vindictive slaveholders—the life-guards of Pandemonium. The ashes of Franklin, Rush, Rittenhouse, their tombs and memories are now in the keeping of a mob, encouraged and sustained by the knights of the lash.

I trembled for you, your wife and children. I have shed tears of joy that you and yours are safe. What is property compared with your precious lives. I have been through a somewhat similar scene.

Will not God overrule this outbreaking of the wrath of man, for the advancement of the great and holy principles of eternal liberty? The plough has, indeed, gone, beam-deep, over Philadelphia. Now you can conquer your hardened

155

city. Men will come to their senses. This will add thousands of bold and true friends to our cause. Slavery itself
will be burnt out at last.

Oh, what a tale to float on the four winds of Heaven!
what an act to be related in the old world!

It would be a proud spectacle to see you draw a draft for
a new and nobler hall, while the smoke of the first ascended
like that of a mighty furnace to Heaven. Give my most
profound and affectionate respects to all your co-workers in
this holy enterprise. Be of good courage. The great moral
battle is yours. God is with you. The voice of the civilized world is with you. The eyes of angels and men of the
upper and this lower world are on you. The eyes of posterity
will often moisten as they read the tragic page in which you
are the conspicuous actors. But, go on. The slave and the
freeman all look to you to build a second hall to Liberty. I
feel identified with your new Phœnix temple. They will not
burn another. Public sentiment will roll over them. . . .

16 *June*, 1838, UTICA.

DEAR FRIEND:

I snatch the first moment that my pressing engagements
and a journey, in and out, of 1,200 miles, with my wife and
daughter, have allowed, to enjoy the satisfaction I now feel, in
answering your second and third letters, which have imparted
great pleasure to me, my family, and others, who have had the
opportunity of listening to their highly interesting contents.
There is something so ennobling to find you acquiring fresh
strength and new vigor, by the persecutions which lower and
thunder over your head and those of your noble coadjutors,
that all you have suffered, and we by sympathy with you,
seems to be a cheap mode of purchasing the development of
those lofty points of character, that unflinching firmness, that
holy boldness and unwavering constancy amidst the whirlwind

of human passion and interests. Yes, such remarkable virtues as these can only be known in the hour of a nation's peril—can only be understood at the funeral of Liberty, and only seen at the grave of humanity. The great virtues are not to be used in the days of prosperity, but are to be brought forth for the sustentation of truth and justice in an hour of distress, when the surface-springs and bubbling brooks show us nothing but dusty and forsaken channels.

On that night when the troops of slavery—a northern mob —howled through your streets, instead of sacrificing on the altar raised to liberty and consecrated by us in the temple of free discussion, their first sacrifice being the temple itself to the god of fire and darkness, whose willing subjects they are, how I have rejoiced, in such an hour, to see you, deliberately sketching, by the dying light of the first temple, a second one still more illustrious and beautiful.

I came from Philadelphia home. The next week I went to the Herkimer Circuit and acquitted a woman charged with murder, and successfully defended a breach of promise of marriage case. On Monday, 28th May, I started for Boston, and attended, three days, the New England Convention. A Convention which will do much good in carrying out the permanent quarterly subscriptions, the libraries, the petitioning Congress and the State legislature, in adding to the ranks of members, and, last, though not least, in inducing political action. All these points are to be made practical. Saturday, after Convention adjourned, I addressed the ladies of Boston, and added to the roll of members. Sunday, I addressed the people of Dorchester ; Monday, those of Duxbury ; and, Tuesday, those of Plymouth Rock, the place of the landing of our forefathers. Wednesday, I went, at urgent solicitation, 104 miles overland to Concord, New Hampshire, where the State Society met on Thursday, and the legislature on same day. On Thursday I spoke three or four hours, and on Friday, our

friends asked the legislature for the State House for me;
but I lost it by thirteen votes—115 to 128. Last year, out of
150 members, our friends could get but 15 or 16 to vote for
our having the hall.

Gov. Hill yoked temperance and abolition together, and
abused both objects shamefully. On Friday, our friends
insisted that I should review the opinions of their governor,
delivered in his message the day before, and the conduct of
the assembly in refusing us the house. I did not spare them,
I assure you. Some forty or fifty members present. Saturday, I came some sixty miles to Groton, Mass., delivered an
address on Sunday, two on Monday, and on Tuesday, went
to Boston by Lowell, forty miles, and spent the day, and in the
afternoon and night went to New York—saw the Executive
Committee of the Parent Society and talked to them two
hours, and got home on Thursday, at three P.M. The thermometer in the shade has been all the time for the last eight
days, at from 80 to 90° Fahrenheit.

Be encouraged, dear brother ; you are engaged in a mighty
work. Do not disturb the ruins of the Hall, if the corpora-
tion will let them stand, for the space of five years to come.
These burnt and ruined walls will make men *think*. The
nation is fairly waked up. We will make politicians feel so,
that they will be the first to run with their buckets to put out
our blazing halls. Write, and believe me ever thine.

———

UTICA, June 26th, 1838.

I thank you most kindly for the box to which you allude
and the minerals from Pennsylvania Hall therein contained.
We are very thankful that you have any scrap of oak or pine
from that Hall, the memory of which will last. That Hall
seemed to be too noble and glorious a monument for this
age ; and, instead of lifting itself as a mark of the tempest

and a target for the thunder-bolt, standing from century to century, a great *moral landmark* on the coast of time, upbraiding the surrounding churches and public edifices, as unheedful of the cries of bleeding humanity, forcing the world to see that the slaveholder had locked up the northern churches, and public halls, and strutted in bold defiance with these keys hanging from his girdle ; instead of standing such conspicuous beacon from age to age, our Hall, when the slaveholders demanded the key, as if conscious of the contamination, *blushed* into a blaze of indignation, and expired, only to live on the pages of history, being satisfied that she had done more, in the four days of her existence, for the cause of humanity, than all the halls and churches erected in the land.   .   .   .

REPORT OF A SPEECH

DELIVERED BEFORE A

JOINT COMMITTEE OF THE LEGISLATURE OF VERMONT,

Raised to inquire into the propriety of reporting and passing Resolutions addressed to Congress, praying that body to abolish the internal Slave Trade between the States, Slavery in the District of Columbia, and in the Territories of the United States, and to prevent the admission of new Slave States, and Texas into the Union, by special request and invitation from the Vermont State A. S. Society, on the 25th, 26th and 27th of October, 1838.

The resolutions passed the Senate by the following vote: "Yeas, 22; nays, 0." In the Assembly they were carried by acclamation, and no negative was called.

SPEECH.

HONORABLE GENTLEMEN OF THE JOINT COMMITTEE: You are clothed with power for the most exalted purposes; not to inquire into the propriety of a bridge over a river, the suitableness of granting a bank charter in this or that town, of increasing or diminishing the tax on this or that district or county; no, your duty extends to eight times as many people as those who constitute this sovereign and independent State, who are your countrymen, your brethren, your fellow beings, born in the republic, not to its rich inheritance, but its orphanage; not to its glory, but to its dishonor; not to its rich treasure of knowledge and religion, but its utter intellectual bereavement and heathenism; not to its liberty and independence, but its slavery and loss of all things; not to its bright and glorious hope, but its blackness of darkness, in despair. In behalf of two and a half millions of your wretched fellow men, found in your own glorious but disgraced country, the cry for pity, help and mercy is wafted in every southern wind which blows over the lands of chains and tears, and has brought to Vermont the deep lamentations of the unpitied, the unwept, and the unmourned.

THE FREEMEN OF VERMONT.

To what friend should the slave sooner go than to the freemen of these vales and mountains?

The dark, unbroken wilderness, which half a century since covered this beautiful land, was not removed by a generation of unpaid slaves—no, the white man alone was the pioneer. The sturdy birch, the majestic elm, the solid beech, the noble maple, the hated massive hemlock and the cloud-propping pine—the Anakim of the vegetable kingdom—have fallen before the freemen of Vermont, and made the earth to tremble in their *dying groans*. Ye middle-aged and aged men, turn to your early remembrance, when the valleys and hills at midnight were illuminated with the funeral piles of these forest giants; who was high priest, who presided at the sacrifice? The sunburnt and hard knuckled freeman of Vermont stood in his sombre linen frock, his sacerdotal robes, and performed the duty. No unpaid slave ever heard the cruel sound of the master's horn call his unrested limbs from his piles of straw to his miserable toil in Vermont. No; your mountains would have held their breath, and refused an echo to that hated sound. Vermont was the first born child after the Revolution. Although she came into the confederacy amidst storms and tempests, which lowered upon her birth; yet she was born perfect in all her limbs; her moral faculties showed that the Declaration of Independence was her noble sire. She was not like her next sister, Kentucky, who came misshapen, limping, half made up, with rickets before her birth and ever since. Yes, those moral rickets, slavery, have sadly disfigured that sister, and her unwillingness to be cured of her complaint, proves that her mind is as badly affected as her body is deformed. Poor Kentucky is not ashamed to steal, but too proud to work, and too dishonest to pay those who do!

Vermont has penetrated to the central line, between the equator and the pole, and on the outer line of the nation, in the far North, last year, sent up her resolutions to Congress against slavery; those resolutions were truly the moral *aurora borealis*, the true northern lights, to alarm the proud, terrify the wicked, enlighten the ignorant; yea, to intimidate those rickety imps and monsters who feed and gorge themselves on human flesh and blood.

Vermont, in presenting those noble resolutions to an American Congress, in face of so much leagued malice and cruelty, appeared like an angel of mercy walking upon the high places of the earth. Who might not, on that day, have coveted the honor of a birthplace in your State? If seven cities of antiquity contended, each, for the honor of being the birthplace of Homer, then may the man of Vermont be justly proud that his State was the birthplace of these resolutions, and stood in the front rank of humanity, and first as a State which mounted the parapets of slavery.

Vermont, before her existence as a State, had tasted of oppression. She struggled into existence under twelve acts of outlawry passed against her by the State of New York.

You had a double war for your independence—yea, treble —with the British Empire and the State of New York and New Hampshire, each claiming jurisdiction over you. Your mountains and forests were your abiding auxiliaries in these contests, these mountains, the native abodes of liberty, the oldest citadels of humanity, the blessed homes of struggling, persecuted and unsubdued freedom. Look at this State in its infancy, sixty years ago, with but 5,000 men who could handle the axe or the sword, tearing down the forests, an unacknowledged community, contending for an existence, while England, New York and New Hampshire sought to take it away. Yet Vermont, the real Switzerland of America, came into existence when political and personal liberty were prized, next after the salvation of the soul, as the greatest good human authority could confer. Slavery, in no form, ever sprouted on this soil. Physicians assert that certain persons are predisposed to certain diseases, so I may say of the citizens of this State, on the great question of humanity now pending before the American people, they have a predisposition to join against any cause or question in which liberty is threatened with destruction or overthrow; to range themselves against the oppressor, and with the oppressed, to seat themselves by the side of the prisoner, and lock arms with him who is ready to perish. She is ready to say to the bondman, "Entreat me not to leave thee, or to return from following after thee, for whither thou goest I will go, and where thou lodgest I will lodge; thy people shall be my people, thy God shall be my God; where thou diest I will die, and there will I be buried; the Lord do so to me, and more also, if aught but death part me and thee."

VERMONT FOREMOST FOR LIBERTY.

The resolutions, adopted by the legislature of Vermont, addressed to Congress, last year, covering the extent of ordinary constitutional action, on the part of the confederacy, cheered the heart of the philanthropist, and armed humanity herself with a new power to march to the terrible contest between the forces of light and darkness, truth and falsehood, liberty and slavery. In the character and spirit of those resolutions the slaveholder must have seen shadowed out, in coming

days, his indictment, trial, and final overthrow. Then he saw
a sovereign State march into the field. Then the slaveholder
found out that the falsehood of the *addleheaded* charge, that
the Abolitionists were only a few decayed old women, subject to hysterics, and a few moon-struck, fanatical men, who
nursed and fed themselves on visions, and spent their time in
trances, or lost themselves by diving into the mysteries of
prophecy, and second sight, or in writing commentaries upon
Mormon Bibles. But these noble-minded men of the South,
whose minds soared into the lofty regions of chivalry, where
women-whipping is one of the most distinguished features or
employments of that *chivalry* (for except in those peculiarly
gay and gallant regions women are not whipped) through
John C. Calhoun, the prince of nullification, raised the cry,
that before the Vermont resolutions were considered, by the
Senate, a string of resolutions, all split out of one log, and by
Mr. Calhoun, must first be considered, as a counter statement, to those from Vermont, as a sort of breakwater to
prevent their consequence! Thus the culprit, arraigned by
Vermont, was determined to open his case, introduce his
evidence and sum up his cause, and make the most of his
argument, before the prosecution was heard, and thus fore-
stall the judgment of the court. I have no doubt, this new
and improved mode adopted by the slaveholders in Congress,
of trying a criminal, would relieve the gallows from bending
under the weight of many a pirate, and the State prison from
the confinement of many a scoundrel. These highly cultivated
slaveholders deny the slave's right of petition on any subject,
any more than mules, dogs or horses, on the ground that
slaves have no rights to be violated; no matter what is done
to the slave by any one, he as a slave having no rights, nor
any interest in any rights, which can be violated, therefore
cannot as a slave assume to ask for the redress of any
injuries, because he, the slave, has nothing which can be

injured. He has nothing which can be the subject of legislative address, on his own prayer, for to admit it, would be admitting there was something the master had not crushed and destroyed, in appropriating the slave to himself. The slave, says the master, cannot petition for himself for anything, therefore the freeman can ask no greater right for the slave than the slave could for himself, *therefore* the freeman cannot petition for him. And if it be right to deny the petition of the slave, in person, or the freeman for him, therefore it must be right to deny the petition of a sovereign State, who asks for the same thing, yea, the whole nation, if it ask for anything in behalf of the slave who has nothing, and is entitled to nothing, on the ground, that the nation is agent for the State, who is agent of the freeman, who is agent of the slave, or nothing; this whole matter resting on a legal *nothing*, no matter how high you pile considerations upon nothing, and extend the boundaries of nothing, to nothing it must come at last. In this bark-mill circle southern mind revolves, on the question of slavery. We know not which most to wonder at, the gross inhumanity it manifests, or the shallow logic by which they affect to maintain this proposition. ·Let us examine for a moment one of the prominent reasons, why there appears to be such a numerous and active force upon the floor of Congress, ready to contend for propositions, which, for absurdity, are only exceeded by their cruelty, and seem to mock all the pretensions which civilization and Christianity ever claimed in their advancement of the human race.

THING-REPRESENTATIVES IN CONGRESS.

The American Congress is, without doubt, an anomaly as a deliberative body, in the civilized world. In that most august representative body of twenty-four sovereign and independent States, are twenty-eight members elected, in consequence of two and a quarter millions of slaves existing in one part of the nation from whence these twenty-eight members come, not to represent them, but to oppose any plan or project which might tend to the benefit of those slaves, to whose very numbers these twenty-eight members were indebted for their seats. By counting five slaves as three white or free persons, as the basis of Congressional representation, these twenty-eight members of Congress hold their seats as the chattel representatives, or as the representatives of things and not of men, and possess or claim the power to silence their chattel or *thing-constituency*, when it asks or seeks to become a *man-constituency*, and also claims the high prerogative of silencing their associate members of Congress, who would seek to elevate the *chattel-constituency* of the twenty-eight to the man basis. The twenty-eight claim that it is a distinct portion of their official duty to countervail the sympathy and humanity of the age, when it shall manifest a desire to elevate their constituents to the common right and privileges of mankind. These twenty-eight men come to represent nothing but the congregated absurdities and all the marked moral obliquities of this period of the world. Let it not be supposed I am a stranger to the fact, that the twenty-eight assert that three-fifths of their slaves are added to the rest of the population, as a constitutional rule, for the purpose of fixing the basis of representation, the same as women and children are counted at the North, for the purpose of fixing the rate.

These twenty-eight men come as a sort of body-guard to lust, laziness, unpaid wages, ignorance, heathenism, the rights of the lash, amalgamation, prostitution, the shooting down unpaid laborers for leaving their employments, divorcing husbands and wives, separating parents and children, the selling men, women and children by private contract, or by public outcry; yea, the right of vending unborn generations; yes, the exalted privilege, peculiar to the slaveholder, of selling his own children, his own brothers and sisters, cousins, nephews and nieces, into the most miserable slavery, and all and every the right of duelling, chivalry, assassination, murder, and generally all and every and each of the varied and multiplied rights embraced within the circle of the most unbounded inhumanity.

These twenty-eight Congressmen are the chosen gladiators, to dispute every inch of ground, which the humanity of Congress may desire to occupy. These are the men, whose votes are employed to gag the House of Representatives of the nation. These are the twenty-eight men to lead the House on the forlorn hope of suppressing debate, and take the liberties of the nation by storm, and lead them into captivity without the hope of ransom. These are the men, to deny the right of petition, when it affects their *thing-constituency.* These are the men, elected different from all the rest, not to favor but to resist all measures offered by others, for the benefit of their thing-constituency. These are the men who, under the pretence of *preserving* order and quiet, in the glory of representatives, produce wild chaos and primeval night, amidst their maniac screams of *Order!* ORDER!! ORDER!!! These are the men who, with oaths, at their private boarding-houses, on the 21st December, 1837, swore that "if any man from the North (as your able Slade had done) should bring in a resolution, or a law, to abolish slavery in the District of Columbia again, they would put him to death!!"

Their notions of government may be inferred from their favorite maxim, that "slavery is the corner-stone of our republic." If slavery be " the corner-stone," it is not difficult to predict of what materials the side, the end walls of this edifice would be erected, if these twenty-eight gentlemen were allowed to remodel the fabric of American institutions.

There are six republics on this continent, in North and South America, which are without those "corner-stones," so much valued by these far-seeing politicians.

Beside the peculiar duties which have been assigned to the twenty-eight *thing-representatives*, they are expected to do a certain amount of bullying, hectoring, gasconading, threatening, challenging, duelling, rifle-trying, pistol-practising, so as to compel from northern members, their profound respect for the peculiar institutions of the South. They, the twenty-eight, are mechanically, as the clock strikes the hour, at least one hundred times, in a session of Congress, to *threaten* to split the Union all to shivers; and at least on one hundred different questions, from the question whether a dead horse, killed in the late war, should be paid for, up to that of the abolition of slavery.

They, the twenty-eight, are ex-officio the wardens and keepers of the wedges and beetles, by which they will undertake to split the Union into pieces or parts to suit purchasers, from a State down to a school district.

The great slave wedge, we are assured by these nation-splitters, would easily rive and sunder the Union, from the capes of the Delaware to the Mandan towns. If these men will sacrifice the Union for their love of slavery, we will sacrifice slavery for our love of the Union. We hope, by the goodness of an overruling Providence, that we shall be able to add two and a half millions of new votaries and supporters of a republican form of government, who, having tasted all the ills which may be practised under it, may also enjoy all the blessings which by any possibility it may confer.

DISTRICT OF COLUMBIA.

MAY IT PLEASE THE HONORABLE COMMITTEE: We will now look at slavery in the District of Columbia. This district has been a sort of man-menagerie, in which the grand experiment has been tried for thirty-eight years, by the consent of the nation, to see whether men can be converted into beasts, or things, by putting them into the same legal scale, annexing the same legal consequences to their acts—except where cruelty is to be practised, for there the punishments would, from their variety and rigor, assume that the offenders were above men, yea, the compeers of angels.

One would think the 200 years of slavery and debasement, on this continent, of man, in the shape of a slave, was a period of sufficient length, to settle the question, whether slaves could be learned to walk on all fours, like the beasts, or not. But no, the grandeur of his celestial descent, his heavenly lineage, the capital of mind the slave receives direct from God, will forever make an impassable gulf, between this noble, though abused immortal, and the beasts which perish.

To suppose it necessary, to make a parade of constitutional learning, to convince any man, who feels and acknowledges the common import of words and sentences, is to suppose that nothing can be made certain in the English language.

It is clearly expressed in the Constitution of the United States, that Congress has power, given by the Constitution, to "legislate in all cases whatever, over the District of Columbia," and therefore has a right to abolish slavery; the same right that it had to establish it, because that Congress adopted it, and therefore has a right to abrogate it. To say that Congress has not the power to abolish slavery in the District, is a crime against the English language, as well as our common humanity. The language is explicit beyond the most malignant carpings of the most fiendish criticism. To say it is contrary to the spirit of our Constitution, is to say that the preamble to the Constitution is false, which says "it was ordained for the purpose of establishing *justice* and *liberty.*" It is as clear as though it had been written, "Congress shall have power to abolish slavery in the District of Columbia." It is one of those cases where the proposition is itself more clear, than any argument, evidence, or illustration assumed as true, can make it. "*Clarius luce*," more clear than light, as the Roman orator once said. Whoever undertakes, by other arguments than the text of the Constitution itself, to make it appear that Congress have, and should exercise the abolition power it possesses, for the benefit of 7000 persons, would make the question more doubtful by words, and might as well undertake to prove the existence of the sun, by his light reflected from the moon, rather than by his own shining, in all the glories of noon.

But many will assert it inexpedient to abolish slavery in the District of Columbia, because the slaveholder is opposed to it.

Shall we wait till the slaveholder is willing, where the nation has the power? Shall we reverse the first principles of our government, and allow the minority to rule, and commit crime, when the majority should rule, and must be responsible for all the wrong and misery which they have power to prevent?

Is the friendship of wicked men and slaveholders more important to a majority of the nation than an approving conscience, which is the voice of God, and the opinion of good men all round the world? If the free States refuse (having the power as they really possess it) to abolish slavery in the District of Columbia, it becomes, truly, the sin of the North, of the free States, and on us rests the responsibility of every pain of mind or body, which may be endured by those 7000 slaves, which they would not suffer, were they free; yea, more, of the horrid countenance we seem to lend to the slaveholders, in the States, where they, as States, claim to have the only power to abolish slavery. Yes, slavery may put forth a very plausible defence of the system, by saying

that the North, without profit from slavery, permit it to
exist, when they have power to abolish it, therefore, they of
the North cannot consider slaveholding very wrong, or they
would abolish it, where they have the odium of its existence,
without the profit of its continuance.

DUTY OF THE STATES.

Gentlemen of the committee, we now come to the legislature of Vermont, asking it, with great respect, to embody
and express to Congress the desire of this sovereign State,
that slavery should be immediately and forever abolished in
the District of Columbia. Your citizens of this State have
besought you by their petitions on this subject to lend suffering humanity a helping hand.

The peculiar posture of affairs in the present Congress
seems to invite the States to come forward in their highest
legislative capacity, and rescue the Constitution of our common country from the most gross violations; violations for
which every patriot should tremble for the perpetuity of our
blood-bought liberties. The citizens of Vermont, as well as
those of the other free States, have sent thousands and tens
of thousands of petitions to Congress, praying for the abolition of slavery in the District of Columbia, and the internal
slave trade and for kindred objects; all of which, in the past
year, have been laid upon the table, unread, unreferred, unprinted, undebated, and unconsidered.

CONSTITUTIONCIDES.

Thus have the members of Congress, from the free States,
bowed themselves lower, in base submission, to the footstool
of slavery, than on all other propositions ever before united.
But the northern members, who voted the Patton gag, before
they got so low, had to grope their way down on a ladder
of perjury. There was no other invention by which they

could have debased themselves, and found for themselves
so abject a point.   It was only by jumping the life to
come.

The Constitution has secured the eternal and Heaven-
descended right of petition to the people of this country;
not that the Constitution gave or conferred this right; no,
sirs, it barely spoke against its violation, it threw its powerful arms out in defence of this right, coëval with man.   But
these members of Congress who voted for the resolution of
the 21st December, 1837, to lay the petitions of the freemen
and women of the North on the table, unread, unconsidered,
and unprinted, must stand on the page of history in all coming time as the assassins; yes, the perjured assassins of their
country's reputation, for the infamous purpose of upholding
slavery in the capital of the nation, and the slave trade
between the States, in its most diabolical form which this
world has ever seen, in the long range of 600 years.

'The regicides of Charles the First—many of them perished
at home on the scaffold, others died of misery and want in
foreign lands, the objects of the world's contempt and scorn,
for having tried, condemned, and executed their sovereign.
These regicides alleged that they destroyed the king, and
broke through the Constitution of England, in vindication of
humanity outraged, and for the delivery of liberty from
chains.   But how much greater judgment should be awarded
against those members of Congress, who, on the 21st December, 1837, laid their sacrilegious, polluted hands upon the
written Constitution of their country, after they had solemnly
sworn by the retributions of the eternal judgment to maintain its provisions—then to turn round and violate that Constitution; not as the regicides did to aid human liberty, but
for the malignant purpose of transfixing liberty to a cross,
and make her expire in her own temple, as a mark of open
shame!   Before these *constitutioncides* could withhold the

consideration of the wretched slave's case, they had to walk over the dead body of the Constitution of their country.

This generation is so overcome with the bewildering cry raised against the Abolitionists in behalf of the southern rights, that they have not yet opened their eyes and ears to the greatest crimes which have ever been committed on this continent; and those crimes, to add to their malignity, have been committed under the forms of the Constitution.

But when truth shall triumph over delusion and the fanaticism of a mistaken and slavery-ridden age, then shall some philosophic Hume, in the next century review the distressing transactions of this; then will the 21st December, 1837, be reckoned the most gloomy and disastrous day which has distinguished the annals of this nation. If the 4th July, 1776, be a day standing preëminent for the grandeur of those principles which we then adopted, the 21st December, 1837, may stand as an inauspicious contrast; if the former was the birth of American liberty, the latter appears like its funeral.

Behold the monstrous crime committed by the majority of the House of Representatives of the United States, as each member responded " aye " to the famous, or rather *infamous* resolution of Patton of Virginia, on the 21st December, 1837. This resolution was passed under the tourniquet of the previous question, or strangled debate. The previous question, according to parliamentary law, is intended to put an end to a useless and protracted debate, after all have been heard, and the question viewed, in all those shapes and forms through full and free discussion, in which they may wish to present it. Then, if garrulous and prating members are disposed to wear out the patience of the House, and waste its time, the previous question may be moved, which puts an end to the exhausted debate. But here the most important question which ever came before a deliberative body of men, was taken, before a word of debate, under the call or motion of the previous question, by which the House of Representatives agreed that all petitions, on the subject of slavery, unread and unconsidered, should lie upon the table.

Behold five crimes committed by each member who said " aye " to this resolution, in the same breath. 1st. The Constitution was violated on the subject of petition. 2d. The previous question was prostrated to an object diametrically opposite to that for which it was intended, by which the members opposed to the Patton resolution (which was a violation of the Constitution), were constrained to give a silent vote against a mighty infraction of the Constitution, without being able to speak a single word to beseech the House not to take this most fatal and unconstitutional leap. 3d. The members who said " aye " committed perjury ; for they violated that Constitution which they had sworn to support. 4th. There was a special inhumanity, amounting to a hideous offence, in refusing to inquire into the condition of two and a half millions of slaves, or any part of them, or the laws by which they were deprived of the inestimable boon of liberty. 5th. There was moral treason committed against white and black, bond and free, every man, woman and child in the republic, in violating their rights, their liberties, their humanity struck down through the sides of the Constitution ; yes, it was high treason against the age, the humanity of this nineteenth century, and the everlasting commands of the great Jehovah.

What monosyllable ever pronounced by man in any day, in any place, was so big with destruction to all the precious hopes of man ? Yes, before this high decree, the slave and the freeman, the sovereign State, and an American Congress, all alike, stood speechless. This was despotism in its most solemn form, which orders the victim to be silent, which it intends for sacrifice. If the victim, the Constitution, could have spoken through its friends, and pleaded against her own violation, her brightest jewel would not have been ravished from her in silence.

Open the black and bloody pages of despotism, recorded in the annals of past ages, and let us see whether ever in one day, Nero, Caligula, Domitian, Dionysius, Aurelian, Bajazet, Robespierre, and Bonaparte, *those flails of Almighty God*, did roll back the car freighted with the most precious interests and hopes of man, as far into the night of barbarism and blood, as these members of Congress, who, on the 21st December, 1837, said " aye " to the Patton slave resolution.

The amazing criminality of this transaction appears more dreadful, when it is considered that this resolution barred the only avenue of the wretched slaves, or their friends, to the District of Columbia, and denied all access to the slave territories, it cut off the humane from the hope of abolishing the internal slave trade, and impliedly forbid our protesting against the annexation of that stranded mass of villains, the cullings of the world's prisons, Texas.

THE POWER OF CONGRESS.

The very reason urged by the South for her counting five of her slaves the same as three of our citizens, was, that it might form a counterpoise to that power, given by the Constitution to Congress, " to regulate foreign commerce, commerce between the States and the Indian tribes." The South contending that the North, only being interested in commerce, would regulate it to the injury of the South, whether foreign or domestic, and that the South must have an additional number of representatives, in Congress, by counting their slaves, to countervail the action of the North on questions of foreign and internal commerce.

Under the power to regulate foreign commerce, we abolished the old African slave trade. Under the power to regulate internal commerce between the States, we petition

Congress to abolish the internal slave trade between the States. Now the South denies that Congress has the constitutional power to regulate commerce between the States, so as to confine the slaves to the States, where they now are. Yes, after we have purchased this power so dearly of the South (which gives the South twenty-eight additional members), we now find the South denying its very existence; in fact, the very consideration money, if I may so speak, for the privilege of counting five slaves as three free persons, is denied.

Why do the South deny it? Because it is the great door to the slave Bastile, left in the side of the constitutional temple, which, when we have power to abolish it in the District of Columbia, we shall have, the same day, power to enact a law, that no slave shall be taken or removed, or sold from one State to another, under the penalty of perpetual imprisonment or death. What is to be the effect of such a law on slavery? First, to confine the slaves to the States, where they are on the day of the enactment of the law. The States of Maryland, Virginia, Kentucky, Tennessee, and the western parts of the Carolinas have, for twenty years past, maintained themselves by selling their surplus slaves to the States of Georgia, Alabama, Louisiana, Mississippi and Arkansas, and not by selling the productions of slaves, but by selling slaves themselves, as the great article of commerce to the great cotton and sugar districts of the far South. Now if these slave-growing States, in the north end of the slave section of the country, were unable to sell slaves, the master and slave could not live together, the slaves of Maryland and Virginia would eat up their masters, and the masters must emancipate in self-defence, to save themselves from destruction. Again, the States of Alabama, Louisiana, Mississippi, and others, if they could not import slaves from the north end of the slave region, there is such havoc annually by death among the slaves of the great planters, by the unhealthiness of the climate and the cruel treatment of overseers, that in less than seven years, if no slave could be imported, into those southern regions, one half of the plantations would lie uncultivated for want of slaves.

This power to regulate commerce between the States, is one of the mighty powers of the confederacy which has lain . hitherto, in a great degree, dormant, although purchased at such a cruel and bitter expense, now amounting to twenty-eight members of Congress; yet it may, if properly wielded, become the great battering ram to knock down the fortifications of slavery. The power to regulate foreign commerce was the battle-axe with which we sundered the neck of the old African slave trade, in six successive cuts, of Congress, enacted at different periods from 1808 to 1824.

Let no one say that the word "regulate," as used in the Constitution, may not mean to alter, change, destroy, abolish, or annihilate. That question has been settled in favor of the above definitions by every department of the government, by both houses of Congress, the President, yes, and several times by the Supreme Court of the United States. These questions of "regulation" under the Constitution, have been up for consideration by our Senate, in forming treaties of peace; declarations of war by Congress, embargoes, non-intercourse acts—this word "to regulate" foreign commerce, and commerce between the States, has drawn forth an immense amount of ingenious reasoning to restrict the word in its meaning, but the Supreme Court of the United States, as well as the other departments of government, have declared that Congress have power to annihilate and destroy any branch of commerce, for this is one mode of regulating it, if Congress in their wisdom see fit to adopt it. The abolition of the old African slave trade had no constitutional authority for its exercise, except what was derived from the Constitution, which confers on Congress the power to regulate foreign commerce. The regulation Congress adopted, was the utter abolition and annihilation of the trade.

By the abolition of the African slave trade, the internal slave trade sprung up in this country, with more than all the horrors which belonged to this bloody commerce on the African shore.

THE MARTS OF BLOOD.

The bloody slave coasts of the Gambia, and Senegal of Africa, were transferred to the Potomac, the James, the Pedee, Cooper and Ashley, and the Savannah rivers. Washington, Georgetown, Alexandria, Richmond, Charleston and Savannah were the marts of blood, where those human-being contracts were made, where wives and husbands, parents and children were torn asunder, and uttered a frightful shriek and farewell of despair. Yes, these towns have been the grand slaughter-house of the holiest of the human ties. When inquest shall be made for blood, well might these Chorazins, these Sodoms and Gomorrahs, cry for the Alleghanies to fall on them, and hide them from the accusing ghosts of ruined and thrice murdered families? This trade in slaves on the high seas, or on the coast of Africa, American law and American humanity has pronounced to be the greatest crime which man can commit against man, and has declared its horrid perpetrators, pirates, and punishable with death. Oh! honorable inconsistency! That which is a crime of piracy three thousand miles off is changed by our laws by the same lawgivers and a part of the same code, when transacted at home in our own sight, and so far from being the highest of human offences, it becomes respectable business, not inconsistent with the duties of a private citizen, a judge, a President of the United States, a member of any of the Christian churches, yea, a minister in those churches; such a mighty change takes place in the criminal code of the United States by sailing through some forty degress of longitude, from the coast of Africa to the capital of the United States at Washington.

SOUTHERN THREATS.

Georgia and South Carolina threatened their sister States that they would not come into the Union, unless the Constitution of the United States guaranteed the continuance of the old African slave trade twenty years after the adoption of the Constitution, because they alleged they could purchase slaves direct from Africa, or catch them in Africa, for half the sum they would have to pay the old States of Virginia and Maryland for slaves; and these States further urged that they would not come into the Union, unless the free States would consent to become kidnappers, and catch the fugitive slaves for them, when they ran into the free States. For as they had run the slaves down in Africa, and conferred so great a blessing on the country by bringing them over, therefore, to encourage the South in its laudable undertakings, the South insisted that the North, or free States, were to act the part of shepherds' dogs, to scare, catch and return their wandering flocks, when they came into the northern parts of the land. So these chivalrous States insisted on three points as " *sine qua nons !*" 1st. The African slave trade should be extended twenty years. 2d. That the free States should deliver up fugitive slaves; and 3d. That they should count, for the basis of Congressional representation, five of their slaves the same as three of our citizens. Before the adoption of the Constitution, a constant system of threatening was kept up, that unless all the humanity of the world was violated, they would not come into the confederacy; and now the cry is, that unless we permit these same States to be considered honorable pirates, they will go out of the Union. It has always been held over our heads, *in terrorem*, first, that they would not come in; and now that they are in, that they would not stay in. And so, these chivalrous States have kept the North holding its breath, occasionally having *conniption fits*, lest the chivalrous human-flesh importers should become so enraged at our northern maxims, contained in the Declaration of Independence, that they would run out of the Union *down some steep place, and get choked in the sea.*

THE GREAT POLITICAL DIVISION.

This nation will, in a short time, be divided into two great parties which will swallow all others up, to wit, an anti-slavery one on one side, and a pro-slavery one on the other; the first holding that all men are created equal, and that labor is honorable in all, and liberty the right of all; while the latter or pro-slavery party will hold that one portion of the country is born to be slaves to the other; and that labor is dishonorable, and a badge of meanness, and a kindred principle with slavery.

The liberty-loving, labor-honoring party; the slave-holding, labor-despising party—to this complexion the people of this country must come at last. This will be the grand division between the political parties of this country.

Ye men and women of Vermont, I know I need not ply you with arguments, to show which side of this important alternative you should espouse.

You have always been on the side of humanity and justice in this great question of slavery. Everything here teaches you liberty; these rocks and hills, these inexorable winters—all command you, as from above, to be industrious, laborious, frugal, and just. Your position and soil are perpetual guaranties that you will be industrious, that labor must be considered honorable ; where those things exist men will love liberty and hate slavery, or history is a lie and experience without instruction.

EXPEDIENCY.

Our fathers have left us one of the most instructive lessons ever given to mankind, showing the folly of expediency ; and, its wickedness when adopted by a nation, in opposition to the plain command of God, and the dictates of humanity, and the sober counsels of exact justice. It may not be unprofitable to glance at some of these governmental gales of expediency, into which our fathers and the present generation of public men have been betrayed, under the notion that present expediency required us, as a nation, to use it to commit crimes, at which, as individuals, we should shudder. At the time of the Declaration of Independence, the nation was like the great deep at the time of the flood, broken up from its foundations, and casting off the allegiance that bound us to the British empire. Society was resolved in this republic into its original elements. 3,000,000 being the entire population; 500,000, or one sixth of whom had been, and were held as slaves.

All men must have seen by our Declaration of Independence, and almost every state paper, all Congressional resolutions, manifestoes, petitions, appeals, and remonstrances connected with our struggle with the parent country, or the formation of States, by our State constitutions replete with the general topic of liberty, which was on the tongues of all, and in the hearts of many, that the times declared the general expectation, that if our independence was ever acknowledged by the British king and other powers of Europe, that liberty, universal liberty under the control of law, was to be the portion of every human being in the land. Consistency, decency, self-respect, justice, and the pleadings of our common humanity all conspired to make us believe that the grave which we had dug for the manacles intended for our hands by England, should hold those which for 150 years had bound the slave.

The war of the Revolution was over, the last gun fired against a foreign foe, the States formed their constitutions, with bills of rights, attesting the doctrines of the Declaration of Independence, full of the most lofty professions in behalf of human rights. The confederation of the States, a mere rope of sand, lasted from 1777 to 1789, twelve years. This was framed during the midnight of the Revolution: but out of regard to the slaveholders, nothing was said about the slave. Let us secure our own independence first. But in 1774, the first Congress thought of the slave, so far as to forbid the old aforesaid slave trade after the 31st December, 1775. This resolution was a dead letter. Nothing said about slavery after, during the Revolution; all still; till the Major General was to be appointed for the armies of the United States; the North said, our Bunker Hill generals must stand aside to oblige the slave province of Virginia, and bring the South heartily into the measures for the Revolution. [Let no one think I intend disrespect to the memory of our immortal countryman by the statement of this fact; far from it.] Again, when the Declaration of Independence was to be drawn, the honor must be conferred on a southern slaveholder, and its composition has, for its great merits, given a glorious immortality to its author.

How small a matter it would have been for Congress, at some one of its sessions during the Revolution, to have declared the slaves free immediately, that they might be armed in defence of the country which had made them free-men. History abounds in examples of this character, in ancient and modern times. Admitting the proposition for a moment, for the sake of the remark (but not as a truth), the

Congress of the Revolution might have declared them free under the unlimited war power a nation possesses over the men and treasure of a nation which is fighting for its existence. This principle must have been familiar to the old Congress of the Revolution. But supposing the former masters, after the Revolution, had petitioned Congress for relief or compensation, how easy to have set off the land now composing two or three States. But our fathers let these golden opportunities pass, for fear of offending the South. Then came the formation of the Constitution of 1787, when twenty years were added to the African slave trade, to accommodate the South, and five slaves counted three whites, as the basis of Congressional representation. Then was the time to have insisted on the abolition of slavery, instead of yielding, and adding tenfold vigor to the insatiate hatred against the *ebon* race. What if three or four of those States had refused at first to enter the Union? Did not two of them do it after all our coaxing, cringing, and miserable expediency? They would have come in within three or four years after, and without slaves.

The other States would have marched forward to grandeur and greatness, untrammelled by this awful system. And the very fact that we had parted on grounds so honorable to us, would have given to the world a most glorious exhibition of our devotedness to the great principles of justice and humanity. We should have had God and all good men on our side; yea, the approval of our own consciences. We should not have had a generation at the North at this time one half of whom seem to be debauched in their notions of right and wrong, in relation to human liberty; as much, I fear, as the besotted masters of the South. It was a corrupt agreement of the majority of a nation, with a minority, to crush humanity. It was the most guilty compact, for twenty years, against the guiltless poor of injured, unoffending Africa.

Suppose we had stood up for God and our consciences while the slaveholder had separated and formed his slave oligarchy, without the aid of northern freemen to subdue the insurrection of the slave. The troops and navy of Great Britain kept the slave of the West Indies in subjection, and not the planters; and so it has been in this confederacy, the military force of the North and the free States have restrained and held back the southern slave from his liberty. Again, the slaves, without the clause of surrender in the Constitution, which was another crime of expediency committed against the law of God and our common humanity by the North, would have fled to us on the long line of Pennsylvania, Ohio, Indiana, and Illinois, not to be pursued with southern vengeance, and met by northern law, northern justices and constables.

No, if we had withdrawn all connection with the South, all countenance, and held back the loan of our non-slaveholding character, as a cloak to cover up the rottenness of her most loathsome deformity, the South would long ere this have abolished slavery herself, from the disgrace it would have been to her institutions. Suppose she had cut loose from the joint inheritance purchased by the valor of the Revolution because we would not participate in her crimes, she would then have stood such a monument of corruption and avarice, murder, meanness and feebleness, that there would not have been a nation in Europe so lost to self-respect, as to have entered into treaties with, or acknowledged the independence of a community whose foreign commerce was kidnapping, piracy, murder and blood; whose domestic pursuits were nothing but lust, women-whipping, robbery, and extortion, who paid their labors in kicks, curses, and lashes, who sold their own children, brothers, and sisters, by private contract, or public outcry. No; the nations of the earth would have regarded them as " *hostes humani generis,*" the enemies of the human race, as the outlawed bandits of the world, whom to have destroyed by been considered as the greatest of public virtues.

But they have been preserved from the universal contempt and war of mankind by their confederacy with the free States.

But whatever has gone to save the South from the execration of the world, has been exactly so much deducted from northern virtue and character. Slavery has always been maintained at the expense of northern character, until Europe now regards the pro-slavery men of the North, and the slaveholders of the South, as on a par, and a stench in the nostrils of mankind. The admission of Missouri, Louisiana, Mississippi, Alabama, and Arkansas were all base bowings to expediency, at the expense of our poor sable brother. They were departures from, and violations of, the spirit of the Constitution. What have we gained by blackening the valley of the Mississippi with slavery, feebleness, shame, dishonor, sorrow, and an unspeakable amount of human misery? The country at the North and the South is every way the worse. Again, we bowed to the South under the famous tariff compromise, by which the North sacrificed more than five hundred millions to the slaveholding South. They now desire a hard money government with which to overthrow northern credit. We lost from fifty to seventy-five millions in the late revulsion in moneyed affairs, by the unnatural credit the slaveholders obtained at the North by pilfering from the future, and anticipating crops to be raised in 1839 and 1840, from the large masses of slaves and land held by individuals, whereas, if each man had had his one, two or three hundred acres and his own hands, and his sons, or one or two hired men, as in the North, nothing of the kind would have occurred.

EXTRACTS FROM A SPEECH,

BEFORE THE GENERAL ASSEMBLY OF THE PRESBYTERIAN CHURCH,

At Philadelphia, in 1839.

THE SLAVE'S FALL.

FOR a man to fall into slavery is to descend as far below the lowest point of Adam's fall, as Adam's fall carried him below the dome of Heaven. For a slave falls out of himself. A slave falls below the capacity of getting up or inquiring where he is, or how he came there, or how he may get away; he falls so long through moral space that when he touches bottom, the laws of South Carolina and Louisiana say he is not to be regarded as a sentient being. Adam's fall left him at the point of knowing good and evil as he had practised them both, and he was a sentient being and could perceive it. The slave's fall is immense, as he goes so low he loses his manhood, and yet retains his shape; he has left behind him all rational companionship, and is found in the same field and on the same level with the braying ass, the bleating sheep, and the grunting swine. He hears the neighing of the horse on one hand, and the lowing of the ox on the other. The man has become a brute.—He is stock, property, a thing—and can claim no interest in the legs with which he walks, the legs are another man's—he has no owner-ship of the eyes with which he sees, they belong to another man—the ears with which he hears, are another's—and if anybody should rob him of his eyes or ears or hands he uses, he has no interest in the question, as they belong to another, who, if the slave has lost his eyes or ears, or hands or legs, must sue for them and implead the offender, but the slave who was using them at the time they were bored out or exscinded, has no interest in the question. If this male chattel lives with a female chattel, and they should happen to have some little likenesses of themselves, they would be called young chattels, who would belong to the owner of the old chattels, and might be sold by the pound.

DUTY TO PARENTS.

God says, "Children, obey your parents;" if the slave parents were to order their children to go into the free States or Canada, Jamaica, Mexico or Barbadoes, and these children were to obey, that would soon pull out the foundation of our Republican form of government, if it rests on slavery, and let the beautiful superstructure of chattelship to the ground, with all the rising hopes of the New World.

I hope that the seven commands I have pointed out as inconsistent with the institution of slavery, will not be regarded as the device of an army of fugitive slaves, lately escaped out of slavery, by even the upholders of slavery of the present day. I hope it will not be urged that the command " children obey your parents," is not of celestial origin ; and that there has been an interpolation or expurgation, and that it should read, " children obey your masters that your lives may be long in the land which the Lord your God shall give your masters."

DUTY OF CLERGYMEN.

Ministers of the Gospel have no business, say some, to interfere with the political institutions of their country, nor common Christians, say others ; the men of this world cite them to such expressions as these " Render unto Cæsar, the things that be Cæsar's." "Fear God and honor the King." "Be subject to the powers that be."

To be sure there is an immense difference between insurrection and reformation.

A general submission does not foreclose inquiry into principles, theories, or dogmas of government. Who is so proper as a good minister to cry aloud and spare not, and show the people their sins, whether in organic law or *statute cruelty*? The ministers of Christ should stand on the watch-towers of the nation, and point out that part of the constitution and laws, which runs athwart the ordinances of Heaven, and publish the crime and probe the conscience. Ministers of all denominations, in a slave State, should join in a universal outcry against the slave laws. For, otherwise, they cannot have a conscience void of offence; and they become the greatest of sinners, recreant to the authority of their high commission, and prove themselves unworthy ambassadors of Christ. The silence of ministers in relation to the criminality of slave laws becomes unpardonable. That silence is a dagger to the soul of the slave; that silence destroys his hopes and blasts his expectations; that silence is moral cowardice, which may have lost the master and minister their souls. Again, this silence soon becomes acquiescence, which soon is apology, which is soon defence, which is soon vindication, which at last turns into a political truth maintained by the authority of the Holy Scriptures, and the minister becomes commentator, conscience keeper, expounder of hard sayings, until the Bible lies, at last, in the southern country, at the bottom of slavery, and the text-book of authority for its support.

It is a libel upon the Deity to suppose that it is a part of his system of Divine government that one man should make his fellow-man *his brute*. To say, that God, who made of one blood all nations of men under heaven, and commanded man to love his neighbor as himself, and that we should do unto others as we would that others should do unto us: should tolerate American slavery, with all its odious deformities, is a flight, not up, but down, below the dark foundations of hell, which is paved with Slaveholding Divinity—yea, tracts full of such theology would make Lucifer light his brimstone lamp to read them—and he would distribute them to each ruined maniac spirit, chained in his eternal cell, throughout his dark dominions, whose terrific yell of fiendish delight would make the pit, box and galleries of all perdition tremble with an improved sensation.

JUDICIAL MURDER.

The unoffending fugitive, who is outlawed by a southern county court proceeding, if he does not return to his master by a day certain, (and as a matter of course he knows nothing of this legal farce, of which he is never notified), he becomes as a "*caput lupinum*" a wolf's head, any man may shoot him down. As though the natural ferocity was not enough in a slave holding country, I have seen in the last two years not less than six cases, in which the master offered a reward of from $20 to $100 to any one who would hunt and shoot down his outlawed slave and bring him the head of the slave, so that he might identify him. What shall be said of the editor or the printer who could prostitute the art of printing, and who, for two dollars, the price of printing such a notice, could become accessory before the fact, to a murder? What can we think of a community which would patronize such papers, or of the state of religion and morals, where the law declared murder lawful, as in these cases; or of the judges at the county court who could prepare a general commission authorizing the whole community to spring upon and murder the most innocent and defenceless man in the world, whose only crime is, that he thinks he has a better right to the use of his legs and hands than any mortal on earth. Fellow-traveller to eternity—fellow-Christian, this is a part of the judicial system, supposed necessary to thunder forth from Slavery's Vatican its decrees against the man who is unwilling to be beaten, whipped and starved as a slave; but prefers his liberty.

I am prepared to say there is not such a God-contemning, heaven and earth-insulting statute to be found out of the southern States, in the four quarters of the civilized or uncivilized world.

The various modes of murder of the fugitive slave, judicial or otherwise, have no parallel in the annals of the nineteenth century; and where we boast over the ancients of our steam, which has made the ends of the world neighbors, despising currents, laughing at tides, and disobeying the winds; which carries, at horse-race speed, a brigade of men across the land on a railroad, by the partnership power of a cord of wood and a hogshead of water, with all the other wonderful things, still this moral blot is wider, and throws into the shade more true greatness, than all the discoveries of the world could or can boast.

These bloody laws carry us back to barbarism—ah! barbarism itself would be so ashamed of such laws, that it would open to the right and left, and beg these slave States to pass through their ranks without claiming any authority or precedent for these refined acts of legislative and judicial murder from any act of barbarism, ancient or modern.

SLAVEHOLDING CATECHISM.

Let our catechism be altered so as to read " Man's chief end is to glorify God, and enjoy him forever, except when he is a slave, then his chief end is to obey and honor his master, and avoid all the misery he can, and *dodge as many of his master's blows as will be safe.*"

RELIGION AND LEGISLATION.

The legislation of a nation will rise just as high on any question, as the majority of the religionists of that nation see fit to put it. If the professors of religion of this country, or a majority of the same, had declared slavery as it is, a sin against God, and a crime against man; that the slaveholder was to be ranked with the highest criminal; Congress would, under its power to regulate commerce between the States, have said that man could not be an article of commerce, and that he could not be bought and sold, and whoever did sell or use a man as an article of property or merchandise should be punished with death, or in the State Prison for life; slavery would have been brought to an end notwithstanding the power of State institutions, as the Constitution of the United States, and the laws made under it, are paramount to the constitution of the States, or their legislation under them. Are not the leading denominations, the Methodist, Baptist, Episcopalians, Presbyterians and Congregationalists (the last two considered as one) equal to two millions of members, who would influence, directly, at least eight millions more, to which add the two millions of professors, making ten millions of the Republic: a large majority of the whole are thus brought under a salutary restraint, and a correct moral opinion. Look at the principle I seek to establish. What do the clergy, and professors of religion say, in relation to murder, robbery, stealing, false swearing, fraud, swindling? The good man, in the pulpit or out, utters the condemnation of these crimes, and legislation follows and prescribes.

The clergy all speak against the desecration of the Sabbath day, and profane swearing; legislation followed to pass penal acts to punish those offences.

Duelling in all the northern States has been the frequent theme of pulpit remarks and condemnation; laws of a high and severe character now do honor to the northern statute book; and the offence is now unknown. · The clergy and religious men thundered their denunciations against lotteries; and legislation came and obeyed the public will, and lotteries are unknown in the North.

Legislation rises and goes forward in all countries, whatever the form of religion; whether Roman Catholic, Mohammedan, Hindostanee, Pagan, Jew, or Christian, exactly as high on all questions of morality, prejudice, superstition or true Christianity, as the public sentiment of the general religion of the country will carry it.

This being an admitted truth, what a tremendous responsibility rests on the majority of the professors of religion in this country? Slavery would long since have ceased to have covered this land with misery, wretchedness, crime and heathenism, had the Christian public bodies and individuals expressed their detestation of the crime, and its criminals. That black cloud surcharged with artillery of the upper world, would not have been ready to descend on this doomed land; it would have passed away before the Christian rebuke of this nation; but no, the poor slave has not had the Christian's pity, nor his enemies the Christian's censure. Had Christians performed their duty, and expressed their abhorrence of slavery in their united and individual capacity, we should not have seen our young and noble Constitution disgraced by a shameful violation of the important right of petition, for three successive winters. Nor should we have witnessed official perjury in members of Congress, who were guilty in the face of their recorded oaths, in heaven and on earth, by meeting the petitioner at the portal of his country's audience chamber, and denying him admission and shutting that door in his face, by the command of the dark spirit of slavery.

Nor should we have seen eight new slave States admitted to the privileges of this confederacy, nor should we have seen

500,000 slaves increase to three millions, unchecked, nor should we have seen Presidential candidates, on their prostrate knees, licking up the saliva of the monster, and see and hear the candidates saying to the monster, " your froth, your whips, tears, blood, murder, are the beauties and sweets of civilized life." You would not have seen the priest of the country bowing before this horrid boaconstrictor, praising the beauty of his folds, the grandeur of his coils, and the richness of his spots ; and as if that was not enough, tell him that he is of Bible origin, and that he is a *lineal descendant of the famous anaconda* who held the dialogue with Eve in the Garden of Eden.

THE SLAVE'S CONDITION HERE AND HEREAFTER.

We act for him, who is the most helpless creature in the universe of God, the most despised, the most scorned—the slave. This is the poor prisoner; he is sick, he is naked, he is hungry, he is in prison; let us feed him, let us clothe him, let us visit him ; and we are promised, that, in so doing, we do thereby visit, clothe, and feed the Saviour of the world, whose representative the slave is, sanctified by the Holy Ghost. Who are so much to be loved and pitied, as one of those followers of the great Redeemer, who by slavery has suffered the loss of all things—of property, of wife, of children, not dead, yet torn from him, himself a slave, subject to mockings and scourgings, who is unpitied and unrequited by the being for whom he toils the live-long day ; nay, he is cursed, abused, whipped—called hard names, eats the mouldy crust under the wall, sleeps on the straw; his unrested limbs are called to renew their painful work before the glories of the rising sun have quenched the light of the last star, and through the day he broils in a sultry sun till the beaming stars of heaven burst through the mantle of evening, and so day follows day to the last of his existence. Child of sorrow, child of want, destitute of all things esteemed, but rich in a celestial expectancy, standing on the lowest stair of human existence, yet the owner of a heavenly mansion, furnished by a Saviour's love; though a prisoner here, he is a freed man of the upper world; though covered with stripes here, he has a garment pure and white, washed in the Saviour's blood; though he mourns and weeps here, he shall have a new song put in his mouth there; though he is faint and hungry here, he will soon be fed on the nectar of immortality; though imprisoned here, he will soon range the illimitable paradise of God; though sick here, he will soon revel in eternal health; though friendless and unbeloved here, he will soon join that innumerable army of friends, who will love him with everlasting love; though a powerless slave here, he will soon be a prince crowned with glory and immortality.

Shall we despise the son of the King of Glory, in exile, soon to be brought home, with the shouts of the redeemed? No, God forbid. Let us do all in our power to lift up our brother from the dark and noisome dungeon, into the sunlight of equality, liberty, religion and law.

SPEECH, REVIEWING THAT OF MR. CLAY,

THE voice of the slaveholder can be heard for the hour together, without interruption, or those hyena cries of " Order, Order !" so often uttered by the meanness of despotism, to drown the cry of throttled humanity. How often has liberty tried to speak, when she has been howled down ? As liberty shrieked in Congress, the fist of the slaveholder was thrust into her mouth. I say *shrieked*, for liberty has never been allowed to articulate a sentence, lest the secrets of the prison-house and the crime of the ravisher should be published to an avenging world. Only broken sentences, cries of smothered murder, crying " ho! help !" are all which has yet escaped, in snatches, in whispers and screams, from that windy bastile, an American Congress, where liberty is brought to the table or block and beheaded fifty times in a morning, to show the blasphemous contempt the representatives of the American people have for their Constitution and Declaration of Independence.

Yes, the Congress of the United States, the most astonishing absurdity, the unrivalled despiser of the institutions which gave it existence. A temple dedicated to the profanation of every principle in practice, which the nation professes to adore, in the abstract.

Liberty in the abstract is slavery in the concrete. American constitutional justice and liberty on parchment, mean atheism and despotism when two and a half millions of the people ask for the benefit of the pretension. They extend their hands to seize those beautiful apples, there is an *awful yell* made in their ears, and, in bewildered consternation, the apples which they forced toward their mouths have become ashes and poison. It is a castle haunted by the genius of deception, who pretends to have married the goddess of liberty, who receives the adoration of all, except the two and a half millions of slaves who carry and hold up her long train when she comes down into her temple to be worshipped.

But when Mr. Clay, the candidate for Presidential honors, wishes to present a petition against the poor slaves of the District of Columbia, all is silence—the elite, the national beauty, the glory of the metropolitan city, yea, the Senate is attent, and the House of Representatives leave their hall to witness the labors of the American Cicero, standing up to defend and perpetuate the greatest crime man ever committed against God, and the greatest crime man ever committed against man.

Behold the inhuman monsters of the District of Columbia! They prepare a petition signed by a few slaveholders, who live on the robbery of the helpless—yea, eat, drink and wear the proceeds of unpaid and whip-extorted labor; they have the unparalleled impudence to place their names on the roll of imperishable infamy, and petition the nation—for what? Ah! that they may live by plunder, robbery, by enslaving and kidnapping their fellow-citizens through all coming time; and when this audacious paper is prepared, why do they not hunt the most distinguished *brigand* or *pirate* on the globe, and send him to the Senate, so that it may be presented by a senator whose notions of right and wrong run contraband to the civilized world?

But whom do these metropolitan desperadoes select? Henry Clay, the man whom they supposed, with his deep-toned, organ voice, honeyed periods and the long-reaching sweep of oratorical sentences, might prepare this wretched dose, and persuade the nation to take it down, however awry its grimaces might be in swallowing, and leave the effect to time, when it was fairly under way on a journey through the system. This was something humbling for this great disciple of liberty, as he pretends in his speech to be, for he appeals to the Searcher of all hearts for what he says as true, when he asserts that every pulsation of his heart beats high for liberty, and that he was no friend to slavery. How cruel to force such a man into the Straits of Thermopylæ!

In undertaking this massacre, this murder of what he loved—" liberty "—ye little souls, judge what it cost this great lover of liberty to have made a speech for perpetual, yea, everlasting slavery, slavery to-day, to-morrow and for-ever, with that burning love of liberty which consumed his very vitals from the intensity of its heat and the fervor of its flame, and baked his clay till it melted. No ordinary individual could be selected for this task. If I am not much mistaken, this petition was gotten up at the instance of the slaveholding orator, to furnish the gentleman an opportunity to make a speech, the popularity of which should settle, in his own estimation, the question of his being the next President; so that, in the fortieth year of the nineteenth century, a speech is made expressly by a candidate for the Presidency of this country, in which the great leading thought is to make the most outrageous slavery—American slavery—perpetual, as long as the sun and moon shall endure, as long as this earth shall make its annual journey through the ecliptic around the sun, continuing to double every twenty years, increasing at the rate of five per cent. per annum, which is Mr. Clay's estimate, and will amount to 5 millions in 20 years; in 40 years to 10 millions; 60 years to 20 millions; 80 years to 40 millions, and 100 years to *eighty millions*—outnumbering every slave, serf and boor in the civilized or savage world. Look at the number in 120 years—160 millions; in 140 years, 320 millions; in 160 years, at the same rate, 620 millions—outnumbering the inhabitants of China—yea, of Asia and Europe united; and, in the opinion of many, equalling in number the present inhabitants of this planet.

Look at 180 years, you see 1,240 millions of slaves if the whole earth could feed them, and if each slave of this vast number was to endure only an average amount of misery and injustice inflicted on the slaves of this generation, surely the everlasting hell itself would cry out that its horrors were outdone by a slave-ruined world.

This is the institution sought to be pressed upon the rising destiny of the New World, and for so urging it upon our perpetual acceptance, and fostering, he asks the office of President. Let us examine this petition, as analyzed by the pacificator.

It is signed by the principal men in the city of Washington, the mayor and several hundred citizens. Many of those persons *conscientiously opposed to slavery*, who are grieved and astonished out of measure that misguided individuals should press on the consideration of Congress, the abolition of slavery in the District of Columbia, and who state, that when they wish it, they, of the District, *will let Congress know.* They say it is a question *purely* municipal, between the District and their own legislature, Congress.

The slaveholder can embark all the respectability of piracy in his favor. The mayor, and all officials stand by him. Secondly, those *conscientiously* opposed to slavery. How *many eternities* it would take to abolish slavery, did it depend on these conscientious opposers, who have petitioned for its continuance, till the sun shall grow dim in years, till the centre of gravity yield up his old dominion!

These conscientious men, *love liberty* so intensely that they petition for *slavery* ; their souls burn for that high behest of all men, liberty, and to gratify that darling wish, they petition the highest legislative tribunal of their country that men and women may become things ; that they may be marked like horses, asses and oxen, for nothing, by their owners, and that they may be scourged, their bodies cut into haggard scars ; that husband and wife, for a few pieces of gold, may be parted to see each other no more, and if either endeavors to run away and see the other, the husband the wife, the wife the husband, the child the parent, or the parent the child, that the bloodhound may pursue and overtake and tear their flesh from their quivering limbs, and if the slave-hunter pursues, and the fugitive flees, most deliberately may the death-dealing rifle be raised and brought to a level, sure aim taken by a *fiendish squint*, the report is heard, and a wild scream of death is the *finale*, and the slave becomes a *freeman of the unseen world*. " Where is my father, where is my mother ?" inquire their little children, as the slave-hunters return from their excursion of blood and murder. Can they answer this question ? If they can, truly these are the only persons who can, in the three kingdoms of Heaven, Earth and Hell. These men " conscientiously opposed to slavery," and yet petition for the perpetuity of a system, which makes us the scorn of man ! This is the *conscientious* opposition that tigers have for kids, wolves for lambs, hyenas for blood. Such solemn duplicity on the high places of the earth ; such a mixture of pretensions of lofty humanity, stooping to the perpetuity of all that is horrible in time or punishable in eternity. The assurance of the bold, the impudent and successful impostors, which has been able with the *horrid accents* of pretended devotion to liberty, republican law, and veneration for the sanctity of our religion, to blot out all distinction between right and wrong, upset the ten commandments, make the Scriptures a cunningly devised fable, humanity a by-word, the Declaration of Independence an absurdity, the Constitution a rope of sand, the laws a nose of wax, the English language a liar, the name of an American a reproach. The American has not his true name as yet; but the world are preparing to christen him and give him a cognomen, which will make him hang his head with shame, and at best he will enjoy but a contraband and furtive reception into respectable circles of European society.

But we are informed that the reason why many of those who are " conscientiously opposed to slavery," signed the petition for perpetual slavery in the District, and in hostility to its abolition is, " because they justly respect the rights of those who own this description of property;" such men must be very *conscientious ;* why not respect the rights of the slaves ? Why is this conscientiousness *all for the master*, who has purloined the earnings of the slaves through several generations for 200 years ?

Another reason why these conscientious men petition is, that those who have petitioned for the abolition of slavery in the District of Columbia *live out of the District*, and therefore have no business to interfere with it ! Repeal the slave laws enacted by the Congressmen of Vermont, New York, New Hampshire and Massachusetts in 1800 and 1801. Abolitionists simply ask Congress to repeal its own laws which it has made; and was it ever known that a legislature might not repeal its own laws ? Let Vermont and Massachusetts stand by their representatives, where they did before they helped to enact the slave laws of the District, and no more is required. Slavery will then be dead in the District. Vermont and Massachusetts by their members of Congress enacted slavery into a legal system in the District of Columbia. The moment the jurisdiction of the territory was ceded by Virginia and Maryland to the United States and accepted by the Union as the seat of government, *eo instanti* in point of law, the slave system and all of the laws of those two States in the District were annihilated. Now from this point we start; if Congress had no power to create the relation of slave and master, then, for near forty years, the colored man has been deprived of his liberty by unconstitutional laws. If the law was constitutional, the States, by whose means, through their representatives, this most malignant system was introduced, owe it to the slaves, whether the slaveowners were willing or unwilling to repeal the system immediately and make all the atonement in their power to helpless innocence. One cannot but be astonished at the slaveholding effrontery in always refusing to regard the slaves as any part or parcel of the *inhabitants* of the Territory. The nation is responsible for the system of slavery in that District; therefore, " those conscientiously opposed to slavery," who petition for its everlasting *continuance* in the District give as another reason for wishing to perpetuate slavery against their conscience, their " deep conviction that a continued agitation by those who have no right to interfere with it has an injurious influence on the community, and upon the well-being and happiness of those held in subjection." Here are three evils or reasons which the slaveholder, " conscientiously opposed to slavery," gives, for petitioning for the endless continuance of slavery in the District.

1st. No right to interfere by those who organized the system and put the yoke on the neck of these guiltless poor. You created the system, but have no business to uncreate. You legislated the system of iniquity into existence; but it would be interference to legislate it out.

Second reason given by these slaveholders who are " conscientiously opposed to slavery," why it should endure forever in the District, is, that the agitation of the question of abolition " has an injurious influence on the community."

If it has an injurious effect now, when there are say, " but

7,000 slaves in that community, it would be twice as injurious, arithmetically speaking, twenty years hence, when the slaves shall be 14,000 in number, and the whites proportionally increased. It therefore follows that the injury to the community is at the minimum, or *ounce notch at the bar*, and any delay to abolish slavery will only increase this difficulty with increasing number, so the weight would be forever sliding back into the *pound notches*, and so on to the end of the bar, the longer emancipation is delayed. For it is often said that the reason slavery was abolished in the northern States, was because of the paucity of the slaves. The more slaves there are, the greater is the number of whites and blacks who must have their social relations broken up and changed. The difficulty of emancipation increases in the ratio of numbers, whether emancipation takes place with or without compensation. If without compensation, then the loss will be less to individuals, the smaller the number of slaves; if compensation is adopted, the difficulty increases with every hour of delay; for if the laborious part of the community are to maintain themselves and to pay a sum, which, put at interest, will maintain the masters, as well as they now are, the fewer of those masters, and the fewer slaves owned by those masters, the less the sum will be to pay. Whether expulsion, colonization, separation or manumission on the soil, there is one proposition on which the ultra-slaveholder and Abolitionist and men of all intermediate shades of opinion must concur, to wit, if slavery is not to be eternal, then the best for the slaveholder, the slave and the remainder of the community, is, that abolition should take place before the number of slaves shall have increased.

The third reason urged by the slaveholder " conscientiously opposed to slavery " in the District of Columbia, is that the agitation of the question of slavery by the petitions of the freemen of New England, Ohio, and New York, in praying for its abolition, " will have an injurious effect upon the *well being and happiness* of those held in subjection " by slavery.

The master, conscientiously opposed to slavery, thus testifies his ardent love for liberty:

Do the masters fear that, in consequence of the agitation of this question by the constitutional mode of petition, they shall be obliged to add to the severity of stripes, hunger, nakedness, or deprive the man of his wife oftener; separate the mother from the children for a longer time; for they must refer to corporeal ills of this description; because, in relation to the immortal mind, slavery has done its worst, no greater injury can be done to the well being of the undying mind, denied all access to books, all knowledge of divine or moral truths, penalties on penalties for teaching the child who is a slave to read. These things have no parallel in the annals of brutality; for the first offence, teacher and taught are to be whipped thirty-nine lashes on the naked back, if both are slaves; for the second offence, one hundred lashes; and for the third, death.

Slaves, do *you* complain that your " happiness and well-being," are injured by petitions presented for your redemption? " No, we have no happiness and well-being to be injured—and were every petition presented in our behalf a blow laid on with violence, we would pray their numbers to be increased—yes, we beseech you, our friends, by the rich boon of liberty, for which we pant and pray, never to faint or grow weary in well-doing; to you our eyes are turned, living and dying; for our sake, for our children's sake, for unborn generations' sake, do not cease, day and night, to bombard this dreadful bastile. We are more than prisoners, we are slaves—we are at the bottom of the wheel and can find no lower depth."

Or, does the District petition presented by the senator, mean,

that the master vents his spleen, which boils up from the bottom of his atra-bilious soul, on the poor slave, because he hates
the petitioning Abolitionist, whom he supposes is in sympathy
with the miserable and undone slave.

Mr. Clay says that he has differed in opinion with the
course of the House of Representatives in relation to the
reception of Abolition petitions. While the House refuse to
read, print, refer, consider and report thereon, he, Mr. Clay,
would do all always by sound argument, coming a little
more circuitously to the prompt conclusion of the House—the
entire and absolute rejection of the petition; but this was to
be done by an argumentative appeal to the good sense of the
community. This is Mr. Clay's medicine for the plague of
slavery. Let us see for a moment how this thing might be
made to appear if the course pointed out by the trans-montane
orator had been adopted. It is said that fighting is a business that two men can play at. The amount of Mr. Clay's
proposition is that an argumentative appeal made to the good
sense of the people of the United States would entirely satisfy
them that slavery was a good institution, as though the reason, that some are dissatisfied with that system at present is
their ignorance of its excellence, and it only requires to be
explained to be admired, only portrayed to be embraced, to
be dressed in its true colors, and philanthropy will run to salute
it, humanity will pillow it on its bosom, while justice will
rock it to quietness, when querulous republicanism herself—
fair daughter of the Revolution—will hold it up to an admiring world, as her darling, her first born, the armament of the
nation in time of peace, her glory and sure defence in time of
war. In this successful argument addressed to the American
people, Christianity herself must be called to the stand as a
witness, while she says " God made of one blood all nations."
" Do unto others as ye would they should do unto you,"
" Love thy neighbor as thyself," " Break every yoke, let the

oppressed go free," "He who stealeth a man let him be put to death;" and in Babylon was found, "cinnamon, and odors, and ointment, and frankincense, and wine, and oil, and fine flour, and wheat, and beasts, and sheep, and horses, and chariots, and slaves, and souls of men." She further says, that, in the synod of Georgia and South Carolina, as my ministers of the Presbyterian Synod certify, there are 100,000 persons who never heard of Jesus Christ. To be sure, it is by southern law, a crime, to be punished with stripes, for slaves to be found reading the Saviour's sermon on the mount, or for one to be found teaching another to read the Lord's prayer or ten commandments, punishable, for the third offence, in some of the States, with death; to be sure, God says of the marriage relation, " what God hath joined together let no man put asunder;" and children are commanded to obey their parents; slaveholders sell wives from their husbands, and make children obey masters and not parents. To be sure slaveholders murder their slaves, when they attempt to run away and they cannot stop them without; to be sure, they, the masters, bid up bounties to be given those who will shoot dead outlawed slaves, who are hiding themselves in the wilderness from the terrors of their masters, half starved; to be sure, there is not one schoolhouse nor three churches in all the South for the three millions of slaves; to be sure, no man is permitted to preach to slaves without making the obedience of slaves to masters as a stepping-stone to immortal life, disobedience, eternal death; the Alpha and Omega of a slave's theology is to obey their masters in all things, right or wrong.

To be sure, labor is despised at the South and considered degrading and ignoble, except in the slave. To be sure, there are more duels and assassinations among the aristocratic whites than there are days in the year, which are the gentlemanly employments of southern citizens, and are the standing schools kept to teach men politeness and educate men to a lofty bearing. To be sure, there are 500,000 slaves whose masters are their fathers, and brothers, and sisters, being one-half, three-fourths, six-sevenths and nine-tenths white; and in all cases of this sort, slavery wears its most attractive and winning form—for if a father, or brother, or sister, has not a right to whip, beat, shoot, murder and sell his own child, his own brother, his own sister, *there is no object in having children*, brothers or sisters; this is one of the most interesting inventions made in this age of fruitful discovery. The father is, in the language of Horace, "faber ejus fortunæ." If the father, at the North, of ten children, could sell them as they grew up for $1000 each, it is easily perceived he might wallow in wealth, instead of dragging life out in "chill penury." Again, it is eminently calculated to make men obey one of the oldest commands, to wit, multiply and replenish the earth. Christianity herself feels bound to testify in behalf of slavery, that this command is obeyed with a *singular faithfulness* and devotion. The money for which a parent may sell his son or daughter, especially where the African tinge has disappeared, and a larger proportion of the father comes out in the progeny, will amount sometimes to $2,000 or $3,000, and furnish money for a summer excursion for the father at the North, and will allow him to pass several times up and down the North River, and make him gape with admiration at the everlasting Palisadoes, and inquire the altitude of the lofty peaks of our cloud-propping Appalachians, and then inquire into an analysis of Saratoga waters, and promenade the porticos of the eating and sleeping palaces of the land, walk abroad and listen to the sound of the sea as it seems to murmur in the tops of the lofty pines, then a tour through Lake George, Ticonderoga, Crown Point, Lake Champlain, St. Johns, Montreal and Quebec—the military classic region—and then return by the Niagara Falls, and so down to New York, in time to attend the Board of Commissioners of Foreign Missions, and to display his generosity in giving $50 of the remnant of the purchase money of his daughter, to carry the Gospel to the benighted Georgians beyond the Black Sea, who are so barbarous and so unenlightened, as to sell their beautiful daughters to be immured in the seraglios of the nobles of Constantinople, or the harem of the Grand Seignior. Illustrious benefactor of Christianity! Let no man say it is the duty of the Board of Missions ever to inquire whether the money given them was acquired by the cunning of the gambler, or the arts of the courtesan; by the success of the highwayman, or by the slaveholder selling his daughter into slavery.

What can be more admired in this age of the 19th century than to see a brother sailing over the ocean and dashing through all the fashionable rounds of dissipation in London, Paris, St. Petersburg, Vienna and Rome, maintained the whole tour by the avails of a poor broken-hearted sister, who was sold before commencing the grand expedition, for $5,000, to a gentleman in New Orleans?

But the young traveller wanted money; she was the most valuable piece of stock he owned. He, however, gave £20 at the anniversary in London, after hearing an eloquent speech, to aid the Magdalen's Society.

A sister sells a brother to carry the *hod* for the bricklayer to the fourth story of the house, and languish and die under the visitation of the lash, to supply her with laces, wedding rings and ornamental dresses for the bridal day, when she shall wed a man who has sold his sister for money to buy a chariot and four, in which the bride and bridegroom may roll their honeymoon away, in going from watering-place to watering-spring, or in search of mountain air, or sea beach side by moonlight, where they may listen to the ocean's everlasting song, and see the moonbeams dance upon the waves, and enjoy the delicious reverie in nature's witchery, and read the last novel, as they course along day by day, and enjoy the reviving power of ether and musk when her sympathies overcome the bride in listening to the well-depicted woes of romance and suffering of bygone days of chivalry. Look at the interesting pair; you may overhear them speaking, with most sovereign contempt, of those miserable northern families who are interfering with our peculiar institutions. Says the bridegroom to the bride, "Those fanatical monsters at the North would fain have prevented me in selling my sister for this chariot and four, so well caparisoned, in which we ride." "Yes," says the bride, "these same meddling monster fanatics would, if they could have had their wish, have prevented me from selling my brother into slavery, by the avails of whose sale I am made so charmingly interesting to you, my spouse, and am now flashing in diamond rings, necklace and splendid tiara! Monsters! I believe they will dissolve our Union, if they do not cease this officious intermeddling! What an advantage we have, my dear," said the thoughtful bride, "in having our lives cast in pleasant places; for if we had been born at the North, you and I would have been poor, and could not sell our brothers and sisters. Only see," continued she, "the good sense of our ancestors and their legislators, whereby the whole of the family is not obliged to be poor, but certain brothers and sisters are authorized to sell the rest of their sisters and brethren into slavery, and become opulent and grand; whereas, at the North all are free and all are poor! With our institution of slavery, and the power of one branch of the family to sell the rest, no family is in danger of losing its caste and elevated position in society, and it enables us to do something for benevolent objects, in carrying religion to the benighted pagans of the old world, who have not enjoyed the high privileges we possess, in this land, where 'all men are created free and equal.' "

Suppose the above dispassionate appeal should be sent forth to the nation, by the committee to be appointed on slavery, according to Mr. Clay's project, revealing some of the choice beauties connected with the institution of slavery; is it not believed that the mighty spirit that rides and directs this moral storm, would forever abandon the pursuit of liberty for the American slave?

But suppose a committee appointed, as Mr. Clay suggests, clothed with a general power to pry into all the secrets of this dreadful prison-house, and armed with the usual right of committees of this character, to send for persons and papers.

Suppose this committee had made up their mind to glean facts from the following and distinct sources; what would the facts warrant as their general conclusion?

1st. Let the committee send for the statutes of the thirteen slave States, and have extracts made from the legislation of each State, showing the servile law, or law of slavery.

The 1st point.   All the statutes would show a slave to be a thing, a mere chattel, and that he ranks with horses and hogs, and he and his increase is his master's.   2d. That he or she never can be a witness against a white man for the greatest wrong done him or her.   3d. The greatest violence done to their bodies or limbs is a matter for which they can seek no redress.   The master has all that is got.   4th. The courts of civil and criminal justice are never opened to them as against a white man, any more than courts are open for goats and hogs to come and prosecute.   5th. For the reason they themselves have no rights for which to prosecute.   6th. A slave may be separated from his wife—his children may be taken from their parents.   7th. It is a great crime by the law for a slave to teach or be taught.   8th. In most of the States, slaves cannot meet for worship unless more whites are present than slaves.   9th. A peck of corn, costing 12½ cents, is the amount of sustenance the law requires the master to give the slave per week.   No man could board a dog at the North for a less sum, per week.   .10th. In some States, twenty, some forty, and others seventy-eight, crimes are punishable with death in the slave.   11th. It is death in many States for a slave to raise his or her hand against a white person, no matter how great the provocation or necessity.   12th. The slave, in cases that take his life, or capital cases, has no trial by jury.   13th. The master has unlimited power to flog and beat.   14th. The master has power to kill on the slave's raising his hand. 15th. The master has power to shoot dead the slave running away, and he is guiltless.

2nd. Inquiry.   Let the committee subpœna the clerk of every county in the slave States, ordering them to bring their dockets and records, to see whether there was ever a white man convicted and executed for the murder of a colored man or slave.   It is averred there was never one.   It is averred there never was half a dozen convictions of murder in the thirteen States, since the Revolution, for the murder of slaves. Though it is averred there have been more than 100,000 murders, which would have been called murders, had the victims been white men instead of slaves—by overworking, under-feeding, want of clothing, cruelty, violence, and by deliberate murder.

3rd. Let the committee send for 100 slaveholders from the different States, and examine as to their feeding, clothing, holidays; the hovel of the slave, the modes of punishing, the number who die annually, the average whippings of males and females; the difference between plantation hands and house hands; the general power conferred on overseers; the number of fugitives, the number of bloodhounds kept, tho number of slaves mangled and killed by them, the number killed for running away, lifting their hands against the whites, executed according to law, and for what offences, and before what tribunal tried; the number outlawed in the county courts for running away.

4th. Examine at least one hundred overseers and their books as to the number of men and women on cotton, rice, sugar and tobacco plantations; on all the questions put the master; his mode of punishing; the hours of labor and rest; the beds and clothing; the crop raised, the deaths—the usual increase; the distance of plantations on which man and wife live, owned by different masters; the clothing, the difference in clothing between field hands, and those who are tavern or body, or house slaves. When do children begin to work, and how soon does the female after accouchement, take the hoe in the field? What is overseer's wages—what number of persons who are slaves have white blood? How many have been sold in the last three years? How many families been separated, wife from husband, and children from parents?

5th. Examine twenty negro merchants, who live by buying and selling human flesh.

1st. How many families have you broken up in the year past—separated portions? Do you bind them in couples, do you not whip those who weep and mourn for their wives or husbands, or children left behind, until they dry their tears under the lash? Do you imprison, and where? Do you buy children by the pound? Do you make them drag an iron ball and chain? How are those females treated who become mothers on your journeys?

6th. Let one hundred persons living in slave States for twenty years past, in the different States not related to slaveholders, come forward and testify. As to the inferior class of slaveholders owning two, three, five, or ten slaves, who hire the men out by the month, day, or year; women by the day, at washing or other handiwork. Do these small slave-owners work? And generally put all the questions before put. What is the effect of slavery on the whites, as to duelling, bloody rencounters, and murders? Does it not destroy the character and standing of poor white men? Does it not degrade the white labor? Is not labor esteemed dishonorable in a white man or woman? Are there not one quarter of the white adults who cannot read and write in the slave States? Is not agriculture in a wretched condition in the slave States? Are there not large districts of country, once esteemed fertile, which are now abandoned and worn out? Is not slave culture eminently calculated to render the land sterile? Would there not be double the amount of labor performed under the stimulus of cash, than what is done under the lash? Is there not a promiscuous concubinage between the white males and the slave females? Is not the Saxon blood increasing every year among the slaves? How many persons do you know held as slaves, men and women, who are as white as people generally are who give no evidence of African blood? Is not the institution of slavery mutually debasing to the master and slaves? Have you not known many persons or masters killed by their slaves? But did you ever know or hear of a slave killing his master, mistress, or any of the family, *after they were set at liberty?*

Let the questions be put to each of the witnesses as to the general practice of masters and mistresses on large plantations sleeping with pistols and swords under their heads. Is burning a punishment common for a slave who is to be put to death?

7th. Let 100 free colored men be called before the committee from the slave States, and examined on many of the foregoing points, and let them be asked: 1st. Have you not known every year free colored people kidnapped, reduced to slavery by having their free papers torn up, and carried off a distance and sold

—if yea, who were they?   2d. Are you not in perpetual fear of being kidnapped? Have you not been struck by white persons, and abused frequently, without redress? Are not free colored females subject to most flagrant insults from white men? Do not the laws allow the mayor of a city, or sheriff of a county to banish you from the State in fifteen days by proclamation, and if you return or do not go, to sell you into perpetual slavery and confiscate your property, real and personal? Are you allowed to send your children to any school? Are you not under the same penalties as to teaching and being taught, that the slaves are? How many of your relations are in slavery? How many fugitives, whom you knew who have attempted to escape, succeeded?—how many were taken back?—how many died in the woods and swamps?—how many were torn to pieces by bloodhounds?—how many were wounded?—how many outlawed and shot dead in the woods? Are many of the free colored people of the South who are adults, married to slaves?

8th. Let 100 fugitive slaves who have escaped to the northern States or to Canada, be sworn to all the sad vicissitudes attending their escape from Georgia, Alabama, Mississippi. Let them state the two, three, four, and five months in which they travelled the length of the nation in the night, not in the roads but through woods, swimming rivers, with nothing but the north star to direct them, the hunger, rags, hairbreadth escapes, regarding the vast South as one jail yard, and every white man, ferryman and gate-tender as authorized to arrest the fugitive. The annals of the world do not furnish such noble daring for liberty as hundreds of cases now in Canada might attest. What were the special wrongs which induced you to run through 1,500 miles of dangers? Was there ever a day since your remembrance, in which the desire to be free has not been prominent in your mind?

9th. Call 100 slaves from every State and every description of business; let them be asked: "What do you most desire? Show your backs; how many times have you been flogged, and for what? Have not your wife and your children been whipped at different times, by the overseer's orders, before your face? How long does it take a back to become sound and heal up from the time of a cruel flogging? Is not stealing often necessary to support life with comfort? Have you not been ordered out of your bed, that a white man might occupy your place? In addition to these, put a great variety of questions which will readily suggest themselves to an inquiring mind.

Let the committee make a digest of the evidence which these nine sources of information of slavery would furnish, and it would be a book of 600 pages, and if after giving the evidence impartially to the nation, the committee would dare to report in favor of the institution of slavery, we might call this a doomed land, whose judgment and destruction linger not. No, the committee might as well call all the men of clear vision in North America to swear that the sun had shone on this land since the 19th century began, and after hearing this evidence should then report that there had been uninterrupted darkness, without sun, moon, or stars since the 31st day of December, 1799, as to report, under the weight of the evidence which must be drawn forth from the course above suggested, that slavery was an institution which ought to be continued another hour in this land. They must report against it, or the stones in the street would cry out. For, the slaveholders, and slavery and its apologists, would, one and all, be crushed by the mountain of evidence, and buried in one common grave, so deep that the imagination would reel in descending that awful and unexplored depth.

It is thought remarkable that the Abolitionists should have

seized hold of the right of petition—a right broken down, invaded and utterly denied. Denied by a formality of Congressional proceeding on the 21st December, 1837, which, for solemnity, has no parallel in the life of the confederacy. For what offence was this oldest right of man, this darling attribute of humanity, the right of petition, condemned and brought to the block? Was it because she raised her voice against a republican form of government? Had she denied that the people were the source of power, or did she wish the nation to reswear its allegiance to England, and put on its colonial sackcloth, or to cover the name of Washington with ignominy, or that Texas might be received into the arms of the Republic, or that the laboring men of the North might be made slaves? No! No such things. She simply desired, through the media of well-written memorials, that Congress *would be pleased* to abolish slavery in the District of Columbia; or, in other words, repeal certain laws which Congress itself had enacted in 1799 or 1800, establishing slavery in the District of Columbia. She asked that liberty might be given to 7,000 most wretched slaves, who were flitting and sneaking around this ten miles square—this drawing-room of the nation—a spectacle of disgrace to our every pretension as a republic—7,000 slaves to be seen by the representatives of the nations of the earth, each slave, a standing, moving, *crawling* witness, of the base hypocrisy of our national diploma. Each slave should make us hang our heads with shame; each slave here makes the representative of despotism tread with a firmer step; each king of the earth finds his throne more firm when he sees republicanism lean on slavery. Each slave proclaims that republicanism is a trafficker in flesh and blood; each slave shows we are cruel, proves us base, selfish, that we pursue robbery as a trade, piracy as a livelihood. Each slave proves we are unfit for freedom. To avenge his wrongs, the judgments of God follow hard upon the footsteps of the slaveholder. The slave tells you that where he lives the white man is ferocious; the common rules of slaveholding propriety are vindicated by the bowie knife, sustained by the pistol, and asserted by the rifle. Assassination is the arraignment, trial and execution, among slaveholders.

They enslave their own children, sell them for provisions, *eat them up by circuity; they are anthropophagi, second-handed.* So do the crocodiles of the same region eat their young, until they are strong enough to escape. The whole ten miles square echoes with screams and flagellation; a man beating a woman to extort, unpaid, from the quivering flesh, labor in some field, or over some wash-tub, enough for his support; in another direction a woman, with jewels in her ears, is beating a man to extort labor, unrewarded, to maintain Madam in idleness. In another quarter, the coffled gang of slaves are marching to enter the bastile erected on this ten mile square. Their groans ascend night and day amidst the cracking of whips, and the cursing of land pirates—these body and soul dealers. There is mourning, the wife torn from her husband and children to see them no more. There the loving child whose garment is fastened to the body in bloody stripes, mangled for mourning the bereavement of her parents. Is this a sight for the foreigner to behold? Oh, my country! how degraded! Oh! my God! when shall these scenes come to an end? Shall we become a proverb? Shall the minions of power in the Old World sneer at our kidnapping morality? Shall our *native Indian* forever despise civilization, built on such criminal injustice? Well may he prefer the wigwam of the wilderness to palaces, built by money coined from the slaves' tears and blood. Well may he prefer the Great Spirit to the Christian's God, if the southern professor has not defamed the Divinity he professes to adore.

The orator divides Abolitionists into three divisions : 1st. The harmless Quaker who is opposed to slavery, but is also more opposed to any noise and disturbance in effecting it. There are, truly, some such *frosty* Quakers, but this is not their general character. There is a large body of this respectable denomination, who would not be so alarmed at the outcry of ferocious slaveholders, foaming with fury and threatening, in powerless impotency, as to be deterred from an energetic and unconquerable pursuit of those merciful constitutional provisions, which open up a passage from the hideous dungeon of slavery. No! never can we suffer those noble-minded Quakers to be misrepresented by the flattering orator, who would rob them of those priceless honors purchased amidst dangers by day and by night in opening their doors to the hunted fugitives, and closing them on their bloody pursuers; who have bound up their wounds, fed, clothed, pitied, nourished and cherished, and then have taken those who were ready to perish, and carried them, night after night, on their way to the land of freedom, in their carriages, and putting money in their hands have referred them to the next man with a broad-brimmed hat, as a place of mercy, and pointing their finger to the North Star, which never sets, and always shines as the *slave's compass*, hung out in the heavens to direct the abused man in his lonesome night wandering, on his way to the land of the Lion and the Unicorn— directs them to the land where the eagles of British mercy will inclose them beneath their ample wings, and make them free by the power of British law ; where the pursuing slaveholder will cease from troubling and the weary slave will bo at rest.

These men, who, in the last thirty years, have been angels of mercy in conducting 50,000 fugitives to Canada, will not thank the senator for his left-handed compliments.

Mr. Clay will do well to remember that the Friend, the

Quaker, abhors war, and no war so much as the continued war between master and slave, and that even Quakers are not such profound lovers of the peace of the Union, and the power of the States, but what they would not fear to jeopardize the former and curtail the latter, if, by so doing, slavery might end.

The second class of Abolitionists named by the orator, he says are only "*apparent*" Abolitionists, because the right of petition is supposed by them to be violated, and therefore he seems to infer that these men have run on board the Abolition ship, until the nation has passed the danger of violating the Constitution on the right of petition, and after that difficulty is over, they will all be out, hurrahing and huzzaing, for slavery whips, and unpaid labor, again. This class of men I am an entire stranger to, having never seen one of them; I cannot say but what Mr. Clay is right. His knowledge is great, and his candor in describing a third set of Abolitionists must make us believe that he cannot be mistaken. . . . .

LETTER TO THOMAS W. GILMER,

GOVERNOR OF VIRGINIA,

In answer to his Proclamation offering a reward of $3,000 for the delivery to the jailer, at Norfolk, of Peter Johnson, Edward Smith and Isaac Gansey, men of color, residents of New York, attached to the schooner Robert Centre, charged with stealing a negro slave named Isaac, the property of John G. Colley, 1841.

His Excellency Gov. Gilmer, of Virginia:

Sir: As a citizen of the State of New York, and as a member of this Republic, I cannot deny that I feel a deep interest in the issue which you and the lieut.-governor of your State, have seen fit to create and tender as between New York and Virginia, on a topic of the most solemn interest, involving the dearest rights of men, the personal liberties not only of the citizens of the State of New York, but also of those of other States, together with those of the stranger and visitor from other countries. The question is one of such magnitude, that I trust it will be considered a sufficient apology for the humblest citizen to run and shut the door against the approach and entrance of such ill-omened principles, which, for the first time, by ingenious constructions, are seeking admission into that group of fraternal maxims, under whose benignant sway we and our fathers have lived, protected at home, and have been defended when abroad.

Your predecessor, in July, 1839, demanded three colored men then attached to the schooner Robert Centre, to be surrendered up by the governor of this State to the authorities of Virginia, " for having feloniously stolen from one John

G. Colley, a certain negro slave named Isaac, the property of said Colley." Mr. King, mayor of Norfolk, certifies that Colley, of Norfolk, made an oath before him, of which the above is the form and substance, on the 22d July, 1839.

These are the facts. This is the case made by Virginia. On these facts you reiterate the demand of your predecessor, that the three men should be delivered up as felons, and that you intend to make the world believe you are in earnest, for since the governor of this State has refused compliance with your demand, you have offered a reward of $3,000 to any person in this State, or your own, to kidnap them and surrender them to Virginia, and thus violate the sovereignty of New York, while the individuals capturing, kidnapping and surrendering these men, would subject themselves to be indicted for a felony, and imprisoned, from five to ten years, in the New York State prison.

It may be added as a part of the facts, in this place, that a search was made on board the Robert Centre, a ship lying in the port of New York, by the master of the slave Isaac, or his agent, where, Isaac being found, the master or agent, in defiance of the law of Congress of 1793, without examination before any court or judicial authority, and in defiance of the laws of this State, committed a felony, punishable for several years in the State prison, in taking Isaac from this State without lawful authority and in defiance of our laws.

But dismissing for the present the reward of $3,000 offered to violate the sovereignty of New York, and the crime of abduction and kidnapping committed by the citizens of Virginia on Isaac, we will return to the consideration of the affidavit made before the mayor of Norfolk, which contains a statement of your case, as you see fit to make it, after having been admonished by the governor of this State, that it might be in the power of the authorities of Virginia to amend the affidavit so as to state at *what time* Isaac was stolen—the affidavit being silent on those two important particulars, as to the *time when* or place *where* Isaac was stolen.

On a case which is entirely silent as to what time, in the course of this century, the crime was committed, or as to what place on this globe the offence was perpetrated, whether in Virginia, Vermont, Jamaica, France or Africa, Virginia demands, on *such a case*, a surrender. Virginia does not pretend that she can improve her affidavit, on reflection, by fixing either time or place of offence; but demands that the governor of New York, with the aid of our sheriffs and constables, should break into the houses of these three freemen at midnight—take, bind, fetter and deliver these citizens to the waiting authorities of Virginia.

It is one of the fundamental rules of merciful justice, inherited by us from our ancestors, that every intendment shall be made in favor of the innocence of the accused until the contrary is made to appear. Might not New York appeal to the candor of Virginia, and ask if the delivery of the accused would not be the prostration of this principle? Would not the surrender have been an admission of what Virginia dare not assert, that the slave was stolen from her jurisdiction?

There is no *time* shown when this pretended felony was committed, whether one or ten years before. It is presumed, therefore, that if the offence were not outlawed by lapse of time, the same would have appeared.

For it will not be pretended, if it appeared that it was impossible to convict the accused on the face of the papers accompanying the demand, that there would be any obligation on the part of the New York executive to surrender and allow Virginia to drag her citizens from 500 to 800 miles, to one of her tribunals, where the individual must be acquitted. This would be solemn trifling, as between the States, while it might be destructive to the peace and prosperity of the acquitted citizen!

But the case made by Virginia, presenting the great inter-State proposition by which she intends to abide, *nolens volens*, though the confederacy is dissolved in its maintenance, is simply this: If these men had taken Colley's slave from him on his middle passage from the banks of the Gambia, in Africa, under the line of the equator, on the high seas, and should have brought him back to New York, Virginia could demand his surrender; for, if this affidavit is sufficient to demand the accused now, it would be in the case supposed. Suppose these three men had found Colley in Africa, in his own cabin, throttling Isaac and putting his fetters on, and should have delivered Isaac, and have afterward been found in New York, this affidavit, if held good now, would in that case compel New York to deliver up.

Suppose these men to have taken Isaac from Colley, in this State, while the master was at Saratoga Springs, if this affidavit is valid for the surrender of these citizens now, then, in that case, Virginia might take cognizance of criminal offences committed in this State; yes, she might draw before her tribunals offences, real or imaginary, committed against her citizens on the high seas, Africa, New York, or Vermont, in any time past, within the memory of man.

Virginia's proposition is, that for a wrong done her citizens, or her laws, no matter when or where committed, whether on this side of the Atlantic or the other, on this side of the Equator or the other, wherever the cold freezes or heat warms, if the culprit is found in any one of the twenty-six States, the Constitution compels the executive of the State where the accused are found, to surrender them.

Is this a provison of the Constitution of our Union, so highly lauded? No, if a provision had been offered by the Convention of the American people, as wide in its power of mischief and unchecked tyranny, as Virginia now contends for through you, the American people, in their State Conventions

for consideration of the same, would have vetoed such a provision with such a roar of disapprobation, as that its last
echoes should still break in upon the slumbers of executive
despotism and repress the first yearnings of slavery's grasp
at universal dominion. Must slavery be maintained at the
expense of universal liberty? Is it not enough that your
hand is at the throat of your trembling slave? Must the
liberties of the North be offered as a sacrifice to such a
horrible institution? Am I not in danger, if your construction of the Constitution were right, of having this newspaper,
if perchance a stray copy should reach your Excellency, laid
before a Norfolk mayor with your affidavit that in this paper
I had refused to acknowledge that slavery was *jure divino*,
and that I had therefore called on your slaves to rise in insurrection against their masters, by implication, or more like the
present affidavit, you should swear to a legal conclusion, that
I had excited insurrection, and that, in legal contemplation,
you might for the purpose of a demand of my person from
the executive of this State, swear that there was not a head
left on a slaveholder's shoulders in Virginia. According to
your affidavit, it is no matter when or where I produced the
insurrection. No matter, says your affidavit, if I caused an
insurrection of slaves twenty years ago, and in the West
Indies, the governor of New York is yet bound to deliver
me up on your requisition. The doctrine of the King of
England, as far as time is concerned, must apply to Virginia,
Nullum tempus occurrit Virginia. There seem to be attributes belonging to the sovereignty of Virginia, which belong
to no earthly government besides. All governments, except
Virginia, seem to feel, that, however lawless their desires,
still, a prudent respect for the opinions of mankind compels
them to respect time and place. But Virginia, in defence of
that singularly amiable, evangelical and democratic institution of slavery, asserts the right of putting on the attributes

of Omnipotence—which disregard *time* and *place*—or time and space. It seems, then, that it is time for mankind, on this and on the other side of the globe, in every parallel of latitude and longitude, savage or civilized, Christian or Mohammedan, pagan or idolatrous, to open their eyes to the consideration of a new power which has arisen on the earth. It takes cognizance of all transgressions affecting the slave-holding rights of Virginia—that she has a legal ubiquity—no time, no space can fetter the application of her vindictive visitorial criminal power, when put forth to protect that lovely institution of unpaid labor, extracted from men and women by the singular properties and blessed agency of the Republican Constitutional cart-whip, placed in the hands of Virginia, as the governing motive, to induce her to enter the confederacy and adopt the Constitution.

But it is hoped that Virginia will be as mild and forbearing as the necessities of the " peculiar institution " will permit, in relation to her sister States, and the other states and kingdoms of the world, and not enforce the rights of Virginia with too much rigor, while mankind are recovering from the surprise felt at the discovery of their new position. For the people of this country, at least of these States, if your affidavit is held good, must feel that they hold their existence subject to a new dangerous tenure, and they may add in their liturgy a prayer, that " from sudden death *or transportation to Virginia*, good Lord deliver us."

I come to a second question which has grown out of this transaction, which I hope may not be considered improper, even for your Excellency, to look full in the face. And that is, by what authority, the man Isaac—not slave—*the man* Isaac, was taken in the port of New York, from the ship Robert Centre, by the two white men of Virginia, who, on finding Isaac in this ship, without any judicial process whatsoever, took and kidnapped him and by a forcible abduction, the said Isaac, against his will, was carried from the free State of New York, into the State of Virginia, and made a slave of. Isaac was brought before no authority. No judge, court or justice ever gave a certificate, in this State, that Isaac owed service to any person in Virginia.

It was one of the clearest cases of kidnapping which can be imagined. By the Revised Statutes of the State of New York, 2d vol., 664th page, 28th section, the offence and punishment are described in these words: " Every person who shall without lawful authority forcibly seize and confine any other, or shall inveigle or kidnap any other with intent either 1st. To cause such other person to be secretly confined or imprisoned in this State against his will, or 2d. To cause such other person to be sent out of this State against his will, or, 3d. To cause such person to be sold as a slave or in any way held to service against his will, shall, upon conviction, be punished with imprisonment in a State prison not exceeding *ten years*." Here is a most horrible crime committed by the insolence of slaveholders breaking in upon the sovereignty of New York, and forcibly carrying away a human being, under the protection of our law as much as the governor of this State. And the sovereignty of New York, and the majesty of her laws, would have been no more injured in the abduction of the governor or chancellor of this State, than of the man Isaac. By the constitution of this State, all men are equal in the eye of our laws; all, equally entitled to her beneficent protection; the highest man is not above her power; the humblest is secure beneath her protection. With our constitution, as a question of protection, there is no high, no low, no black, no white, no slave, no master; no, the law is, like the atmosphere, stretched over the entire sovereignty of New York, furnishing vitality to all, it is the poor man's palladium, the aegis of the rich; the poor colored infant, sleeping in its cradle, is defended against the prowling kidnapper, with the same tender solicitude, which* would defend the bishop ministering at the altar.   However despised the human being may have been in foreign lands, however scarred with the slaveholder's whip, however broken in spirit.   Yes! no matter if he has been made ignorant of his high destiny by law; no matter if he has been sold on a thousand auction boards, as a chattel; or been out-lawed for seeking liberty; or a price offered for his head by ferocious brutality; or if wounds inflicted by bloodhounds are yet unheeded; or if hunger and poverty have left but the *uncovered framework* of a man; or the light of knowledge has never broken in upon the dark chambers of his soul, yet, the moment the ship brings him within the headlands of New York, the great folds of her constitutional liberty encircle him as a garment, her humanity lifts him up, benevolence feeds him and pours oil upon his wounds, while the law, stern, inflexible, becomes his sentinel to guard his every step by day and defend his sleep by night.   There is no recognition in this State of that infernal maxim, worthy of a Jeffreys, which prevails south of Mason and Dixon's line, by which a colored man is presumed a slave until he proves the negative.

All men are presumed free in this State.   Now look at the crime committed against the constitution and laws of the State of New York, yes, against every man, woman and child who breathes within our limits, by the forcible abdica-tion of the man Isaac by two Virginia kidnappers.   It will not help the matter for you to say he was Colley's slave. That was the very point judicially to be proved under the act of Congress, 1793, and under the statutes of New York, be-fore you attempt to remove him.   *Have the slaveholder's words, that a man is a slave become judicial proof*, record evidence?   Is liberty nothing?   Suppose it had appeared that Isaac had been kidnapped ten years before from this State, and carried to Virginia, and been sold a dozen times, he would have been a free man still, and so our courts would have decided. There are a dozen other ways by which a man who is a slave may become free. But these kidnappers seemed to think that there was no mode so acceptable as the original one by which slavery was created and introduced into the world—*the knock down and drag out title ;* the club-law title deed—and under that title is Isaac now held. Virginia is in duty bound to return that man Isaac to the authorities of this State, where the kidnappers found him, and if Colley had any claim on Isaac, the courts are open for its assertion.

Again, have we any reason to believe Virginia would deliver up the kidnappers, on the requisition of the governor of this State, on an indictment found against them for kidnapping? Virginia may have the opportunity in less than six months to see what she will do ; but there is not the least reason to believe that Virginia, who talks so largely about constitutional compacts, would surrender these men up. These men should be indicted for kidnapping a man in the State of New York and carrying him away into perpetual and hopeless bondage, while the three men you have offered the $3,000 bounty for, according to your own account, stole a man out of slavery to bring him into the daylight of liberty, into a free State. Look at the character of the offenders. One set of men, whom you demand to be delivered to Virginia, their crime is in aiding a poor slave to the recovery of his long-lost liberty—the most holy, precious right of man—helping a poor, miserable slave to escape from bitter slavery, a life used up and wasted for the convenience of another, helping him to escape cruel scourging, hunger, nakedness, ignorance, brutality, unrequited toil and all the uncomputed sorrows of a slave. The kidnappers of Virginia, for gold, in violation of the laws of the Union and of this State, ruthlessly, without a particle of authority, laid their cruel hands upon Isaac and forced him back to suffer the vengeance of an enraged master, who will glut his rage on the unoffending and quivering flesh of poor Isaac, for having committed high treason against his authority, for the great crime of having preferred liberty to slavery. The deed done by the three New York men is worthy of being commemorated as the three men of the Revolution were honored, who delivered up Major André. These men, if they did what you allege, to aid their poor countryman to escape slavery, deserve the thanks of the civilized and Christianized man throughout the world; for they are like the poor widow whom the Saviour commended for throwing her mite into the treasury: she did what she could—these three colored men did what they could to miti-gate the cruel fate of poor Isaac.

The insulted sovereignty of New York is wounded, through the sides of poor Isaac, and cries, like the blood of Abel, to Heaven for vengeance against those assassins of liberty, violators of law, who have robbed the State of New York of her peculiar glory of defending and protecting the lowest of our species from all injury and violence, unless done by the intervention of the due process of the law. But these kidnappers of Virginia will be demanded, but will not be surrendered.

But, sir, there is one point in this controversy, which strikes me as the most alarming feature in this whole transaction, and manifests, to my mind, the reckless daring of Virginia through her governor which is unparalleled in the annals of State intercourse: I mean your offer of $3,000 reward for the men you are pleased to call fugitives. To do you no injustice, your proclamation is here given verbatim:

"BY THE GOVERNOR OF THE STATE OF VIRGINIA—PROCLAMATION:

"Whereas, a felony was committed at Norfolk, in the State of Virginia, in the month of July, 1839, by PETER JOHNSON, EDWARD

Smith and Isaac Gansey or Garsey, men of color, at the time attached
to the schooner Robert Centre, and believed to have been residents
of the city or State of New York, where they may probably be found,
and the said Peter Johnson, Edward Smith and Isaac Gansey or
Garsey have fled from justice and are now going at large; therefore,
I, Thomas W. Gilmer, governor of the State of Virginia, have thought
proper to issue this proclamation of $1,000 to any person or persons
who will apprehend and convey to the jail of the borough of Norfolk,
any one of said offenders; of $3,000 upon the delivery of all of them
to the jailer of said borough of Norfolk. And I do moreover require
all officers of this State, civil and military, and earnestly REQUEST all
persons *within or without* the limits thereof to use their. utmost
exertions to apprehend the said felons, that they may be brought to
justice.

"Given under my hand as governor and under the seal of the State
at Richmond, this 13th day of November, 1840, and the 60th year of
the commonwealth.

"THOMAS W. GILMER.

"'National Intelligencer' will please insert six times.—Nov. 17th."

This proclamation is a renunciation on the part of Virginia,
of the Constitution of the United States, at a time when she
is pleading with New York for its punctilious and most
solemn observance in relation to these same three men for
whom you have offered this enormous reward. This is a new
mode of appeal from the decision of the governor of New
York. The governor of New York says to you, "These men
have committed no felony or crime acknowledged by the
laws of nations, or of this State, and cannot be delivered up
to the authorities of Virginia, in pursuance of the Constitution and the laws of Congress." You then offer an enormous
bribe to any miserable caitiff who may be found in Virginia,
New York, or in any other State, or in fact to any foreigner
who has the brutal courage to commit the crime of kidnapping on these men, and a high-handed felony against the laws
of New York, to deliver these innocent men into your pos-

session. Whoever should be deluded, in this State, Virginia, or elsewhere, to arrest and convey these men under your proclamation to Virginia, would come within the tremendous penalties of the statute of this State, already cited, especially the 2d clause of the 28th section, which says, that, whoever shall, without lawful authority, forcibly seize or confine another; " to cause such other person to be sent out of this State against his will, shall be punished in the State prison not exceeding ten years."

You therefore perceive, that you have offered $3,000, not to honor the law, but to break the laws of a sister State, and involve the transgressors in the most serious calamities, from having been seduced by your gubernatorial bribe. And these men-thieves, if Virginia did not throw off the obligations imposed by the Constitution, must be delivered up as kidnappers, who had been seduced by your bribe to the commission of this crime.

This law of New York was made to protect her citizens and its own sovereignty, against the machinations of foreign intruders, whether they be governors or individuals. You could not refuse to deliver up those who earn your bribe and flee to you for protection; for it will not be pretended, but that, by the laws of Virginia and the law of nations, the violent and forcible abduction of free men by an unauthorized force from their own State to a foreign one, is, and always has been, regarded as one of the highest crimes which could be committed.

But there is one point of view connected with your extraordinary proclamation, which, I cannot deny, excites in my mind a most tender commiseration for your own personal safety, in case your bribe to rob these three colored men of their liberty should be found effectual, and they should be carried out of this State. I am serious, sir, when I tell you, that your own personal liberty is in danger every moment;

for if the colored men should be carried off to Virginia by the stimulus of your bribe, you could, yea more, you would be indicted in some one of the counties of this State through which the colored men were abducted, as the procuring cause of their arrest, as the principal felon; for you say in your proclamation, that you "earnestly *request* all persons within or without the limits of Virginia to use their utmost exertions to apprehend them;" and you say they are probably in the City or State of New York. Your object is, therefore, relieved of every ambiguity; it is to get, by the means of these 3,000 pieces of silver, the innocent betrayed into your hands.

There is not a lawyer in the United States who is entitled to the appellation, who would not agree in pronouncing judgment against you, as the main felon, under our law, in case these men were arrested by that proclamation in this State and carried to Norfolk jail, in Virginia. You "entreat" A to murder B—you "entreat" C to burn the house of D—you "entreat" E to rob F of his purse; if your entreaties are complied with, is there a criminal authority, in England or this country, which would not pronounce you a murderer in the first, guilty of arson in the second, and of robbery in the third cases supposed? You must remember, you have no authority in the State of New York, unless our governor delivers the fugitives to you on your requisition. By entreating another to kidnap and carry these men off, you become a trespasser, "*ab initio;*" and come within the maxim, "*Qui facit per alium, facit per se.*" Remember when an indictment is once found, the offence will never be outlawed, although you might refuse to deliver yourself up for two or three years to come, while governor; but that is a long road which never turns, and the moment you ceased to be governor, your successor's first act, if he did his duty, would be to deliver you up on the requisition of the governor of this State, to come here, be tried, condemned, and undergo, for ten years or less, in our State prison, a felon's fate, and there learn to sympathize with the three colored men whom you wickedly caused to be dragged from their own State to waste their lives in Virginia's penitentiary cells, for an act which the Creator of all men had declared to be one of the duties of man to man, " to deliver the oppressed."

And who has converted one of the duties enjoined by our common Creator into a crime? A community of slave-holders. Why all this trouble and distress, which seem to threaten this Republic and individuals? The answer is as easy to give as it is disgracefully painful to state. Slavery, the principle of taking man and converting him into a chattel, into property, by thrusting him down from his lofty estate, to stand on a level, in a legal point, with the lowing ox, and neighing horse. To talk of regulating such an institution as slavery, by constitutions, just and equitable laws, in which two communities must administer these constitutions and laws, the one a community of freemen, sensitively alive to personal liberty ; the other a community of slaveholders, who, have to reverse, as it regards one half of its own population, all the rules of morality and justice, and apply the rules which govern beasts, to men; *these States must necessarily be in eternal conflict* until liberty conquers slavery, or slavery overturns the liberty of all. The vicious principle which has been admitted into the Republic of slavery, forbids the possibility of our complicated system of liberty and slavery, in juxtaposition, surviving the shocks to which it must be constantly exposed, in endeavoring to maintain propositions in eternal hostility to each other.

As to the great argument put forth by Gov. Seward, it is a perfect justification of the course he has adopted in asserting that the offence charged by Virginia is not one known by the laws of this State or the law of nations, and that Governor Seward is to be the judge whether the alleged offender has committed such an offence for which he will surrender up or not.   If the argument of the governor of New York is not sound, personal liberty rests on a foundation of sand, and we are in jeopardy every hour.   My remarks were intended for the *defects in the affidavit of time and place,* which Virginia refused to amend, if she could; being determined to extend by that operation, the dominion of slaveholding over a territory hitherto unconquered from liberty.   2d. I examined the high-handed and unauthorized transgression of our sovereignty in kidnapping Isaac by citizens of Virginia. 3d. The unparalleled attempt by the corruption of a large bribe, on your part offered by proclamation, by which you entreat persons to come here and abduct, in defiance of severe laws of this State against the offence, the three men. Hoping that you may, in the calmness of retirement, review your course and turn your eyes to the tremendous machinery which has been called into line for action against these men, to wit, your immense bribe, your State legislature, and your auxiliaries, the other slaveholding States; all of this array of force is about to measure swords with the free State of New York to compel us, by appealing to our fears, since you have failed to convince our understanding, to acknowledge the unlimited diminion of slavery over liberty herself.

However this matter may eventuate, it will be the consolation of Gov. Seward, that he did what he could to vindicate and defend the liberty of the Republic from the assaults of a grasping and relentless despotism, seeking to override the great barriers of constitutional freedom, purchased by the blood, and defended by the bravery of our ancestors.

AN ADDRESS,

BY THE "NATIONAL COMMITTEE OF CORRESPONDENCE,"

APPOINTED BY THE CONVENTION WHICH NOMINATED JAMES G. BIRNEY FOR PRESIDENT, AND THOMAS EARLE FOR VICE-PRESIDENT OF THE UNITED STATES, IN APRIL, 1840, AT THE CITY OF ALBANY.

To the friends of Liberty and of the oppressed in the United States, who intend to honor the " high obligation resting on the People of the Free States to remove slavery by moral and political action, as prescribed in the Constitution of the United States," the following address is most respectfully submitted by the National Committee of Correspondence.

MEN, BRETHREN, FELLOW-LABORERS, FELLOW-CITIZENS, AND FRIENDS:

The work of republican reformation is begun. Humanity, a new element, has been found in the ballot-boxes of 1840. The voice of stern justice is beginning to speak from a new place. The power which will overthrow slavery has been discovered; it is the terse literature of the northern ballot-box.

The groans of three millions of bondmen have penetrated the-ballot box, the abode of the sovereign's opinions. The ceaseless cry of the slave is respected in a new quarter. Every independent freeman is an American sovereign, and is proprietor of a portion of that power which can destroy slavery. It is his sovereignty, his manhood, his abstract right, enforced into a stern reality; it is his ballot in the box. There have been found, for the first time, in 1840, electoral tickets for President and Vice-President of the United States, in the ballot urn, the names of men who would employ all

234

just and constitutional means to elevate the chatteled slave to
a fellow sovereign—a freeman.

All men are ready to inquire, can slaves be made into
freemen, at the polls ? We answer, YES : and six thousand
voters, at the late election, in our free States, have said the
same.

Six thousand men have refused longer to make the condition of the slave more hopeless, by clothing his master and
the pro-slavery man with power to further crush him down.
But these six thousand men have said by their votes, "We
will employ our power to *deliver*, not to bind; to set free,
not to imprison; to make freemen, not slaves; to make a
republic, not a despotism; to make men, not things; to
increase our wealth, not our poverty; to sustain our religion,
and not abolish it; to preserve the Union, not to dissolve it;
to make the New World the abode of freedom, and not the
habitation of voiceless bondage."

These six thousand men hope, with the assistance of others,
to present 8,000 specimens of slave chattels, in the District
of Columbia, converted into men, with an "inalienable right
to life, liberty, and the pursuit of happiness."

To secure this glorious object, every freeman in the United
States is invited to come to our assistance, at every corpora-
tion, village, town, county, State, and Presidential election,
from this hour until the general jubilee shall ring from Lake
Memphremagog to the waters of Ponchartrain; from the
Penobscot to the Colorado. For these six thousand men
believe that to secure this grand object, the voting literature
of the nation must not be false to freedom, containing slaveholding and pro-slavery names, which is the substance of the
present emission of the ballot-box, and must be expurgated.
For who would believe that for half of a century, the majority
of names found in those boxes, who have governed this land,
was in favor of aristocracy founded on the skin, caste, unpaid

wages, violence, blood, sale of human flesh, separation of husbands and wives, parents and children, ignorance, irreligion, infidelity, atheism, adultery, stealing, robbery, hunger, nakedness, broken limbs, crushed hearts, lunacy, idiocy, mutilated limbs, scourged backs, the slash of bowie knives, duels, assassinations, war, murder, the pursuing of slaves with bloodhounds, idleness, licentiousness, coërced amalgamation, poverty, pride, contempt of labor, insolvency, gambling, cockfighting, horse-racing, piracy sanctioned by law, outlawry for love of liberty, with coffles, whips, fetters and chains, as the badges of undone men.

These law-makers have seen the South taking from the North, under the shape of credit, for twenty-five years past, ten millions per annum, to supply the deficiency which the whip could not extort from their own slaves, never to be repaid. Northern manufactories are now standing still for want of money *abstracted* by the South to maintain slavery in its idleness, and despotism in its dignity, and free laborers are thrown out of employ, for the benefit of those who live on the unpaid labor of the slaves.

The slave power in the halls of our national legislature has so molded the political economy of the country as to cripple the interests of free labor, derange northern capital, and reduce the free North, as far as possible, to the level of the enslaved South, and thus secure between the free and the slave States that balance of power which, on a system of equal legislation, the South could never attain.

We have here set down some of the curses of slavery, which have so many distinct names in our language. Each of these vipers has been sustained by consent of American law makers, in sucking the warm heart's blood of this nation, until the country staggers from debility. We have seen the frown of heaven lowering on this land, in the tempests of the ocean, in the tornadoes of the land, the fires in our cities, our villages, our steamboats, wasting pestilence, and bloody wars. We have seen a thousand savages maintaining against us a five years' war, while the bones of our youth are left to whiten amid the everglades of Florida. We have seen the value of property changed from the most extravagant estimation to the lowest depression; bankruptcies unparalleled in the history of a civilized people; States as well as individuals dishonoring their engagements in foreign lands, as well as at home; general ruin has stared all men full in the face; and these things, it is believed, are sent from the armory of the Almighty, as avengers of his wronged and insulted people, whom we have crushed as slaves under our feet, and have refused to listen to their cries, in our pulpits, our press, our State or Congressional legislation. Yes, the present Congress has broken down the Constitution of the land in its zeal to silence the voice of petition. In this, our Republican representatives have outstripped the boldest and wildest flights of despotic fanaticism—have attempted to legislate away human nature itself—have taken to themselves a seat beyond and without the pale of civilized legislation among men. And all this, to show their humble devotion to the slave power.

The great political doctors of this land have felt of the nation's pulse, looked her in the face, inquired for all symptoms, modes of diet, manner of repose, and her sort of amusements and various exercises. One set of these pro-slavery physicians profess to have discovered nothing but a corn on one of the toes, while the other thinks a little more exercise would give a finer flow of animal spirits, and relieve the patient from a certain dyspepsia or sleeplessness which he has discovered. In vain do we point them to the festering sore that must be probed to the bottom, and without delay, lest the deadly gangrene ensue. We are told that the patient was born into the world with that ulcer, that although it has increased five-fold, and is abstractly an evil, and might abstractly be considered the cause of an abstract ailment, and an abstract lingering, and may be followed by an abstract death, but surely nothing *more*, unless it was *abstractly* buried in an *abstract* grave. The pro-slavery doctors have hunted for all causes for the afflictions of their patient except the right one.

To drop our figure, it seems plain that one million two hundred thousand laborers, especially if they are slaves, can never maintain four millions five hundred thousand idle people, who have so many extravagances to gratify. If slavery were abolished this day, the slaves, as freemen, would from the stimulus of reward, produce double what is now extracted from them, and with vastly less pain. Again, there is nearly one million of idle poor men and women in the South, who are very poor, but still refuse to work, as it is disgraceful for white people to labor, in a slave country. This million would rejoice to labor for its reward, when its disgrace was removed. The South and North would immediately flourish, and at least fifty millions of permanent wealth be added to the nation annually; and the solid happiness of the nation doubled, besides being relieved from those periodical spasms and insolvencies which so seriously convulse it every seven or eight years. The danger of insurrection at home, or invasion from abroad would be removed to an interminable distance.

Each of the great parties in this country, for the sake of political power, has bowed with the most fawning submission to the two hundred and fifty thousand piratical janizaries, the men-consumers of the republic, and agreed, for the sake of power, to stand guard, night and day, as sentinels, armed to the teeth, on the confines of man-chattelism, to defend the two hundred and fifty thousand men-appropriators in their heaven-abhorred villainy, against the insurrection of the oppressed, or the invasion of holy and legal philanthropy.

The present Whig party, which has swept over the land with the power of a tornado, has acted in subservience to the slaveholder. The northern ballot-box is crimsoned with the blood of the slave, both parties having laid him on the altar of venality, as a sacrifice to propitiate the goddess of power, and have thus sought her favor, the one party by the dexterity with which they laid on the wood, while the other, not to be outdone, displayed a cultivated vigor in binding the victim. The successful party, who bound the sacrifice, will move around that altar, and install their high priest in solemn form, when he will be called on to swear to defend the victim and the altar from intrusion, by the blood of Bunker Hill, by the retreating, shoeless, blood-tracking soldiers of the Revolution, and as he marches around the blue flames, will further swear by the Goddess of Liberty and by the liturgy of equal rights, by the length of Mason and Dixon's line, by the awful and unrevealed mysteries of the implied compact, by that uplifting faith which grows stronger and stronger, as the evidence on which it rests grows weaker and weaker, by the high commands of the unwritten part of our Constitution, by its wonderful power to repeal the written portion, by the surprising wisdom each white man possesses to make a constitution for every black man, as he runs along, by all that is glorious in *white*, by all that is contemptible in *black*, by all that is tremendous in color, by all that is sublime in straight hair, by all that is horrible in *kinked*, " I, William Henry Harrison, President of the United States, as Martin Van Buren did before me, will forever protect the altar of slavery, with its victims, from all encroachments by the humane; I, the said President, affirm there is no human arm so mighty, no constitution so strong, no philanthropy so penetrating, no democracy so flagrant as to be able to unbind one of those chatteled victims." The President and Vice-President of the United States elect, have declared, yea, pledged themselves to maintain the greatest lie in the universe—that a father can chattelize his own child, into a slave; that the insolence of piracy is true southern chivalry; that a human flesh-proprietor has a right to make others groan with pain that he may sing for joy; to make others go hungry, that he may be fed to the full; to wear out others that he may be well preserved; to make others lie on the cold ground that he may lie canopied on his bed of down; to cause other men's wives to be sold to buy ottomans for his own; to send his own colored children to be sold in a market that his white ones may be educated in a college; to send other men's sons to be wasted with toil in the fogs of a rice swamp, that on the avails his son may whirl and dance in the circle of fashion.

It is held to be the prerogative of constitutional highway-manism to have the custody of treason's beetle and wedges to split this Union from end to end. These patent right Union-splitters follow their profession, for the profits of the pursuit, from the instinct of gain, as a mode of aweing northern free-men to silence, while they more quietly devour their domestic prey. It is a part of the slaveholder's birthright, that if the business of slavery is in danger of being shorn of its profits, he may embark in high treason as a kindred pursuit, but more exalted, as a man who has served an apprenticeship in the destruction of the rights of men must necessarily have a greater prospect of success than other men, when he raises the standard of treason, and seeks to enslave his country and rob it of its independence, as he has individuals of their liberty. A slaveholder must be indebted for his prosperity either to the destruction of the freedom of his country, or of single persons. He is a liberty consumer, either by retail or at wholesale. It is by force of the foregoing principle, that the South have supplied the ten millions of deficit of their own slaves, by thrusting their greedy fingers into the pockets of northern industry. Violent changes in the general policy of this nation they have always promoted, as the bankruptcies consequent thereon, and the great uproar of distress, have enabled them to charge to the account of the government, that which has sprung from the ruinous credit obtained by slaveholders in the North, to supply that inability which slavery has to maintain itself. Thus we have been in the roar and noise of embargoes, non-intercourse laws, war, a United States Bank—expiring as unconstitutional, a tariff as necessary, a Bank of the United States again chartered as constitutional, again overthrown as unconstitutional, a high tariff imposed by the South, till it was discovered by them to be unconstitutional, nullification, splitting the Union, secession; till Henry Clay and John C. Calhoun compromised the tariff to death. The South, by its vote declared the late war, in opposition to the desire of the merchant and the sailors, from the pretended yearnings of humanity, to rescue and protect six hundred seamen, impressed into the British service under the plea that they were British subjects, where they received the accustomed wages of seamen; while at this very time the South depended for their very existence upon the labor of two millions of men, women, and children, impressed, yea, enslaved by them, without wages—and said slaves were themselves property. Thus we went on; amidst the confused din and hideous uproar of these multitudinous changes in fifty years occasioned by the systematic disturbance by the votes of the South of any and every settled policy. In this endless fluctuation and change has the South robbed the North of two hundred and fifty millions of dollars to maintain her dreadful system, thus taking by fraud the labor of the free to make up what the slave could not earn. All this has been done to allow no particular branch of business to wear itself a safe channel before the South proposed a change. These changes in legislation are southern apologies for those enormous unpaid balances due the North, which changes were procured for the sake of the apology, to defraud the North, which has been running down the frightful precipice of bankruptcy in caravans, in consequence of these things.

The mighty and powerful party newly arrived at the palace of power, has reached the same by promising to guard, perpetuate, and even strengthen the great walls of slavery, while they fortify its outposts.

This great party has supplanted its rivals in the affections of the South.   Yet we lament that this powerful party should not have reserved even a formal salutation for liberty.—No, the cause of liberty must not expect more from this party than its predecessor.   No, not one fetter will be broken, not one tear wiped away from the cheek of the friendless slave. We suppose the Whigs will reprint, as a second edition, the Democratic programme of northern subserviency to the South, of which they once so loudly complained.   But we feel assured there are thousands and tens of thousands in the Whig party, who find themselves there from ancient position, whose hearts throb with the most tender desire for universal emancipation, who will be soul sickened, when they see their party crouching beneath the slave power, swimming with such a ponderous millstone about its neck.   They will abandon their party, we hope, on such painful discovery, and come and join the liberty party, never to desert it.

Look at the perfidy of the treacherous slaveholder, who, after tempting Martin Van Buren and his party to forsake the great highway of Democratic principles, to "bill and coo" in the forbidden and polluted paths of slavery, and now, having drawn the Democracy out of sight and hearing of the doctrines of the Declaration of Independence, slavery deserts them, and leaves them at the greatest possible remove from their own well avowed principles and the great landmarks of their professions.

Mr. Van Buren and his friends are not to be pitied ; they had no right to barter their principles, their humanity, their justice, for power possessed or expected, when conferred by the slaveholder as the price of political integrity to the slave. The Democracy is rightly punished, by the desertion of the slaveholder, and a perfect prostration of Mr. Van Buren and his party. The case still proclaims, in tones loud as thunder, the want of gratitude and the treachery of the slaveholder, and shows that whoever leans upon him for support, reclines upon a " broken staff, upon whose sharp point hope bleeds and expectation dies."

The South has been so kind to the Democrats as to relieve them from standing on guard, to protect the jewels of slavery from the depredations of Abolitionists, and have been most graciously pleased to permit the Whigs to cover themselves with glory in that desperate and honorable service ; supposing that rotation in office of such high distinction, would be peculiarly desirable in this ambitious age ; (and who could so nicely adjust with propriety to the honorable ambition of our times, those delightful duties which must be performed from one end of Mason and Dixon's line to another, in Congress and out, with such peculiar judgment and taste as good, pious, patriarchal Democratic slaveholders) ? The highest post of slaveholding elevation will be conferred in all suitable times and modes as befit so distinguished a service, on the most reckless defamers of Abolition, the equal rights of men, and the Declaration of Independence. The slaveholders will now be able to judge, which of the two great parties can discharge the laborious duty of traducing the slave and the slave's friend with the greatest skill ; which of the two parties can produce the ablest argument showing that the colored man is nothing but a connecting link between a man and a monkey, the ablest essay proving that a black man has no soul, and a mulatto has but half of one, and a man whose blood is three quarters of African descent has but a quarter. Also, an ably-written essay will be expected, to show that a colored man ought not to learn to read or write ; another book show-ing that the slave's mind and memory is so retentive that he does not need a Bible, hymns or psalms in books, as he will be able to remember all he hears read or said by others, in the way of "oral instruction." Another book will be required, showing that the southern slave is happier than the northern laborer. Another work, in 2 vols., 8vo., showing that slavery is a happier state than liberty, if a man has food to eat when well, and physic to take when sick. Another constitutioual argument showing that freemen in the free States have no business to petition for the abolition of slavery in the District of Columbia, or anywhere else; the second volume should be a luminous argument supported by authorities drawn from history, the laws of nations, and Confucius, that a man had better mind his own business, and let other people's alone. Another powerful book, entitled, "The Authority of Mobs Vindicated to put down Abolition ;" finally, there should be a work written, showing the propriety of what exists, and why a man south of Mason and Dixon's line should have double the amount of political power of one north of the line, or why 450,000 men south of the line should have as many electors of President as 1,000,000 north of that line. To which add a short-hand catechism for vulgar slaveholders, by which they may swear Abolition down, by firing their oaths at it, as at a mark.

But the Democracy of this country have been taught a bitter, but instructive lesson. They should not have sold Joseph into Egypt for a mess of Presidential pottage. The Abolitionists have been endeavoring to reduce Democratic abstractions into substantial realities. We invite every Demo-crat in the land to aid us in reducing their beautiful theories to practice. We believe every innocent man upon earth has the best right to himself, his wife, his children, his earnings, his labor, his liberty and life, and do not Democrats believe the same? This is Abolition; and is not this Democracy? Democrats profess to be anti-monopolists; what monopoly so great as for 250,000 slaveholders to monopolize the labor of 3,000,000 of people, without compensation?

May our merciful Father forgive our erring brothers, who have gone as they say, "for this once," and voted against the poor slave, for a Tyler or a Johnson. May they be forgiven by Him who treasures up in everlasting remembrance the sorrowful groans of the slave mother, as she, on the day they voted for a slaveholder, listened to the piteous cry of her first-born, beaten by the fierceness of avarice, the cruelty of lust, the unfeelingness of a slave-master. That inarticulate sorrow of a bleeding heart is transferred to that great ineffaceable record which will be read and published from the centre of eternity. Oh! forgive all who have voted that this mother's groans and her child's cry shall yet for four years more ascend from this blood-stained and tear-watered land, that a Tyler may rule. May the brother who has prayed with us, worked with us, suffered with us, petitioned Congress for aid and God for help, come back and vote with us. Brother! do not give that slaveholder more power to smite God's guiltless poor! Come back, brothers, and go with us, and we will love you. Come back from the *blood-bubbling* feast of the cruel! Come with those who will embrace you and do right. If you will go into this glorious army, raising for our enslaved brothers, you have a commission sealed with the blood of Christ, ready to be delivered to you. No self-denying and benevolent labor for the slave shall be unrewarded by Him, for even a cup of cold water given to His representatives, for His sake, shall not be forgotten. Blessed is he that considereth the poor. The Lord shall deliver him in time of trouble.

Come, Brothers, let us haste to the glorious rescue of the Declaration of Independence, of our holy religion, our Bibles, and three millions of fellow men in bondage. For if slavery is upheld it must be by a perverted Bible, and a false religion, and by some unknown God, "whose attributes are rage, revenge, and lust." To suppose, as the majority of the southern clergy do, that this hell-concocted villainy is a Bible institution, approved of by the God of heaven and earth, would in twenty years, if believed, drive all Christendom into the arms of blank atheism, frightful nothingness, eternal sleep, endless chance, which would be infinitely more consistent than a slavery-approving God. Such is not our God, who loves all his children, and did not confer power on one to maltreat the other by making him his slave. Come brothers, with your hearts filled with courage and love to man, and help us fight for hated truth, abused truth, despised truth. A lie cannot last forever. Slavery is the greatest lie in the universe of God. It is unalloyed wickedness. It embraces every crime which may be committed against man or his Maker. It is the fittest emblem of hell that can be found on the earth.

Never did the East foretell brighter signs of coming day. The seven years of persecution are ended. The nation is' about to arise and deliver. We are on the eve of a great victory over Gog and Magog. Bone is hastening to its bone. Slavery must die. It is doomed. The roaring shout of gladdened nations will ascend, as broadside after broadside of the walls of slavery come thundering to the ground.

Is not the day at hand, when the apocalyptic Babylon's overthrow may be applied to American slavery. "And I heard another voice in heaven, saying come out of her, my people, that ye be not partakers of her sins, and that ye receive not of her plagues. For her sins have reached unto heaven, and God hath remembered her iniquities. And the kings of the earth who have committed fornication, and lived deliciously with her, shall bewail her and lament for her, when they shall see the smoke of her burning, standing afar off for the fear of her torment, saying, Alas! alas! that great city, Babylon, that mighty city, for in one hour is thy judgment come. And the merchants of the earth shall weep and mourn over her, for no man buyeth their merchandise any more; the merchandise of gold and silver and precious stones, and of pearls, and fine linen, and purple, and silk, and scarlet, and cinnamon, and odors, and ointment, and frankincense, and wine, and oil, and fine flour, and wheat, and beasts, and sheep, and horses, and chariots, and SLAVES, and SOULS OF MEN."

LETTER TO SAMUEL WEBB, ESQ.

10th October, 1842.

DEAR BROTHER: I cannot but regret that such a space of time has gone by since I held communion with your spirit, so alive to every great and good thing. But I have been a bird of passage from one part of the anti-slavery hemisphere to another. I have never so entirely consecrated myself to the slave as I have done this year. I have been instant in season and out of season; I cannot tell you that my progress has been equal to my sanguine wishes. The times have been put so horribly out of joint by slavery; money is so uncommonly scarce that our agents in the cause could scarcely keep their noses out of water, and have lain at the edge of the water in a sort of snorting and strangling state, and I would be obliged to pass to their part of the country and *pump* the water out of them, and lay on warm clothes, and beg for a sort of *mineral* air to inflate their lungs with, and then they would rise and run again as though nothing had happened to them.

Slavery has undone us. She has crawled into the Constitution; has paralyzed the Church; broken the compact; silenced petition; overthrown morality; blotted out humanity; really dissolved the Confederacy, and left the nation undone. I have attended a vast number of conventions this summer all over the land, and placed in all its astounding forms the modes by which slave labor manifests its malignity to free labor; by which the Clay and Calhoun Compromise Act has alone wrung and crushed out of existence one thousand millions of dollars in the North, and reduced us to a position of misery from which twenty years of unbroken prosperity could not lift us up to that summit-level we occupied in 1833. The people approvingly admit that all I say is true, and admit that we only perpetuate our wretchedness and misery by electing either of these slaveholders, Clay and Calhoun, to the Presidency; men who, by being fathers of the Compromise Act of 1833, thereby thrust their bowie-knives into the national heart from opposite sides, where they met and *struck fire* in the conflict of opposition, until the points of their blades each pricked through from opposite sides, and for that act, each claims the Presidency, and each is equally entitled to rule a slave-loving and a slave-ridden people. I say men will listen and hear the proofs I bring that these two men are the great destroyers of their country's glory and happiness. Yes, and men will admit it is all so, and then go away and join their parties' shout for the one, or hurrah for the other! What destiny awaits this wicked land! I solemnly believe there is more positive crime committed against God in wronging man, in this Republic every day, than in the sixteen governments of continental Europe, with their two hundred and twenty-four millions of inhabitants. If the sun went around the earth as the ancients supposed, I think he would pause with amazement in his diurnal career over *Brazil, Cuba, and the United States.* But I mean to do what I can, in my little day and generation, to crush this great monster, though I confess I tremble for my country. Our election is the 8th of November, I hope we may gain some over last year. If we could go as high as seven thousand votes, I confess I should feel we had done nobly. But I fear we shall not, though I have worked *so hard.*

Allow me to hear from you soon, and believe me as ever, your assured friend.

LETTER TO DR. BAILEY.

April, 1842.

Dr. Bailey, Editor of the "Philanthropist:"

Sir: Pardon the freedom of a stranger, in bringing before you the sentiments of a coöperative in the great field of human rights. Perhaps by comparing opinions more frequently, on the subject of American slavery and its remedy, we may find that those who are separated by many degrees of latitude and longitude, may view this great crime and its cure not essentially unlike. That which is the oftenest considered, will be the best understood, and what is intended to be embraced in the great issue now making up between liberty and slavery, is a question in which the character of this nation is deeply involved, and on which the happiness of tens of thousands and the freedom of millions may depend; and must be one always claiming and summoning to its consideration, the most patriotic and far-seeing of her sons. If this communication should be the means of your placing your views before the world on the momentous question alluded to by me, one of the greatest objects of this letter will have been accomplished.

The work of the Revolution was fairly staked out, embracing the political freedom of the colonies—the personal liberty of each one—in the immortal Declaration of Independence:—but that great work was but half completed.

The great Declaration is a summary of colonial and personal injustice. The sword in seven years cut loose the colonies from their bondage. The dismemberment was ratified. Our country took her seat at the council board of nations. The young Sovereignty *limped* up into the temple of nations, with the Declaration of Independence spread, in her right hand, with a whip and fetter in her left, followed by a slave, while the blush mantled on her cheek, and revealed the struggles of her shame; and what she lacked in the sincerity of intent, she contrived to countervail by a certain impudence of pretence—and what she lost by force of position, she would fain make up, by the ingenuity of her abstractions. Theoretically, the relation of slave and master, king and people, was dissolved. The Declaration of Independence struck up, and the *hand* of the king fell off; it struck down, and the hand of the master was unclenched. Slavery since then has been constitutional man-stealing and legal kidnapping; slavery, though once laid out for interment, was not buried, but was in fact, an ill-omened resuscitation of a fungus on the body politic and was strapped and bandaged up with the other sores of the Revolution, and instead of excision, it now claims the dignity of being a " peculiar institution," whose increasing weight makes the body politic, by which it is nursed, reel and stagger under its ponderous load. The past year has given some encouraging premonitory symptoms of that final and frightful collapse of a system of crime, which has battened on the tears and blood of men, from century to century.

Great injustice will not last forever. Accumulated sorrows of swelling hearts, will burst out somewhere. In a single morning of August, 1831, *eighty-four* disembodied spirits were summoned from the Southampton massacre, to stand before the Eternal, as witnesses of justice long denied, and hope crushed in the bosom of the slave. Were the green earth of this nation carpeted with Decalogues beaming with celestial light from every word; were the blue heavens of this land curtained with aphorisms of eternal truth, and the leaf of every tree in the forest, or the field, instinct with declarations of the equality and universal liberty conferred by God on man, still one guiltless slave held as a chattel, by the law, would give the lie direct, to this festooned and emblazoned hypocrisy of high sounding moral assertion. The abstractions of this nation are divine ethics, but the practice iniquity's rules of action. It seems to be thought important that a man's abstract belief be right; then his practice is his own affair, for which he is not accountable.

It is difficult to define the position of a nation whose morality terminates in the orthodoxy of its abstractions. No nation in which the religion of Moses and Christ prevails, was ever rich enough to perform its labor by slaves. Slavery will cost a nation its self-respect, also the loss of the labor of those who rely on slavery for support, also the loss of the poor freeman's labor, who will not work where labor is disgraced as the business of slaves. Slavery will bankrupt its community every ten years, because slavery will not and cannot do enough to maintain a community, where the majority are idle. The deficit which slavery does not supply, must be purloined by stealthy credit, and paid in repudiation and bankruptcy. Slavery blots out the line between *mine* and *thine*, and elevates the greatest crime into a " peculiar institution."

The commerce of such a country is quickened into life by the whip; the groans of fathers, the tears of mothers, are the indications of its progress.

The cracking lash from twice ten thousand cotton-fields, is the mournful music of their progress from day to day, to life's end. The slaveholder cramps the immortal powers of his slave, to make the animal portion more available. I repeat, no nation is rich enough to use immortal man as property. He is too valuable for the base purposes to which he is applied. What farmer could prosperously *till* his cornfield with a golden plough, with handles of orient pearl? It may be asked, if slavery expired on the 4th of July, 1776, how has it come down to us, with so much brass on its front, claiming the assistance of the Constitution as its great patron? The answer is, there was no days-man, no saviour, no Granville Sharpe, to stand up between the oppressor with power and the helpless oppressed. Had God seen fit to have raised a Sharpe to have proclaimed that slaves could not breathe in these United States, the first moment they touched our soil, the abiding electricity of the great Declaration might have melted their chains; there was a divinity in its language, and a force in its terms, that casuistry could not resist or robbery prevent.

Lord Mansfield, who, for more than 30 years, ruled the judicial mind of Westminster Hall, by the supremacy of his own, twice in the King's Bench, on solemn argument, pronounced slavery a part of the law of England. But the great Granville Sharpe consecrated himself to the noble work of exploring the deepest spring of English liberty, the waters of whose fountain when by Sharpe presented to this same court, Lord Mansfield declared to be the true nectar of English liberty, and from that day henceforth forever, no slave could breathe who had placed his feet on the soil of beetle-cliffed England. That was the *eau de vie*, the water of life; and Somerset's case will be regarded to the world's end, as the re-discovery of the long-lost spring of English liberty. If we had had a Sharpe to have taken a slave, on a writ of habeas corpus, before the first Chief Justice Jay of the Supreme Court of the United States in 1789 or 1790, while the great truths were *yet* in the memory of men, while gratitude to God was felt for the white man's deliverance from a foreign yoke, before the cotton gin—the black man's curse—was invented, who can tell but what the slave might have been proclaimed free!

But alas! the claimants of human flesh were constitution-makers, law-givers, law-interpreters, and law-executioners.

Construction and definition came mainly, from those interested to perpetuate a crime, as disastrous, in the end, to
themselves and their posterity, as to the victims of this
aggravated villainy. Slavery has eaten out the very soul of
words, and every intendment raised, in behalf of liberty, and
every presumption raised against cruelty and injustice is
broken down, by violent construction, shamefully at war with
the benignity of the common law. The common law presumes all men free, till the contrary appears, without regard
to color. Slavery presumes a colored man a slave, until *he
proves himself free.* I solemnly believe if the Constitution
were to be interpreted by the judges of Westminster Hall,
slavery would cease in a single day in the District of Columbia; and it would be told, it could not derive a single power
to hold a colored man by virtue of that instrument.

Has there ever been a judge at Washington, who delivered
a judicial opinion, in which the rights of the slave were
involved, but came to the consideration of the question,
under the horrible weight of injustice, so deep, that the
loftiest intellect might flag and falter, by the debasement of
its employment, which instead of weighing out the justice of
Heaven, is basely employed in lending its sanction to the
clutchings of robbery, the greediness of injustice, and the
baseness of avarice. Look at the pompous prowling white
man, and the poor powerless black one, contesting their
rights in a slaveholding forum! Could the black man have
summoned as much influence and power as the white, and
employed able counsel to vindicate his rights, what glorious
triumphs would truth and liberty have made over falsehood
and tyranny; the world would have rung with the grandest
efforts of mind which had ever arrested the attention of mankind, from the time of Demosthenes to the days of Cicero;
from Paul to Luther, or from Bacon and Raleigh to Edmund
Burke and Patrick Henry.

But no, the colored man's oath could never be heard in the Sanctuary of Justice, for wrong done him by one of the Caucasian race. He was poor, he could employ no counsel to aid by strong arguments to drive deep the stakes of liberty. In the last half century, there have been wrongs enough inflicted by the white upon the colored race, to have kept all the courts of the civilized world well employed, in administering and weighing out natural justice to these injured ones.

We therefore, as Abolitionists, should never make a single admission, in relation to the construction of our Constitution, which might tell against the slave. It is craven to admit anything against the colored man, in favor of piratical legislation. Every act, organic or legislative, morally, so far as it bears on the slave, is clearly null and void in the court of conscience, it being made to take rights from him, without his consent, and which natural justice would declare wrong. It is ethically wrong to admit that the slaveholder has one right, however acquired, when that right is carved out of the natural ones of the slave, no matter how strongly the slaveholder's right may be upheld by a covenant or league on the part of the free States. For neither the slave or free States had any moral jurisdiction over the African, to reduce the quantum of his political and personal rights, below the average of the great community. But when we point to the Constitution or laws of the Union or States, as evidence of rights secured to the master, to the disparagement of the slave, whose whole life, and that of his race, have been a continued protest against and dissent therefrom, our act is morally preposterous in the extreme.

No doubt many tender consciences suppose there is something perversely radical in the above proposition, and that such doctrine is dangerously immoral; and these persons seem, although subject to an abolition influence, anxious to atone for their small spice of abolition, by asserting the validity of the master's claim, whatever it may be, when propped by constitutions, legislation, or judicial decisions. This looks too much like being as liberal as a prince in another man's house.

The ground I take, is, that all slave laws being made in derogation of all right, human or divine, and by the robber against the robbed, of the strong against the weak, and without consideration or consent express or implied, on the part of the slave, and for the entire profit and advantage of the master, and to the never-ending injury of the slave, therefore it seems to me, that the facts here assumed as entering into any law to uphold slavery, directly or remote, are of themselves evidence of the most stupendous fraud which can be committed through the instrumentality of one class of men upon another. Then we may refer to the civil law, the law of nations, the common law ; and it is the unbroken current or authority of all these laws that *fraud* avoids all contracts and all proceedings however solemn, as a judgment, or decree of the highest courts ; and even acts of parliament when procured by *fraud*, are all null and void, however high the authentication of their solemnities. But slavery, so far as written laws come to its support, is always stamped with fraud, as clearly as though in the preamble to the law it was to recite, that " Whereas, it is right for the strong to rob the weak, the powerful to deprive the helpless of themselves, and appropriate them and their posterity to their own use ; and whereas morality and honesty in the transactions of men are exploded truisms belonging to an obselete age, and the man, who by night or day, or by the most flagitious fraud can circumvent this fellow-being, is well entitled to the fruits of his knavery ; therefore be it enacted, that if A is stronger than B, he has a better right to B's body than B has to himself; if A by fraud, stratagem, or force can violate B's natural right, that is to be taken as evidence that B was not made for himself, but for his stronger neighbor's use."

Again, is it not the essence of absurdity, for us to contend that the constituted powers of this nation are constitutionally capable of being employed to uphold slavery, but these same constituted authorities are constitutionally powerless to do justice to the slave, and restore him to his liberty?

We never should admit that we are under a *moral* obligation to do wrong, and have *therefore* no legal power to do right. Many are in haste to admit we have conspired by *compact* against the liberties of the colored man, and that morality requires we should be pertinaciously and wickedly consistent in carrying out the original knavery of our contract, to crush forever the rights of two and a half millions of men, and that we exhausted our power to do good, in the great evil we undertook to perform ; therefore, if indeed we desired now to do right, we have no power ; or at any rate, morality demands we should be villains, because we *so agreed*, rather than become just and honest men, at the expense of breaking a murderous covenant. We have thrust the innocent man into the dungeon, but have no power, say some, to lift him out. Our constitutional power being exercised to destroy the rights of man, is a *spent power*, and when a sense of our crime appears to us, and we would desire to redress the wrong we have done, some tell us, alas ! we have no space for repentance, because we are constitutionally moral bankrupts. Every admission made of constitutional inability to redress any and every act of injustice, direct or remote, affecting the liberties of any of our countrymen, touching any point wherein we have heretofore wronged them, is as cowardly as it is untrue. It has, however, often been done to propitiate slaveholding and pro-slavery wrath ; but we have always lost in self-respect, more than we have gained, by our pusillanimity. It is wrong to make merchandise of even a legal opinion which goes to confirm the conquests of the bucaneer. The proposition cannot be doubted that we have power to take back everything wrong in the Constitution or law, to which we or our fathers have lent their sanction, affecting the rights of colored men. We can abolish slavery in the District of Columbia and between the slave States, because these two kinds of slavery derive their power from the Constitution, whether rightfully or wrongfully I will not stop to inquire. The fugitive slave act of 1793, by which the free States have become the hunter's great forest of human game, can be abolished by Congress. The internal slave trade, and the act of 1793, abolished, slavery could not stand five years. Then there is the war power of Congress, the treaty power, and the guaranty in the Constitution of a republican form of government to each State; who dare affirm or deny that some of these powers may be equal to the abolition of slavery in all of the States?

Without pausing to reason for a moment, on any of these remedies, I may be permitted to say no reasonable Abolitionist should ever suffer his mind to be perplexed for a moment with the notion that we have not power to undo all the wrong which we have inflicted on the slave. The bare discharge of the free States in money and men from all obligation to aid in suppressing slave insurrections and to deliver up fugitives, would compel the South to manumit for their own safety. The South, were they to rely on themselves for protection from insurrection, would be compelled to *dot* its whole territory with forts; not less than 2,000 would be required, to protect the women and children. The forts required, at $20,000 each would be $40,000,000, and the munitions, arms, etc., to furnish in a small degree each fort, could not be less than $10,000 each, or $20,000,000 more, which added to the cost of forts would amount to $60,000,000 —strange mode of extorting labor in the nineteenth century!

Secretary Upshur refers to this mode of defending the South in his late report. If the forts were built, the slaves would find them as good points to rally for insurrection, as the master for protection.

Again, the great staple of the South, cotton, has found a competition in the British East Indies, where enough probably will be grown in a few years to supply the necessities of men, at about half the price at which cotton has heretofore been sold. To enable the southern planter with his reckless mode of conducting his affairs, to compete successfully against the cheap free labor of India, would require cotton-gin and slaves to be given to him, as a governmental bounty, or donation, in the start.

The first streak of light which appeared after the Revolution was a lurid one, shot forth some twenty-six years since; and men have disputed from that time to this, whether it was a prismatic ray of the ascending glories of the sun of liberty, or whether it was not a false light flung up from the pent fires of slavery. It is called the Colonization Society. A few good men in the North had a hazy, indistinct idea of the immeasurable wrongs of slavery, and could find no measures for its redress, except expatriation beyond the Atlantic, of those freedmen, who had once been its victims. The North thought they saw in this society the colored man elevated on the other side of the globe, and the slaveholders saw something more congenial; they saw the freedman, by them hated, because he was free, cut off from all sympathy with the slave, no more to be the bondman's eyes and feet, the slave made safe, his value increased, his escape impossible. This society was a strange confusion of benevolence and fraud, of northern indefiniteness and southern avarice, glossed with good intentions, controlled by southern sagacity, as heartless as it was specifically selfish, believing in the safety-valve for troubled consciences, and a sure way to make slavery valuable and perpetual.

About this time, or shortly after, the slaves, it is supposed, organized two distinct missions, one the free State, and the other the Canada mission. The object of these missions appears to have been to send off slaves to liberty. These societies, without funds or agents, or the countenance of a single member of Congress, or a doctor of divinity (but the whole constituted authorities of this country, by sea and land, armed against them), have done a very spirited and successful business (*although the slave trade is forbidden*) ; the society deals in nothing but slaves, and has sent away to these missions five persons, where the Colonization Society has sent one to Africa. The Colonization Society seems to be a sponge, to absorb the unregarded and floating sympathy, which men feel, to do something to wash out the vileness of slavery. When men cease to delude themselves with the folly that the expatriation of a few thousand freedmen, is the same as the emancipation of two and a half millions of slaves, *then*, and not till *then*, will the Colonization Society be powerless, for the purpose of mischief.

Long continued injustice done to man, must burst up somewhere, sooner or later. Witness the Southampton massacre. Slavery did it. Slave insurrections on sea or land with murder, is a part of the shocking system. In 1832, a few northern noble spirits, deeply pitying the condition of the slave, and perceiving the hopelessness of colonization, determined that the only remedy for slavery was unconditional emancipation. And in the last ten years there has been performed an amount of labor by the Anti-Slavery Reformers, without a parallel in any of the past ages of benevolence in the world.

Both of the great parties who contended for the mastery of the Republic hoped to flatter the South by a base and profound acknowledgment of various Constitutional compacts implied, upholding slavery, which never existed, and by abusing Abolitionists without stint or measure—this was the competition between these great parties, who from that day to this have poured from a thousand presses concocted and deliberate falsehoods, to bereave the friends of man of their characters for humanity, sense, patriotism, and every quality which can elevate or ennoble. These parties have set mob-ferociousness upon us, demolished private buildings, destroyed the sanctuaries of the living God, and devoted to the flames the most beautiful temple ever erected to Liberty on this continent; they laid their Vandal hands upon printing presses and destroyed them; and above all, they inflicted dreadful scourging upon our most worthy men; they levied fines contrary to law on some, imprisoned others, and finally murdered Lovejoy, the martyr.

We were compelled, poor and sparse as we were, to erect and maintain presses, papers, and publish books, pamphlets, reviews, magazines, and in fact to create in self-defence, and that of the rights of our race, a literature of our own, in which to embalm the sorrows of insulted men. We have been refused the columns of papers to refute the vilest calumnies which those same papers had originated or circulated. The public mind was so far misled, as to the objects of Abolitionists, as to believe slaveholders to be the innocent victims of position, and that Abolitionists were justly deprived of trials by jury, as monsters too great to be entitled to anything but the headlong vengeance of lynch law.

The Abolitionists of the United States, on bended knees, besought the great denominational divisions of the church to throw open the doors of their churches, and view the poor slave as the representative of their ascended Redeemer. This great honor we tendered them in the imploring bowels of compassion, and in every form of entreaty, argument and remonstrance. These churches have been besought to tell their brethren of the same sect or connection in the South, that slavery was a sin against God, a crime against man ; and to let the oppressed go free. But these churches refused to admonish and do the glorious work, and preferred union in iniquity to schism for the love of God and man. Had the church, as her character imports, opened her arms for the pleading and bleeding slave, long ere this, it is believed, the work of emancipation would have been complete; and political action by a liberty party rendered unnecessary. But she declined the Heaven-descended honor; she refused in most cases to hear a message from him just ready to perish, or give notice of the meetings in which to listen to the tales of his long unheeded sorrows.

We then besought the authorities of our national capitol with uncounted petitions asking Congress to exercise the constitutional power it possessed to break the slave's yoke. When the frank and fearless petition of the slave's friend was read in Congress, the slaveholding representatives sent up a shriek which pierced the capitol dome, and for about the space of two hours, they cried out "Great is Diana of the Ephesians !"

Two hours did I say ? Have they not so cried from that day to this, in behalf of slavery ? Have they not walked over the prostrate Constitution of their country ? Have they not, unread, unprinted, unreferred and unconsidered, sent petitions signed by more than two millions of our citizens to the Congressional sepulchre ? Have not the most solemn appeals, for the last eight years, praying the emancipation of thousands of our native-born citizens from slavery the most awful, been treated with an indignity surpassed only by a fanaticism which could break down the barriers of the Constitution to strike down the imploring slave; in the first moment of his trembling hope, when the first ray of light fell upon his chains, it was to be extinguished by a darkness which cast its common shadow over the Anglo-Saxon's constitutional hope, and the poor African's only expectation.

But this entombment of a nation's recorded philanthropy is not a final rest; it shall have a resurrection with the flush of injured immortality on its cheek, defying her assassins; and shall publish the glory of her redemption, where there is a slave to be set free, or a freeman to rejoice.

We have appealed to the church, and she has declined the honor. We appealed to Congress, and she threw us back our petitions, mixed with the broken fragments of the Constitution. We have appealed to the slaveholder; he points to the fagot and the flames. What shall we do?

The nation is about to become all slaves or freemen together. The thirteen slave States have found slavery too expensive a mode of existence without practising, at least decennially, on mankind, that robbery, through bankruptcy and repudiation, which they continually inflict upon their slaves. These slave States are insolvent; showing their deformity abroad, and revealing their nakedness at home.

They have struck down by tariff legislation that prosperity in the North, which they had neither the power to imitate, nor the firmness to pursue.

The North, by its wretched alliance, through its Siamese ligature, walks with a feeble step; as it carries helplessness along, it is itself borne to the same miserable end.

The nation is rushing upon the crisis of her destiny with a momentum augmenting the velocity of her speed, proportioned to the increasing light of her criminality. For already the man of Vermont and the citizen of Michigan hear in the sigh of the south wind the cry of the South, saying, " Cease to prevent my escape; cease to oppose my insurrections for that liberty for which your fathers fought and bled ; cease to provide the southern fort and arsenal, by your taxes, to keep us down;

vote me free; remember me at the ballot-box, where you stand one of the sovereigns of this empire of slaves; you have the power—God give you the will!"

Congress, by means of slaveholding bullies, has lost its character as a deliberative body; it is the national bear-garden; a more licentious body than the French Constituent Assembly when torn by Girondist and Mountain factions; for those murdered their sovereign; these, our Constitution and the nation's character.

Slavery has ruled this land. The robbed Cherokee has been driven from the council-fires and graves of his forefathers, by the slaveholding bayonet, to find a new home in the land of the setting sun, and leaves behind, the legacy of a wronged and ruined people's curse; and as band after band of the brave Seminoles are forced from their everglades to the solitudes of the distant West, we may well fear the seven last plagues of the Apocalypse will be poured upon us, for the wrongs committed against *them*, and the slaves of this land.

We have tried the inapplicable system of questioning the political candidates in this land; hoping by that lever to pry open the prison doors.

A new kind of political literature sprung up in the North, in which the Jesuits were fairly distanced, in their own celebrated art; the catechism of humanity was answered by the political catechumens in such mode as " to keep the word of promise to the ear, and break it to the hope."

There was as much honest complaint against the askers of questions as the answerers. Bad faith was the result on the part of the voter and *voted*—crimination and recrimination had brought us to the border of ruin. We were determined for a while, that the Whig and Democratic parties should perform this exalted work of humanity, and we seemed to think, by a sort of political expediency in barter, that the anxiety felt for our votes, by the candidates nominated by those parties, would revolutionize their sentiments, and make them sincere advocates of the rights of the slave. We never, by this course, gained truth an advocate, or humanity a friend. Ten candidates either before or after the election apologized for any seeming abolition tendencies in their moral framework, or by force of position, to *one*, who has avowed his fidelity to our principles.

The truth has been, both parties have been so corrupt as to employ all their ingenuity to fix on their adversary the stigma of upholding abolition; while each sought to wipe out the blot of *humanity*, by some bold impudent blow, struck full in the face of Liberty, as an atonement for the suspicion of being just. The effect at last was that a genuine Abolitionist of either of these parties, could not be nominated for a law-making trust, but was put under the ban of proscription. And when a man was nominated, who by any accident bore the proscribed cognomen of Abolitionist, he was found almost uniformly to be a man, who from the futileness of his powers, could render our cause no service, and would, if a man of some talent, always as between abolition and party, in a *pinch*, go for party and sacrifice the slave, at the very moment his strength was most wanted; these men, when nominated, were stool-pigeons to catch our votes. But did such a Whig candidate inspire confidence enough in a Democratic Abolitionist to obtain his vote; or vice versa, in a Whig Abolition voter, if the candidate were Democratic? So nothing but harm was gained. We boxed the compass of expedients. The Church, Congress, the candidates, were all broken reeds. We had made the experiment complete; and had set down satisfied that we could not bribe men to do right, for the hope of gaining or fear of losing our votes.

This brought the Abolitionists to a solemn pause. They looked all around the horizon for help; they saw Liberty everywhere in the dust; the moral and pecuniary resources of the nation evaporating; the Republic, through its great parties and denominations, with her literature both in Church and State, bowing down before the great monster slavery. What should be down? Was this god-like enterprise to be abandoned in despair? Must the avenging sword, the midnight flame, the forlorn shriek of despair, be the only remedy for this crime.

God forbid, that the fair plains of the South should be delivered over to the vandalism of such a terrible necessity. We found on review, that heretofore we ourselves had voted for President and members of Congress who had refused to lift an ounce of the weight that crushed the slave; yea, more, voted to *continue* the fetters *on*, and, in fact, were the bodyguard of slavery.

By a little reflection we saw ourselves through the ballotbox forbidding the slaves deliverance, and refusing the repeal of a single law, by which he was bound.

In looking this question over in its amazing breadth, we, in the fear of God determined to discharge our own duty, without any relation to measures of subtle contrivance, or of expediency; and if we did our individual duty, on others than ourselves must be fixed the sin of the continuance of slavery.

We are born under a selfocracy, and came from our Creator with a charter commanding us, at the age of majority, as law-makers and as sovereigns, and law-givers, standing with these high responsibilities bound upon us, commanding us to do the greatest good to the greatest number; "to love our neighbor as ourselves;" and "to do unto others as we would that others should do unto us." This is believed to be one of the highest religious duties we can perform in this world. We are bound to select and vote for those legislative and executive officers, who will employ their best faculties, and all the constitutional power within their reach, " to break every yoke, and let the oppressed go free." We stand at the ballot-box legislating ; for our representative is but our agent, our servant, the mere reflection of our concentrated will.

Every prayer, argument, speech, gift, or act, this side of the ballot-box, is but moral suasion; if the vote is cast for a liberty candidate, then we test and prove the sincerity of the prayer; then we perceive that moral suasion has done its work. Our prayer, argument, or moral suasion, with its infinite appliances, may be likened to a cause in a court of justice, the opening, the evidence, the pleadings of the counsel, and charge of the judge; this I call moral suasion. But the verdict of the jury is like the vote at the ballot-box ; that is the great *fact*, this is the great *act* of prayer. But the man who talks of argument, prayer and moral suasion, and still votes for a President, or a member of Congress, who will vote the fetters of the slave continued *on*, that the slave still weep for blows inflicted, that he still be deprived of his wife, child, Bible, and hope, and will not vote a chain to be taken off, on this voter, prayer and moral suasion have never had a controlling effect, or he would not so vote ; for his agents voting this way, or refusing to vote that, is the act of the voter as much as the representative's.

The voter votes in Congress yea or nay through his representative. In voting for a member of Congress, or President, or a member of the State legislature (who votes for the senators in Congress) our acts affect for weal or woe every bondman or freeman in this great country. What other act in the even tenor of a common man's life, can equal this ? Is it not in his ballot that he demonstrates before God and man the piety and purity of the act ?

Let us look at the anti-slavery and pro-slavery law-givers standing at the ballot-box, ready to deposit their votes, for

President or a member of Congress. The Liberty Party man has on his vote the name of a genuine Abolitionist, as a candidate for Congress, and in that name is concentrated his whole code of Christian humanity; in that name on that ballot is impliedly these words by the voter: "I vote for the greatest good of the greatest number; I vote the Declaration of Independence a solemn and practical reality; I vote the right of petition be restored; I vote a slave is a *man* and not a *thing*, and has a better right to his own body, and its labor, and to his wife and children than any other person on earth; I vote the slave have his own Bible, and be permitted to read it and worship God as he sees fit; I vote that his little children be sent to school; I vote slavery abolished in the District of Columbia, and in Florida, forthwith; I vote the internal slave trade between the States be abolished, that the infernal trade be punished as piracy on the high seas; I vote for the repeal of the act of February, 1793, by which the slaveholder pursues the fugitive slave in the free States; I vote that the Republican form of government guaranteed to each State in the Constitution, is one in point of form described in the Declaration of Independence, in which the government is made for the benefit of the governed; and that all men are created free and equal; I vote all acts of the several State legislatures conflicting with the republican form of government aforesaid described, be declared null and void, even if it set every slave free as its consequence; I vote that if it becomes necessary for the common defence of our country under the war power, to take the southern chattels, called slaves, and convert them into men, and put arms in their hands; I then vote the same will be a constitutional mode of giving them liberty, and to hold the converse of this is to declare slavery must be continued, and that it is more important than the salvation of this nation from a foreign foe, or the integrity of the Union in case of domestic insurrection; I vote that either the war power or the treaty power, may, in certain contingencies be competent sources of power for the abolition of slavery in this nation." The vote goes in, and the voter's legislation and control over the slave are irrecoverably gone, for two years.

Let us see what is contained in the eye of Reason, in the *name* of a pro-slavery candidate for Congress. The pro-slavery voter stands likewise the legislator of two years, at the ballot-box, and on that vote of his in the name of the candidate is written, in the eye of experience, these other words: "I vote that my candidate for Congress, if elected, act with and under the dominion of his party, and if it be necessary to preserve the power of our party that in casting his votes, he bow down to the slaveholders, then I so vote; I vote the Declaration of Independence is a rhetorical flourish, and that all men are not born free and equal; I vote that slavery be *continued* in the District of Columbia, and the internal slave trade be prosecuted; I vote that a master has a better right to his slave, and to that *slave's wife* and children, than the slave has to *himself or them ;* I vote the slave have no Bible; I vote that the whip, cudgel and fetter be used as the master sees fit; I vote the act of 1793 remain unrepealed. In fact I vote slavery remain one of the 'institutions of this country.'" The vote has gone in, the voter's power is spent, and that vote has sent a torpedo shock through the frame of the most remote slave, who dips his bucket in the waters of the Mexican Gulf, or lifts his hoe on the banks of the Perdido.

How can a man pray and plead 729 days for the slave, and on the 730th day, when he is armed with the power of a sovereign, when he is about to do an act which has more power and efficacy, than all he has said and done for two years past, prostitute it and go and vote for the master?—

vote all he has said and prayed for the slave to be bald hypocrisy? What would the master say to such a voter? "Ah! well done good and faithful servant, you keep your prayers, tears and pleas for the slave, but in the trying moment, you give the *power* to me. It is all I ask." If the slave were to upbraid an Abolitionist, who had voted for the master, or a pro-slavery candidate, would not such a voter have to apologize and say, "Oh, slave! have I not talked, plead and given my money, to wake up the public to your case, for 729 days, and do you suppose I am also to vote for you? No that is *too much:* my 730th day is my own, my vote I give to my party, and *your* master." "But," says the slave, "give your 729 days of prayer, moral suasion and alms to my master, and only vote for me by casting your ballot for an Abolitionist, and I am content." Have we not tried these parties long enough? On the free States rests the crime of slavery. There are 1,700,000 law-makers or voters in this land, and more than one million of them live in the free States. We can elect President, Vice President and a majority of the House of Representatives, and 26 Senators from the free States, who, with the Vice President, make a majority of the Senate. Is not the mighty power of legislation contained in a vote as applied to this amazing question, one which involves all that is vital in Christianity, dreadful in the day of everlasting retribution? Does not this voting assume an aspect as sublime as the Christian religion can make it, in discharging our duty to our fellow-man, whose shackles we can strike off or retain? We consider it a most glorious revolution, in our own minds, by which we see this law-making or voting to be a duty which exceeds in its consequences to our brother man, any other act which we can perform, touching the liberty and hopes in time and eternity of two and a half millions of our race—a duty big with the most important consequences, being for good or evil, the greatest, yes, infinitely the greatest act we can perform for or against man in passing through this world.

We have treated voting and politics heretofore, as something doubtful in morals, but at all events, as a subject on which there was no accountability to God. We have acted as though voting was a sort of neutral act, in which there was neither sin nor holiness, right nor wrong, however done. We have acted as though voting was an act performed on a neutral territory, where the power of God did not extend on the one side for approbation, nor on the other for condemnation. The American Ballot has been treated in such a way, in the pulpit and out, that a stranger might suppose we were political infidels.

Now, may we not thank God that the anti-slavery cause has been the means of opening our eyes to the dignity and responsibility of legislating with the fear of Him before our eyes. We cannot bind and load our brother with fetters at the ballot-box, and be less guilty before God, than he who does it on a plantation. Alas, alas! for 52 years, or 26 times, the American voters have gone up to the ballot-box and taken the awful sin and crime of slavery on their own souls, by refusing to listen to the souvenir of the slave, but have joined hands with the wicked master, and silenced the mournful cry of God's unpitied poor, and added law to law, weight to weight, to his insupportable burdens. Let each man legislate under his deep accountability to Heaven, and there would never be a pro-slavery vote cast again.

ARGUMENT, ON THE QUESTION

WHETHER THE NEW CONSTITUTION OF 1844

ABOLISHED SLAVERY IN NEW JERSEY.

Supreme Court of New Jersey.—THE STATE *vs.* EDWARD VAN BUREN, *Writ of Habeas Corpus.*

THE STATE *vs.* JOHN A. POST, *Writ of Habeas Corpus.*

Before the Justices of the Supreme Court of New Jersey, the Honorable Chief Justice HORNBLOWER, *and Judges associated,* NEVIUS, CARPENTER *and* RANDOLPH.

E. P. PALMER, Esq., *Petitioner for the Slave and Apprentice.* ALVAN STEWART, Esq., *of the State of New York, Counsellor and Advocate for the slave and apprentice, admitted to argue these causes by the courtesy of the Court.* A. O. ZABRISKIE, Esq., *of New Jersey, Counsel for* VAN BUREN ; ALVAN C. BRADLEY, Esq., *of New York, Counsel for* JOHN A. POST.

These causes were argued before the Hon. Justices of the Supreme Court, at the Capitol in Trenton, on the 21st and 22d days of May, 1845, Mr. Stewart occupied about eleven hours, and the defendant's counsel five hours, during two days and an evening.

The argument in these two causes, in behalf of *Mary Tebout,* held in the first case, as property, until twenty-one years of age, her mother being a slave, and she being nineteen years of age ; and in the second case, *William,* a colored man, claimed by John A. Post as a slave for life, being about sixty years of age. Returns to the Writs of Habeas Corpus were duly made on Wednesday, the 21st of May, 1845, in these causes respectively, before the justices aforesaid. These writs had been granted on a previous day, on motion of Alvan Stewart, Esq., in open Court.

The object of those writs was to test the institution of slavery in the State of New Jersey, which the counsel for the slave and apprentice contended was abolished, by the first section of the Bill of Rights, in the new Constitution of this State, which went into operation the 2d September, 1844. The defendant Van Buren, by his counsel, returned to said writ, that he held the said Mary Tebout, by means of several intermediate conveyances, from a person who owned the mother of said Mary; the said mother being a slave for life, and that the said Edward claimed to hold the said Mary, as his property, until she was twenty-one years of age, she now being nineteen years old, by virtue of a Statute, passed for the gradual abolition of slavery, in February, 1820, by which all slaves born previous to the fourth July, 1804, were slaves for life, and all children born of said slaves after 1804, were declared free, but to be held by the owners of their mothers as apprentices were; who were bound out by the overseers of the poor, males till twenty-five years of age, and females until twenty-one. The said male until twenty-five, and female until twenty-one, were held by their owners, their administrators and assigns, as property, or as other slaves are, until their time was out.

The return in the case of John A. Post was the same in substance, that he held the said William, a colored man, as a slave by virtue of the law aforesaid, being born before 1804. To these returns general demurrers were put in, alleging the institution of slavery was abolished, and that the returns did not state sufficient authority to authorize the defendants to hold said persons. To which there was a joinder in demurrer.

Both of these causes were argued together, depending on the same laws for their support, and for the purpose of obtaining a judicial decision, overthrowing the system of slavery in New Jersey, in all its parts. The following pages are the substance of the argument and reply of Alvan Stewart, Esq., of New York, who appeared for the slave and servant, as their counsel.

The first article of the new Constitution of New Jersey, of September, 1844, is entitled "RIGHTS AND PRIVILEGES."

"All men are by nature free and independent, and have certain natural and inalienable rights, among which are those of enjoying and defending life and liberty, acquiring, possessing and protecting property, and of pursuing and obtaining safety and happiness."

It was supposed there were from seven hundred *to* one thousand slaves, and from twenty-five hundred to three thousand servants or more, whose liberties were involved in the argument and decision of these causes, as well as the institution itself.

ARGUMENT.

Alvan Stewart, Esq., arose and invoked the kind consideration of this Court, while he endeavored to break into a new, and almost uncultivated region, to explore and investigate the long neglected rights of man to his own body and soul. The courts of our country had sounded the depths of human learning, and all the vast stores of history, and the remains of antiquity had been overhauled, sifted and analyzed, with metaphysical sagacity, to determine with judicial accuracy, all the rights which men had to property, lands and tenements, corporeal and incorporeal. Everything in the shape of human acquisition had been again and again labored and belabored by the highest talents of the land, until learning and genius could do no more, to add to man's possessions; while the great right of *man to himself*, while innocent of *self-ownership*, under all circumstances, is a great question, which has rather been *grazed* than lifted up, shunned than embraced, or duly considered, in all its mighty amplitude, and its solemn importance; and then only at distant periods of time, and under the greatest disadvantage in point of time, place, position and circumstance. The controversies about lands and estates, and the personal rights of *freemen*, with all the subtle ramifications of the schoolmen, of various legal questions of our age, have been pressing the highest judicial forums of our land for decision, and constitute much of the drudgery of counsel, and labor of the judges. A modern legal opinion of counsel or judge is, that it is *his opinion* that he has clearly discovered what was the *opinion* of Chief Justice Mansfield, or Lord Thurlow, on this question, when

Lord M., or Lord T. saw fit to express an *opinion* on this subject.

Considering the mighty questions of human liberty placed under the control of twenty-seven State constitutions, their laws, and the Federal Constitution and acts of Congress, and the ten thousand forms in which human liberty may be abused, from the most horrible slavery, to the slightest invasion of a trespass; it seems passing belief, to be told, there is not one volume of reports, arguments and decisions, touching the great inalienable rights of man, invaded as they are, by communities, states, and individuals, as a regular commerce carried on in crushed and violated human rights, assaulted in every direction, overthrown, trodden under foot as they are, at every step and angle of passing life. The attention of our countrymen seems to have been turned to the contingencies and appurtenances of our race, rather than to man, and the elevation of the race itself. Congress has shown more anxiety to protect the hats, the boots, and the coats which men wear, than the heads they cover, the bodies they surround, and the feet they inclose. That grave assembly can dispute from Christmas to dog-days, about the tariff, protection, free trade, and revenue, while a petition to abolish slavery in the District of Columbia, to give a man to himself, a wife to a husband, and children to their parents, is received with profound astonishment as a moral anomaly, and when the House has recovered from its surprise, the petition being so completely at right angles with the course of a Republican Congress, that unread, unprinted, undebated, and undecided, it is ordered to lie upon the table, until the clerk removes it to its sepulchral silence in one corner of the capitol, to rest with the other entombed memorials of a nation's dishonored humanity.

Nothing has been held so cheap as our common humanity, on a national average. If every man had his aliquot proportion of the injustice done in this land, by law and violence, the present freemen of the northern section would, many of them, commit suicide in self-defence, and would court the liberties awarded by Ali Pasha of Egypt to his subjects. Long ere this, we should have tested, in behalf of our bleeding and crushed American brothers of every hue and complexion, every new constitution, custom, or practice, by which inhumanity was supposed to be upheld, the injustice and cruelty they contained emblazoned before the great tribunal of mankind for condemnation; and the good and available power they possessed, for the relief, deliverance, and elevation of oppressed men, permitted to shine forth from under the cloud, for the refreshment of the human race.

Yet these laws and constitutions should have long ere this felt the weight of judicial pressure, and their good or evil been made prominent to the men of America, and the breadth and depth of the stream of national justice ascertained, so that we might know the exact distance between our self-glorifications on our pompous anniversaries, and the pretended magnitude of our personal liberties, as compared with the stern and inexorable mandates of judicial decrees; or what was the difference between an abstract dogma of liberty, and a practical decision of tyranny.

Alas! said Mr. S., how vast the distance between an abstraction and a practicality! Oh! when shall we see that glorious day, when the lion and the lamb shall lie down together? that day when the law, with its mercy, shall be extended to all, when none shall be so powerful as to override its injunctions, none so *low* as to fall beneath its merciful protection; defending all in their possessions; the rich man in his castle, the poor man in his liberty, and the value of his labor, whether in the wilderness or in the city, on the highway or in the closet · let this law of liberty brace the strong man on his journey, and its precious breathings fill the lungs of the infant in the cradle.

Oh, for the glorious day when we shall have freedom for all, wages for labor, education for all, mercy to all, justice for all, and God's religion in all! It was a horrid thought, that in the nineteeth century there should be found educated men who were so weak, or so ignorant, as to suppose the title to the great, inalienable, God-given rights of life, liberty, and the pursuit of happiness, depended upon the complexion of a human being, whether white, black, brown, red, or in combinations of these, with curled or long hair, thick or thin lips; the body is the casket, the soul, the immortal mind, is the jewel. The jewels are homogeneous, the caskets may be infinitely diversified. To deny the existence of the jewel, from the casket's being more or less plain than some other we have seen (when we know the jewel is within), is not more absurd than to make a man's right to liberty depend upon the color of his skin. But, such is the raw material of apologies for gross wickedness, and the vileness of the material is never improved by its manufacture. The raw material, its manufacture, the manufacturer, and the consumer, of such strange productions, ought to be bottled and hermetically sealed, where they might be seen through a glass case as *certain lusus naturæ*, or as a calf with two tails and no head, are seen in some of our museums.

In order to understand the blessings which the new constitution of this State confers on the subject of liberty, it may not be amiss to look, for a few moments, at the past ages of the world, on the subject of slavery, and see how the men of antiquity saw and treated this terrible perversion of human rights. The ancient world, before the advent of our blessed Saviour, was filled with this awful crime. All pagan lands abounded with idolatry and slavery. But the glorious new religion, wherever it made a lodgment, amidst cruel scourgings, the fagot and the flame, the block and the cross, the dungeon and the gibbet, obtained the ascendency; and this dreadful institution fell before the mercy of the cross. From the conversion of Constantine in the fourth century, until the twelfth, Christianity fought her victorious battle with slavery, and came off conqueror, and drove it from the entire regions of continental Europe, or wherever Christianity obtained a foothold throughout Christendom. To be sure, there existed, owing to the Feudal Law, a sort of serfdom, in some countries, which was different in application and character from the chattelhood of slavery. Time fails to tell how the various devices of pope, pontiff, bishops, ecclesiastical councils, decrees of councils, of kings, diets, and parliaments, accomplished, during what is called the dark ages, this most glorious work.

But the ever-memorable year of 1492 came, forever to be reckoned the most wonderful in the history of our race since our Saviour was born—a new world was discovered by Christopher Columbus, the grandest man of his race.

The human passions burst into a mighty flame, fed by the accursed thirst of gold, discovery, and conquest. The peaceable and inoffensive red man of the islands of the Antilles was forced as a slave to do work in the fields and in the mines; and of that age of innocent red men, a whole generation found that mercy in death, which their Spanish conquerors denied them. The good Las Casas, moved by a considerate sympathy for the red man, absurdly recommended to his prince and country, to repeal slavery as to the red man who could not endure its cruelty, and in lieu, *abduct and kidnap* laborers from the burning tropics of Africa; and from 1520 this dreadful wound was opened in the side of Africa, which has continued from year to year, and from century to century, to flow on without intermission, until this very hour. For more than 300 years has Africa been despoiled of her people by the kidnappers from the nations of Christendom, until Christendom in three centuries had made it the *law of nations* to rob the men of Africa of life, liberty, and the pursuit of happiness, and made and revived the extinct law of slavery, and with armed bands marched into defenceless villages on the Senegal and Gambia, set their habitations at midnight on fire, and with pistols, swords, fetters and ropes, pursued and overtook the distracted people and bound and sent them to this continent amidst hunger, thirst, contagion, disease, and death, the survivors in the pirate's ship, and in a land of strangers, they were sold to drag out life on the plantation of the haughty, the thankless, and the cruel. By such deplorable means has this continent fought against her own prosperity.

Mr. Stewart then said he had two cases in his mind, which illustrated what all knew respecting slavery, and few whose opinions were entitled to respect would dare deny them.

Said he, lifting his head and turning to the northeast, directing all to look, and see what they could behold on the last day of November, 1620, on the confines of the Grand Banks of Newfoundland—lo! I behold one little solitary tempest-tost and weather-beaten ship, it is all that can be seen on the length and breadth of the vast intervening solitudes; from the melancholy wilds of Labrador and New England's iron-bound shores, to the western coasts of Ireland and the rock-defended Hebrides, but one lonely ship greets the eye of angels or of men, on this great thoroughfare of nations in our age. Next in moral grandeur was this ship to the great discoverer's; Columbus found a Continent; the Mayflower brought the *seed-wheat* of states and empire. That is the Mayflower, with its servants of the Living God, their wives and little ones, hastening to lay the foundations of nations in the occidental lands of the setting sun. Hear, the voice of prayer to God, for his protection, and the glorious music of praise, as it breaks into the wild tempest of the mighty deep, upon the ear of God. Here in this ship are great and good men. Justice, mercy, humanity, respect for the rights of all ; each man honored, as he was useful to himself and others ; labor-respecting, law-abiding men, constitution-making and respecting-men ; men whom no tyrant could conquer, or hardship overcome, with the high commission sealed by a spirit Divine, to establish religious and political liberty for all. This ship had the embryo-elements of all that is useful, great and grand in northern institutions ; it was the great type of goodness and wisdom, illustrated in two and a quarter centuries gone by ; it was the good genius of America.

But, look far in the southeast, and you behold on the same day in 1620, a low, rakish ship hastening from the tropics, solitary and alone, to the New World ; what is she ? She is freighted with the elements of unmixed evil ; hark ! hear those rattling chains, hear that cry of despair and wail of anguish as they die away in the unpitying distance. Listen to those shocking oaths, the crack of that flesh-cutting whip. Ah ! it is the first cargo of slaves on their way to Jamestown, Virginia. Behold the Mayflower anchored at Plymouth rock, the slave ship in James River. Each a parent, one of the prosperous, labor-honoring, law-sustaining institutions of the North ; the other the mother of slavery, idleness, lynch-law, ignorance, unpaid labor, poverty, and duelling, despotism, the ceaseless swing of the whip, and the peculiar institutions of the South. These ships are the representation of good and evil in the New World, even to our day. When shall one of those parallel lines come to an end ?

Mr. Stewart then proceeded to the definition and origin of the word slave. He cited the encyclopedia under title, slave, as authority. The word, according to Vossius, is derived from *sclavus*, the name of a Scythian people, called the Sclavoni. The Romans called slaves *servi*, from *servare*, to *keep* or *save*, being such as were not killed in battle, but were saved to work or yield money. A slave bred in a family was called *verna*, hence our word *vernacular*, or the slave's tongue.

A Roman slave being set free, took the cognomen of his master for his sur or sir-name, and his slave name for his Christian—hence, our surname means the name of the lord or sir. So curiously has slavery interwoven itself in the affairs of men, that all men are made most singularly to feel the disgrace of the institution in their paternal name. The Romans had those called *mercenarii*, who had been rich, but having become poor, sold themselves for a time.

The Greeks had those called Prodigals, who, having lost their estates by their extravagance, were sold to discharge their debts by law, for a longer or shorter time. Delinquents to the revenue, or unfaithful subtreasurers of the Roman Empire, were sent to the oar as slaves. But Tacitus describes the most remarkable slaves ("De Moribus Germanorum,") called enthusiasts, who were gamblers, who having staked and lost their money, goods and lands, finally staked their own bodies, and if they lost, the strong and the young lifted up their hands and received the fetters thereon, from the aged and weak, and were marched off forthwith to the slave market and sold by the winner as slaves for life. This was done under the code of a gambler's honor.

Those are the two kinds, among the ancients, of slavery, voluntary and involuntary. Some think slavery did not exist before the flood. But Alexander Pope thinks differently, and says:

> "Proud Nimrod first the bloody chase began,
> A mighty hunter and his prey was man."

A man has no right to sell himself, and if he had, he could

not bind his posterity. A man is not allowed to kill himself.
Blac. Book 1, C. 14 ; *Montesquieu's Spirit of Laws*, b. 15,
c. 2, and 6. Both say, if a man might be taken in war and made
a slave, this war-right of the captor could not extend to the
captives posterity. This alone would abolish slavery. The
Romans exercised the power of life and death over a slave.
So do slaveholders in the United States under certain circumstances ; if the slave refuse to work, he, the master, may, by
slave law, whip and beat him until he is dead, unless he sub-
mits to go to work ; or if a slave attempt to run away, and
the master commands him to stop, and he refuses, the master
may shoot him down, and the slave laws of more than ten
States say, *amen.* The Romans were very cruel, and had an
island in the Tiber, where by law, they might send *old, useless
and sick* slaves to starve to death or die. It said as an evidence
of slavery's hardening of the heart to human suffering, that the
elder Cato sold his superannuated slaves for any price rather
than maintain them. The Romans had slave dungeons under
ground, called " ergastula," where the slaves were worked in
chains. The same in Sicily, which country was cultivated by
slaves in chains. Eunus and Athenio excited an insurrection
of 60,000 slaves and broke up the dungeons.

But we are more immediately interested in the light in
which our English ancestors viewed these great questions of
human rights, and we have derived most of our ideas of law
and liberty from that interesting source. The case of Somerset, to be found in the 20th vol. of British State Trials, also
in Long's Reports and Burrows', is one of manifold interest.
It was justly said by that great lawyer and civilian, Mr. Hargrave, the counsel of the slave Somerset, though greatly aided
in his brief by that eminent philanthropist, Granville Sharp,
" that slavery corrupts the morals of the master by freeing
him from those restraints so necessary for the control of the
human passions, so beneficial in promoting the practice

and confirming the habit of virtue." It is often dangerous to the master, as exciting implacable resentments on the part of the slave.

Slavery communicates all the afflictions of life to its victim without leaving scarce any of the pleasures; it depresses the excellence of the slave's nature, by denying to the slave the ordinary means of improvement and elevation in the social scale of existence; it brings forth the gross, malignant, cruel, mean, deceitful and hypocritical portions of human nature, without a counterpoise or a power of suppression. The slave is always the natural and implacable enemy of the State; he owes it nothing but deadly hate.

Instead of the Constitution and the laws being his shield and his inheritance, they are employed to strip him of his natural rights, of life, liberty and the pursuit of happiness, existing antecedent to all human compacts; and what should be employed for his protection and defence in the shape of law, is used for his prostration and destruction. It is the element of constant fear to the family and the State, and is therefore real weakness to the State from the constant apprehension from insurrection at home, or invasion from abroad, when it is always expected the slave will range himself in the ranks of the invader of the land. The slave has no country, no real home for which he will fight. Judge of the surprise of General Lafayette, when on the first day of being introduced to the American Congress in Philadelphia, in the summer of 1777, he listened to the extraordinary request of South Carolina to be released from raising and equipping the quota of troops designed by Congress to be raised by that State as her proportion in the eventful struggle of the Revolution, on the ground that if she spared that number of troops from the State, it was feared that there might be a servile insurrection; that it was necessary the troops should remain at home to restrain a domestic enemy in her own bosom. If all the States had been under the weight of slavery like South Carolina, our Independence could never have been achieved. Such States as South Carolina may bluster and threaten their brethren in time of peace with nullification and revolution, but when war comes, her power to act out of her own territory will be in the inverse ratio of the noise and threats she made in time of peace. The enemy of her own household will furnish a good market, not only for her capabilities but her courage. If the home market is the best one, she will find one at her own door, as ample as her productions may be abundant.

In the late war, about midsummer of 1814, this nation was overwhelmed with shame, grief and astonishment, at the capture and sack of the city of Washington, by a body of British troops, soldiers, sailors, and marines.

The public authorities had sufficient notice of the enemy's intention, the militia of the three cities of the District, and of the surrounding counties in the adjacent portions of the old States of Virginia and Maryland, could have driven the British force into the sea, had not a report been universally circulated on the morning of the battle, and on the battle-ground at Bladensburgh, that the slaves of the District and of the adjacent counties, from which the militia were drawn for the defence of Washington, were to rise that day in insurrection in the absence of their masters. The moment the British approached our troops, President Madison, with the Secretaries of the Departments, fled from position to position, abandoning, as all who know the ground may see, one favorable place after another, and finally retreated eight miles, from Bladensburgh to Washington, and at last the retreat became a general rout; each man having his mind on the danger he feared in his own house or plantation from the insurrection of his slaves, rather than the immediate work of defending the Capitol of the nation. This is a perfect solution of that disgraceful affair. It was the natural consequence which the weakness of a servile population creates, and the fear in a day of adversity which it will inspire.

Mr. S., said he learned the cause of our disaster in 1818, while going over the ground of this disgraceful retreat, with a general, who was a brigadier on that mortifying day, and who assigned the above reasons to him as the cause of this most shameful result.

John Locke declared a right to preserve life is inalienable; that freedom from the exercise of arbitrary power is essential for the exercise of this right.

In the sixth year of the reign of Edward III., 1334, a law was enacted declaring that all idle vagabonds should be made slaves, fed on bread and water or small drink, and *refuse meat*, and should wear an iron ring around their necks and legs, and should be compelled by beating, chaining and otherwise, to perform the work assigned, were it never so vile; the spirit of the English nation could not brook this, as applied to the most abandoned rogues, and repealed the law in two years after its enactment. But nothing places the judiciary of England on higher ground, than its patient work in extirpating villenage from England. It was an institution connected with the feudal system, and the Norman Conquest of 1060, and the other conquests obtained in previous ages, and was nearly allied to slavery, in everything but the name, so that it is supposed that at one period, there were not less than three quarters of the population of the kingdom, who were either villeins regardant, or villeins in gross. The dishonor of such a state of things has been so deeply felt by thousands, who are descendants of these bondmen in England, and who now rank high in the scale of society, that there is rather a desire to conceal than reveal the odious state in which our ancestors existed; therefore, David Hume and Sir William Blackstone are very niggardly in dealing out information on an infamous and obsolete institution, so humiliating to our ancestors, and humbling to their descendants.

But, to understand the terrible hardships endured and suffered by our ancestors, for many generations, and the glorious way of their deliverance by the judges of England, may furnish us with valuable deductions, which may be applied to solve any difficulty growing out of the causes under consideration, by learning what use a court may make of *law* to establish justice.

A villein in blood and by tenure was one whom the lord might whip and imprison. The villein could acquire no property except for the lord. "*Quidquid acquiritur servo, acquiritur domino.*" A villein regardant passed with the land of his lord, on which he lived as a kind of property like the trees, but might be severed and sold when the lord pleased.—*Co. Littleton*, 117 *a*. If he was a villein in gross, he was an hereditament, or chattel real, according to the lord's interest, being descendable to the heir, when the lord was absolute owner of the soil, and the executor, when the lord was possessor for only a term of years. The common law held, if both parents were villeins, or the father only, the issue were villeins. The child at common law followed the condition of the father, *Partus sequitur patrem ;* while the civil law held, *Partus sequitur ventrem.* Therefore, it was a departure from all principle, for the slaveholders of the United States, who, if they inherited anything from England, inherited the common law, to substitute the principle of the civil law, because they could make more money by it, and say the child in slavery should follow the condition of the mother, when the common law said it should follow the father! But why reason on a subject, when brute force and selfishness stand in the place of right reason and truth ? Had the doctrine of the common law been followed, slavery, from its *mulattoism*, a significancy of the times, would have been in its *last quarter*. The object of drawing this all but obsolete learning from past centuries, was not to make a public parade for the sake of its strangeness; but to show in the great struggle, in past ages, between slavery and liberty, how the judiciary of England conducted itself in those encounters between the powers of light and darkness.

The Courts of Law in the British Isles, from the Conquest down, employed every intendment of humanity, every device, every fiction, in behalf of the unfortunate serf. One rule was, for the court always to presume in favor of liberty; but in some thirteen States of our Union, if a man is of African descent, he is presumed a slave, until the victim proves a negative. In England, the *onus probandi* lay on him who asserted slavery or villenage. If a villein prosecuted a writ of *Homine Replegiando* against his lord, on the trial the lord had to prove affirmatively that the plaintiff was his villein, and the villein, though the plaintiff, might stand still in court till that was done by the defendent. The lord's remedy for a fugitive villein was the writ *Nativo Habendo*, or *Neifty*. If the lord seized the villein by his writ of *Nativo Habendo*, the villein procured the writ of *Homine Replegiando*, or *Libertate Probanda*.

By the writ of *Nativo Habendo*, the master asserted slavery, and if the master was *once nonsuited*, he could never sue the serf again, and the villein might plead the record of nonsuit as a perpetual bar. Not so, if the villein was nonsuited on the writ of *Homine Replegiando*, or *Libertate Probanda*. He might sue again for his liberty, and the record of nonsuit, if made ten times or more against him, could never be pleaded or used against him. The slightest mistake on the part of the lord, or accident, was laid hold of by the court to defeat the recovery of the lord.—*Somerset's Case*, 20th vol. of Haswell's State Trials. So this honorable court of New Jersey should do, under the new constitution of this

State—the constitution adopted by the people in 1844. This court, in accordance with the noble example of England's judiciary, should make every intendment in behalf of your bondmen, as between the selfish and cruel demand of slavery and the ceaseless cry of liberty. Give the slave the benefit of every sensible doubt, which may cloud the mind of this honorable court.

Sueing, or being sued by a villein, freed him. The lord's granting him an imparlance, manumitted him, or asking an imparlance of the villein did the same. Almost the last case of villenage reported, was near the year 1600, on the accession of James I. Crouch's case is reported in Dyer. All of these obstructions thrown in the way of this sort of slavery, are most interesting legal relics of servitude, showing the metaphysical dress in which it was clothed by our subtle and ingenious ancestors. These were patterns of extinct fashions of opinions, now only to be found in the ponderous tomes of antiquity, garnered up in the library of the legal antiquarian; as the visors, steel and brass armor, of the 10th century, disclose to us the mode and appearance of the knights on the field of battle in the days of chivalry.

To establish villenage, the villein must be proved such by two other male villeins, *ex eodem stirpe*, from the same stock, or the villein might confess in open court, being a court of record, that he was one. The female villein was not allowed her testimony to prove a man a villein. A villein was called *nativus*, as well as *villanus*, from the lord's villa, *nativus* from being found on the soil—a native. The lord, on declaring on a writ *Nativo Habendo*, had to bring his two witnesses with him at the same instant he declared, and if he did not, the villein went forever free. A man might plead bastardy, in himself, father, grandfather or ancestors, and if the plea be true, that, alone, manumitted the villein, for the *filius nullius est filius populi*. For if there was a link of illegitimacy, it set the line of descendants from the bastard free, because the lord could not show that he was the son of his bondmen in particular.

Another plea of the villein was called *adventiff* by the Norman French Law, showing that a person was born off from the *manor*, and if true, it set the man and his descendants free.

Sir Thomas Grantham, about the year 1684, bought a monster in the East Indies, and brought him to England as a show. The monster had, growing on his breast, the entire parts of a child, except its head. The monster being carried through the kingdom as a show, was baptized, and he brought a writ of *Homine Replegiando* against his master, and was set free.

I have done with villenage in England—such in a dark age was the view which learned jurists and judges took of this important matter. The judiciary in many countries have been, at different periods of civilization, the last branch of human government, to feel the force of popular opinion, in behalf of liberty, or employ its power in accelerating the march of freedom, or the overthrow of strongholds of fortified oppression. It is not a matter of complaint that the judiciary is the *hold-back power* of the State, or conservative in its character, but with all that, it has a high mission to discharge on the part of liberty. And the English judiciary have shown the world during those dark ages what they understood to be contained in their commissions, touching England's bondmen, even, under the iron rule of the haughty Norman and his imperious descendants, who, by rights of conquest, and by the subserviency of supple parliaments connected with the agency of the Feudal System, had reduced four-fifths of the inhabitants of England to the condition of villeins regardant, and villeins in gross, attached to the soil, or the person of some grandee of the realm, as slaves, whom their lord might scourge, sell, or transfer with the soil, or at will.

The judiciary of England became the Temple of Mercy to which these unfortunate bondmen cast their imploring eyes for relief through a succession of five cruel centuries, during eighteen generations of men. The courts of English·law during this long period, employed all the subtleties, fictions, and presumptions, in which the English Law abounds, in behalf of the liberty of these grossly injured men, so that at last, the sublime moral spectacle was presented to this world, of many unrepealed statutes, and the common law still in full force in favor of villenage, while the bloody useless fetters hung on the tyrant's dungeon walls, but the last bondman of the three-fourths of the population of a mighty kingdom was enfranchised from captivity, by force of England's glorious judiciary alone. The king, and iron-mailed barons, the land-owners, and man-holders, were foiled, and their prey taken from their power by the resolution of the judges, who, being determined, did administer *justice through the law.*

Montesquieu says that Aristotle, in reasoning to sustain slavery as derived from war, cites authorities from barbarous ages, and appears in this matter as unphilosophical as he does in the nature of the thing. The war-power to be the source of a right, when the war is prosecuted for no other motive except the value of the captive, is as rational as to give the robber title to his spoil, because he had the courage to take it—making a crime the most bold and daring, the parent of a civil right. Behold bleeding Africa, for three hundred years her wounded side has flowed, and yet flows on, unstaunched by the humanity of the nations. Behold this accursed crime which has crawled up with brutal impudence, and enthroned itself as one amongst the laws of nations. *Laws of nations!* What was this law of nations? That Christendom had a common right to plunder, burn, murder, enslave irredeemably, and make property of the inhabitants of that ill-fated continent, in and through all coming generations of their posterity. A *law of nations!* that all law, justice, mercy, humanity, should be suspended, as to one quarter of the globe; a *law of nations*, that piracy, murder, fraud, arson, kidnapping, ravishment and stealing, should be considered lawful as an injunction of the law of nations, to be honored and obeyed. A law of nations directly at war with every other law constituting that code; a law of nations, striking justice down, and sending it into eternal banishment from the world, subverting the decalogue of God, blaspheming Omnipotence, brandishing the powers of perdition in the face of the Allseeing, calling this bold defiance of the Almighty, the law of nations! Out upon such infinite perversion, such inexpressible criminality. Russia, Prussia, Holland, Austria, England, France, Sardinia and the United States, in the last forty years, as it regards themselves, by treaty and legislation, have abolished their respective portions in this frightful law of nations, while Spain, Portugal and Brazil, three of the basest kingdoms of earth, are now retrograding into the darkness of barbarism and infamy, and without competition are now almost the exclusive proprietors of this law of nations and its abounding criminality. Look at Spain three hundred and fifty-three years ago, as she stood on the day of Columbus' discovery, head and shoulders above the powers of Europe. Conquest, avarice, slavery and idleness, which she introduced to the new world, re-acted on her, and in our day, she has been stripped of her mines, her provinces, viceroyalties, kingdoms and one half of a continent, and is now reduced to the island of Cuba, with its crimes of flowing blood, slavery, idleness and avarice; these relatives have been punished in so signal a manner, in the case of Spain, by Him who rules the destinies of nations, that to deny it, is a proof that our ignorance is only surpassed by our infidelity.

The court will pardon me in these remarks, which in the first instance may appear remote from this question, yet when we consider the character of the human mind, they will all be found to bear on the great question in the Constitution of this State. What do we mean by liberty and independence? Infinitely absurd to say, a man has power even in himself, by contract, to dispose of his own liberty and all the rights he possesses. Society has claims on him, his wife, his children, and his God, which he cannot cancel by selling himself to another. Yes, coming generations have a voice in the question. He has no more right to sell his body than he has to commit suicide, for, by so doing, he passes from manhood to thing, or chattelhood, and becomes a piece of breathing property. The great rights of manhood are not given to us by our Creator, to give, sell, and barter away. The powers of life, liberty, and the pursuit of happiness, cannot be resigned to a power inferior, to that of the one, from *whom* they have been received.

As to the consideration that might be given for those God-inherited rights, described in your Constitution, as inalienable, who is rich enough to buy them, who is able to make title to them? Suppose that some Crœsus owned this continent, and the mines of Golconda, and should offer them to me to become his slave, according to the laws of South Carolina and Louisiana; at the same instant, he executes for the consideration of my person, a deed of the continent and mines to me, and I execute to him a deed of my body. The purchaser of me, by the operation of the slave laws, instantly becomes repossessed of what passed to me by grant, under the maxim that the slave and all he hath, or may find or acquire, belongeth to the master, therefore, I the slave would say, that the consideration having failed, and by operation of law, my master having become reseized of his continent and mines, I am free again. Thus, it would be found impossible to make a bargain resting upon equity, for the sale of one's person, as the whole subject revolves in a circle of never-ending absurdities, justice leaving the parties where it found them : man with equal success having attempted to quadrate the circle, create perpetual motion, and make a contract for the sale of a man, by his own agreement, on consideration of value for value received by the slave upon the principles of slaveholding law ! If a man could not perform the act of making himself a slave, how could another do it for him, or a State or a government, without doing an act repugnant to that law of nature spoken of in the first article of your new Constitution?

When I applied for these writs of *Habeas Corpus* some days since, to one branch of this court, it was remarked by one member of the court, that this case would require great consideration from its effect on the towns of this State, as it might subject said towns to the maintenance of worn-out, aged and infirm slaves, in the shape of paupers. That contingency is possible, but forms no ground against awarding to the bondmen that constitutional justice, so long withheld by the consent of these towns, as well as the avaricious masters. It was argued in the Somerset case by Mr. Dunning, the counsel of the claimant of Somerset, that if this slave was set free by the judgment of the court, there were then at large fourteen thousand slaves in England, belonging to gentlemen in the West Indies, who, for their own convenience, had brought them to England, and valuing them at £50 per head, they would amount to £700,000, or $3,500,000. What was the memorable reply of Lord Mansfield ? It was, " that a man's natural relations go with him *everywhere*, his municipal, to the bounds of the country of his *abode*." And in answer to the suggestion of a loss by the proprietors of the 14,000 negro slaves in England, said Lord Mansfield, "*we have no authority to regulate the conditions on which law shall operate.* We cannot direct the law, the law must direct us."

So, the *argumentum ab inconvenienti* should not apply in this case. If these slaves have been worn out by the consent of the public, if that public have folded their arms in silence, and witnessed the robbery of these men, from year to year, of their earnings (which might have supported them in the evening of life), it is right that the same public should support them when they can toil no more in the enjoyment of their just liberty. For it is always dangerous to men to see liberty struck down in others, and because they do not taste its bitterness personally, passively to look on without resistance. It will sooner or later strike back on themselves. That man is not worthy of liberty, who will not fly to the rescue of his brother when he sees his freedom struck down or assailed. Our liberties are always invaded when the humblest individual is deprived of his, without our making all the resistance within our power.

At the time of the argument of the Somerset case, in 1771, the world was full of slavery, especially the West Indies, and the colonies of this continent—it was tolerated in all. But behold what may be done by the indomitable perseverance of one man, if that man be Granville Sharpe. He was a gentleman of small means, but of a great heart, and had for some time made the study of human rights a subject of great consideration. He had read, thought, and written in their behalf, and was the prosecutor who interested himself for Somerset, the slave of one William Stuart, a West India planter, and prepared much of the brief of Mr. Hargrave, and obtained the writ of *habeas corpus*, returnable in the Court of King's Bench, at his own expense. The court heard the argument patiently the live-long day, and decided against the slave, on the authority of a case in 1749, in Lord Hardwick's and Lord Talbot's time. Nothing discouraged

Granville Sharpe ; at the next term he brought up Somerset a second time, and the question was so important, that the court heard the argument a second time, and decided, as before, against the slave. Poor Granville Sharpe, still contended that a slave " could not breathe in England," and having spent some months in deep study, upon the law of England, though a layman, he brought up Somerset for the third time before the Court of King's Bench, which had Lord Mansfield for its chief, who did not meet poor Sharpe and his counsel with a rebuke for his unconquerable fanaticism and obstinacy, nor did the court throw down the common impediment to the march of mind and further consideration, by saying " *res adjudicata*," " *res adjudicata !*" No ! where human liberty was concerned, or the great rights of self-ownership staked upon human reasoning and judicial determination, Lord Mansfield was not in haste to say " we have decided against human nature." The cause was argued a third time for a day in Westminster Hall, and Granville Sharpe had, since the last argument, descended into the deepest wells of English liberty and brought up a draught of the waters of life, liberty, mercy, and law, so pure, that when it was commended to the lips of the judges, they were made wise, the scales fell from their eyes, and they saw in its length and breadth the mighty truth beaming on the forehead of justice herself—" that slaves cannot breathe in England," and the light of that day has shone on with increasing strength and beauty, until we can now say, that the sun which never sets upon the realms of the British Empire, beholds in his circuit through the heavens, no slave to crouch beneath her vast illimitable power.

But oh ! what shall we say of the sublime humanity of Lord Mansfield and his compeers, who were not afraid to confess they had been wrong, and had the magnanimity to say it before a slaveholding age ? This day saw the longest stride which British greatness ever took on the highway of human glory.

Would to heaven that all courts might imitate the illustrious example in administering justice in the sublime humility, which dignified the court and exalted our kind, as in the case of Somerset! The great principles established in the Somerset case awakened the philanthropy of England, and put forth its strength in 1783, 1788, 1792, 1796, 1797, and finally, in 1806, was successful in the abolition of the African slave trade by Parliament. Wilberforce, Pitt, and Fox were foiled again and again, in Parliament, the theatre of their eloquence, and seat of their power, but justice finally prevailed. This was the first great blow struck for the man of Africa, in three hundred years, from the beginning of his American and West Indian enslavement. But from that day, the vindication of his rights has been *onward*. Congress, in 1774, recommended the *ceasing* of the African slave trade in December, 1775, but it was not abolished until January, 1808, by a law passed the March before, in 1807. Three acts of Congress were passed in 1814, 1820, and in 1824, increasing the penalties against transgressors, until it finally declared that all who were engaged therein, were pirates, and subject to the pirate's doom. An act of Congress passed in 1787, declared that involuntary servitude, or slavery, should never exist in the Northwestern Territory, comprising the present States of Ohio, Indiana, Illinois, Michigan, and the territories of Wisconsin and Iowa. These early acts of national legislation show which way the mind of the nation pointed at *this* time.

A slave is a rational human being, endowed with volition and understanding, like the rest of mankind, and whatever he lawfully acquires and gains possession of, by finding or otherwise, is the acquirement and possession of his master. —4 *Dessaus.* 266; 1 *Stewart Rep.* 320. Slaves cannot contract matrimony; their earnings and their children belong to the master.—*Slave Law.* Indians are held as slaves in New Jersey.—*Halstead's Rep.* 374.

Behold the shameful injustice of the Law of Slavery.

If it be found by a jury on inspection, that the person claimed to be a slave is white, the claimant must prove him a slave or he will go free; but if the jury find the person to be of African descent, the law of slavery presumes the person a slave, by whomsoever he may be claimed, and the burden is thrown on the alleged slave to prove a negative—that he is *not* a slave.— *Wheeler's Law of Slavery*, 22. The owner of a female slave may give her to one person, and the children she may thereafter have to another !—*Law of Slavery*, 2. A slave cannot be a witness before any court or jury in the land, against a free white for the greatest injustice. This is one of its most horrible features.

Look to the case of an alien white child. Suppose her to be the daughter of parents of the lowest class of those who migrate from Ireland to America, and that these parents should die on their passage over the Atlantic, leaving to the mercy of New Jersey laws, and the good people of Perth Amboy, their daughter, twelve years old, who cannot read or write, barefooted, destitute and friendless. Under your laws, the overseers of the poor bind her out, to the mayor of Trenton; she has lived with this rich, popular and influential citizen but one little month, when by violence, she is dishonored by her master, the mayor. Is he safe from the retributions of justice? Is she deprived of her oath? No. She comes, friendless and lonely, and knocks at the door of your grand-jury room. Humble and feeble as is that knock, it is quickly heard by the acuteness of humanity's ear. She enters the vestibule of the great temple of justice, and immediately the majesty of the entire law of the land, not only of New Jersey, but of this vast empire, stands in its mighty invisibility around for her protection, ready to be revealed in its power. She is invited, on oath, to tell the story of her wrongs, the indignant grand-jurors listen and believe, and find a bill against the mayor; she goes and comes under the law's broad shield. This haughty man is found by the officers of the law, is arrested by its power, and brought before a court to plead to this indictment. He is tried; a second time, she, the friendless, comes and tells the tale of her dishonor; confiding justice, humanity, loving and honoring men believe her story; he is convicted and attempts to fly the power of the State and Union, which is by that child's oath already set in motion, and will prevail against money and mobs of rescue, all of these cannot save the big criminal from the vengeance of the law; to the penitentiary for ten long years, he must and does go; yes, the merciful majesty of the law shines gloriously on the head of the friendless foreigner. This is being born free and independent by the law of nature, under your Constitution.

But not so of the poor injured slave, man or woman, native born though they be, however cruel or terrible the wrong inflicted on them, by their owner or other free man, the slave is not to be heard to tell his or her story, however true, before any human tribunal in the land against a free white person. Is this being free and independent by the law of nature? Is this possessing the safety and happiness described in the first article of the new Constitution, which your organic law declares to be a portion of all, of woman born? Slavery imports perpetual obligation to serve another! Does that look like being free and independent?

Slavery, is so abhorrent to all justice and mercy, that all the intendments of law and justice are opposed to it; so that the legal writers of slave countries say that it can only exist by force of positive law. The *lex scripta* must be its foundation, and that I think you no longer have. The *lex scripta* must be the source of all of that mischievous power, which

ouo human being can exercise over another, by making a
fellow-being his slave, his chattel. The foundation of slavery
which sprang up in our colonies, had, as a general rule,
nothing but the barbarous custom of a few inhuman planters,
in its origin, which custom was one within legal memory,
and ran not back to that unsurveyed point of antiquity, transcending all human memory, where its source was hidden in
the night of by-gone ages. It has not that common law
authority for its support, which was supposed to be handed
down from generation to generation, in the libraries of
judges and lawyers, as copies, as some conjecture, of obsolete, worn-out and extinct statutes. As the soul survives
the body, so it is supposed these customs called common law,
are the souls or spirits of departed statutes, the tombstones
and graves of which can no longer be found. *Cineres peri-
erunt.* But their imperishable souls still remain to guide
and direct us on the journey of life, and as far as they speak in
the language of authority over this land, they forbid in trumpet tongues, the existence of this vile institution of slavery.

Institution of slavery! Institution of horse-stealing, institution of gambling, and the institutions of highwaymen,
sound equally sensible, to a just and philosophical thinker.
But slavery is within the memory of men, so far as its advent
to the new world is concerned. We track it from the
middle passage to this hour, from its first unholy foot-print
at Jamestown to the last ones made this day by those now
held in New Jersey; and if the court finds, existing, a well-
grounded doubt as to the authority for this institution which
is trying to nestle down on our soil, and is taking rank with
your scientific, religious and agricultural institutions, then
give humanity the advantage of that doubt, and put the system to death. As between strength and weakness, power
and imbecility, if a strong doubt arise in the minds of the
judges, the mercy of the law says, decide in favor of imbe-

cility and weakness; "those who are ready to perish," let their blessing come upon you. Every intendment is in favor of natural rights, until the contrary doth most manifestly appear. If the new Constitution has seriously drawn in question the villainies and crimes of this complicated institution of wrong, then this court, acting within the spirit and scope of American institutions, are bound to give the slave the benefit of that doubt and set him free. A solid doubt should secure emancipation. But thanks to the freemen of New Jersey, the court is not obliged to look through clouds to see the clear sky of Liberty beyond, for its Constitution, in its first section, asserts in the strongest form of the English language, the explicit principles put forth in the Declaration of Independence, when our country was introduced into the family of nations, by which we declared the great self-evident truth to be, that all men were created free and equal, and possessed of certain inalienable rights, among which are life, liberty, and the pursuit of happiness, which is the proposition of the Constitution of New Jersey, expressed so distinctly, that *cavil* itself looks on in humble silence, and hangs his head in mute despair. For these great man-rights, as I have said, there is no buyer, no seller, no market. They are a trust confided to man by his Maker, in order to place him at the head of the created life, and give him dominion over it; and his rank he can never sell, lose, or forfeit so as to take his station as property among the quadrupeds and animals. In the fall of Adam man never fell so low as the slaveholder would have wished; for, according to the law of slavery, the poor slave in the disastrous fall of the first transgression "which brought death into the world, and all our woes," fell out of his manhood into chattelhood, and fell on till he lost his wife, his children, and in the amazing descent as he further fell, he lost all his property, and all he should thereafter acquire; and as he further fell, he himself became property, and brought not up on solid ground, until he could say to the neighing horse, on the one hand, "thou art, as property, my brother," and to the lowing ox, on the other, "thou art my equal, my peer." Such is the slaveholder's construction of the fall, but this is one of man's pit-falls, and not one of his Maker's.

Mr. S. said he had an argument, which the court might regard as novel, which he wished to urge—that each and every branch of our government, state or national, were under a most solemn covenant with one of the great nations of the earth, to use our best endeavors to abolish slavery, in every part of our country; and we have been living under the weight of that solemn and disregarded undertaking for the last thirty years. I understand a treaty made by the treaty-making power to be the solemn and paramount law of this land, and if I am right in its construction, the duty is imposed upon our nation, and I may well urge it even upon the judiciary of this State, as a coördinate branch of the government, to employ all the power it constitutionally may possess, by its decision, to fulfill this engagement of the nation.

The article to which I refer, is the 10th article of the treaty of Ghent, of the 24th December, 1814, made by the United States of America on the one side, and his Britannic Majesty on the other. Lest there should be some attempt to cavil, and pretend this article of the treaty had reference to the African slave trade, I may be allowed to say there is not one word in the treaty, except in the 10th article, which touches or relates to the subject of slavery, and it is an engagement relating to slavery as to the traffic generally in the two countries, for each had abolished the African slave trade under the most tremendous penalties long before 1814; therefore the treaty referred to slavery generally in the two countries. The words of the 10th section of the treaty of Ghent are as follows:

"10th Article. Whereas the *traffic* in slaves is irreconcilable with the principles of humanity and justice, and whereas both his Majesty, and the United States are desirous of contributing their efforts to promote its entire abolition, it is hereby agreed that both the contracting parties shall use their best endeavors to accomplish so desirable an object.

"*Signed* 24*th December*, 1814.

("Done in triplicate.)

"GAMBIER,
HENRY GOULBURN,
WILLIAM ADAMS,
JOHN QUINCY ADAMS,
J. A. BAYARD,
H. CLAY,
JONATHAN RUSSEL,
ALBERT GALLATIN."

United States Laws, 1st vol., 699.

This treaty, so long dishonored on our part, has been most faithfully respected and obeyed on the part of Great Britain. They immediately began to adopt means for the subversion of slavery as a system in the West Indies. To be sure the violence, disorder, and lynch law of the slaveholders of the West Indies defeated the kindness, and deferred the approaching justice of the English nation for some years. It was astonishing to see the impudence of the West India planters threatening dismemberment of the empire, revolution, and treason, as often as the mother country originated a measure in any degree preparatory to emancipation. These contumacious slaveholders did all in their power to frighten England from her high purposes, 1st, by asserting that the slaves would cut their master's throats if emancipated; 2d, that the slaves were so brutified, they would all starve to death, and die from laziness, and could not take care of themselves; that the slaves were thieves and drunkards; that the whites would have to abandon the island if they were set free, and lose their estates; in fact that slaves were not men, and had no souls. Amalgamation, house-burning, and universal desolation would be the first fruits of such procedure.

The Moravian, Baptist and Methodist ministers exposed themselves to great rage from the slaveholders in attempting, as Christian ministers and good subjects, to preach the Gospel to the slaves, and aid them in information, and in furthering the objects of the mother country. Baptist and Methodist meeting-houses or churches were torn down and burnt, and these blessed ministers were in constant peril of losing their lives, and were occasionally imprisoned and banished from their homes and families. In fact, everything, which is said against emancipation and abolitionists in Mississippi, Georgia, and South Carolina, was said in the British West Indies thousands and thousands of times by the press, resolutions of public meetings, the Island Legislatures, and the voice of man, against emancipation and British abolitionists; but on the passage of the great Reform Bill of England in 1833, about 500,000 new law-makers or voters were added to the old parliamentary constituency of England, and when this fresh stream of popular power flowed, it rose so high, that on the bosom of its flood it carried into the new Parliament men deeply sympathizing with the great principles of justice, and one of their first act of legislation was to declare slavery abolished in the West Indies, paying £20,000,000 sterling to the slaveholders, and giving them, the masters, six years more the service of the slaves, so that emancipation would not take place until the first of August, 1840. This apprenticeship system, regulated by a most complicated law, with especial justices to stand between master and apprentice, proved, if possible, more bitter than slavery itself. Nothing could have been more unfortunate, or fraught with greater injustice to the colored people.

The master's avarice and cruelty arose in proportion to the

shortness of the time that he could exercise his despotism. The special justices intended for the slave apprentice's friend, eat sumptuous dinners with the planter, and decided controversies in his favor. The humanity of the government in the apprenticeship system, was entirely defeated by the greediness, cruelty, and avarice of masters. The horrid flogging, the treadmills, and other instruments of slaveholding vengeance and torture were in full play during the probationary state. The mother country had been overreached in paying twenty millions of pounds sterling to see the objects of their solicitude so shamefully treated. The mistake of the home government was in supposing it possible to ingraft a system of apprenticeship, education, and a preparation for freedom, on the old tree of slavery, and in having confidence in those brutal, cruel, and avaricious slaveholders, who, with their twenty millions of pounds, and six years of labor, only hated the poor slave the more as his liberty advanced day by day in his chains. Finally, in January or February, 1838, the British minister wrote to the governors of these islands, requesting them in the coming spring and summer to convoke those insular legislatures and ask them forthwith to abolish the remaining two years of the apprenticeship system, if the islands wished for the future good will of the slaves, or in fact, the protection of the parent country, in case of insurrection. This stringent measure brought the obstinate slaveholders to their senses. The West India Island parliaments were convoked, and the final acts of emancipation passed, to take effect simultaneously on the 1st of August, 1838, except the island of Antigua, whose parliament, with great good sense, abolished slavery and apprenticeship both, in 1834, in an island of 30,000 blacks, and 5,000 whites—six to one. Great kindness, love, education and prosperity followed this island. However, the eventful first of August, 1838, at last came, and instead of blood and insurrection, as prophesied by

the selfish and cowardly, the blacks throughout the British
West Indies, to the number of 800,000 human beings, who
had been slaves, met in the evening of the 31st of July, 1838,
and there continued in a solemn and quiet manner until the
moment of midnight came, when the bells of the churches of
the British West Indies struck and played from island to
island, while cannon were roaring throughout the great
Antilles—they were the glorious peals of freedom, the joyful
freed men raising notes of thanksgiving and praise to heaven
from bended knees, falling with hysteric transports of wild
and delirious joy, into each other's arms. No mortal tongue
or pen can describe the overflowing ecstasies of these naked
and scourged bondmen, now standing up as British freemen—
slaves no more.. They sung, they cried, they danced, and
thus in wild and rapturous joy they passed the terrific bourne
so long wished for by them—so long feared and dreaded by
the guilty white man. But the first drop of the white man's.
blood has not yet been shed, by this deeply abused and
emancipated people. Many thousands of these long-injured
people are now proprietors of two, four, eight, ten, and fifteen
acres of land. Their wives and children stay at home and
cultivate and raise enough for the family's food and clothing;
the father works, or some older sons, on some neighboring
plantation—the money he or they earn pays for land :—his
wife and children create subsistence from his own fields.
Hundreds of schools and many churches, have sprung up for
the adults and colored children. Once the planters raised
nothing but sugar, molasses, rum, and coffee, and bought all
their provisions from abroad ; now the laborers' families raise
provisions on the island. Less sugar, to be sure, is raised,
but two-thirds of the sugar goes, as a money question, further
now than all did in slavery, as more than one-third, sometimes one-half, was spent for provisions which are now raised
at home. So they have gone on with remarkable prosperity,

both master and freedmen. The plantations have risen, some twenty, thirty, and others forty and fifty, and many sixty and sixty-five per cent. above their slave value. In fact, the English government now feel that they acted unwisely in giving the twenty millions of pounds; for the lands alone of those slave islands are now worth more than slaves and land both were in 1830. Indeed it is a matter of regret now, that the slave had not received what England had to give.

On the same day, the fetters fell from the slaves of South Africa; from the Cape of Good Hope, six hundred miles north, inland, the institution expired on the last acre of British supremacy—from ocean to ocean. On the 1st of April, 1844, England, by her East India Company's mighty powers, struck slavery dead through her Oriental regions—twelve millions of slaves, serfs, and caste—crushed beings, lifted their unfettered hands to God to bless his power, and that of England's, which, amidst a population of one hundred millions of Eastern Indies, left them in chains to pine no more. Has not England most gloriously, in thirty years, from 1814 to 1844, performed her high and glorious undertaking with these United States in the treaty of Ghent? Has she not blotted out that great dishonor of our race from her vast dominions? What have we done to fulfill our part of this great national covenant? When the Abolitionists presented from year to year, petitions clothed in dignified and respectful language, praying Congress to abolish the internal slave trade between the States, in the Territory of Florida, and in the District of Columbia, signed by tens of thousands of names, unread, undebated, unprinted, and unconsidered, they were laid upon the table. This being esteemed too a great a privilege for humanity, during three years, these petitions, by a rule of the House of Representatives, were forbidden a reception by the House. The Abolitionists, for endeavoring to fulfill the paramount law of the land, the 10th article of the treaty, were defamed in Congress and out, their names cast out as fanatical and incendiary, they were mobbed by the countenance of men in high places, their churches destroyed, their halls burnt, and their people imprisoned and murdered! If slavery not only forbids and restrains a nation from performing its most solemn treaties, but violates them, and thus endangers the peace, prosperity, and happiness of the whole people, can it be doubted that it contravenes the 1st article of your Constitution, which assures us that man has the right of " acquiring, possessing, and protecting property, and of pursuing, and of obtaining *safety and happiness.*"

Can *safety*, *property*, and happiness be maintained by men or nations who violate faith, who are truce-breakers? Is not that *slavery* which hazards the peace of the nation by refusing obedience to the highest law of individual and national preservation, something that is contrary to the great law of *nature?* Every branch of our government — legislative, judicial or executive—should have lent every encouragement and aid in their power to the removal of this cancer, battening with its roots in the jugulars of the Republic. But instead of presidential and gubernatorial messages urging Congress and the State legislatures, under this standing paramount treaty-law, to do all in their power within their respective jurisdictions to abolish slavery, slavery has mounted the highest places of power, and has rescinded and annulled the treaty, and compelled presidents and governors, by messages and inaugurals to forewarn the legislative assemblies and the people to violate this treaty, and turn their entire power and legislative action against those who had petitioned for the abolition of slavery. Is not this high treason against the State and man's best interests? Has not slavery caused these high dignitaries to commit official perjury? And is not such a terrible institution hostile to man, his safety and happiness as a man and as a citizen, and is it not within the inhibition of the first section of your Constitution, and does it not violate that freedom and independence conferred upon him by the law of nature, and does it not stand between you and the enjoyment of the first article?

What is that law of nature by which all men are made free and independent? Allow me to define it as I understand it. The law of nature is that great omnipotent law of God, ever in full force amidst the busy hum of thousands in your emporium, or in the solitudes of the wilderness, on the sea, or on the land; it follows man down into the mines of the earth, it ascends with him to the Chimborazo's top; it has no latitude, no longitude, no length, no breadth; it is truth, and is as earnest in its pleadings, amidst the inhospitalities of polar cold, as in the boundless prodigalities of the burning tropics; it is the everlasting justice and mercy of the Eternal; it is the great imprint of God upon man, which can never be counterfeited, erased, or repealed; it is so immutable that it never changes, *man cannot* repeal it; it is a part of each human being's inheritance, which, without crime he can never spend or squander; it abides with him, though unhonored, under all circumstances of bereavement, and guarantees man's right to life, liberty, and the pursuit of happiness as inalienable.

The law of nature is taken up and recognized by the good people of New Jersey, in the most solemn form as a rule of action, in her organic law. This first section declares that amongst man's inalienable rights are life, liberty, and the right of acquiring property. What, can a slave have safety, or acquire property? he who is nothing but a chattel, a piece of property himself, can he acquire safety? No; of all the innumerable murders committed by white men and women upon the slaves of the South (and there is no day goes by in which there is not more than one murder in each slave State, on an average), not a single white person has yet been executed for the murder of the colored man. The white is frequently hung in the slave States for stealing slaves, but not for killing them. Oh, sum of all human villainies, let the curse of God rest upon it, let every wind of heaven be charged with its destruction, every rising sun be its destroyer, the rolling seasons its executioner!

Slavery is the *exact converse* of every proposition contained in the first article of your new Constitution.

Slavery throws down every human right in the market to the highest bidder. If slavery (or semi-slavery, in the shape of children of slaves, in this State continuing to be slaves, males until twenty-five, and females until twenty-one years of age, and this operation is to pass under the name of being born free, and persons forty-one years old and upward be retained as slaves for life), and slaveholders are to stand asserting their wicked power, then the first great section of your Constitution is converted into a vapid and senseless abstraction. Shall your Constitution be withered by the power of slavery? Shall this Constitution stand gilt with the gold of high pretension, while within it is full of ravening and dead men's bones? Shall this slave institution continue to exist in hostility to so plain a provision? This frightful institution claims to exist, by the apology of some, since the 2d of last September, even since this Constitution went into operation, without a platform on which to place its accursed feet. The best foundation I can see for slavery in this State, at this time, and the length of time it should continue, should be the amount of time it would take the people of this State to recover from their astonishment at its inexpressible *impudence.*

The institution of slavery is the converse proposition of the Ten Commandments—it is the essence of injustice and meanness in its most compact form; and it would seem that no nation not struck down by a mortal paralysis, would wait a moment before rising and felling the monster, the first instant they discovered his seven heads and ten horns emerging from the forlorn regions of "Eldest Hell."

Which shall stand—the great written, organic law of liberty, or the unwritten and inexpressible villainy of slavery? Which shall stand—the natural God-inherited rights of life, liberty, property, safety, and happiness for each human being in New Jersey, or that of an institution which subverts every object for which a good constitution was ever made?

A constitution, *ex vi termini*, imports a covenant made by the whole people, with each person, and by each person with the whole people, to protect and defend their God-inherited rights of life, liberty, property, and safety from violence and invasion. A constitution is made for the defence of human rights, and not for their destruction; a constitution is the highest evidence of man's weakness; and intended to combine society's strength for the defence of each individual. How is it possible that a constitution, whether of this State, or of the United States, which was created on purpose for the protection of life, liberty, property, and safety, can exist and be entitled to the name, without overthrowing every institution, villainy or stratagem created or made, intending to cheat man out of life, liberty, property, safety, and happiness?

The men who framed the old State Constitution of New Jersey, in the year 1776, were not such hypocrites as to stamp that Constitution with the protection of human rights. No, they said nothing on that subject, for they knew there was no inconsiderable class of the population of this State who were wedded to the insatiable desire of appropriating the labor of others, without compensation, by compelling negroes, mulattoes, mustees, and Indians, to work for them for nothing, and make chattels or property of their persons, their wives and children—yes, of those human sinews, as a marketable commodity, men were to be degraded and forbidden, under penalties of thirty-nine lashes, from wandering from their masters' homes on Sunday, for the infliction of which stripes, by the order of a justice of the peace, a constable did, and yet does receive from the master the sum of $1 for performing the brutish service. To add to all other ignoble acts on the part of the State, was a provision forbidding emancipation of the slave, if forty years old or more, for fear of the distant contingency, that this freedman might become a public burden to the township, by being a pauper in his old age; and rather than subject the towns to that, they preferred to let the man and his posterity remain in slavery. Such was the gross inhumanity of the age; thus cheap were human rights held by the people of this State at large. Gross inhumanity to the master himself; it took away his *locus penitentiæ*, his space of repentance. And if slavery is not abolished, this infamous provision is still in full force. The reason why slavery was not abolished by name in Massachusetts and New Jersey is to be found in this, that the conscious shame of the fact restrained the framers of those constitutions from immortalizing their own disgrace by admitting slavery's previous existence, in and by its distinct abolition. They therefore put it to death by suffocation by the hands of liberty, without a name, hoping the judiciaries would attend its funeral and burial, and forever remove its unsightly corpse from the sight and smell of men, with as little parade as possible; and further hoping that a generous posterity would disbelieve their early public history, and consider it as apocryphal and slanderous of their illustrious ancestors, as the constitutions of these States do not so much as name so great a moral blemish on their historical fame.

Said Mr. S., by the statute of this State (which he contended was repealed by the first section of the new Constitution) passed February, 1820, all children born of slaves after 1804 were to be free, but were to belong as servants, and to be held as apprentices, and bound out by the overseers of the poor to the owners of their mothers, their administrators, executors and assigns—males till 25, and females until 21. These persons were property in every sense of the word, until their time expired; they are purchased and sold in private and at public auction, pass under the insolvent acts and bankrupt acts, the same as oxen and horses. What is the difference between this Mary Tebout and her mother? Nothing, until Mary has passed 21 years of unrewarded toil. She is called a servant, she is said to be born free, is now but 19, and has been sold three times. The southern States call slavery involuntary servitude, or persons bound to service by the laws of the States. The domestic institutions of the South, the patriarchal institutions and the peculiar institutions of the South—by such soft hypocritical use of words, do they mean to make the English language a partner in their guilt, by using it as a cloak to conceal the hideous visage of that frightful monster, whose mouth is filled with spikes, and face covered with iron wrinkles, with burning balls of fire for eyes, whose every hair is a hissing serpent, whose fetid breath would kill the Bohun Upas, whose touch is ruin, whose embrace is destruction, who is fed on blood, tears and sweat, whip-extracted, from unpaid toil—her music is unpitied groans of broken hearts, of ruined hopes, and blasted expectations.

Away with such artifice to shield deformity, by those cruel and wicked States, boasting of their republicanism, and rights of man. Even New York and Pennsylvania once held persons born free, whose mothers were slaves, the males till 28, and females till 25, as slaves. Terrible nick-naming of human rights, as in bold derision of them. These New Jersey servants are property, in its base sense, slaves for years, the parents deprived of all jurisdiction of their offspring, all direction of their education, and paternal tenderness; the law confining these poor servants, and obliging them to live with those who have owned and abused the mother who bore them, and are still continuing to hold their parents until death, as slaves. The master can sell his servant and horse together. This servant-woman at 15, and the male-servant at 18, contract marriage, and when the woman is 19, and man 22 years of age, having three little children, the father is sold to one end of the State, and the mother to the other; their little children left in the street, the marriage relation broken, the paternal and maternal relation dissolved; these little ones not to see their parents for two years or more; the husband cannot see his wife or little ones, nor the wife her husband or babies for two years to come. Call you this being born *free?* The man is deprived of his wife, and the wife becomes a widow, and children orphans, according to law, to satisfy the claims of certain old slaveholders in this State! Is this being born free? This looks none like respect for the law of nature, by which we are born free and independent. We can never honor or respect the new Constitution, till we feel there is meaning, power, vitality, in those blessed words of justice, truth, mercy, freedom, safety; and further, feel that there are no birth-impediments, or interest of others in the use of our bodies, inconsistent with our own happiness. Each individual should be left to fulfill the object of his mission to this world in the best way he may; society should not load him with burdens for the benefit of others, but should give him every facility to run his race of existence, with dignity to himself, and thus truly serve the ends of society and his own creation, in passing from the great eternity of the past into the illimitable future.

Here, we are not left in the dark, as to the meaning of the words of the New Jersey new Constitution, for it is almost an exact copy of the first section of the Massachusetts Constitution of 1780. The first section of the Massachusetts Constitution is in these words:

"Article 1st. All men are born free and equal, and have certain natural, essential, and inalienable rights, among which may be reckoned the right of enjoying and defending their lives and liberties; that of acquiring, possessing, and protecting property; in fine, that of seeking and obtaining their safety and happiness."

Here Mr. S. asked Mr. Zabriskie, counsel for the claimant of Mary Tebout, if he contended there was any difference between the two sections of these Constitutions? Mr. Zabriskie replied, he did not.

The New Jersey Constitution has in the 10th Article these words: "The common law and statute laws now in full force, *not repugnant* to this Constitution, shall remain in force until they expire by their own limitation, or be altered or repealed by the legislature."

Further, Mr. S. said that he relied on a portion of the Constitution of the United States, for emancipation, by this honorable court, to wit, the Magna Charta portion, where it asserts "that no person shall be deprived of life, liberty or property, without due process of law."

The case of Winchendon *v.* Hadfield, *4th Mass. Rep.*, 123, is the case of one Edoin Landon, in relation to the question as to which of the towns should support him, he having been a slave in Massachusetts, and sold eleven times, enlisted twice in the Revolutionary army, the second time for three years, his master receiving his bounty and his wages—also, *4th Mass.*, 539. Chief Justice Parsons decided in this cause that slavery had been abolished by the first section of the Massachusetts Constitution, as had been decided in former unreported cases. This is legal authority, in effect, on the very words of the New Jersey Constitution, 1st article; Massachusetts has shed from the lamp of her judiciary as pure, bright and steady a light as any court in the new world, and has done her fair share in elevating the science of the law. I repose with great confidence upon this authority; it covers the whole controversy.

The case of the slave *Med*, 18*th Pickering*, 193, known under the name of Commonwealth *vs.* Thomas Aves, presented within the last half dozen years this same great question collaterally. The argument was elaborate, and the opinion of Chief Justice Shaw luminous.

Chief Justice Shaw says, Massachusetts in 1641 abolished slavery, except of *captives taken in lawful war* or guilty of crime. But slavery grew up in Massachusetts, and in 1703 an act was passed in that colony, imposing restrictions on the transmission of aged and infirm slaves; and by an act of 1705, a duty was levied on the importation of slaves, showing slavery in full force until abolished by their Constitution of 1780. The Chief Justice, in this case, says it is now well established law that slavery was abolished by the Constitution of 1780, and before the adoption of the Constitution of the United States, slavery being *repugnant* to the principles of justice, of nature, and the declaration of rights, which are a component part of the Constitution of Massachnsetts. Slavery, said he, crept into Massachusetts by force of custom existing in the West Indies and in several other States, encouraged by the mother country (miserable apology better than none, even in Massachnsetts).

Chief Justice Shaw says, " Slavery is a relation founded in force and not in right; existing, where it does, by force of positive law, and not recognized and founded in natural rights." Slavery, he says, " is contrary to natural rights, to the principles of justice and humanity." He then says, " Bond slavery cannot exist in this Commonwealth, because it is contrary to natural right, *repugnant* to the Constitution and law, designed to secure the liberty and rights of all persons who come within the limits of this State, as entitled to the protection of law."

But what case can I have stronger than the opinion of Chief Justice Marshall, himself a slaveholder? Borne down by slaveholding construction as he was, still his innate integrity triumphed over cultivated wrong, and compelled him to define slavery as contrary to the law of nature, for the definition of slavery by the civil law, showed it an institution contrary to the law of nature, which law of nature New Jersey has adopted. In case of the *Antelope*, 10*th Wheaton*, 120, Chief Justice Marshall says, " That slavery is contrary to the law of nature will scarcely be denied; that every man has a natural right to the fruits of his own labor is generally admitted, and that no other person can rightfully deprive him of those fruits, and appropriate them against his will, seems the necessary result of that admission." Chief Justice Marshall quotes the definition of slavery in the Latin from the civil law, which, with his own opinion, would seem to put the question in this case for ever to rest. It is this, " *Servitus est constitutio juris gentium qua quis Domino alieno* CONTRA NATURAM *subjicitur.*" Slavery is an institution by the laws of nations, by which one is subjected to another man, as master, *contrary to nature.* Slavery strikes down and repeals, if it could, the law of nature referred to in the 1st article of your Constitution; what can be stronger and more complete?

Here Mr. Stewart gave way for an adjournment until 3 P.M., for dining.

The court being present at 3 o'clock, P.M., Mr. Stewart resumed by saying: Has any lawyer the courage to say that the legislature of New Jersey could create the institution of slavery to-day in defiance of the new Constitution? Perhaps most, if not all, would say No. Why could not the legislature enact such a law so as to create the relation of slave and master? It would be correctly answered, and by all, that it would be *repugnant* to the new Constitution and its first section. Do not we discover that a law sustaining slavery is equally repugnant to the new Constitution, whether passed ten years before it, or ten years after it? and that the repugnance is not a question of past or present time? If it is repugnant, it is equally so in the one case as the other—"it is so odious nothing but positive law can sustain it," says Lord Mansfield.

Mr. S. said that he had confessed himself to have much respect for a *being* so highly honored as man by his Maker, a being created in the image of God, who showed at all times the grandeur of his descent, and the illustriousness of his lineage by that great unimpeachable record written upon his countenance sublime, by the finger of God, which no poverty, sorrow, or crime, could erase: its marks of origin were open to all, read of all, and should be comprehended by all. In the first place we must look at the immense natural wealth, or God-given possessions, which belong to the meanest man, who prints the green earth with his foot, or drinks from its waters, and renews life every moment from the unbought atmosphere—is fanned by the wings of the wind, cheered with the eye-possession of the universe; yes, his every-day existence could not be sustained, at a less expense than the fitting up of two worlds, for his accommodation, the earth and sun; the bread he eats, the wool, the flax, and cotton he wears, is warmed into life by rays of light from the sun, sent over ninety millions of miles in profusion, without stint, each ray having its definite office and distinct commission to aid to life, strength and joy, a single human being. If there were but one man on this globe, these vast structures of two worlds must be reared in all their architectural grandeur and fitness. This globe must revolve around on its own axis

every twenty-four hours, and shoot along upon the vast plain
of the ecliptic, at the inconceivable rate of sixty-eight thousand miles per hour. Man perishes, if the globe were to
revolve around the sun at the rate of thirty-four thousand
miles per hour; man could not live in these regions with a
year of seven hundred and thirty days, with the unbroken
severities of a double winter, or the scorching heat of a protracted summer.

The outlay of Almighty power, which sends this noble
earth careering round the sun with such prodigious force,
and brings it back to the same point, in absolute space with
infinite precision, with the punctuality of God, is a portion of
each man's inheritance; and all the powers ever displayed
by man, exerted by beasts, felt from winds, or overwhelmed
by tornadoes, or moved in tempests, or lifted or sunk by
earthquakes, swept by tides, or driven by inundations, put
forth since the morning of creation, would not furnish a
sufficient force, to propel our globe on its everlasting journey,
a single day. Yet for man these high demonstrations are
made, to fit him up an abode with the finish of Omnipotence,
commensurate with his every want; it is his God-inherited
estate; and were the poorest man on earth to exchange that
estate, for the power of Bonaparte, when all Europe shook
beneath his tread, and trembled at his power, this poor
man would be undone, by the exchange; the property is too
great for any one to buy of another; this is the benevolence
of Heaven to its honored creature, man. When each man's
God-inherited estate is reckoned and computed, though possessing nothing else, and compared with that of any other
man's God-inherited estate, they are equal; and if one possess a million of pounds, and the other no money, still when
their whole possessions are considered, one has one hundred,
and the other but one hundred and one. This proposition or
statement will forever vindicate the goodness of Heaven, and

show the absolute equality of all men, if considered possession-wise.

Therefore it seems to me, that the Declaration of Independence in asserting that all men are created free and equal, is true as a proposition, and is not a rhetorical flourish, but a sublime estimate, no less grand than true, when we refer to the vast possessions of each human being; and that any accidental variance by the acquisitions of one, of more wealth than another, does not disturb the great result any more than the dust which may fall upon one of the scales shall change their general equipoise.

All men are created equal, and shall a being of such amazing dignity and immense possessions, of such grand lineage, be made a slave? God forbid. Equality, life, liberty of locomotion, the rights of acquiring happiness in every way we see fit, not violating the rights of our brother man, or the edicts of heaven, with the God-inherited estate, constitute what your Constitution and that of Massachusetts and the Declaration of Independence, describe as rights *inalienable*. Is it not so? What kind of a deed must that be which should attempt to convey my right and title in the wind, atmosphere, earth, and my share in the power that propels this ponderous globe around the sun?—my title to the exhaustless fires and light of that great luminary, and of those rays which might fall on me or on the earth and produce my raiment and food? Is there not deep and philosophical truth in asserting the *inalienability* of rights like these, so essential to man's existence, and his everlasting accountability to the Father of all, for his abounding munificence, with which man can invest no other being, or divest himself. Can it not truly be said that a being who is born to such great possessions, is born free and *independent?* The greatest blot on American character is, to have been deluded by slaveholders into a belief that those great words expressed by the men, who wrote and adopted the Declaration of our Independence, were mere abstractions and the flourish of oratory, where they declared the great self-evident truth " that all men are created free and equal, and are possessed of certain inalienable rights, among which are life, liberty, and the pursuit of happiness," and that the same were meaningless. These truths are self-evident, and why ? They are evident in every breath of air we respire through our lungs, every step we take, in every object we behold, printed on every tree, written on every cloud, bursting forth in every falling drop of rain, reflected in every ray of light, by which the universe is warmed, and in glory lit up, and by the succession of day and night, summer and winter, seed-time and harvest ; in fact, its self-evidence is stereotyped in eternal beauty upon the earth, the sea, the mountain, the valley, upon the moon, the sun, and stars of heaven. This constitutes the great record of ever-during *self-evidence*, that all men are created free and equal, and are possessed of certain inalienable rights, etc.

This rises to a moral, if not a mathematical demonstration ; and that a great nation should, so far as individuals, forget the dignity of their origin, the vastness of their inalienable possessions, and should hunt for arguments to force their debasement and search for reasons to *undervalue* such a being as man, especially in a great *selfocracy*, where each man is a sovereign, is, among all strange things, one which would exceed belief were we not met by the strange phenomenon at every turn of human affairs. Had we incorporated the divine sentiments of our great Declaration into our minds, as an everlasting first-principle, and lived under the sway of its glorious dominion, no slavery would then have disgraced our magnificent country ; no half cultivated, forlorn and deserted sections of slave States, would have told the world their melancholy tale. No *coffled* gang of slaves would have dishonored our nation, driven from State to State, for sale. No, our prosperity, riches, glory and moral elevation, would have presented so imposing an example of man's capabilities for his own advancement, that king-craft aristocracies and all of that coarse mode of working, taxing and governing men, as family-jobs, would, long ere this, have been thrown into the rear of the camp of human progress, and new forms of self-government would have succeeded, in which the governed should have been the governors, and the interest of the governed would have prevailed, in the true advancement of the human race.

We have terrible penalties to pay, for abandoning principles so glorious, so wise, of which we have had a full view, and for saying, most shamefully, that the Declaration of Independence is a formula and not serious, the poetry of excited minds. By thus forsaking these great truths, certain and as practical as the decalogue, we fell back into the arms of a low, base expediency, and *re-lived* forms of crimes and follies of former ages, holding these sublime truths as abstractions, fitted only for the meridian of heaven, with angels for their operatives, to carry them out, while we fed ourselves upon the husks of former absurdities, rejecting truth, holding it too beautiful for practical use.

Will not this court set the nation the shining example of doing right, on this question, by acting up to the full measure of their judicial and moral power?

A nation may lose its liberty in a day, and not miss it in a hundred years; this nation lost its true liberty, the clear light, the first moment the great words of the Declaration of Independence ceased to be honored and respected as household, every-day truth, the fundamental rules of action, as the political and moral mathematics of the nation.

Although we make several hundred volumes of fourth of July orations, poetical self-glorifications and boasting eulo-

giums for the home-market, yearly, in which the most beautiful descriptions are given of the dress and form of liberty, as
a wonderful unknown goddess, and amuse ourselves in
describing her altar, the costliness of her sacrifices, and the
riches of her perfume, and the curling smoke of her incense;
yet if in the everyday intercourse of man with man, of courts
of justice with causes, in expounding the doctrines of the great
declaration and of legislation, in framing new rules of action,
we should with one consent, have asserted that in the
Declaration of Independence and other national and State
Constitutions containing the same thoughts, that liberty was
sincere, in declaring the freedom and equality of all men, and
the inalienability of the rights, of life, liberty and the pursuit
of happiness, we should not have lost liberty; for not so doing,
we have lost liberty, though we do not miss it; we have only
liberty's casket, but the jewel is gone; we are playing and
satisfying ourselves with forms when the substance has
departed. We make the loud acclaim, we fire the cannon of
salutation, crackers burst under our feet, our toasts may be
drank in three times three, in the wildest uproar of animal
excitement; still these demonstrations are worse than senseless, because they make us think we are true believers in
liberty and the divine dignity of man, while we are only
high-heeled hypocrites and fanatics, spinning in concentric
circles, like brain-turned dervishes around an abstraction of
liberty, being neither flesh nor spirit, being the great *indefinable*, our adoration increasing with our ignorance, until the
beatitude of our worship is made complete in the perfect
idealess. Still, for a pretence, we make long speeches about
Republicanism and Democracy, while we have nailed and
crucified, in and through our colored brother, Liberty on the
cross. We have so long been absent from *true* liberty, that
we should require a formal introduction before we should
dare address her, for she is not that tawdry dressed cyprian

bearing her name, who had sold her charms to demagogues, pimps, panders, pirates, buccaneers and slaveholders, whip in hand, who have declared that slavery is the chief corner-stone of our republican institutions; while the clergy of the south have most impiously averred slavery to be a Bible, God-honored, Christian institution, to be kept. Shameful impiety and desecration of the fountain of Eternal truth.

The court will pardon me while we look for a moment at the sublime teaching of that wonderful and holy book, the Bible, so often lugged in to uphold piracy at the expense of the Eternal's justice and man's happiness. The Almighty has done a thousand fold more, to express his infinite abhorrence of slavery, than of all other crimes and offences against his law. He has suspended the laws of nature, and in one instance of time, smote two and a half millions of people with death, and caused the sea itself to retreat before the fugitive slave, and made, as predicated on these amazing exercises of power, a direct revelation of himself, and immediately caused our revealed religion to be produced, to express his everlasting detestation of a crime which would unthrone Him, and crush his creature man, and place him beside the beast of the field. Our maker destroyed the first edition of mankind. In the second emission and publication of our race, Egypt became the schoolmaster nation of the human race, and the great instructor of mankind. The nations of the earth, on camels and dromedaries, came, in the infancy of antiquity, to Egypt, to exchange their rude materials and ignorance for the Egyptian works of art and knowledge. In fact, no opinion was considered worthy of general acceptance, by the surrounding barbarians, unless it had an Egyptian indorsement, and their wise men's stamp and mark upon it.

It appeared that the Israelites, in near four hundred years, had increased to two and a half millions of people, as would seem from the number of men spoken of in their Exodus.

The Pharaohs had a slave market for centuries. The poor Jews had become slaves of the most distressing type. They had their overseers, their distinct tasks ; they were scourged, and had every mark of human debasement and slavery inflicted. The day of their deliverance was in an age, in which the passion for public structures, imposing in their magnitude, wonderful in their display of high-wrought efforts of genius, constituted the chief employment of their kings, and great men, for centuries. The poor Hebrews had often laid their petitions before Pharaoh through Moses and Aaron, asking to be permitted to go into the wilderness, and worship their God. But Pharaoh, as a slaveholder, stood between this people and their conscience, and refused to let them go. Slavery strikes down the rights of conscience always, for there is not a slave in the United States, who is informed in any reasonable degree in the Christian religion, who does not remain in slavery, contrary to the plainest teachings of his own conscience. The Almighty having warned the Egyptian government of the great crime of holding men in bondage, was determined, in the early ages of mankind, to settle the question of his infinite abhorrence of slavery, in a manner so elementary and signal, that the stamp of His finger-marks should remain uncrasable through all coming ages. For slavery overthrows the *will* of the victim, and the claim of the Almighty to the adoration of his creatures ; and no power can get in between God and man, and interfere on this subject, unless it is slavery. Slavery breaks down the will, volition, and choice of its victim ; the slaveholder steps in between the slave and his Maker, and says, oh, slave, talk not of conscience, your religion, or your God ; do my will, or die ; my will is your law, and not your God's ; my will you must obey, or die. Slavery always disputes our Maker's supremacy ; warning after warning, miracle after miracle, had been lost upon the obduracy of Egypt's king.

One morning, as the population of that kingdom of fifteen millions of people arose and looked at their beloved Nile, lo! and behold, it was one vast river of blood, from the cataracts where its tumbling torrents of blood fell in mighty roar, and pursued their sweeping course for 600 miles to its seven mouths, where the Mediterranean, receiving its tribute from this ancient servant, blushed for twenty leagues around, at Pharaoh's impudence. The stranger from afar, the traders, seekers of knowledge, and the citizens, stood that livelong day, and wondered at the bloody Nile; and as reasons were asked and given, I think I hear them say, the reason why the Nile runs blood is that Pharaoh holds the Hebrews as slaves, and the Hebrews' God demands their release, and shows his anger and his power at Pharaoh's refusal. The stranger would carry this news to the utmost bounds of living man, saying, one entire day I saw the Nile run blood, to express the abhorrence of the Hebrews' God against the crime of slavery.

Again, the heavens were darkened at noon by the gyrations of armies of locusts, which shut out the sun, and they consumed the vegetation of this fertile land ; men cried for mercy, and in a few hours this army of destructive locusts was carried on the wings of a strong west wind into the depths of the Red Sea, not one left. The Egyptian and the stranger knew that the Hebrews' God had done this, to cause these poor slaves to be delivered from the mighty monarch's cruel power.

On a certain other day the obstinate Pharaoh refused after many promises to let the poor Hebrew slaves go free. It is noon ; the burning power of a June sun strikes the land; anon, all eyes in Egypt are turned to a black cloud rising out of the west, over the Lybian desert. This was the first thunder-storm in Egypt, and the last, for it neither rains nor hails in Egypt, owing to the great Lybian desert of sand on the west, and the Arabian desert on the east, as philosophers suppose. It skirts the western heavens, and the terrific clouds raise themselves higher and higher; men turn pale; anon the low and solemn tones of thunder are heard; men tremble and say it is the voice of the slaves' God—in a moment the flashes of forked lightning play with infinite quickness, men fall on their knees and declare it is the flashing of the angry eyes of the Hebrews' God at the Egyptians' cruelties. The clouds rise to the high altitude of noon; the lightning, the winds, and roaring thunder send consternation into the hearts of affrighted men. It appears like night, nature in agony, men fear to speak, and believe they are on the eve of doom; men and beasts hide themselves in extreme terror; the thunder makes the earth, tremble from pole to pole; the pyramids rock from their deep foundations, the rains descend, the hail beats the earth, fire and ice leap from the clouds, while the lightning strikes down the trees, plays round the pyramid tops, smites the sphinx, and runs along upon the ground, men in agony, praying for deliverance; Pharaoh and his court lie prostrate in the palace, the earth seems shaken out of its place, and all nature in convulsions. The king implores mercy, and the Father of all hears, pities, and delivers the faithless king and people, and ere the sun went down, that storm and desolation had forever gone by, and the last cloud sunk below the horizon in the Red Sea, while the beautiful sun rolls down the western heavens, smiling in mercy from and beyond the dark solitudes of the interminable Lybian sands. This storm, all men knew, was an evidence of God's displeasure at slavery. But Pharaoh would not let the people go.

It is in Egypt and is midnight when the young wife, but two years married, awoke and placed her hand on the shoulder of her youthful husband; he was as cold as marble, he would not awake at her mournful cry—he was dead, he was the first born of his parents. She arose in wild despair, she lit a flambeau, and looked at her little babe on the mattress; the fixed smile was there, rigid in death, never to be relaxed; *he* was the *first* born of his parents; she flies to her father's and mother's bed in the next room, she awakes her father, but none but the archangel can arouse her mother from death's sleep, most profound; she was the first born of her parents. She sends her man-servant to her neighbor for help in this awful hour; the servant enters the neighbor's, a light is there, wailing and horror meet him. The aged father of the second house was the first born of his parents, and is dead, and the infant first born is also dead. No contortion, no groan was ever heard of all who fell in a single instant, on that dreadful. night; they lay with all the peace of eternal sleep upon them. The servant finds another servant in this second house of death, they go out, they hear the survivors' wail, and see the baleful torch lit up in every house around; they ascend a tower on the banks of the Nile, high above and all around, as in a moment, for forty miles, as far as eye can measure light upon the earth's dark face, the beams of the death torch of that direful hour from all directions strike their wretched eyes. The lamentations were loud and long; and when the morning sun arose, the angel of death for long hours had been gone from the abodes of man and beast, and there was not one house in all the land of Egypt in which there was not one dead, or about two and half millions—one-sixth of the people, or a life of one of Egypt's slaveholders had been taken, for each Hebrew slave *detained.* No mistaking the power and will of the God of the bondmen longer, and the affrighted Pharaoh and his court cry to these slaves, " up and begone, or we are all dead men." The funeral, the most terrible in time, then followed. Nothing like these deaths or funerals in the history of our race.

The fugitive slaves had marched to the northeast and reached the Red Sea, and were in great fear, reposing on its banks between two mountains, the one on their right, and the other on their left. Solemn hours! As they rested we may feign that young Hebrews climb to the mountain tops, and saw the rising clouds of dust on the southwestern edge of the heavens. That army is led on by Pharaoh's generals, of chariots and cavalry, the notes of trumpets fell upon their ears, and the young men cry to their friends below, "They come! they come! we hear their trumpets on the plain!" Then the desponding fugitives cried, "Were there no graves in Egypt?" The night came, portentous; a mighty cloud rested between the slaveholders and the trembling fugitives. On the side next to the poor slaves, the cloud beamed as from a pillar of fire, all light, the smile of heaven. On the other side of the cloud the pursuing slaveholders saw it all dark, lugubrious, presaging to them the horrors of their last day. This was another finger-mark of Divine power. The morning lowered, and, in clouds, to these sad and impious slaveholders heavily brought on that day whose end they would never see. The trembling fugitives stood looking nine miles across the intervening Red Sea, whose waves broke in melancholy murmurs at their feet. Despair was on every face. When Moses spoke, "stand still and see the salvation of the Lord," another finger-mark of Omnipotence was made, and Moses stretched out his rod over the Red Sea, and anon a long line of subsidence of the waters appears. Every fugitive eye saw it. Then the reflowing of waters from that central line, the piling of waters follow; the waters ascend and pile, ascend and pile, until the naked bottom across appears with perpendicular water walls of great height, by Omnipotence held up, and probably one mile wide is left like a clean beach. The fugitives pass down on this untravelled road, and finally division after division rose upon the further side. At length the weak passed up, the cripple climb the bank, and lo! there see those little orphans pull themselves up by twigs, and that poor old man on his crutches, they help pull him up—they are all up and over. Now rises the wildest, grandest, and most sublime music which ever burst from human lips—the fugitives' song! The headlong vindictive slaveholders, burning with rage, thirsting for revenge, follow on the fugitives' track into the sea; and as they were at the central depths of the Red Sea, gravitation was permitted to re-assert her ancient law, when down came these mighty mountains of waters to their forsaken bed. Pharaoh and his haughty hosts expired in the centre of a miracle. For forty years the Almighty fed these poor fugitive slaves directly from His own table.

The God of Heaven, as in mercy to man, that he might never again commit the atrocious crime involved in slavery, caused Mount Sinai to quake from its deep foundations, and amidst the thunders and the lightnings, the Almighty, with his own finger, wrote the tables of the law, his ten eternal orders, which are most eminent Anti-Slavery in character, that the crime which had shaken Egypt to its foundations, might never occur again for want of a Divine prohibition. This was the decalogue, " Love the Lord thy God with all thy heart, mind, and strength, and thy neighbor as thyself." This command obeyed, destroys all the slavery in the world. What slaveholder can kindly love his slave unless he manumits him?

The preface to these commands, in the sixth verse of the fifth chapter of Deuteronomy, " I am the Lord thy God, which brought thee out of the land of Egypt, and from the house *of bondage.*"

" Honor thy father and mother." No, says the slaveholder, I will sell your father and mother, you must obey your master.

"Thou shalt not kill."   I will kill, says the slaveholder, if it is necessary, by flogging to obtain submission; or if the slave will run from me when I tell him to stop, I will shoot and kill him, and Southern law says amen.

"Thou shalt not commit adultery."   I will commit adultery, and break the marriage covenant between my slaves, and compel them to marry over when my interest will be promoted, or separate man and wife by sale or purchase, and make them marry again.

"Thou shalt not steal."   I will steal, and appropriate, says the slaveholder, all that man hath, all he can earn, and the *man himself*, when *my* interest can be promoted thereby.

"Thou shalt not covet."   I will covet that man's or that woman's body, and I will possess myself of them, and appropriate them to my own use, says the slaveholder.

Look at the condescension of the Almighty.   He made these poor fugitive slaves the librarians and custodians of the revelation of his will to mankind.   Slavery treads this revelation under foot, and quotes the Bible to prove slavery, when there is the most incontestable evidence that there never would have been a revelation in the decalogue, but as the finishing stroke of those awful wonders and miracles, on the faith of which our religion rests, all originating, converging and terminating in that great fundamental proposition, that God infinitely abhors slavery, because it supplants his direct authority over the will of His child, and throws His child, with an immortal mind, made in his own image, into the category of brute-beasts, thus forever overthrowing the fundamental relation of God to man, of man to his neighbor, and of man to himself.   To vindicate the character, power and justice of the Supreme, and bring man home again to his true relations, was well worthy of a display of such awful power, introducing Himself as God to the ancient world.

Mr. S. said there was another proposition which he wished to glance at in passing. That was the Constitution of the United States, for were he before the King's Bench, in Westminister Hall, he would there insist, and he believed with entire success, that there was not a slave in New Jersey, or in any slave State, who had been deprived of his liberty according to law. I mean slaves as they are generally and at large, and not those who have been convicted of crimes ; and therefore there is not a slave, if you admit him a person, as slaveholders contend, but must be discharged by a judge or a court, on being brought before said court on the ground that he has never been deprived of his liberty by due process of law, according to the Constitution of the United States. That record must be produced, originating in a decision or an indictment of a grand jury, and the finding of a petit jury, and the pronouncing of judgment thereon, by a court of competent jurisdiction. This, Sir Edward Coke, and Judge Story on Sir Edward's authority, in his Commentaries, 440, says is the meaning of due process of law at common law, as used in *Magna Charta*. But I am willing to reduce the character of the court, and even strike out the petit and grand jury from the instrumentality—and then I say that "due process of law" means a court or some judicial personage, one or more making a court, who have adjudicated the man to be a slave ; and if that record cannot be found, the man must go free ; or the individual must not lose his liberty without due process of law. That record cannot be found in this land. Will any man pretend that plantation and cart-whip discipline is due process of law? Will any pretend that being deprived of the right to learn to read, or write, as in some of our States, under the penalty of twenty-five lashes on the naked back of the teacher and the taught, is due process of law? Yes, for the mother to teach her child to spell the name of the Saviour, for the second attempt, mother and child are to be whipped one hundred lashes; for the third offence, the punishment of death. Is this the due process of law, named in the Constitution of the United States? The pursuing of fugitives with bloodhounds cannot be the due process of law of the Constitution.

The separation by sale of husband from wife, and wife from husband, and children from both, to suit the convenience of the master, cannot be due process of law? The being born of slave mother, on a slaveholder's plantation, cannot be due process of law? The being torn away from home, kindred and friends, and sent by the middle passage to a slave auction in South Carolina, and sold on the boards into hopeless bondage, cannot be due process of law?

Is not slavery a punishment or an infliction on men beyond the track of the common misfortunes of mankind, of sufficient magnitude to have it left to some mortal man, in the shape of a justice or judge, to adjudicate a man into the great dragnet of slavery? For, we find it takes the strongest judicial power in the land to get him out. Slaveholders claim him under the word " person " in the Constitution, because they say, there is no other word by which they can denote slavery. The word person I have, in this argument in relation to due process of law, used in the slaveholding sense, which is, after all, downright perversion.

The word person, in the Constitution of the United States, means a human being possessed of the natural rights of life, liberty, and the pursuit of happiness. The word person means a human being in the fullness of his natural rights, and nothing more. The Greeks, Romans, and English, whether using the word in law or in common parlance, mean this, and nothing more; and you can legally no more express the idea of a slave by it than you can that of a king. A man who is a slave, according to slave law, has lost his *personage,* ıf I may so speak, and has passed into chattlehood, or thing-hood, and all the rights of person are annihilated, or in a state of suspended animation, until the pure air of liberty inflates his lungs again. The Constitution of the United States is an Anti-Slavery document, in its general spirit and tendencies; and under other auspices and circumstances would have been called a great act of universal emancipation, and have set every slave free in the land, being paramount law, without doing the thousandth part of violence in con-struction which has been done by a slaveholding interpreta-tion, by which it has been made into a slaveholding document, - to create the horrid institution by reënacting the slave-laws of the two States of Virginia and Maryland, thereby cover-ing the two sections of the District of Columbia, in creating and regulating by territorial laws, slavery in eight of the. new States; five of which, Florida, Louisiana, Mississippi, Arkansas and Missouri, were not a portion of the United States or its territories at the adoption of the Constitution of the United States. The Congress of the United States under slaveholding dictation created slavery, therefore, in Kentucky, Tennessee and Alabama, a portion of our territory at the adoption of the Constitution; and in the other five States the nation purchased the territory and created the institution in them as territories, and the Congress then brought these five slave States into the sisterhood of the republic. And now we are told slavery is a State institution, and is beyond the reach of any power of Congress, for its extermination; that is, that Congress has power to create and fasten this infernal institution on a territory, but has no power to abolish it anywhere, after it has enacted it once into existence, either in its territorial or State character; it has no power to lop, restrain or eradicate slavery from a State or territory, but is bound to foster and nurture it with parental care, as one of the *patriarchal, domestic* and *peculiar institutions* of the South. Permit me to assert, as it regards these States, that Congress had no more power to create slavery there in the beginning than it had to create an autocrat in either of those States or territories, in whose hand and his heirs all power, legislative, judicial and executive, should be centred forever, with full power to sell or dispose of the bodies of all the people or inhabitants who should or might come within the bounds of his territory or State. For the power exercised in the case of slavery by one half of the inhabitants over the other, is precisely the same in degree and kind as that described, only the number of the autocrats is increased. Each autocrat has a less number of subjects, but the power exercised is precisely the same in extent, and in relation to those on whom it operates, is the same precise autocratism, as though there was but one despot. Now I deny that Congress has lawful power to do any such thing.

Many persons run to the Madison papers published in the last few years, to ascertain the meaning of the framers of the Constitution, who met in Philadelphia in 1787, as a mere committee of the nation, sent out to report to the people the form of a Constitution for their adoption in the summer of 1788. I deny in any event, the right to resort to this mode of interpretation, to contradict the noble and glorious text of that document; but supposing this a correct mode of getting darkness into the room to show the light, still it is not applied at the right point. Thirteen State conventions were held in the year 1788, by the authority of their respective legislatures, to adopt or reject what had been framed, by a committee-convention of the nation, as a body of draughters of the form of the Constitution, who had been sent to Philadelphia, during the summer of 1787, to do that very work; not to adopt that Constitution, but to report the form of one, to the people of the States.

In the summer of 1788, the people, in their thirteen State

Conventions, by the constitutional number of nine, adopted this Constitution; and if this rule of interpretation now sought to be adopted, could be made applicable anywhere, we should have to go to the *adopters*, and not the framers. What, and how did the *adopters*, the people, understand this instrument when they adopted it? Did they understand it in any sense different from what it imports on its face? Where are the secret intentions, private understandings, those implied guaranties and curious fanciful compromises of those thirteen Conventions of *adopters?* Have they ever come to light except in some long speech of some southern slaveholding orator? How came the descendants of those slaveholders of 1788 to be made the special depositees of all those secret guaranties, compromises, and implied understandings, in behalf of slavery, now spoken of with a confidence as startling as the information communicated is important, novel, and false. This was not so. These are mere after-thoughts of despotism. No man has ever shown one word from the adopters, conflicting with the text. Shall a committee sent out by the nation, affix to well understood language of the common law, and of every day use, some secret cabalistic meaning in hostility to the text; and then get the people, through their Conventions, to adopt the Constitution for the beautiful principles it expressed on its face, and after that was accomplished, to wait till the framers and adopters are dead, and then to come out and say, ah, the people have adopted this Constitution, for what it purported on its face, but we, the sons and grandsons of the southern framers, have a cabalistic key left by our grandfathers in the South, by which, when the word justice appears, our grandfathers meant *slavery* or *injustice;* when we used the word *persons* we meant *slaves* sometimes, and sometimes *free persons;* when we said "no person shall be deprived of life, liberty or property without due process of law," we *there* understood a slave to *be* a chattel or a piece of property, and not *a person;* we had a sliding-scale by which we used the word person for slave when the interest of the slaveholder is to be promoted, but when the language can be applied to him as a person in another part of the instrument, and thereby set him free, the intendment is to be against liberty, and we did not mean that he should have any of the blessings of the Constitution, but only its curses and its cruelty. When the word person means *bitter*, it is the slave's portion; when the word person means *sweet*, he has no lot or part in that matter. Although the word person never meant slave in any written document before we affixed it among ourselves, or our grandfathers did, in this *peculiar* sense, and refused to use the word slave. This was the secret opinion of the drafters, who supposed they could thus *deceive* the adopters into adoption. When we enacted that Article by which we said " the United States shall guarantee a republican form of government to each of the States," we knew the old and true meaning of a republican form of government to be one in which the government was made by and for the benefit of the governed, and that each person in a republican form of government was born free and equal, and entitled to life, liberty, and the pursuit of happiness. This, we knew, would by force of this provision in the Constitution of the United States, if faithfully honored, blot out slavery from every State constitution, and every State upholding a proposition of slavery by State legislation, it being diametrically opposite to a republican form of government; therefore, it was agreed secretly, as a compromise, by the framers of the Constitution, as one of the secret compromises or implied guaranties, against liberty, that this should be an *unexercised article*, or an *unused function* of the Federal Constitution, as a sort of fifth wheel to a coach; because, if carried out, it would cut up slavery, root and branch, in the old States then made, and in the new *to be made*. Therefore, says this secret compromise-keeper, we, at the session of Congress in 1845, in pursuance of our secret compromise of interpretation of language, with its *use* and *disuse*, and under the suspension of that article of the Federal Constitution guaranteeing a republican form of government, admitted Florida as a State, as we had several slave States before, in which we permitted this Article of the constitution, guaranteeing a republican form of government to each State, to be overridden and totally disregarded, as though it did not exist; and in the Florida constitution, slavery is held such a sacred and central right among her institutions, that it is placed out of reach and beyond the control of her own legislature, and that colored freemen coming into that State from Maine, Massachusetts, or other free States, may be sold as slaves; and the right the Constitution guarantees to each citizen of one State in enjoying all the privileges of citizenship in another State, says our secret compromise-keeper, means, as it was understood by the framers in the cabalistic catalogue, that this part of the Constitution should never apply to a Massachusetts or Rhode Island citizen, if his great grandmother had a drop of African blood in her veins; and that although the Constitution of the United States had abolished attainders in this country, still, so far as free colored citizens were concerned in coming from free to slave States, they were to be regarded, in defiance of the Constitution of the United States, as attainted—yes, the victims of a *colored attainder*, and subject to the awful judgment of perpetual slavery for showing their colored heads, with no helmet but the Federal Constitution for their protection, in a slave State.

And if the old State of New Jersey had had the benefit of the Federal Constitution before the adoption of your new Constitution of 1844, and if Congress had given this State the practical benefit of a republican form of goverment, by abolishing in Congress your State slave laws, as contrary to a republican form of government, it would not have been necessary for me to have troubled your Honors, the legislation of Congress being paramount to all State constitutions and State legislation on all points within its constitutional jurisdiction. And although the constitution of a State may be silent on the subject of slavery, still, if slaveholding legislation dishonor the State statute book, then Congress has jurisdiction to abolish such State law, as renders the form of that State government hostile to a republican form of government. The form of a State government may be republican in its constitution, but legislation may spring up in that State, by which one half of the people may assume to own the other half, in direct hostility to a republican form of government, and the United States is then bound, by some exercise of sovereign power, to restore to the people of New Jersey, a republican form of government, either by legislation in Congress or by the exercise of judicial power through the Federal or State judiciaries; and if through the latter, then I am in my proper place to contend here, this day, that this old law of slavery was unconstitutional ever since the adoption of the Constitution of the United States, as being contrary to the fundamental guaranty of the Republic, and all State laws conflicting with said guaranty of a republican form of government are null and void, as much as a State law violating the liberty of conscience secured by the Constitution; and if this ground be a sound position, the slave laws have been void from the adoption of the Constitution, as being in direct hostility to the solemn guaranty in the Constitution in favor of a republican form of government. Give me a republican form of government in the Constitution and the legislation of a State, and I defy any man to hold a human being in that State as a slave, according to the law of that country, until the meaning of language is revolutionized.

The very idea of a Constitution of the United States in an enlarged view would be replete with consequences full of glorious import to the bondmen of this land. As has been said by me before in the course of this argument, a Constitution springs from our weakness and need of protection, and is a covenant of the whole people with each *person*, and of each *person* with the whole people, for the protection and defence of our natural rights, of life, liberty, and the pursuit of happiness. Is it possible to conceive that a people meeting from their natural weakness, and after coming together, conclude to make a charter party of piracy? That, although they agree to protect and defend five-sixths of the people in their natural rights, yet, as it regards the other sixth, they solemnly covenant and guarantee, to give them no protection or advantage therefrom, but covenant to 'strip said one-sixth of their natural rights of life, liberty, and the pursuit of happiness; and reduce them to chattels, men-breathing-property, so that they would be infinite losers by forming a Constitution. Instead of having their natural rights protected, they are stript of the right to themselves, and delivered over to masters, who, drunk or sober, reasonable or unreasonable, sensible or foolish, are to make for them Constitutions and laws, in the height of passion, prompted by lust, avarice or meanness, from hour to hour, and day to day, until life's end. The slaveholders contend the Constitution of the United States secured them these terrible advantages. If it did, and the adopters had so understood it, I do not believe a single State would have seriously entertained an idea of its adoption for a single moment, north of the State of Delaware.

To be sure, we have lived under an *invisible Constitution* of slaveholding construction for fifty-five years, which we have never seen, but have often bitterly felt—the good honest anti-slavery Constitution which should have gone into

operation on the fourth of March, 1789, as it was honestly
adopted, and if carried out, in the integrity of its high and
glorious purpose, would, long ere this, have extirpated
slavery from this guilty land, and made it the paradise of the
new world. But the government, from its adoption, has
been under, as a general proposition, the control of slaveholding Presidents, Vice-Presidents, Speakers of the House
of Representatives, who organize the legislative power with
five millions of whites at the South, and ten millions of whites
in the North. The South should have had three of the nine
judges of the Supreme Court of the United States, but they
have five and the North four; they have two-thirds of the
foreign ministers, the principal officers on the sea and on the
land. The South have furnished the spiracles through which
the government has breathed, yes, and the eyes with which
it saw, the ears with which it heard, and the tongues and
pens by which it spoke and wrote. It is no wonder the ship
lost the track of its contemplated voyage, and became the
abused organ of a section of the land whose supposed interests prosecuted an implacable war upon human rights, or in
other words the basis and prosperity of whose peculiar institutions were quickened into life by tears and blood, and
found their proper aliment in crushing and prostituting the
rights of one half of their own population, and holding human
labor in contempt, by which three millions of their own
population, being white men, could not labor by the side of
the slave without disgrace; and they, the whites, having no
capital but their labor, sunk down to a point of degradation
but little above the slaves—no schools, they became the
lazaroni of this continent; while some forty thousand oli-
garchists, owning most of the land and the slaves, and being
prompted by ambition and money, moved by the common
spirit of slavery, the true bond of connection and source of
their political power—these men have snatched this Consti-

tution from the nation, and have given us by the force of
suppression, violation, construction and interpretation, com-
mingled with their fanciful guaranties and compromises, a
Constitution as by them administered, bearing a faint resemblance to the one given us by the fathers of the Revolution,
with their wounds yet unhealed from the battle-fields of
freedom. The preamble of the Constitution of the United
States must have been adopted after the whole document had
been prepared by the framers, as the grand exponent of
intention ; and as so much is said by slaveholding casuistry,
I have often thought that the framers of that instrument had
a melancholy foreboding, that attempts might be made by
the crafty and designing of an after age, to pervert that
document, so plain and so full of good sense and virtuous
principle, to some sinister purpose ; therefore, as an everlasting *finger-board* pointing to the straight road of intent, they
virtually said—"Here we unlock our hearts, as to object
and design, and we say, Trust not those who tell you this
is not the truth. This is our design : We, the people of the
United States, in order to form a more perfect union, establish
justice, secure domestic tranquillity, provide for the common
defence and promote the general welfare, and secure the
blessings of liberty, for us and our posterity, do establish and
ordain this Constitution for the United States of America."
What purity and nobility of object ! How much have we
had practically, of this Constitution, by slaveholding construction ? Let us see how it would read if made for the
object intended by slaveholders and their apologists, and as
we practically see it administered. " We, five-sixths of the
people of the United States, in order to secure a union among
ourselves, which shall make the other sixth curse the Union,
and to establish justice for five-sixths by the most cruel
injustice to the other sixth ; to provide for the common
defence of five-sixths, by taking away all public and private

defence from the other sixth; to promote the particular welfare of five-sixths by destroying the entire welfare of the other sixth; to secure the blessings of liberty to five-sixths and the curses of never-ending slavery to the other sixth, do ordain this Constitution for the United States of America."

What would the adopters in the thirteen States have said to such a draft of a Constitution? Most of the thirteen States, on organizing the conventions of 1788, for rejection or adoption, would have resolved to have let the common hangman hang this Constitution on the gallows, with caricatures of the leaders in the convention of 1787, and closed the scene by burning it up, and have adjourned *sine die*. Another convention of the United States would have been called by an indignant people, and the first article would have abolished slavery, by name, in the United States, as an everlasting disturbing cause, no longer to be trusted to disgrace our soil.

Many seem to think, that we derive our natural, as well as citizen rights, from a Constitution. That cannot be so. Our natural rights are derived from our Maker, and the Constitution is like a fence around them to protect them from the invasion of others. Men derive title by letters-patent from the supreme power of the State, to their land, and the fence is placed around it to protect it from the wandering herd. Constitutions may also be said to be of American origin, and it is not possible we were so corrupt in the morning of the science. To be sure England talks of our Constitution; she speaks of the *Magna Charta*, obtained by fierce and ignorant barons, in the year 1215, with sword in hand, from feeble John; also the introduction of the Protestant religion, by Henry VIII., and the Revolution of 1688, and some other important epochs like the Reform Bill, which added to the current stream of imperial legislation, all considered, being "*moles indigesta*," make the sum and substance of what an English-man means by the Constitution of his country. France made several Constitutions during the political paroxysms and revolutions of that curious people, during the latter end of the eighteenth and the beginning of the nineteenth centuries, but at last this gallant people revolved in a circle of element ary expedients, from 1789 to the war of the barricades in 1830; making organic experiments, to collect the true sense of the nation respecting the safest place or hands in which to lodge power, from which the greatest amount of protection might be expected with the least burden to the people. Different forms of primal law were submitted to the people for adoption or rejection.

But look at Russian, Prussian, German, and Italian States ; here each person is looking to imperial, royal, or ducal pre-rogatives, for that security of life, liberty, and property, which should never have been absorbed by the Crown, but should always have constituted a fundamental *layer* of human rights, coming from, and adopted by the people, as their wall of defence.

Our colonies were in the habit of receiving gifts of a poli-tical character, carefully sent over the Atlantic after them, in grants, patents, bills of rights, and charters ; the very rights which they could not have left behind them, and *been men.* These constitutions, anywhere and everywhere, as a general rule, are made to defend human rights and not to crush them. The very idea of a constitution is like a life-preserver, made to save men in their danger in the water, and is not to be loaded with lead to sink them. There are innumerable modes by which human rights have been crushed, without calling in the very thing which should protect them, with which to accomplish so diabolical a purpose. To suppose ships made on purpose to preserve five-sixths, and expressly to drown the other sixth who sailed in them ; the bridge to precipitate

its sixth passenger over it into the river; is not more absurd
in supposition, than to suppose a United States Constitution
to be an instrument of ruin and destruction to every sixth
man who sought its protection.   Instead of an asylum he finds
it to be a dungeon with fetters; that he is to be bereaved,
and his posterity in all coming generations, of all capacity to
have natural rights; the forlorn victims of avarice, lust,
cruelty, and contempt; *himself*, property owned, and in the
most abject form, shorn of the power to assert the strength
heaven gave him to protect his most valuable rights. Rights!
Amazing! He has no rights but the right to be abused, to be
whipped, to starve, to suffer, and to die!! This idea of a
constitution being used as a death-warrant to execute human
rights, is a horrid solecism! incomprehensible, yea, a sublime
absurdity; the greatest insult ever offered to the human understanding; and certain men pretend such is the Constitution of the United States.

If the Constitution was an animated being, with reason
and a voice, and if you were to ask her to speak and say, was
she made to uphold slavery, and destroy human rights, she
would answer, " As to slavery I know not what you mean by
the word, I never used it in my life; I was born and brought
into this world for the single purpose of protecting the rights
of persons, defending men from the violations of their human
rights, from invasion from abroad, or forceful wrong on
the soil. I know no one except as a *person* possessing the
rights of life, liberty, and the pursuit of happiness, and for
their protection I put forth my power. When the free men
and women of this country are counted as a basis of representation in Congress and for Presidential electors (Indians not
taxed excepted), and three-fifths of all other persons are to be
counted, and though States or individuals call those three-
fifths, slaves, serfs, *or connecting links between men and mon-
keys*, and even treat them as such, I only know them as I do

the rest of mankind—as persons; my eyes can only see men as persons, my ears can only hear the cry of men as persons, possessed of natural rights. I cannot be used to destroy the liberties of any innocent man. It is not within the range of my power, unless I am perverted to purposes contrary to my instincts." "Who dare affirm," says she, "that I guarantee slavery and make compromises for its support? Oh!" says she, "it is all false, it is directly the reverse; I guarantee to each State a Republican form of government, which confers the equal right of life, liberty, and property to each innocent human being in each of the twenty-seven States; that is my right, my power, my nature, prerogative, scope, end, and object of my existence; and slavery exists in this country to my unutterable confusion, by my violation direct, and by reason of the people of this land having refused to allow me to prostrate slavery through the judiciary or Congress, under my guaranty of a republican form of government to the States. *Persons* bound to service or labor by laws of one State, I say, shall not be withheld, but shall be delivered up on claim of him to whom such service or labor is due. Here I deal with persons again. If the wife, the son, the daughter, the apprentice, the prisoner from his bail, escape into other States, I order all of these persons to be delivered to the husband, or the father, or the master, or their bail, to whom such labor and service is due, and for this purpose I am a perpetual treaty between the States, to accomplish these just objects, and save the effusion of blood. If," says the Constitution, "a slave is not a person within the protection which I afford to all persons where I say 'no person shall be deprived of life, liberty, or property, without due process of law,' then he is a being I have no right to touch and deliver up, for I can only deliver up persons bound to, or who owe service or labor as persons and not as slaves; and if these persons are slaves, then I am under the most solemn promise

15*

and obligation not to explain away, but to see that slave-persons, if you please, are not deprived of life or liberty, without due process of law, which must have been some distinct adjudication that the being was a slave, by a court, acting on the principles of the common law. No such court has been organized in this land, no such judgments have been rendered. If he is within the protection of the *magna charta* part of my character, then I will not deliver the man to his master, as you are pleased to call him, until a judgment of some kind, showing that the man owes service to another, and has been deprived of his liberty by due process of law. Some record of that kind must be shown, or I cannot deliver him up."

Said Mr. S., I demand that these persons be delivered up to enjoy their liberty, on the ground of the declaration in the Constitution of the United States, declaring that " no person shall be deprived of life, liberty, or property, without due process of law. There is not a slave or servant, so held, of the four thousand of both sorts in New Jersey, but who is entitled to his liberty by the Constitution of the United States.

It is a curious and ridiculous idea of some, that our fathers had *secret thoughts* of crime against man, which they had not the courage to express, under the name of intentions, when they drafted the Constitution of the United States; and that we, out of respect to the unrecorded, unwritten, villainous intentions, and wicked wishes of our venerable ancestors, should take those wicked thoughts and unrecorded intentions of crime against the rights of man, as our Constitution, under the idea of intention, rather than the beautiful text itself, so full of life, liberty, and justice. The Constitution of the United States, on its own face, is safe, and more to be relied on to explain its own meaning with justice to the framers, adopters, and us, their posterity, than all we could learn from each drafter and each adopter, could we summon-them before a court of justice to explain it as they understood it, on the 4th of March, 1789, the day it went into operation. To be sure, if the adopters ever thought of slavery, they did not think to name it, and must have supposed it near its end, and they did not wish to disgrace the nation by the admission that so foul and base a thing ever existed. It is truly lamentable to think the human mind is yet in such a low state of civilization, that from this point to enter *goose-hood*, would be elevation, and that men should delight to lay hold of such absurd views, as the one exposed, to justify themselves in the perversion of that glorious instrument, to some low and grovelling purpose, pecuniary or political.

Mr. S. said that he felt mortified to think it should be necessary for him, in the nineteenth century, to stand in Republican America, the live-long day, before one of the highest courts in intellect, learning, and station, to prove a human being a man, and not a thing. The proposition that the colored people of this State held in bondage, are men, born free and independent, by·the law of nature, is one above all demonstration, outstrips all logical deductions, and addresses itself to our every perception, for its truth, which can gain nothing from analogy, and borrow nothing from illustration ; comparison cannot aid in its development, and similes cannot make it more clear to the human mind. Antiquity and to-day utter the same response. It is the same yesterday, to-day, and forever. Every degree of latitude and longitude renders the same verdict, whether at Timbuctoo or at Trenton ; whether in mind or in body, for time or eternity, they are men and women, creatures of hope, gazing on the same bright, strong, beautiful, and ancient heavens, on ˙which Adam, and Solomon, and Daniel, and Paul, Copernicus, and Columbus, turned their admiring eyes ; the frames of colored men, their human countenance divine, containing the same unerased lineaments, vindicating, in celestial heraldry, the grandeur of their descent, the greatness of their origin— showing that God is their father, that all men are brethren of one blood ; that the sweets of life, the joy of liberty, the hope and pursuit of happiness, are the gifts of the Great Father, to all, and each of his children, with a power and privilege forever to climb the ascending heights of eternity, through the merits of His Son, increasing in happiness and knowledge, through the endless day of Heaven.

The greatest announcement affecting the interests of man ever made since the advent of the Redeemer, was the synopsis of the rights of man, made by the immortal signers of the Declaration of Independence, on the 4th day of July, 1776.

The announcement was antagonistic to the opinions of all former ages, and the then existing powers of this world. Russell, Sidney, Milton, Cromwell, and Locke, were permitted to ascend the mount of Discovery, and behold, as by prophetic sight, in the land of the setting sun, beyond the vast Atlantic, a people asserting what these philosophers believed ; that all men were created free and equal, and possessed of certain inalienable rights, amongst which were life, liberty, and the pursuit of happiness. What they hoped for man, we have seen and heard. When this sublime declaration was made on the 4th of July, 1776, it was high treason, and political atheism, in every other government on earth.

To all other governments with birth-born kings, birth-born legislators, birth-born judges, this declaration of the American Revolutionists was a thousand times more formidable than war or revolution itself. This was a great fundamental proposition, placing all men on a level, and as equals, on the start of the journey of existence ; stating the value, the riches of their elemental capital, which no insolvency could

divest, no bankruptcy carry away.   Slavery, or the inherit-
able dominion of man over man, with its complicated train
of truckling dependencies, artificial distinctions, the iron-
railing of caste, were in one day, by the great proposition of
the 4th of July, struck down as false in principle.   This was
the sentiment of a New World, and the signers of the
great human being *postulatum*, spoke for themselves, and
the unborn nations of this broad continent, respecting this
great Americanism of the new hemisphere.   The glorious
sound went careering through the world, that all men are
created free and equal.   The Massachusetts slave heard its
music, and joined in the chorus, and his freedom was confessed.   The slaves of New York and Pennsylvania listened
to the joyful acclaim ; the man-chattel of New Hampshire
caught the still small voice, and joined in thanks to heaven,
that all were free.   Congress caught the sound, and said, the
African slave trade should cease on our part forever, and that
no slave should tread the States of Ohio, Illinois, Indiana,
Michigan, and the territories of Wisconsin and Iowa.   The
angel of deliverance flew with the mighty scroll in her right
hand over valley and mountain to the vast lands of Mexico,
and proclaimed from the summit of her smoking volcanoes,
that all men were born free and equal ; and in one day,
50,000 black slaves, and two millions of enslaved Indians, in
their *repartimientos*, in the mountains, in the mines, in the
workshops, and on the roads, in their chains, heard the glorious decree, and they all in chorus joined, and sung, " that
all men are created free and equal," and in that instant they
stood up free.   The angel cried again in Guatemala and
Peru, from the depth of the blue heavens, " that all men
were created free."   The black and red slave heard his
voice, from the mountain and the mine, the hill and the hollow, that all men were created free and equal, and their fetters fell from their delivered hands as they lifted them to

heaven; and then they sung, "all men are created free and equal," for they were free.

Along upon the mighty Andes the angel flew, and from Chimborazo's icy top, she cried again so loud and long that the tens of thousands of poor bondsmen of Chili heard, some in those unvisited regions, subterranean, damp, dreary, digging gold ore and veins of silver far under the floor of the roaring Pacific, who never saw light; while others were delving in the depths and bowels of the Andes, to satisfy the accursed thirst for gold; others in smelting-houses loaded with chains; others driving, as serfs, their master's flocks of goats and sheep on the mountain's side, and the loaded mule along; others with loads upon their heads, in the rounds of common life, who wore out their being for thankless masters; others to galleys chained; others bound to posts, whose backs were being scourged; others in a deferential form were listening to the raging words of graceless masters. All heard the long, the loud trumpet sound, "that all men were created free and equal." All around the whips and fetters fell, and in one joyful hour, in time, up went the glorious chorus of response from men who were slaves no more, who said and sung "*all men are created free and equal.*" The joyful proclamation, by the angel made, and the sublime chorus, and Humanity's reply, rolled over the great mountain, and down its eastern slant, and the slaves of Guayaquil, Colombia, Venezuela, and Bolivia, learnt to sing the holy notes, "that all men are created free and equal;" and in one day deliverance came to all these sons of sorrow and of toil. The angel then to the West Indies flew, and the men of Hayti said, throughout that island, all men are free, and one million stood up enfranchised; the anthem of deliverance was sung in each British Isle on the 1st of August, 1838, and 800,000 slaves in one moment became 800,000 British freemen. The angel flew to the Cape of Good Hope, and sung her celestial song, and in one day 100,000 bondmen cried from the Cape inland 600 miles east and west, from sea to sea, "we all are free." The angel balanced on her pinions, flew and cried in the ears of the Bey of Tunis, and in the Egyptian Ali Pasha's, "that all men are created free and equal." These sons of Mahomet heard, and the Heaven-made-decree obeyed, and in those lands of darkness and of death, in one day each slave cried out, "I am free! I am free!" On the 1st of April, 1844, the angel of peace and good will toward men, blew a louder and longer blast than she ever yet had done; it was heard over the hundred millions of East Indies, saying, "all men were created free and equal." In a moment the hereditary serf, the caste-marked million, and slaves by descent, for ages, in all 12,000,000 told, started into life and joy, amidst rattling chains and broken fetters falling from them, their eyes streaming with tears, grateful to Heaven as they flowed, and they all joined in the glorious song which they now sung, "that all men are created free," and "that they were slaves no more!"

We live in an abolition age, when the dungeons which have incarcerated suffering humanity are being broken in and unlocked, in every corner of our benighted world, and the captive bid come forth ; and may I entreat this Honorable Court to share in the unfading glory of opening this castle of slavery, New Jersey, with the key of the new Constitution, and the other keys I have the honor so submit to this Court, by which to let oppressed men go free.

Here Mr. S. closed his opening argument, having spoken until six o'clock, P. M.

The Court adjourned until Thursday morning at ten o'clock. A. M. The Court met at ten o'clock, A. M., on the 22d of May, and Chief Justice Hornblower made a very able, eloquent, and affecting address, to two fine looking young men, who were sentenced to be executed in August next for the murder of Parke and Rasner.

At eleven o'clock, A.M., Mr. Zabriskie opened his argument for the defence of the claimants of these persons, and spoke till half after one, with a good deal of talent and power. The Court adjourned until three o'clock, P.M. Mr. Zabriskie resumed, and concluded at half after three, P.M.

Mr. Bradley, as counsel for the claimants, spoke with much energy and ingenuity until five o'clock, P. M., when he closed.

Mr. Stewart replied from five o'clock, P.M., to six. The Court adjourned until seven, P.M., and Mr. Stewart spoke from seven, P.M., until after ten, and closed.

It is regretted that the arguments of Messrs. Zabriskie and Bradley could not have been given at length, but many of the points which they made will appear in Mr. Stewart's reply. It is not expected we should report all Mr. Stewart said, first and last, in eleven hours of delivery.

ARGUMENT IN REPLY.

Mr. Stewart said, in reply, that he must express his gratitude to the learned counsel, for the kind compliments paid to his intellect, by one who had given us so strong evidence, that he himself enjoyed the singular fortune of a fine mind, embellished with the advantages of a polished education, and what he could not command from research he might still enjoy by the power of reflection.

Mr. S. said the learned counsel had alluded to the fact that the first person they had seen alive, who was an Abolitionist, in the county of Bergen, was the person who served these writs of *habeas corpus*—Mr. Palmer—and the counsel gravely informs us that the people did not *tar* and *feather* him. I suppose this statement is made as a distinguished compliment to his neighbors in that county, and as the highest proof they have ever given of their civilization ; and it is to be hoped they may never, in an evil hour, fall below this high-water mark of their advancing elevation.

Mr. Zabriskie has told us, to frighten and almost alarm us out of this effort in behalf of crushed men, and to make us leave these slaves in the great man-trap, that if your honors shall let those slaves go free under your new Constitution, the courts will be compelled to hear arguments by wives and children, to be set free from the dominion of their husbands and parents. The bare statement of so strange a proposition relieves me from a reply to it.

The gentleman has endeavored to alarm the sensibilities of the court, by a parade of several distinct orders of modern philosophers, known under the name of Fouriers, Anti-Renters, Socialists, Owenites, Fanny Wrighters, Non-Resistants, and No-Human-Government-men, Dissolvers of the Union, Nullifiers, and Infidels. And he would wish to fasten the opinion upon the court, that there is some sort of relation between these philosophers' views and this dry law question, which is, whether slavery in the State of New Jersey is a *legal* and *lawful* institution or not. I confess I cannot discover any more relation between the philosophical dogmas of these different philosophers and the question before your Honors, than there is propriety in the following question: "If it is two hundred miles from this place to Boston, what is the amount of the first quarter's salary of the Lord Mayor of London?" I think when the pertinency of one of these propositions is made manifest, the other will then appear.

But, as there have been several attempts to lock and hook together, during the gentleman's reply, things the most dissimilar and uncongenial, I will take, if the court permit, the present opportunity, to define the liberty party Abolitionists' creed, a body of men who, at the late election, appeared to number about 62,500 voting men, of which body the speaker was an humble member. The liberty party Abolitionists, in the United States, had been a political party, with its candidates, ever since April, 1840; and was formed from necessity, to overthrow slavery, after having tried both of the old parties in vain, *each of the old parties having a slave end to it*, so that it was impossible to get either to undertake this work. The liberty party hold the Constitution of the United States to be, when properly interpreted, an anti-slavery document, replete with tendencies in favor of freedom; but that the slaveholding portion of this country have seized upon the reins of government, and perverted the Constitution's high intent, to the base purposes of sustaining, and increasing the power of slaveholders in every possible way, and have violated the Constitution by employing it to sanction slavery in many ways, and in the overthrow of the right of petition. The liberty party Abolitionists mean to employ the Constitution, and in pursuance of its authority, and not contrary thereto, to overthrow slavery in every way, and by all lawful means. We mean, as a body, and it is a part of our creed, to cling to the Union or Confederacy under all circumstances, and never give it up; slavery in, or slavery out, Texas in or Texas out: we hold on to the Union *and every acre of its soil,* whether it be the sands of Georgia or the mountains of Vermont, for the exaltation, purification, and enfranchisement of this land from slavery, root and branch. It is a cardinal principle from the beginning, never to vote for a slaveholder, or an apologist of slavery, but hold it our duty to vote at every election for men for town, county, State, and national officers, who will employ all lawful power to banish slavery from the nation, for the sake of three millions of slaves compelled to work without wages, as well as three millions of ignorant, poor, and *unschooled* whites in the South, the lazaroni of this continent, who are ruined by the most abject poverty, it being disgraceful for them to labor for wages by the side of the slave. To save six millions of human beings from ruin or desolation, *or one-third of our countrymen,* is the exact object of the liberty party Abolitionists, let it take ever so long to accomplish it. We have no motive for advancing the one, or retarding the other of the great parties, as we mean, in the end, to *overthrow them both*, as soon as we can get our countrymen to adopt our belief; we are law-abiding and law-sustaining men, and there is no more connection between the liberty party Abolitionists, and the list of philosophers just enumerated, than there is between the Chinese wall and the Erie canal. · We believe in short, a man has a better right to his own wife and children, than any other man, and we suppose the curse of slavery has, as a mass, nearly ruined the men of the South, as well as the land of the slave States, and we wish to improve and save our country and our people, by our party organization. And my apology to the court for this statement, defining our position, is the attempt to injure and dishonor as high-minded and pure a body of men as breathe, by making them keep company with those philosophers, however respectable they may be; yet we have not chosen their society, or opinions, in the prosecution of our enterprise.

The counsel of defendant, has attacked New York for calling a State convention. I can see nothing ULTRA or radical, once in a quarter of a century, in a State's reviewing the ground it has passed over, and thus lay hold of the improvements time suggests, or brings to light, for perfecting her great social edifice. The old way to amend the fabric of government in Europe, was on the battle-field, amidst the clangor of arms and roar of artilery, with bullets for *yeas*, and cannon balls for *nays*. I confess I much prefer the mode adopted by the State of New York.

The learned counsel, to get rid of the force of the first article of the new Constitution of this State, says it is a mere abstraction, a rhetorical flourish, and is not a part of the Constitution, in reality, not binding us to do anything. I should like to know where I am to *begin to read* the new Constitution, and how much of it is to be rejected as surplusage.

The other counsel, Mr. Bradley, says this section of the

Constitution is a mere braggadocio, a mere telling England that all men are free and independent by nature, and it is *so* said, to let England know that our people *know* that we are as good as her Lords and Commons, Kings and Queens, and that it grew out of our revolutionary jealousy, of our own importance, when we first inserted it in the Declaration of Independence. This is queer indeed! New Jersey, in her old Constitution, made *two days before* the Declaration of Independence, was perfectly silent then ; when the reason for bragging might have operated, she is very meek *then ;* not one word is said about human rights; but 68 years afterward, in September, 1844, when all danger is forever past, according to the gentleman, New Jersey sticks up her bristles, and says, " I would have you know, old England, yes, old John Bull, and you Miss Victoria Guelph, and Mr. Albert Coburg, that we are as good by nature, and as independent as any of you, *yes, that we be.*" But the sober-minded, brave, and considerate Jerseyman never had such a thought pass through his mind, at the time he voted for its adoption. He had too much regard for his own dignity, and too much respect for England, to employ himself in such a miserable small game of *swelling and surf-making,* to elevate the character of his country. The noble-minded Jerseyman is willing that other countries should amuse themselves with the baubles of kings, queens, and lords, as national dolls and playthings, without considering himself undervalued in the least by not being used for the same puerile and harmless purpose by his own countrymen ; and the last place in the world he would seek to curl the lip of scorn, would be in his own great fundamental and organic law, asserting his own freedom, dignity, and independence.

Mr. Bradley contends that Moses' law sanctioned slavery, and the buying the heathen around about for money. Yes, there was a kind of servitude which looks like buying the heathen by those ancient Jews for money. But the Jewish government was a theocracy, and every law, decree, or order of government, began with "Thus saith the Lord," as a standing formula; whether the document, law, or proclamation, came from the elders, a king, a general, or a high-priest, from a good man, or bad one, whoever had occasion to employ the character of the government, as that was a theocracy, and these rulers always used "Thus saith the Lord," as a universal preface to the law. All of Moses' laws were not from God; but Moses' system was a code of particulars, some from God and others from man. The Saviour settles this question in the case of that law of Moses, by which a man might live with his wife, a month after marriage, and if he did not like her, then give her a bill of divorcement, and send her away, however virtuous and worthy. The Saviour says, "Moses suffered it from the hardness of your hearts, it was not so in the beginning," etc. Now, this month divorce; the case of a Jew being permitted to take a cow, or an ox, which had suddenly died, to the gates of the city, and there sell it to the heathen and strangers to eat (forbidding the Jews to eat it), also the case of taking interest of the heathen, and none of a Jew, are instances. Polygamy is a fourth case, and the fifth is a man's making his captive into a wife, living with her as long as he pleased, and then setting her adrift, as in the 21st chapter of Deuteronomy; all of these cases have thus "Saith the Lord," as much as good laws. These laws Moses suffered this ignorant people to adopt as a matter of expediency, but they were not the laws of God, but are properly recorded, as our laws formerly in New York were, in favor of lotteries, and regulating Long Island horse-races. But the terrible injustice of these laws, proves that man was their author, and not God; but they are recorded under the general appellation of

"Thus saith the Lord," because the government was a Theocracy. This view, Mr. S. believed necessary, to vindicate the purity and glory of God. There was a law of heavenly origin which said, "whoso stealeth a man shall surely die or be put to death," which form he did not recollect, and is found in these same chapters. He did not see how that law of God could be reconciled with American slavery; for every man and woman, or his or her ancestor, had been stolen in this country. Again, if slavery is a Bible and heavenly institution, we should not be *opposed to it in the abstract*, as the defendant's counsel are, but everything should be done to foster and encourage it, and their Honors should resign their seats rather than decide in Mr. S.'s favor, however plain the new Constitution or other thing might be for the slave; for if the Bible countenances slavery, it is abstractly right, and the plaintiff's counsel commit a great sin in opposing slavery in the abstract, which they intend to atone for by going with all their might for it practically, and thus purge themselves for opposing, what the Bible sustains, in the abstract and concrete. If it is a Bible institution, which we have been abolishing in New England, New York, and Pennsylvania, let us repent in dust and ashes, and run down all the colored, the weak, the young, the Irish, the English, and the strangers on their first arrival; and catch our few suffering Indians, who are still straggling as wanderers among their fathers' graves, and make them all into slaves, and their posterity in the free States; and thus secure the blessings of Heaven, that are poured out so bountifully on Virginia, Maryland, and the Carolinas.

Mr. S. said that of all remarkable arguments for ingenuity, he had heard one urged by both of his learned and ingenious adversaries, and, in fact, the main one, on which they sought to continue the institution of slavery, in this State, which surprised, yes, astonished him, by its subtlety and cruelty. In the 1st section of the 10th Article of the new Constitution of New Jersey, among other things, it says:

"The common law and statute laws now in force, and not *repugnant* to this Constitution, shall remain in force until they expire by their own limitation, or be altered or repealed by the legislature; and all writs, actions, causes of action, prosecutions, contracts, claims, and rights of individuals, and of bodies corporate, and of the State, and all charters of incorporation, shall continue, and all indictments which shall have been found, or may hereafter be found for any crime or offence committed before the adoption of this Constitution, may be proceeded upon, as though no change had taken place."

The point the defendant's counsel would raise, is this; admitting that the new Constitution has abolished the old slave laws, root and branch, as being "repugnant" to the new Constitution; still under the name of "claims and rights of individuals" which "should continue," the rights of master and slave are both preserved in the 1st section of the 10th Article of the new Constitution under the head of "rights *preserved*," as defendant's counsel contend. The counsel further contend for defendant, that it is good law without such saving clause in the Constitution; and that all rights are preserved, notwithstanding a constitution, hostile to them on its face, has abolished the laws which created the rights, in so many words, *totidem verbis.* I deny these propositions, *in toto,* as applied to a case of slavery. *Reserved rights!* They would be *reserved wrongs!* and upon that principle a State could not abolish slavery; as for instance, suppose South Carolina makes a new Constitution, and abolishes slavery, and with, or without a reservation of the *rights* of the citizens; according to the argument we hear, the rights of the master are all taken up and preserved in the new Constitution, to the services of the slaves; the rights of sale of labor, or sale of slaves, or their offspring, are the same as before. They alter this Constitution again, and re-assert, ten years afterward, that slavery shall never exist in South Carolina; but the planter smiles at the imbecility of the Convention, and says, "although they have for the second time abolished slavery by the Constitution, and all laws which maintain it, yet according to the arguments of the defendant's counsel, in New Jersey, my rights are all preserved to the slaves, and that is all I ask;" and furthermore, says he, "it is curious to see how the body of this glorious institution of slavery survives its own decapitation. They cannot," says he, "abolish slavery, even in a constitution made on purpose, but the *Divine rights of slavery will survive*, and ride careering over all human attempts at their annihilation; and what," says the South Carolina planter, "is the peculiar beauty of this proposition, is, that by the universal admission of all jurists, slavery can only exist by positive law, for its support; but I have now discovered how it may exist not only without positive law for its support, but in deadly opposition to the most stringent organic Constitutional Law, for its entire abolition and express destruction." Once in a nation, and adopted by law, no form of law can banish it, as it lives under the name of a "right preserved;" yes, it lives and flourishes with an endless life. *It is the real " live-for-ever."* Yes, if this argument is sound, the most monstrous wrong in the universe, for whose destruction a new Constitution was expressly made, flourishes and prevails; yes, lo! the melancholy spectacle is presented to the astonished world, that although the laws sustaining slavery are all abolished, yet slavery has a more solemn and formidable protection, as a reserved right, than it ever had before, and that too in the bosom of its own executioner. The counsel, I have no doubt, hopes the shrewdness of this argument will be its apology for want of solidity. The master never had a single just right to the slave, and the Constitution no more preserves any for him, than it does the *turn-pike for highwaymen*, the treasure in my house for a thief, or the thoughtless young heir for a prey to blacklegs and sharpers.

After this view of this question has been taken, I shall consider the concession virtually made, that slavery is repugnant to the new Constitution; that the Massachusetts decision ends this cause, if good authority.

But slavery has been spoken of by the defendant's counsel with great respect. I regard it as the curse of the nation. Virginia, at the time of the first census, in 1790, had more than double the inhabitants of the State of New York: now it is sadly reversed, New York has about double that of Virginia. Virginia, with nearly double the territory of New York, and more good land than New York, situated in the most benignant climate to be found under the bright heavens, penetrated with large bays, and beautiful, noble, and navigable rivers, stretching to the metropolis of our land, washed by the Ohio; no land whose mountains are more ready to burst with their mineral wealth than hers; whose lead, iron, coal, and copper, lie hoarded in those beautiful mountains, in value beyond the computations of numbers, or the dreams of avarice. But that wealth shall never be explored, raised, or enjoyed by the palsied arm of slavery. No, it is reserved for the vigor of the freeman's strength; not dishonored by the blight of unpaid labor: those treasures will only come at the call of honored and free labor.

Look at hundreds of thousands of acres of fair and valuable land in Western Virginia, which would make noble farms, when free labor shall be honored, now sold at six cents, ten cents, and twenty-five cents an acre. Look at hundreds of old farms within forty and fifty miles of Washington, to be sold from $4 to $10 per acre, with their dilapidated buildings, covered with mortgages and trust deeds; the same land, slavery abolished, and freemen to cultivate, would be worth from $30 to $80 per acre. Look at whole regions and portions of counties abandoned, as commons, in old Eastern Virginia, where you may ride for hours, without meeting an inhabitant in the lower counties of this State, land yet beautiful, if its powers of fecundity were truly developed by freemen, once the seats of joyful hospitality of the last century, now as silent as the ruins of Palmyra and Babylon. The young growth of timber coming up, the wild animals resuming their ancient dominion, the traveller from the old world, as he measured his lonely steps over these forsaken abodes of men, would inquire what desolating wars have consumed the sons and daughters of this fair land ? in what chronicles shall it be found, or what more than Egyptian plague has been and bereaved these uncultivated lands of their proprietors, and has left the fox to come in at the window, and the owl to hoot at noon, and appointed the stork, the raven, the cormorant and bittern, *to perform the hospitalities of these dilapidated homes of departed men ?*   Alas ! the curse of the slave's foot-print has been *here*, unrewarded toil has been *here*, inalienable rights have been cloven down *here*, man has ranked with the ox, in the market, *here ;* marriage rights were trodden under foot *here ;* the father who begot, and the mother who bore the son and the daughter, had no rights in their children *here ;* men had no right to cultivate their immortal minds *here ;* justice and mercy had no abode *here ;* free labor was dishonored *here ;* the lash, the fetter and the chain ruled *here ;* and at last, hunger expelled the oppressor from his home *here.*

The splendid and princely plantation of George Washington, the Father of his country, presents, in forty-five years, one of the most melancholy and remarkable instances of that ceaseless vigilance of Providence, which pursues injustice with unerring certainty, from year to year, and at last overtakes and awards the punishment affixed to fundamental violations of the great rights, which the Father of all has in the welfare of his abused children.

Thousands of acres, and money in vast amount, united in the official station of President; this plantation lying within some ten or twelve miles from the three beautiful cities of Georgetown, Washington and Alexandria, partly surrounded by the majestic Potomac River, bearing on its commercial bosom ships from the ends of the world, freighted with every human want; this plantation was ready to ship at its own door, every redundancy it bore, at remunerating prices. The ambition of General Washington during the last years of his retirement, was, to make this favored place, with his hundred slaves, his abounding wealth, the great pattern plantation of this continent. Having done much to see his high purpose accomplished, in December, 1799, he died, having emancipated his slaves by his will. Judge Bushrod Washington, his nephew, with a large family of slaves, with a salary of $4,500 from the United States as judge for life, succeeded his illustrious uncle; and in 1819 or thereabouts, made a large sale of some thirty to fifty slaves, being near one-half. The nation was incensed at the act; his public apology was, that he was compelled to sell part to support the rest, and thus the process of *anthropophagi*, or man eating man, indirectly commenced; the cultivation was miserable and the bushes encroached; some fields, by 1828 or 1829, at the time of the ·judge's death, began to be given up. John A. Washington, the nephew of the judge, succeeds; the woods still gained; field after field, under slave and master's cultivation, went back to primeval forest. At about 1839 or 1840, Colonel Washington died, and in the month of April or May, 1842, the widow and her children were, like Adam and Eve, from Paradise driven out. "Great Burnam Wood had come to Dunsinane" as in Macbeth; the door was locked, the gate was shut, slavery's curse and the wilderness had expelled them from this ancient home of America's great man. This is slavery, sooner or later, everywhere; the curse of Heaven is upon it.

It would be a fraud on the people of New Jersey, so to construe their new Constitution, as the defendant's counsel had contended. There was not one in fifteen of the seventy-thousand who voted for its adoption, who would not glory and feel elevated by the act. To see these poor bondmen and their children free, must be matter of joy to all. The argument that they would not be so well off, is too stale to be used, in 1845, in New Jersey. For if the argument proves anything it proves too much, and that it would be better for the great mass of mankind to be slaves, and that it is a desirable institution. On that point I have no more to say except that those who believe such doctrines can easily put themselves and families in possession of its blessings, as several of the slave States are so kind as not to refuse to those of Anglo-Saxon descent the *peculiar privileges of that pleasant-spoken institution.*

To illustrate one of the abhorrent features of the institution in the slave States, Mr. Stewart, adverting to one of the positions of the opposite counsel, supposed the following case: An old man, said he, whom we will call Tinkem, lived in Trenton, once upon a time, and not being long for this world, called his ten sons around him and told them, My sons, I have but little to give you of worldly property, and, therefore, in order to start the five oldest of you comfortably in this life, I give each of them one of their five younger brothers, to be his property—in other words, his slave for life, and his posterity after him. And you, the five youngest of my sons, must be the slaves of your elder brothers. I do this in conformity with the usage of the citizens of a large number of the States of this Union! But the eldest son says,

"Father, what are the rights and prerogatives which we shall, in that case, possess over our slave brothers?"

"Oh," said the old man, "you will reduce them to chattels, or cattle—living, breathing property—that is all. It is perfectly legal, and you will be protected in the enjoyment of your property; you are no longer to regard them as sentient beings; you are to deprive them of all education, except the cart-whip instruction; you are to make them know and feel that their every moment is to be regulated by your wish and will, and that they are subject to be sold, and worked, husband apart from wife, and wife from husband; and their children from both. So, now, my sons, take your slaves, and begone!" Now (continued Mr. Stewart), the story of this horrible deed reached the ears of the citizens of Trenton, and the sanctum of its editors. A burst of indignation is the consequence. Everybody and every press exclaims "monster! monster! monster!" with one voice. It is taken up by the people, and the press of Philadelphia and New York, and language grows weak, and imagination weary, in searching for fitting epithets in which to condemn the foul and damning act of this heartless old villain, Tinkem of Trenton! Men come from a prodigious distance to get a sight of so much moral deformity, existing in a single man. The phrenologists come to examine his craniological developments, wondering what manner of man-monster he can be; and the whole nation rings with the story, and but one opinion is expressed, everywhere, in public and in private—that of horror and astonishment. But, your Honors, pause in your honest outburst of indignation. Old Tinkem stands excused, in view of the fact that not a week comes and goes in the regions of the sunny South, that does not furnish a parallel to this conduct. A slaveholding father there gives the children of his own body, by his bond-woman, to be slaves for life, to his children by his free-woman—I mean his wife! It is done in twelve

States out of the seven and twenty of which this Union is composed, whenever the father wishes to endow his heir out of his possessions. And this I hold to be slavery in the length and breadth of its flagitiousness; it is yet but one phase of its abounding villainy. The picture is startling, frightful, revolting; but it is neither overdrawn, nor too highly colored.

Mr. S. replied to several subordinate points made, and authorities cited by the counsel of the defendants, which it is not supposed would materially improve the report of the argument. What is further said is a part of a report made of what Mr. S. said, by Mr. Otis, reporter of the New York "Evening Express," and what followed Mr. Stewart's close is the report of Mr. Otis also.

Mr. Stewart drew his remarks to a close by appealing to the court very earnestly as to the high and solemn duty left to them to perform. It is yours, may it please your Honors, (he said), to put the last, the finishing stroke upon slavery, in one of the noblest old States of this glorious confederation. It is an honor which you should covet. Let no man take it from you. Leave it not to other hands to finish so noble a work. What would the world say, to see a case like this argued as it has been before this court for two days, with the full light of this blessed and glorious Constitution shedding its rays upon it, turned off and decided against liberty, upon the worse than doubtful authority of a few extinct and exploded statutes, which stand repealed in your code by the voice of the people speaking through a convention of their choice—the acts of which they have also confirmed by their solemn votes? May it please your Honors, I cannot believe that such will be your decision. I have too much faith in my kind for this. I feel that New Jersey will hold up the hands of this court in coming to the support of freedom and of free institutions in her borders.

Never can the act be regretted. Conscience will approve it. Time will approve it. Death-bed reflection will approve it. Eternity and heaven will approve it. It has been long, too long postponed. But it is not too late to come up, man-like, statesmanlike, patriotlike, godlike, and declare that it is indeed true, in the language of your now organic law, that within all your pleasant borders, at least, all mankind are, by nature, entitled to perfect freedom in the possession of life, liberty, and the pursuit of happiness.

After Mr. Stewart resumed his seat, there was a pause of some duration. The scene was quite impressive. The auditory was numerous and highly respectable, and such was the impressiveness with which the closing appeal of the advocate for freedom was delivered, that no one seemed to like to be the first to break the spell his eloquence had cast upon the assembly. At length, the Bench arose, the Chief Justice adjourned the court until to-morrow morning, and the hearing of the causes which have occupied our attention for these two days past was terminated.

NOTE.—These causes were subsequently decided against the construction advocated by Mr. Stewart, Chief Justice Hornblower delivering a dissenting opinion.

LETTER TO DR. BAILEY.

New York, Aug. 30th, 1845.

Dear Bailey:

Sir, as you desired occasionally to know how I *treated*, and was *treated* by, the human beings who are travelling that journey, whose limit is a bourne from which no traveller returns or sends back intelligence of the beauties and glories of that undiscovered land, peopled with all the former generations who have made a transit over this sorrowing globe—I hasten, at this point, to redeem my obligation to you, springing from that request, and give you a brief account of a recent journey, from which I returned this week, to the northern part of Vermont, bordering on Canada line, where my four sisters reside. I make an annual pilgrimage to visit them. Their husbands, except one, are thorough working liberty men.

I happened to leave Troy on the morning the shilling boats ran the seventy miles from Troy to Whitehall, on lake Champlain, through the Northern Canal. I found myself on one of our very hot days, thermometer at 89°, Fahrenheit, with a hundred and twenty gentlemen and ladies, crowded into one of the narrow packets. As night approached, we learned there would be no berths for sleeping, as we were a dense mass of living flesh, which filled the boat. Everything betokened a miserable and sweltering night, in which there was no calculating the limits of endurance, or the bounds of forbearance necessary to bring us through this purgatorial state, in which all that was dissolvable or which might be in solution, in each man's composition, seemed not only to exude, but flow in silent currents through the unnumbered perspiratory outlets of our different tabernacles of clay. This night was to be passed in *head-topping or perpendicular sleep.* It was truly a severe night. But to mitigate its horrors, two Methodist ministers of the northern part of the New York Conference, one about sixty-five and the other about forty-five, were found in the middle of the boat, in the forepart of the night, making loud assertions against modern Liberty party Abolitionists, while they justified slaveholders and southern institutions. The younger one, though a man of some talents, seemed a pro-slavery fanatic, so bitter in his soul against Abolitionists, that, had his power been equal to his malice, there would not have been one of us left unburied, whether dead or alive. I first took them for slaveholders peddling the peculiar institutions of the South, in small quantities at the North, to suit purchasers. The first question I put to them, was, is slavery right, or wrong? They both replied, and often asserted, they would not answer that question; that had nothing to do with the question; but they said the question was, what shall we do with the slaves? I pressed these men repeatedly to answer my question, is slavery right, or wrong? But they said they would not answer me. I then told them if slavery was right, we had nothing to do about it, and had no business to intermeddle with it; and it seemed to me (as I by this time discovered they were clergymen and the whole boat was listening), that in men at their time of life, as professed teachers of the entire word of God, the spiritual fathers and teachers in the land, it was a dereliction of duty for them to refuse to let us know whether *it was right* to steal men and women from Africa, and in chains bring them to our soil, and sell them like brutes, work them without wages, and keep them on the most wretched and scanty fare, and work them in the burning sun under the gashing lash, and, if the master pleased, as he often did, whether it was right for him to sell children from their parents, and a wife from her husband, and deprive them of the Bible, and all the lights of immortality, except a selfish, ungodly religion, which was preached to them, saying: "Slaves obey your masters, God commands it, for slavery is an institution of God, and if you, the slaves, wish to go to Heaven, you must work as hard as you can spring for the master, and be careful and never steal any of your master's pigs, chickens, corn, or watermelons." Cannot you inform us, sirs, said I, whether such an institution of robbery of God's poor children is right or wrong, or not; or is it too deep for you to decide? They answered they would not say, whether it was right or wrong. Then for the first time, they had reason to learn both the wickedness and meanness of their position by an overwhelming laugh of contempt which saluted their ears, from the audience. I then stated that there was not a minister in the entire South, who dared preach the most important essential truths of Christianity to the slave! Oh! said they, the ministers of the South do not preach politics to the slaves. That, I replied, was the reason they did not preach the whole Gospel. Why, is the Gospel a political gospel, said they, or one of them? Yes, said I, it is, and I am sorry you do not know it. The first great elementary political rights, are also religious ones; that a man owns his own body and soul, has a right to appropriate and enjoy the faculties of that soul and body, and is bound to enlighten that mind; the man has the political and religious right to his wife, and the wife the same to her husband; and these parents have a political right to train up their children in the nurture and admonition of the Lord. Children obey your parents, is a command of God; and it is a political right of these parents to exact obedience; but slavery says, " no, obey your masters." The right of worshipping God according to the dictates of your own conscience is one of the greatest of political rights—that alone, enjoyed by the slave, would set him free, for there is no slave but feels his right of conscience violated, in serving a master as a slave, by force. Finally, after a great deal of jesuitical pettifogging on the subject, evincing trick, and heartless devices to delude, they said they were opposed to slavery, *in the abstract.* On which, I asked them if they were opposed to the toothache in the abstract? (An overwhelming laugh.) They were angry, and insinuated that this was no comparison at all, and that the audience were not well-bred! They then said they would preach Jesus Christ and Him crucified to the slave. To that I replied, that is the correct doctrine, for everlasting justice was the fundamental of Christ's religion. The younger priest arose and in a rage said, there was no such thing in the Bible—Paul did not say so, Christ did not say so, and that I was wiser than Paul and Christ. The audience cried, shame, horror, shame on such priests and such a religion, and this priest went muttering, in a passion, on deck to get fresh air. " *Whatsoever ye would men,*" etc., I supposed proved the justice of Christ's religion. Much was said in two hours between me and these wicked apologists of slavery—enough to make a small book. But I will say, I never saw an audience so rapidly converted to truth as this audience was, by the shameful absurdities of these ministers, until these two men might fairly and candidly have been said to have renounced the great corner-stone truths of Christianity, to bolster up the abhorred system of slavery. Terrible thought, that a man should strip God of his glorious attributes, in order to make the devil respectable!

A little before daylight, we left the packet and went on board the steamer Saranac, at Whitehall, and at 8, A.M., of that day, at breakfast, while passing over the military classic waters of Champlain, near Ticonderoga ruins, a conversation broke out at the table as to the cause of the city of Washington falling into the hands of the British in the summer of 1814, in the late war, when I replied, it was slavery which was the source of our weakness, disgrace, and defeat on this painful occasion. Two well-dressed men, who turned out to be slaveholders, one from Georgia and the other from Virginia, informed us that no part of our country was better prepared to resist an enemy than a slave State, as slaves loved their masters so well they would fight bravely for them. I felt obliged to deny that this was the history of the country, and to remark that our people, with more men than the British, the President of the United States, Mr. Madison, the Secretary of War and heads of departments, with several thousand of the best marksmen in America, gathered from ten miles square and the adjacent States of Maryland and Virginia, who met the British Commodore with his *liberty sailors* at Bladensburgh—our men retreated over sandhill after sandhill, and the President at their head, with the best opportunity to have met and conquered these sailors, but instead, they retreated to Washington City, and broke in perfect confusion, each man fleeing to his home, leaving the Capitol to be sacked, burnt and plundered without resistance. Gen. Smith of Georgetown, D. C., told me, in 1818, while passing over this very ground in a journey I was taking to Washington City, that he commanded a brigade in this fleeing army of ours, and that the secret of our disgraceful flight was, that a story had been circulated through the District and adjacent counties of the two States, that on that day the slaves were to rise and assert their liberty; and that each man more feared the enemy he had left behind in the shape of a slave, in his own house or plantation, than he did anything else. The officer and soldier had their minds distracted with the possibility of this insurrection, said Gen. Smith, and therefore fled to their homes before an inferior force, and left Washington to the mercy of its captors. In the Revolution,

South Carolina, I think in 1777, sent a committee to the Continental Congress, at Philadelphia, apologizing for not furnishing the quota of the conscription of troops designated by Congress for that State, for fear that their slaves would arise and assert their liberty, when they discovered the weakness of the whites, after sending forward their legal war-contingent to the war of Independence. Where would have been our victory, the same autumn of '77, at Saratoga, or our finally acknowledged Independence, if all had been in the position of South Carolina ? Slavery alone would have made the whites slaves of England for the sake of American whites enslaving the men of Africa. There was a great deal said between us. For the Virginian, I drew a contrast between the State of New York and Virginia. In 1790, Virginia, with one-third more territory, with the finest soil, and the most beautiful climate on earth, had 70,000 inhabitants. The State of New York 300,000 people. Now Virginia 130,000 or 140,000, and New York 2,600,000—double the population—and the city of New York could buy and sell Virginia alone, and they might throw in North Carolina into the bargain ; such was the curse of slave-labor, and prosperity of honored free labor. I proposed to make a slave of the Georgian on the spot, as it was probable I was the strongest, according to his own principles, and inquired for the objection, and what he had to say, why I should not make a slave of him, on the spot. He said that would be wrong, as he was a white man ; but it would be right to enslave an African, although he was only a forty-eighth part African and the other forty-seven parts were Anglo-Saxon. The people raised a shout at his proposition, which learnt him he was on the beautiful free waters of Champlain instead of the slave-bound Savannah.

Our cause in Vermont seems firmly fixed in the affections of the true-hearted.

On Sunday, the 24th of August, I spoke two hours in the

middle of the day, to a large audience in the Brick Church in Cambridge, in that State—six or seven towns were represented, and some of the audience came sixteen miles.

Vermont will do her duty. On my return on Monday, I came twenty-seven miles by 10 A.M., to Burlington, and then passed up the lake to Whitehall, where, at half after 5 P.M., a most respectable body of men and women, between seventy and eighty, went on board the canal packet, to pass through the Champlain Canal to Troy. We were packed away quite densely in the boat: and after dark, the captain, to my surprize, came and said, I heard your combat with the Methodist clergyman, when you went up, and I wish you to speak on the subject of slavery in order to pass the time. I told him I was unwell and had been so used up with the hot weather, that I could not do it. He asked me a second time, and I for the same reason declined. We had gentlemen and ladies from Boston, New Bedford, and ten to twelve English gentlemen from Montreal, several from New York, and various parts. Mr. Randall, an old sea captain and a gentleman of wealth from New Bedford, moved that Mr. Stewart be requested to speak, and it appeared to be carried by an almost unanimous aye, with the exception of two male noes and one female. And these three noes were two slaveholders from Virginia, and the woman a West India Cuban slaveholder. And to this strong invitation I replied, I did not feel able to speak, and declined. These slaveholders at this point spoke, and said, as much, it was well I had declined, for they had paid their money on the boat, and were not to be disturbed with abolition. Upon that, a gentleman moved that all who desired to hear Mr. Stewart speak, should rise up. Every gentleman and lady in the cabin arose as with a hasty spring, except the three slaveholders. Upon that I arose and thanked the firm and pertinacious friends of the liberty of speech. I stated I would now speak as my right had been denied by these slaveholders. Upon that these slaveholding men protested I should not speak; if I did, they would leave the boat and complain to the company. I seated myself for a moment, and the audience took them in hand; and such a tongue-dressing as they received from the gentlemen present, should be a caution to their successors in time to come. The friends of the freedom of speech said to them, do you mean to padlock us as you do your slaves? If we wish to discuss geography, politics, agriculture, religion, slavery, or abolition, are you three beings to sit here and tell us seventy people, what we may or may not say, and when? You are most wretchedly mistaken if you expect to apply your plantation discipline to this boat, and as to your getting out of the boat in the night, that you may do; and as to your threatening that you will tell the proprietors of the boat and the world, to injure this line, we defy your impotent malice —there are men on board of this boat who believe in free discussion of all things, who could buy and sell all the slaveholders who ever did, or ever will pass over these waters. Do you think, said one of the audience, if a boat-load of slaveholders on the Savannah, Ga., River, wished to discuss the inimitable justice of working men, women, and children under the lash, without wages, and it was opposed by these travellers from Vermont or New York, as a disagreeable question to them to hear, would the slaveholders be silent? No. The probability is they would commit murder by throwing the three men overboard to drown. I, being seated, must say I never saw our principles vindicated more practically in my life, and those two men and the woman were perfectly demolished.

The audience said, Mr. Stewart, go on; and as I arose again they gave three tremendous cheers. I drew a picture by comparison between New York and Virginia and the Carolinas, showed our prosperity, riches and glory—the poverty, misery, smallness of population, ignorance of their people, the whipping out labor without wages, the petit-larceny course of things, and the vast districts of forsaken and slave-cursed land, where the fox climbs into the window, and the deer bounds in the thicket of a second wilderness, where, seventy years ago, might have been found the piratical hospitality of those who gave away what they never earned. At this point the slaveholders hissed me. Ah, said I, that hiss shows the malice of the serpent, the intelligence and bravery of the goose. The audience gave a most powerful cheer and made all their canes rattle with approbation. Whereupon one of these creatures said, " you (meaning me) are an ass." Ah, said I, a man who is agitated, often will speak of his nearest connections, and that this fellow had better have been silent rather than to have conferred upon the poor speaker a title which had so long been considered the brightest jewel in the crown of this slaveholder's race, and that from Balaam's ass their great ancestor, who once spoke, to the one you have just heard, there has been an *articulate bray* in the family when any one wished to raise a man who was a slave above the *long-eared brute*.

There was another mighty roar of three times three from the audience, which made these fellows get up and go upon deck, where one of them came and stamped with all his might directly over my head—upon this the captain darted up and silenced him at once. The audience were greatly enraged at this last indignity. I spoke till bed-time ; and when I dismissed I never saw an audience more indignant at slaveholders and their institutions, and the conduct of these men had done infinitely more than I could, to confirm their hatred of slavery and their abominable cruelties toward their fellow-men. This was the topic of conversation until we separated.

You will excuse the length of this letter, and believe me, as ever, yours, etc.

THE ACT OF 1793.

*How came an act so sanguinary to stain the pages of our
Federal Statute Book?*

By this act every inch of the free thirteen States is reduced
to the meanest debasement. By this act, Congress sends the
prowling slaveholder, armed with bowie-knives, pistols,
halters, fetters, and bloodhounds in full cry, through the
free States, pursuing the fugitive slave. The northern State
judges, justices of the peace, as well as those of the Federal
Government, the State constables, sheriffs and deputies, the
United States marshals and deputies in these States, by the
authority of this awful and ferocious decree of 1793, were
commanded to join in the hue and cry of the kidnappers of
the South and to re-kidnap, bind, fetter and certify back to
the prison of the hopeless, the victims of a nation's atrocity.

During the summer of 1787, six weeks were consumed by
the southern delegates at Philadelphia, in that convention
which formed the Federal Constitution, contending that all
laws to regulate commerce must be enacted by two-thirds of
the members elected to the House of Representatives and
Senate of the United States. The delegates from the North
and East declared this government one in which a majority
must govern; and utterly refused to place a perfect control
of the government in the hands of the South, who had little
or no commerce *to regulate*. The South then said if they
surrendered this proposition they must have equivalents.
And they demanded that the Constitution should be so made
that Congress should have no power to interdict the old
African slave trade, from the 4th of March, 1789, until the 1st

of January 1808 ; so that the South might issue her proclamation to the four corners of the globe, summoning all the
villains, pirates, kidnappers and man-thieves, who wandered
over the face of the earth, to come to the great murder feast
of nineteen years, and plunge into the centre of Africa and burn
and destroy her towns, assault and capture her men, women
and children, and make her rivers desolate and leave her
lands without inhabitants, and bring the survivors as slaves
to cultivate the plantations of the southern Democrats.

To this proposition the North consented and basely bowed.
And it was so. The South then said, *one good turn deserves
another*, and after we have risked our lives in robbing
Africa of her people and brought them to our country, we
ought, as a basis of representation in Congress, to count five of
these slaves the same as three whites, and thus make them
into a *dumb constituency*. Agreed, said the East and North.
And by virtue of this slave representation, twenty-five
members now hold their seats in the House of Representatives.

Nearly four years rolled by after the new Constitution
went into operation, and for four years had Africa sent up to
Heaven the lamentations of ruined and rifled nations ; when
the South made her third experiment and found a lower
depth in northern meanness, than depravity herself had ever
sounded, or legislative impudence ever fathomed. The
South told the North that these ungrateful sons and
daughters of Africa, after they had kindly brought them
from a land of Paganism to a land of Christian whips and
pious chains, to a land of human *back-furrowed Democracy*,
to a land in which the Republican master has a better right
to the African's body, wife and children, than the African
man has to himself or to them, still, with all these rights
secured to the southrons by the Constitution, these people will
run to your free States in the North, and we shall lose our

trouble and money in kidnapping them, and bringing them over the breadth of the Atlantic, unless you will kindly, when they flee into your free States, agree by law to be our wolf-dogs, and deny them food and shelter, and run back and howl on their track and re-kidnap them—we shall lose the great object *we had* in forming the Union—which was to spread the ægis of the Constitution over man-stealing, piracy and blood, and thus gain a constitutional respectability in this pursuit, which we could not otherwise obtain. We hope the dear North will not refuse us their aid; otherwise the constitutional provision of nineteen years will be of no use, and the great capital we have embarked in the slave trade will be a total loss; and in fact slavery itself will fall to the ground and must be abandoned, unless the Christian North agree to be our trusty watch-dogs to run fugitives down and take them up. "Agreed," said the North and East; and thereupon in conjunction with the South, passed the nefarious act of Congress of 12th February, 1793.

A half century of crime has all but elapsed, which has no parallel, as between independent States, in the annals of venality or the crookedness of perversion. Forty-nine years rolled to eternity's shore, bearing on their front wrongs done by man to man, not surpassed in outrage, nor equalled in refined malignity, by any invention of our race, in which the contest was between the profoundest abjectness of subserviency on our side, and the most sanguinary avarice on the other.

NANCY'S CASE.

In February, 1842, the Supreme Court of the U. S. at Washington considered this act, in which the following facts appeared. About sixteen years ago, an aged slaveholder, in the State of Maryland, being a man of a kind heart, and having a colored woman possessing many virtues, by the name of Nancy, of the age of twenty years, he emancipated her, as he supposed. This slaveholder, being careless, did not give the young woman her legal manumission papers. She came about fifteen miles from the North line of Maryland into Pennsylvania; where, by her industry and good conduct, she, in the course of a year, recommended herself to the affections of a very respectable free colored man, whom she married. This colored man had a comfortable estate, which, with their industry, maintained them in a very respectable manner. Years went by, and in the course of time they were the parents of four fine children. The old slaveholder being dead, and his son learning that this woman had not received the legal manumission papers the law re-required, and being moved by the infernal avarice and cruelty of slavery, about three years ago took two or three *loafers*, and being armed with pistols and bowie-knives, he went to a Pennsylvania justice of the peace, living three or four miles from this woman, and obtained a warrant to arrest her and all of her children and bring them before the justice; where the slaveholder said he would have it tried to know whether the woman and children were his or not.

The slaveholder and his myrmidons pitched in at an unsuspected hour, about sundown, upon this poor mother and her little brood, and instantly dragged them out of their house; the mother screaming, kidnappers! kidnappers! kidnappers! The children burst forth in the most terrific cries, which were heard by their father in the field, who came running to the house. The wagon by this time, without any explanation to the distracted husband and father, having started, the horses going full jump, and the broken-hearted father following and hallooing to stop, until the wagon passed out of sight in the distance. The father came to a tavern, near the justice, where the kidnappers stopped, and the justice, being from home that evening, the kidnapper told the husband he would take good care of his wife and children until next morning, 9 A.M., when they would go before the justice, and the cause should be tried. The husband, believing what the kidnapper told him, and the doors of his own house having been left wide open, he concluded, at the request of his wife, to go back and shut the doors and secure things at his plundered home, and come back early the next morning ; the slaveholder having solemnly sworn he would not remove the family without the justice decided, on hearing the case, he had a right so to do. But behold the dreadful villainy of a slaveholder : at midnight, when the neighborhood were locked in sleep, he and his gang arose and took the woman and children, and before daylight, he had driven with such speed, that they were secured in one of the great prison houses, to-wit, the State of Maryland. At daylight the broken-hearted husband went to the justice, who told him that the woman and children had never been brought before him ; and from the statement of the tavern-keeper, it was obvious to the poor colored man and his neighbors, that his wife and children had surely been kidnapped without trial ; the husband followed to the Maryland line, which he did not dare pass over ; as by a law of Maryland (though contrary to the Constitution of the U. S.), a free colored man coming into Maryland, might be taken and sold into perpetual slavery. Oh! the sorrows of this *woman* and this *man;* all of their hopes stranded for life ; their free-born children instantly turned to slaves. The neighbors of the colored man, in Pennsylvania were incensed and highly indignant. There is a law in Pennsylvania punishing kidnappers from three to ten years in the Penitentiary of that State ; and under that law, the neighbors of the bereaved husband, went before the Grand Jury of a Court of Oyer and Terminer of the State of Pennsylvania, and got the

Maryland villains indicted for kidnapping. Upon the indictment being presented to the Governor of Pennsylvania, he
made a requisition upon the Governor of Maryland, to
deliver up the kidnapper for trial to the Court of Pennsylvania. The Governor of Maryland refused to obey the requisition or deliver up the felon.

A correspondence finally took place between the governors of the two States, by which it was agreed that their
respective States should pass a legislative agreement on
this subject, into a law, which was done accordingly. The
substance of this agreement was, that the cause against the
kidnapper was to be tried in the Pennsylvania Court of Oyer
and Terminer, and if this court decided against the kidnapper, the cause was to be taken by writ of error to the
Supreme court of Pennsylvania; and if this court affirmed
the judgment against the kidnapper, it was then by a writ of
error to be taken before the Supreme Court of the United
States for an ultimate decision.

The Pennsylvania Courts decided against·the kidnapper
and in favor of their own statute, and sentenced the culprit,
I believe, to seven years in the State Prison. According to
the agreement, the cause was brought by writ of error
before the Supreme Court of the United States, at Washington, in the winter of 1842; where the most remarkable decision was made, by this Court, after hearing the respective
Attorney Generals of the States aforesaid.

I say *remarkable*, for nothing in the 19th century had
transcended the decisions of the 17th, by Jeffreys, Scroggs
and Pollcfexen in the bloody trials of Lord Russell and
Algernon Sidney, until this master and terrific decision of
judicial tyranny flung all the judicial Neros of England into
the regions of forlorn and returnless insignificance. The
court decided that the State decisions of Pennsylvania were
wrong, and annulled them. It further decided that the part

of the Act of Congress of 1793, which required State judges and justices of the peace to issue warrants, at the instance of slaveholders or their agents, against fugitive slaves, and hear the cause and grant certificates of ownership to the claimant of a fugitive, was unconstitutional, null and void; as Congress, the court said, had no right to require State officers to execute an Act of Congress, or of the Federal Government.

I would remark here that every fugitive slave, who has been sent back to slavery, for 49 years, by a State judge, State justice of the peace, recorder or mayor, has been *judicially kidnapped*, and is now held in slavery by force of an unconstitutional decision. Dreadful thought, that the thirteen free States have been obeying an unconstitutional law, and committing the crime of judicial kidnapping, as though the fate of the slave was not hard enough; it seems that every State judge, justice, mayor or recorder, who have done this shocking, bloody and dirty work, had no business, by law, to do it; and that any man would have been justified in going into their unlawful and unconstitutional court, it having no jurisdiction of the fugitive, and taken him away from the State functionary by force, and the State judicial officer could not protect himself or the court; and the individual who had set all such fugitive-State-judicial functionaries at defiance, would have been upheld by the Supreme Court of the United States.—Oh! the poor slave, what hast thou not suffered?

The court decided, however, that a judge of the United States courts might issue a warrant, under the Act of 1793, and arrest a fugitive slave, at the instance of a claimant, and hear the proofs and grant the master or his agent a certificate, returning the fugitive into captivity. There are only three such officers in the State of New York, to wit, Judge Conklin of Auburn, Judge Betts of the city of New York, both district judges of the United States, and Judge Smith Thompson, one of the justices of the Supreme Court of the United States. The court further decided, which is the *truly fearful* and alarming portion of their decision, that the slaveholder, or his agent, may, whenever and wherever he sees fit, arrest a fugitive slave without warrant or any authority from a State or United States judge or justice, or any functionary on the earth, and take the said fugitive into the service of the slaveholder; and no State law, writ of habeas corpus, right of trial by jury, or any State law intended to designate a mode of trial for the fugitive, shall stand in the way of the master: or in other words, the master may seize any person he sees fit, in the State of New York, to call his slave; or the master may walk triumphantly over all State laws enacted for the defence of human liberty, and carry off his prey to his den. According to this dreadful decision, any man in the State of New York, who assumes that he is a slaveholder, may lay his hands on any other man or woman in the State, claiming him or her by word of mouth, as his or her slave, who has escaped from him in some slave State; and although the person claimed may cry and protest, that he or she was born *free* and *white*, and was never out of this State; still no trial, no proceeding whatsoever, can be put in operation to investigate the identity of the person claimed, or look into the matter, or stay the potent slaveholder, but the victim must go to a slave State as a slave, even if it was the son of the governor of this State, or the governor himself; and the court insultingly tells us the only remedy of this kidnapped person, is to be found after he or she has reached the master's home, in a slave State, to sue, in a civil action, the master, in a slave court, for his liberty. Ah! glorious opportunity, to go to a southern lawyer penniless, the master having taken your money, the master holding a pistol to your breast, forbidding your leaving the plantation; and if you do, he may legally shoot you dead, if you will not stop when bidden; you are 1,000 miles from all of your witnesses, and now the poorest man in the creation of God—*a slave*; and then you are told to litigate with your master in a slave State, before slave judges and a slaveholding jury!

Why not stop and have the litigation with the master in this State, where he first sets up his claim, by which the burden of proving you his slave will be thrown on him, and you will have judges and jurors who are not slaveholders, and also your witnesses to prove your freedom, and friends and means to employ counsel? The answer to this seems to be, the great, lordly, sovereign slaveholder must not be hindered by your State court trials—his business is too important for him to be delayed from home to litigate the freedom of a man or woman. The slaveholder has said that A. is his slave and that is enough, and ought and *must* satisfy those fastidious fools at the North; his word and character is like the chevalier Bayard's—above fear and without reproach. Again, if the slave *sues* in a slave State *for* his freedom, the slave will have the burden of proof thrown on him—of proving a negative—that he is not a slave.

If he has any colored blood in his veins, the law comes to the master's aid, with the presumption that he is a slave; and further, if ever so white, and he is doing work as a slave— then if he sues for freedom, the cruel and malignant law of the South presumes he is a slave, or he *would not be* in the *condition* of *the slave*. Now this rule of presumption is in exact hostility to the common law, that great inheritance of English liberty from our Saxon ancestors. By the common law all men are presumed honest, just, and free, until the contrary appears by proof.

It was said when this decision was announced it produced a shock, as though a mine had exploded under the capitol.

There are nine judges of the Supreme Court of the United States; five of whom are slaveholders. It is said six opinions were written at the time, in which a great variety of judgment prevailed.

It is said by Judge Baldwin, that the Constitution executed itself, and that no such act as 1793 was needed, and the act was void. But an *average* of opinion seemed to conduct the court to the conclusions above referred to. If we are to consider that astounding branch of the decision as law, by which the slaveholder comes to the North and exercises the slaveholder's elementary power, not right, the same as in the woods of Africa during the time of the slave trade; then it would seem that while we have declared it piracy and death to take a man with a view to enslave him, on the coast of Africa; that at the same time one man may take another and make a slave of him, in Oneida County, be he white or black, and take him to a slave State and there use him as a slave; and that the only remedy for this kidnapping is a civil suit, prosecuted by the helpless slave against his master, before a slave court and jury. This would not give one in ten thousand an opportunity to escape. For it must be remembered that Pennsylvania and the free States, and ours amongst the rest, have passed laws against kidnapping, by which these statutes have said that whoever shall take and violently carry away any person from this State, or sell said person with a view to enslave him, without lawful authority, shall be imprisoned, varying from three to ten years, and, I believe, in some, for life.

But this decision overthrows those most important laws, enacted for the feeble and defenceless, as the great bulwarks of human liberty, and turns the free or slave States into slave-kidnapping ground; where a man may commit the crime of enslaving, in perfect safety; and his only danger is that the slave may sue for his liberty in a slave State, though that he cannot do without the master's permission, as he cannot leave the master's premises without his consent, and that will never be given to go and consult lawyers to invalidate the master's title. And if the slave attempts to leave the master's premises by force, the master can shoot him dead if it be necessary to enforce obedience or restrain him. If the nation, or the free States dreamed for a moment of the horrible position in which they were placed, by the late decision of the Supreme Court of the United States, under the act of 1793, there would be one universal mustering of all men, women and children for the repeal of the act of 1793; and also for a declaratory act by Congress, abolishing, if in its power, the legal effect of this *monstrous opinion* of the Supreme Court of the United States.

To this frightful precipice has slavery conducted this nation, at last, so that now no man has any shelter left beneath the magna charta of American Independence, for his own liberty, his wife's, or his child's, for a single day; for he may be made a slave in Oneida County, in the State of New York, any moment, and cannot appeal to any law in this State to prevent it. No, the writ of habeas corpus, the right of trial by jury, are all swept by the board, and a man now holds his liberties by no better tenure than a kidnapper's mercy.

Good God, have mercy on us and destroy slavery, for it is destroying life, liberty, property, and the pursuit of happiness. I hope our friends will in the next two years, present the petitions to abolish the act of 1793 for signatures, to every householder, his wife, and children over fourteen years of age throughout the Empire State; going two and two from house to house, pleading for a deliverance of this Republic.

Abolish the act of 1793 and we place Canada on Mason and Dixon's line; or, in other words, we set Canada down on the line of Maryland, Virginia, Kentucky, and Missouri, and slavery would abolish itself in those four great States in three years.   The slaves would have nothing to do but walk over the line.

The abolition of the act of 1793 delivers the North from the basest position ever occupied by States or individuals.   It gives us back our bibles and the riches of immortality, which the act of 1793 makes us agree to forego and renounce. Now, we abjure the doctrines of Jesus Christ the Son of God, breathing mercy and love to all, to become the allies of the cruel, and the stirrup-holders of kidnappers, and the collar-wearers of the southern slaveholders.

3d January, 1843.

REPLY TO THE JUNIUS TRACT

OF THE REV. CALVIN COLTON, 1843.

WE cannot forbear asking Mr. Colton, cannot Congress, who made this law in 1793, repeal it in 1843 ?   There cannot be two opinions on this subject, among learned or unlearned, Christians or Jews, slaveholders or Liberty party men.   If Congress may repeal this law, the Act of 12th of February, 1793, which it has passed, what would be the position of the slave ?   Precisely the same as though Canada was to slide down and be bounded on the South by Mason and Dixon's line—precisely the same as though Canada was the northern boundary line of the slave States.   The moment the slaves passed into Pennsylvania, Ohio, Indiana, Illinois or Iowa, from a slave State, they would be *free*, by the laws of slavery, and the *law* of nations.   They could not be pursued or arrested.   They would be *free*.   How long would slavery stand in the border States of Maryland, Virginia, Kentucky, or Missouri ?   Not five years, if we take away the power of *reclamation*.   This act of Congress in abridging the natural right of the slave to seek his liberty, is the act of the free States in common with the slave.   But for this law, slavery would have been overthrown.   But for the North agreeing to stand as a *bull-dog* sentry on the line between freedom and slavery, covenanting to re-kidnap the fleeing, innocent man and woman, and restore him or her in chains to his oppressor slavery would have fallen to the ground, by the power of *flight alone*.

BALLOT-BOX POWER.

According to slaveholders, their exponents and apologists, every right they have acquired over the slaves by the laws, constitutions and compacts, are ballot-box powers, in their inception, and have all been voted for in the appointment or election of those individuals who created, made or passed these laws, constitutions or compacts. But slavery, though the highest of crimes, is a thing so much more sacred than any other human right, that when once voted into existence by ballot-box power, or if ballot-box intrenchments are thrown up around it, the ballot-box has spent its power, unless it be to fortify the infernal institution, but has no power to overthrow, curb or restrain it; when the ballot-box has once conferred any power on this piratical institution, it must remain inviolable, irrepealable, to-day, to-morrow, and forever!! So say slaveholders, and Mr. Colton and the Whigs, in the spirit of their arguments, in favor of what we might suppose were truly *peculiar* institutions, which, when once made, defy their creator, and become *eternal*. Yes, they are *peculiar*, if having once got into existence, there is no way to get them out. But Mr. Colton has been so kind as to inform us how to get them out. It is by *moral suasion*. These institutions which will not yield to the omnipotence of the ballot-box, may still be kindly flattered out of existence! Yes, they may be persuaded to die, but cannot be killed. The institution being so very humane and generous, it is to be presumed, that, to help justice and humanity, it will agree to *die*, from pure patriotism, and from an abhorrence of its own existence. But the difficulty still is, if Mr. Colton is right, that slavery cannot die, except through the ballot-box power; for if you should persuade each slaveholder to give liberty to his slaves, in the District of Columbia, unless slavery is forbidden by law, what hinders another villain from setting up the business again, under the nose of Congress ? But what is the use in pressing this argument further, or of sending an absurdity in hot pursuit after an impossibility !

THE GREAT VOLCANO.

Look at the absurdity of this reverend and crafty Whig. We are told over and over and over again, from page to page of his argument, that our mission of benevolence might be very proper, if we did not propose to overthrow the general welfare, and trample on contracts, compacts and moral obligations, by casting our votes where we have not the least chance of success, and if we were successful in getting a majority, we are, in all respects, perfectly powerless, as we have not a crumb of constitutional power by which to touch slavery, or even the hem of its garment, in state or nation, it is so sacredly guarded against every approach of humanity ; but still, by voting for these abolition objects, we defeat ourselves and the Whigs, and thus we may "throw the government of the States and nation into hands that will ruin us all, as they have heretofore tried to do, with no small success." What are we to gain by acting with Whigs, after the gentleman has shown us that the Whigs cannot touch slavery even with a pair of tongs, for want of constitutional power; and that all the Whigs can do, with that great slaveholder as President (who swallows daily the unpaid labor of 52 human beings), would be to prop, enlarge, fortify and strengthen slavery ?   Let him not talk of the right of petition—when did Clay, or Calhoun, or Van Buren ever come out iu its favor ?   And if the Whig party had power, and allowed us to discuss every proposition for curtailing and lopping off a branch or a *twig* of slavery, still this great constitutional Whig informs us (and the Whigs have adopted his legal advice by circulating his tract as their opinion) that however full of emancipation, justice and mercy, a Whig Congress might be, it could contrive no way or means to deliver or aid a single slave, without tearing the Constitution all to shreds and shivers, involving the country in flames and blood, from Montpelier to Tallahassee, from the Pedee to the Sabine, from the Montauk to the mountains of rock, where there would be nothing to extinguish the flames of our dwellings, but the blood of our citizens; and this universal massacre, would end in the extinction of black and white, bond and free, and convert this end of the continent into one vast sepulchre where no living man would survive to record the dismal catastrophe, which had blotted a great empire from the map of the world, in defending the constitutionality of slavery! Alas, alas, alas, did ever nation live on the top of such a constitutional volcano before? Yes, a volcano that never casts up its lurid flames and pumice stones, as long as you feed it with constitutional gags, and the twenty slave-elected members of Congress; also by throwing down into its voracious crater throat seven new slave States and Florida, as a mere desert to be swallowed by its unappeasable voraciousness, with an eight years war for the extinction of the noble Seminoles, at an expense of fifty millions; she can contain within her mighty bowels, unpained, the ten miles square, and 8,000 slaves and three slave dungeons; she can circulate the slaves in coffled gangs, or by ship, all through her huge entrails; she can hear within her the crying and groaning of the whipped millions, the mangled thousands and murdered hundreds, as they send up their daily cry to a nation's mercy, unmoved, untouched; but let one petition for mercy or deliverance be presented, and then, oh! the tremendous upheavings, the unearthly sounds, the smoke, the pumice stones and ashes, which put out the sun of Liberty, and make it dark at noon, while the streams of boiling, bubbling, fiery lava pour down, sweeping all before them. And it seems to have been the business of Whigs and Democrats, with the great ecclesiastical denominations of this country, to cap the top of this mighty slaveholding volcano, that the prisoners' cries bound in its caverns, and the rage consequent on a demand for their deliverance, might both be suppressed in eternal silence.

SLAVERY RIGHT, BECAUSE OF DISTRESS IN ENGLAND!

Then, again, this Whig mouthpiece says there is distress in England among the operatives.

Yes, that is true—there is slavery in Brazil, and in Cuba, there is a vast amount of highway robbery in Spain, but Spain does not make highway robbery an organic institution: and there is the burning of widows in the East Indies, or has been till of late, and females have ruined and cramped feet in China, and they murder, sometimes, innocent people in Cochin China, and they flog and work people for nothing in two State Prisons in this State, and men spend their lives in the mines of Mexico, Chili and Peru, and some men whip their wives in New York, some men are daily drunk and miserable, but women-whipping and drunkenness are not defended institutions. What do all these things prove? Why, according to this logician, that every abuse of man, which we can find existing on the earth, or crime committed against his happiness, that to be sure is an example, which authorizes us to adopt that abuse, and to put it into our Constitution and make laws for its defence, as an institution; and if the institution be attacked for its inherent, self-evident villainy, why, then show that it is right? Oh, no, show that some other people, ancient or modern, or individuals of this or that nation, have committed some vile offence against God and man, and that proves slavery a good institution. The abuses of the poor operatives in England are not a part of the English Constitution and laws, compelling them to suffer.

COLTON'S ARGUMENT—PARENT AND CHILD.

But Mr. Colton has overthrown slavery after all; for he says it is like the relations of husband and wife, parent and child, master and apprentice. He says the husband, parent and master have a right to the service of the wife, the child, and apprentice, and so he says has the master to the slave's service, but not to his *body*. He says the slave is entitled to his own body, if we understand him. He, speaking of the slave, says, " the service, not the person, is the property." This is new slave law, of Mr. Colton's—it is on the 8th page of his tract, in which this discovery is made. He says the law gives command of the slave's person, so that the master may get his services. But he says, " neither master, nor father, nor society itself has *property* in the *persons* of men, but God only." If a man owns his body, how can another man get a title to his services, except by contract ? and if any man can show a slave who has made a contract for a good consideration, for himself and his posterity, to work for nothing but the chance of being whipped, beaten, kicked, cuffed, and if he attempts to go away, who then *agrees*, that the master may shoot him, and further agrees the master may sell his wife and children, and further *agrees* the master may pound him to death, if he does not work, and moreover *agrees* the master may sell him from his wife and children, and *agrees* that the master shall withhold all knowledge, and that he, the slave, shall never *own* anything on earth—no, not a cow, a sheep, a hog or a goat, and that he contracted to stand forever, called a chattel, a thing, instead of a man—if he will show me one such case as this, I will agree that this man may be a slave, and his master a knave, and I will not try to change their condition.

The husband and wife make a contract in marriage, which is reciprocal and for the mutual benefit of the parties, but the husband cannot sell his wife, nor the wife her husband. The indented apprentice has a consideration for his services in being taught a trade, receiving a good common school education, and being clothed during his childish years. He receives the amplest compensation for every particle of labor he performs. Can his master sell him? No. Can his master beat him to death under the head of correction and go unpunished? If the master is cruel, his articles of indenture can be cancelled, by the magistrates; but what power, but death, cancels the slave's, even if he be seventy years of age. Who ever heard of binding out a boy or girl for life? Until such cases occur, let no comparison be drawn, where there is no more resemblance than between an iceberg and a steamboat. Mr. Colton and the Whig party, think the relation of parent and child, and master and slave are alike, and the relation substantially of the same interesting character; and slavery appears so amiable, that Mr. Colton and the Whig party could not find a more pertinent case of resemblance and illustration, than the holy relation of parent and child. There are between 300,000 and 400,000 slaves in the United States, whose fathers are their masters. Here the double relation of master and parent on the one side, and child and slave on the other, one would suppose, from Mr. Colton's and the Whig party's notions, on such subjects, must be a state of too much advantage and happiness for the son-slave or daughter-slave, to last or enjoy on this earth—a greater share in the good of this world, than falls to the ordinary lot of mortals. The parent and master, according to Mr. Colton, will act for the best and do the best for his child; and as evidence of his kindness, he considers him or her a slave, and frequently sells his own peculiar picture, as early as a purchaser presents, to preserve the affection of his wife, who is not delighted in seeing living images of her husband, proving that she, the wife, is but the successor of some servile Libyan dame, in the warmer affection of her husband. A father cannot sell his legitimate children, which, perhaps, Mr. Colton may consider a disadvantage, under which the bastard-slave does not labor; for the father of the bastard-slave often sells him or her, and with the money gives the son of the free woman a liberal education at some eastern college, while the son of the same father, his half-brother, instead of graduating at Yale or Princeton, will receive his honors at a cart-tail, where the parchment will be laid on his naked back; where, if he is not made master of arts, he is sometimes permitted to graduate from time into eternity. Perhaps Mr. Colton thinks it a misfortune that parental authority ceases at twenty-one years of age, over the child. The law of slavery is so kind as never to give up the master's solicitude for the slave, even if he should live 100 years. This goes to prove, notwithstanding some trifling disadvantages on the part of the slave, how much more regard the master has than the parent—the latter throws up his care and responsibility at twenty-one, while the kind master pursues the slave through all the narrow lanes of life, with a master's eye, nor once loses sight of the object of his tender solicitude, until the slave exchanges the master's kindly grasp for the still more kindly gripe of death.

The son at the death of his father, whether twenty-one, under or over, inherits his father's property—the slave is *inherited*—the only difference is between the active and the passive *voice*, the difference is a mere question of parsing grammar. The son *inherits* the slave. The slave is *inherited* by the son. But, according to the doctrine of consideration and reciprocity, Mr. Colton and the Whig party would tell us the bargain was equal, for if the young master has inherited an aged slave, what then makes it equal is, the aged slave has inherited a young master. So the inheritance *account* is balanced by its equality. And if the young master sells his aged slave, then the slave has got a new master, which, according to Mr. Colton and the Whig party, is like an old widower getting a new wife. For Mr. Colton compared slavery to the marriage relation, as one of its most fitting illustrations. The master sells the slave's wife and children, whom the slave father sees no more: Mr. Colton, the Whig party and the slaveholders would tell you, that he, the slave, may get him a new wife, for if a man lose his wife and children by sale, may he not get him a new wife? It matters not how the slave loses them.

Mr. Colton is right, in one respect—showing a strong resemblance between a child of the master and his slave. The child at two years of age is ignorant, does not know how to read, write or cipher. So the slave at forty resembles, in these respects, the child at two. Mr. Colton contends the master is bound to feed and clothe the slave. So is the owner bound to feed and stable his poor plough-horse, and upon the same ground the horse can prosecute, according. to Mr. Colton, for neglect to stable and oat him, the same as the slave may sue or indict for neglect to feed and clothe him. True, the community might indict the man who abused the horse, or the slave, out of all reason, if they felt disposed.

But the first case is yet to be seen in a court of justice, where a southern man has been indicted for *overworking, underfeeding, and not clothing* a slave. The first case at the North is yet to be tried, of overworking and underfeeding among the tens of thousands of poor, abused, starved skeletons of horses. Yet the power of redress, as it regards the slave and horse, are exactly equal. The slave has the same right to go before a grand jury and state his case, on oath, against his master, as the horse has. His oath is not allowed against the master, or any white, in any case, or received at all.

SELECTIONS.

ORGANIZATION.

A NEW epoch opens. The straitness of the times tasks the genius of humanity to fresh efforts. The Reformation cannot be carried by the A. S. newspaper, or the hired agent. We commend and love them both, but they are high-priced instrumentalities. We cannot cultivate mountain land with a plough of gold. Slavery has invaded our purses; slavery demands the earnings of Friday and Saturday of the North as a *union tax;* we pay it. Bankruptcy is the return cargo from the South. One man in five works at the South; nine out of ten work at the North, or the nation would perish. The South pay their debts with the bankrupt's certificates— that is their circulating medium, as individuals. Repudiation in a State is piracy in individuals. Slavery slays by violence, one slave in each of the 13 States daily. They fall by cruelty, overworking, underfeeding, and in nameless other ways. The North looks on. She sees the writhing victims on the Union's altar; she hears their groans. These Union victims, whose blood flows on the altar of the confederation, amount to 4,745. The Christian religion is abolished wherever slavery comes to be a legal institution. When Atheism is established by law, the Christian religion is repealed by law. Slavery is the converse of every proposition in Christianity; whoever sustains it in Church or State, does it at the expense of Christianity.

ABOLITION CONVENTIONS,

Our Conventions heretofore held have adopted, whether as

town, county or State, the mode of sending out a committee to report resolutions. These resolutions have generally been affirmative or negative propositions, touching slavery in the Church and State, affirming what we ought and ought not to believe and *do*. Or, in other words, we have spent the last seven years in a circle of splendid abstractions, or golden affirmations of what was or was not the truth, seeming to think if we could once mark a proposition as true, on a ten hour discussion, that was enough ; and, in fact, we have acted as though our ten thousand resolves had, by our vote, the breath of life breathed into them, and that henceforth they would fly like an angel of mercy through the world, under our new embodiment, as a sort of everlasting agent of truth, not subject to any of the laws of our common mortality. But our abstract propositions had no longer legs nor larger hands after we had passed them than before ; and yet we congratulate ourselves in having fifteen or twenty resolutions, discussed or undiscussed. It might often be said that a favorite polemical controversy would spring out of a single resolution, and use up the entire time of a Convention. In reviewing the past, without being too censorious, it cannot be denied that we seemed to act as if we had only to pass a resolution to organize the State, and distribute light in every corner of the same—as though we had really done the work by passing the resolution. We almost mistook our resolutions for their performance. We were too well satisfied with *resolving* to do instead of *doing*. We spent our energies in establishing our abstractions as first principles, and gave but little time to the practical carrying out of the same, infinitely the most important.

THE SLAVEHOLDING OMNIBUS.

The agitation growing out of Texas reveals the fact that this Government was from the beginning, and now is, a mere slaveholding omnibus to carry slaveholders and their baggage, and that we at the North have had to feed the horses, make the roads and keep the omnibus in repair, for the naked reputation of having a right to ride in the omnibus, though we have to go on foot, run in the dust, shouting that we have equal right to ride with those inside. The North have just discovered we are running by the side of the omnibus, which is loaded down with slaveholders, slaves, chains, hand-cuffs, whips, bloodhounds and slaveholding constructions of the Constitution, done up in bundles, labelled, "For the addle-headed of the North." Another bundle, entitled "Slave-holding Constitutional Compromises," lately discovered by the grandson of one of the framers of the Constitution, show-ing that the true cabalistic reading of the Constitution is, that where the word liberty occurs therein, it means "slavery"— where the word justice, there read "injustice or oppression"— where any word soever in the Constitution like these, " the United States shall guarantee to each State a republican form of government," they are to be rejected as entire surplusage, as has been the case in the admission of eight slaveholding new States—practical construction thereon by Congress. There was another bundle entitled "Forgeries or Discoveries," that the words in the Constitution "No person shall be de-prived of life, liberty or property without due process," is falsely printed in all the editions of the Constitution extant, and that the true original was framed and adopted in these words: "Men or women who are weak, Mulattoes, Quadroons, eights or sixteenths, thirty-seconds, or sixty-fourths, or where sixty-three drops of their blood is Anglo-Saxon and one drop African, in origin, and in that proportion, shall be deprived of life, liberty, and property, without due process of law." Also one other bundle entitled, "An astounding discovery just come to light in Florida, said to be discovered in the hollow of a tree, on which fugitive slaves had ascended to escape the rage of the pursuing bloodhounds—a most wonderful document on parchment, showing that the Constitution was made for nothing else except as a slave-breeding, slave-voting, slave-working, slave-selling, slave-pursuing and catching document." The North have made more discoveries about the omnibus and its contents in the last six months than in the last forty years before.

THE GREAT EVERY-MAN POWER.

On the day of the morning of the famous battle of Trafalgar, by Lord Nelson against the French, the English Admiral caused a piece of white cotton about one hundred feet long and twenty-five feet wide, with letters four or five feet long to be inscribed thereon and fastened to the masthead of the Admiral's ship, that it might be seen by every man to be engaged throughout the fleet. The words were :."ENGLAND EXPECTS EVERY MAN TO DO HIS DUTY." Oh! the enthusiastic shout that went up from England's tars at the sight : thousands of whom saw the sun rise this morn for the last time forever. The anti-slavery host expect every liberty man will do his duty. The great secret of successful prosecution of the anti-slavery conquest is yet unrevealed, and where revealed is not believed. The simplicity of means is so amazing, men will not believe it. It is the *great every-man power, the one-man power, the common-man power, the unlearned-man power.* Every honest anti-slavery man has the power of converting some of his neighbors to our glorious principles, in the next five weeks by talking, by tract, newspaper, or pamphlet. A man of the smallest intellect, is a stronger, a wiser and a better man, when armed in the panoply of eternal justice, mercy and equality, surrounded and trusting to these principles, to bear him up, than the greatest intellectual Goliah, who even defied the armies of the living God, trusting to his weaver's beam of falsehood and lies,

polished with the tinsel of the devil's rhetorical varnish.
One ounce of truth will make the beam kick with a ton of
lies.

MYRON HOLLEY.

The Convention at Rochester, on the 12th, 13th, and 14th
inst. (June 1844) was one of the largest ever held in this
State.   In addition to the convention proper, thousands of
the citizens of Rochester and parts adjacent, joined in a grateful tribute of respect to one of the most illustrious men of the
Empire State.   Yes, Myron Holley's shaft of granite, some
11 or 12 feet in height, weighing between five and six tons,
will stand commemorating, from generation to generation,
from century to century, the *high born purposes* of his majestic soul, as long as the quiet Genesee shall glide at the
base of Mount Hope, bearing on its bosom the tears of the
pilgrim-visiter to this city of silence, and will reveal to the
great *unborn, that men* lived on the earth in 1844, who acknowledged the power of genius, and honored a brave humanity, in a pusillanimous age, and have left this imperishable
testimony as an incentive to all who have the inclination and
power to follow his glorious example.

NEW YORK BOWING TO VIRGINIA.

The conduct of Gov. Bouck is looked upon as a base bowing of the State of New York to slaveholding, despotic Virginia.   The craven conduct of Bouck will ruin his reputation
in all coming time—the unmanliness of submitting on our
knees to Virginia, while she holds an unconstitutional law
over our heads, and the heads of all the navigators of our
ships, compelling us New-Yorkers, every time one of our
ships touches her coasts, to pay $10 of *tribute money*, and
give bonds that we will *not steal negroes* while on her coasts,
or in her waters.   Bouck seeks this moment of our degrada-

tiou to make us play the spaniel, and *lick* the feet of our masters by telling them that we will repeal our Jury Trial Law,
the bulwark of Liberty, and pass a Nine Month law over
again, so that Virginia may *bring, work, hire, whip* and *fetter*
her slaves on our soil nine months at a time, in one year.
Oh! degraded New York!   Oh, must New York bend her
gallant Empire head, while women-whipping Virginia puts
the yoke on our degraded necks, *and keys the bow?*

I returned from this last journey worn down, and all but
sick, but feel to-day as though I might still work for the *helpless.*

A CLERGYMAN UPHOLDING SLAVERY.

Another of the most prominent of the clergy fell into a
passion, and very earnestly asserted that "Slavery was a
Bible institution, and its use was proper like any other
institution; and its abuse was the only thing that was
wrong,"—as the relation of husband and wife. was a very
good relation, but the husband may abuse the wife—that
abuse is wrong.   Oh! my countrymen, when such miserable
men crawl into the pulpits, to insult God, and the Christian
religion, and become teachers of the road, not to heaven,
what can you expect but all manner of corruption and degeneracy in the public mind?   What terrible responsibility
must lie on that man who charges atheistically on the great
and good God of the Universe, the horrible crime of slavery?
A crime which unites within itself all crimes, which expunges
the decalogue, and insults and treads under foot the divine
virtues of Christ, and strips the Christian religion of every
beauty, and charges on the deity the crime of giving one half
of his children to be used as slaves by the others.   If the
father of ten sons were to give the five youngest to be slaves
of the five oldest, in the county of Oneida, every man, woman and child, for one hundred miles around, would cry
monster! monster!! monster!!!   Monster, would be writ-

ten on his fence, his house, his barn, if men dared come so near him. This man would be supposed to be a connecting link between Judas Iscariot and Beelzebub. Yes, he would occupy the seat of professor of moral depravity! He would be considered the impersonification of the extinct and forgotten depravities of Sodom and Gomorrah, embellished with all the acquisitions of modern crime.

ORIGIN AND OBJECT OF CONSTITUTIONS.

The different States of this Republic are the only ones who date their political existence from the adoption of written constitutions. The beginning of the nations of Europe, reaching far beyond the era of printing, is generally lost in the mists hanging over distant periods of time, if not absolutely concealed in the darkness of an impenetrable antiquity. Fable and mythology, as to the origin of many of the nations of Europe, constitute much the larger share of their history; and conjecture, at last, amidst the conflicts of tradition, is the strongest light we can bring to bear upon the night of distant years.

The constitutions of the States of this Republic are among the most august and certain of human memorials, or national records; existing in thousands of forms, and in tens of thousands of places, being each but a duplicate of the sacred original. The constitutions of the different nations of Europe seem to be a succession of lost rights, recovered at different points of time; and in some great state emergency, by insurrection, or revolution, have been extorted from the fears or necessities of the ruling prince. These successive recoveries in many of the kingdoms of Europe, go by the name of the constitutions of their countries, which are more properly subversions of some ancient despotism, than constitutions.

But the Constitution of these Republics, both State and national, were formed for the mutual protection and defence of the persons, liberties, and property of the people; not carving these immunities out of the despotic power lodged in the hands of some weak prince, but simply agreeing how to employ the great inheritance given them by the King of kings, and Lord of lords, for the defence and protection of each one, in the enjoyment of his natural rights given to each one by his creator. The distinctive character of the American constitutions, is this, that a State Constitution is a covenant or agreement of the entire persons of the State, with each person, as an individual, to protect and defend him or her in their natural and acquired rights, while each individual covenants and agrees to sustain, with his person and estate, the commonwealth. Or in other words, a constitution for a State or the nation, is a covenant of the whole people with each person, and of each person with the whole people. A constitution is the most solemn expression of human weakness, and of single person's inability to protect and defend themselves from the avarice, cruelty, and violence of others, therefore, the whole confederate with each, and each with the whole, to secure the enjoyment of our God-inherited rights. Constitutions are formed to *protect* natural rights, not to *create* them. Every man has a right to pursue his own happiness, in whatever way he pleases, unless it violates his obligations to God, or the rights of his fellow-man.

It is the great mistake of many, to suppose, a constitution can, or does form the *source* of our natural rights, and that we derive the right to life, liberty, and the pursuit of happiness, from our constitutions. We do not derive our title to our farms from the fences which surround them, but from deeds and patents, originating in the supreme power of the State; so our constitutions, both State and national, are so many walls of defence around our natural rights, which we hold by a deed, patent from the Almighty. No man is capable for himself, or for another, to enter into a compact or a

constitution, to forego, sacrifice, or surrender up, while in a
state of innocence, his natural rights to life, liberty, and the
pursuit of happiness. Can any man believe a man would
concur in making a constitution, which not only refuses to
protect his natural rights to life, liberty, property, and the
pursuit of happiness, but absolutely annihilates those rights.
—yes, instead of obtaining protection for his natural rights,
he comes forward, as some argue, and agrees he has no natural rights, and that they are extinguished. Where is the
man on the wide earth, who was ever found so out of love
with himself and his posterity, and so devoid of reason, as to
consent, in person, or clothe a delegate with power, in making
the fence around his farm for his protection, finally to agree,
that his title-deeds to his farm should be torn up and destroyed, and that he and his family might be turned headlong into the street, and his house and barn be burnt to the
ground?

If no man ever exercised in person or by delegate the
power of self-extinction, in making a constitution, where was
that power acquired in a constitution, which is an agreement
of the whole with each, and each with the whole, to destroy
human rights and blot out the manhood of our race, instead
of nourishing and defending man's natural rights? If slavery
crept into the Constitution of the United States (which is
denied), by what possible means, unless by the most melancholy insanity?

Shall it be said, that part of the people, a minority, instead
of wishing protection for their natural rights, concluded that
their share under this Constitution, should be a perpetual
power on the part of the majority of the great national
brotherhood, to extinguish the natural rights of the minority,
and make them and their posterity slaves and chattels, in all
time, and all that they, the minority asked, was, that this
great compromise might be kept inviolable, in all coming

ages, as the key-stone of the federal arch ? This is sublime absurdity. But where, how, or when, was the power for the creation and adoption of the federal Constitution gained, except by the consent in person, or through delegates freely elected ? Who ever heard of a constitution founded on this continent for the destruction of human rights and the blasting of human hopes ?

No doubt a charter party might have been entered into to prosecute and carry on piracy and man-stealing to and from the ill-fated continent of Africa, for a single year, or a single voyage ; but in what land of civilization, has it ever reached our ears, that a great nation ever met to form a constitution for the protection of the majority, and for the perpetual destruction of the minority ?

The very idea of a constitution implies, that those for whom it is made are to gain thereby, and not become losers! A constitution is to create a national or state partnership ; in which the partners are all equal; each brings the same amount of capital for the public weal, each brings the same right to be protected ; the life, liberty and pursuit of happiness of every one, is, in the eye of the Constitution, equal to that of any other. But according to the theory and practice of the slaveholders and pro-slavery parties of this land, after five-sixths of the population came up to create and adopt the Constitution, pointing out the great self-evident rights each wished more securely to be protected, by this Constitution, the last sixth of the people arrived and declared themselves equally anxious for the adoption of this Constitution, in order constitutionally to dispossess themselves of their natural rights, and get rid of their heaven-inherited legacy of life, liberty and the pursuit of happiness, and wished the same instrument, which brought protection, life and liberty to the five-sixths, might by construction and interpretation of the same instrument, when applied to the last sixth, be construed so as to strip them of all protection, and their natural rights, and make them slaves, chattels and outlaws forever.

But slaveholders and their apologists can find no more substantial grounds on which to place this mighty platform of human rights, than the foregoing absurdities.

REPLY TO THE DEMOCRATIC REVIEW.

February, 1845.

ABOLITIONISTS, THE BALANCE-POWER PARTY.

THE reviewer says, "Abolition has certainly grown now into an important political fact." Again he says, "it is not to be denied that at the late election, partly from accidental circumstances, and partly from its own strength, yet still practically as a fact, it has been able to hold, quivering in its own mad hand, the balance of power between the two great parties of the country." The reviewer then asserts that the Abolitionists of the State of New York held the Presidential election in their hands, and the control of the elections and political power of the Empire State, and had power to have given these rich prizes of human ambition to either side they had seen fit. He then inquires, "has it come to this? Has Abolitionism held in its power the arbitrament of this great national issue?" He says, "political abolition is no joke. It is a something, though it be only a wild bull loose in the streets." Again he says, "we cannot refuse to confess how narrowly we have escaped being fatally gored· by its horn. Should we have escaped if Mr. Clay had not · published his Alabama pro-Texas letter?" Taking the admissions of this literary organ and distinguished mouth-piece of the great conquering plurality and minority of the twenty millions flushed with an unexpected victory, big with buoyant exultation, reposing in the banqueting-house, amidst the roaring of cannon and the shouts of multitudes, about to wield the destinies of the great nation of the new world for long years to come—to them, for good or for evil, the mighty power of the Republic, with its vast responsibilities, is vouchsafed. Still this same triumphant party, in the moment of their wonderful success, admit that the Liberty party Abolitionists might have sent them into a polar winter's night of political ostracism, where they might have had an abundance of time to have made an inventory of their losses, and have compiled their criminating statistics, revealing the sources of their disasters, and the causes of their overthrow by force of the great gorings, and the unspeakable and prodigious roarings of that *tremendous Abolition bull of* 1844.

Let us pause, and for one moment examine, by the light of the foregoing admissions of this distinguished professor of elemental Democracy, as to the fact. What other *balance-power party* has ever been found before, in this nation or in any other, which pursued such a course for its own exalted object, in unshaken neutrality, spurning the golden bribe laid at its feet, refusing by a transfer of its numbers to either side to win, by its preponderance, the casting vote of an empire's power? While two great parties sought power, for the honor and profit of its exercise, limiting its blessings to the Anglo-Saxon caste, a third party refused its acceptance without sharing it with every human being of the republic, high or low, bond or free, rich or poor, ignorant or learned, determining thereby in the end to overthrow slavery, and exalt men to that level where the Declaration of Independence left them.

DEMOCRATIC PROFESSION AND PRACTICE.

What but the consciousness of patriotism could have influenced the Liberty party Abolitionists, and sustained them amidst dangers so threatening, temptations so flattering, opposition so overwhelming? Where is the case known in our annals of a party refusing homage and empire; yes all that could fascinate the vulgar, or charm the refined, excite the selfish or stimulate the generous; for the ambitious there was place; for the sordid there was gold; and the caresses of success might have saluted the huzzas of millions in the pride of conquest.

Yes, the Liberty party was firm in occupying its unchangeable position, taken on the first of April, 1840, by which it refused to give a vote for a slaveholder, or his apologist, from constable to President. Although near two-thirds of their numbers were gentlemen from the Whig ranks, and were keenly sensible that in the last ten years they had received injuries from the Democratic party, which for magnitude and meanness had no parallel; the chronicles of man's history may be searched in vain through centuries before the seeker of truth would have found the same amount of servility submitted to, by so large a number of human beings, since the dawn of civilization in any ten years of a nation's life, ancient or modern, for so small consideration as has satisfied the Democratic party of the United States to be false to herself, unfaithful to her age, and derelict to every abstraction of belief she professed, as if it was her chief joy to place an impassable gulf between practice and profession, and that her works should prosecute a ceaseless war upon her faith.

The President, on the 4th of March, 1837, in his inaugural address, when taking upon himself the official oath—Heaven's sanction for Earth's performance—swearing by the retribution of that great day, when president and people, governors and governed, slaves and masters, should each stand alone, to answer for himself before Omniscient Justice, yet, in such an hour of time, he promises, in effect, to violate the Constitution, and veto any bill that might be passed for the emancipation of slaves in the District of Columbia.

This was the boldest criminality in attempt, this was sacrilege of the high priest in the temple, and high treason in the coronation oath; he abjured man in distress, and foreswore our common humanity and made the Constitution and American institutions, so far as president could make them, by his fiat alone, a cow-hide oligarchy, and the will of the ten millions of the North, and the non-slaveholding white millions of the South, was paralyzed, and the slaveholding *ukase* henceforth was the government, and the title deeds to the blood-purchased institutions of our ancestors were not worth the space they occupied, or the paper and parchment on which they were written.

REVERSE THEORIES.

If we must always make war on what we profess, would to heaven, our political theories could be reversed, and that our abstractions were, universal inequality, and that man had the abstract right to enslave and imbrute his fellow-man, that superior brute force was the great rule of right, and that the strong might do what they pleased to the weak.

DEMOCRATS SUCCUMB TO SOUTHERN THREATS.

In ten thousand ways, for the last ten years, the Northern democracy, until this winter, bowed, with the submissiveness of the scourged slave, at the crack of the whip, to the every command of the haughty slaveholder, with the everlasting threat in their mouths: "flinch in stabbing liberty here, or liberty there; or the executioner, with his basket of sawdust, shall move before you, and when you look again you shall behold the headless trunk of Martin, the supple." Will not such fearful menaces be the best apology the Democratic party can offer to the impartial historian, when the record of man's accountability to man shall be unrolled?

SLAVERY'S DECEIT.

If the slaveholders had not cheated their dupes, at last, it would have been an inconsistency of conduct which criticism itself has never been able to discover or fasten on their *peculiar* institutions.

FANCY STOCK.

Neither party pretended it came within the scope of their commissions, to reduce our American abstractions to practice. Though it is not denied, that either of the two great parties had an immense amount of fancy stock in abstractions, sufficient, if the capital was but paid in, to cleanse the terraqueous globe from all crime, wrong or impropriety, which have disgraced the annals of man.

SERVILITY OF THE DEMOCRATS.

We cannot hope to impress men who are so well satisfied with the objectless victory, lately obtained by the democratic party, as the editor of the "Democratic Review" is—who regard government as a job, made for the benefit of its administrators, who could conceive no higher object in making a canal, than to be the excavating contractors and its lock tenders, nor any higher motive for building a turnpike, than the chance of erecting the gate house, or being toll collector. It may be matter of regret, that men, who so poorly appreciate the end and object of a Republican government, should be intrusted with its control, still we may pity them, in their success, as time lost to their race, during their power; but as a party they have long been bent double in a shameless and craven posture, before the slave power, awaiting the shaking of the crumb cloth; charity therefore, compels us to admit, that the rigidity of their muscles will not bear an instantaneous perpendicularity of the body—from the horizontal to the rectilinear extension of the tendons, and therefore we fear that years must pass before they can *look the zenith in its face.* And you have bowed and cast your modest eyes to the ground, as your masters from these States spurned petitions for enslaved men; reviled free labor institutions, declared slavery the chief corner stone of a Republic, and permitted their twenty-three slave counted three-fifth representatives ever and anon to pull your beards, and threaten the dissolution of the Union, and you said "sweet masters, oh! do not," and trembled.

Has not the Democratic party, by the command of their masters, for twelve years gone by, until the repeal of the 25th Rule—at all times and on all occasions, stood in the centre of the path, with a drawn sword, facing and obstructing every movement of humanity, for the amelioration of the free colored man, the emancipation of the slave, or the rescue of free labor institutions, from the indignities of slaveholders?

The Liberty party go for the Constitution unchanged, as the great palladium of human liberty. We go for the entire Union, slavery *in*, or slavery *out*, Texas *in* or Texas *out ;* we will never give up one inch of the soil of our stupendous republic, to unmanly compromise, but will contend at the ballot box, with rendered reasons in our votes, and arguments in our mouths, made of justice and of truth, to-day, tomorrow and to our lives' ends; and leave the bequest to our children, to purify the pilgrim land of the New World from slavery and make this land the theatre for accomplishing the desire of nations, by raising man through justice and knowledge to the summit level of man's glorious capabilities. Mr. Reviewer, is this madness which alarms, injustice that startles, innovation that terrifies, or sacrilege which profanes, in the organization of a party whose elements are justice to all, mercy to all, protection to all, education for all, wages for all, toleration to all; none so strong as to be above the law, none so weak as to fall below its succor. Just and equal law shall be eyes to the blind, ears to the deaf, feet to the lame, its atmosphere shall brace the strong man in his journey and be respired by the infant in its cradle, and vindicate its supremacy over the assassin's knife, assert its majesty over the madness of the mob, and hear the lowest note of insulted humanity.

ABSTRACT ABOLITION.

But the Democratic reviewer says, the Liberty party has committed great mistakes, and says " he has no reference to the general question pro or con, of the Abolition of slavery," he says " *Abolition* and *Abolitionism* are two wholly distinct things," and that many look with favor on the former who are firmly opposed to the latter.

He says, we ought to hate slavery and love the slaveholder ; and that this is the great and capital mistake of the Liberty party. He understands Abolition—hatred of slavery, in the abstract—to be one thing, while *Abolitionism* is a sincere opposition to slavery and its supporters, taking active means for its overthrow, and a very different thing. This latter sort shocks our Democratic reviewer. This distinction is not so original, as to entitle him to a *patent* for its discovery. But as here lies the great mistake of these "one idea" men, it may be well to fasten our attention to it. The reviewer's proposition, in Democratic English is this, abstract Abolition is a hatred of abstract slavery, without attempting immediately, or remotely, to give liberty to a single slave ; that is prime Abolition, in his opinion, such as will pass current, with the reviewer, and even the slaveholders themselves. He assures us, many slaveholders entertain great respect for Abolition of this type, and therefore the reviewer seems to admit that this kind or sort must be correct. But *Abolitionism*, which forms associations, applies hard arguments, strong reasons, for immediate emancipation, and uses the ballot-box, and all constitutional power, to make itself felt for the overthrow of this terrible sin, this is outright fanaticism and all wrong. The reviewer's Abolition is to *think right* but do *nothing.* To illustrate his position, it is like this : My innocent friend has unjustly been torn from me, and immured in a dungeon, and the reviewer's doctrine is, I may *think* my friend was unjustly imprisoned and ought to be out ; but says one, " why do you not apply for a writ of *Habeas Corpus* and have your friend brought up before the judge, and discharged ?" But I reply, " how dare you give me such mad and fanatical advice ? You talk like a modern Abolitionist. Do you not know, sir, that there is the breadth of the earth's diameter between *believing* my friend is wrongfully imprisoned, and the *taking the first step* for his deliverance? Sir, you are *demented!* I will not take one measure for his discharge, he may lie and rot there, *and the ants may carry his mortal remains through the keyhole of his dungeon* before I move in the matter. I am as much opposed to his being in the dungeon as any man alive, and there my duty ends." Abolitionists not having the faculty to love slaveholders and *hate* slavery, the reviewer says, is our great mistake. A man has a daughter kidnapped and enslaved in a brick yard, she is compelled by the power of the lash, amidst tears and blood, to make brick. A neighbor hears the father of the poor captive calling the enslaver of his child a robber, a thief, a fiend, an incarnate devil. "Hush!" says the neighbor to the father, " you may curse the *enslaving* of your child as an *abstraction,* but you must entertain nothing but love and respect for her enslaver ; he, the enslaver of your child, is an hospitable, chivalrous fellow, generous as a prince in his house, keeps the best pack of hounds, the finest stud of blood and racehorses, of any man in the country ; and just please to remember, there are forty fathers and mothers whose sons and daughters are toiling with your daughter, in the same brick yard, whose children he took and carried off with your daughter; and, again, it is the peculiar institution and the peculiar. mode of making brick adopted by this gentleman." Says the neighbor, " condemn sin and not the sinner, slavery but not the slaveholder."   " Ah !" says the agonized father, " was there ever sin without a sinner, or slavery without a slaveholder ?"   If our Democratic reviewer's ideas of moral responsibility are right, the whole world is wrong; he virtually says, " Hang the murder, and let the murderer most affectionately go free; most lovingly discharge the horse-thief, and send grand larceny to the State prison; set free with a kiss the midnight burglar, and send his indictment for burglary to the penitentiary; the house-burner we should embrace with great endearments, but stretch his arson on the gibbet."   If this is so, society has made a grand mistake, in erecting penitentiaries, jails, dungeons and castles, where the criminals they confine should have never been, but rather should have been cheered by loving smiles, have moved as the *élite* of the grand and fashionable world—the true *beau monde* of high-minded eccentricities.   Then let all the abstract crimes of this world of ours be forever hung, burnt, cropped, whipped and imprisoned in some *lady's thimble*, which would hold it all (*with rooms to let*), and let this thimble stand on some Jesuit's table, warning the generations of men, as they come and go, that the true road to the love and affections of mankind is in the commission of the highest crimes, and that the everlasting writhings of these unpardoned abstractions of criminality, *in the thimble*, stand as in bold relief to vindicate the justice of this world in condemning crimes, and loving criminals.

RE-CESSION OF THE 10 MILES SQUARE.

After expressing great distress, on the part of the Reviewer, at Mr. Calhoun's having nationalized slavery and stripped it of all locality, as an institution, he fears a tremendous eruption of the Northern Abolitionists, into the houses of Congress, by petitions to abolish slavery in the Dictrict and the internal slave trade, at the next session of Congress, and to get rid of such fearful injuries to the Democratic party, and the liberties of this nation, he comes out with his *grand Panacea*, to arrest our Vandal career, that is, by ceding back the ten miles square to the States of Virginia and Maryland, and thus preserve the unspeakable blessings of slavery, and the slave trade, as State institutions, which can no longer be defended as national ones. This is all the great Democratic party, in the hours of its transports at its success, can undertake to do, for the cause of human liberty, and the elevation of the masses in the new world! The world is likely thereby, to be involved in a debt of gratitude, so overwhelming in amount, that insolvency will be the only mode of meeting the interest, and repudiation of discharging the principal.

THE PROSPECTS OF LIBERTY. 1846.

Some very judicious and prudent liberty-men, hope and believe that the coming winter will open a new drama flattering in character, auspicious with new-born hopes, in revealing to us large accessions to the army of liberty, recruited from the ranks of the thinking and considerate, who will forever forswear all allegiance to that baleful and mysterious power, exercised by the slaveholders from the foundations of the Republic, to uphold Southern slavery and destroy Northern freedom. This hope is borne up in the arms of the Wilmot Proviso, by which men could manifest the exact amount of abhorrence each one entertained against slavery, in the most abstract sense of language, without stopping to consider the effect of the Constitution of the Union, State legislation or implied or express compromises.

Such an hour and such a day it was believed had come, when the timid might safely be brave, the weak become strong, when casuistry would lie speechless before frankness, and double dealing would be superseded by simplicity, and truth would walk over the field without an antagonist, while the powers of inhumanity would be tongue-tied from inability to reply to these great aphorisms, that a man is a man the world over, and while innocent has always a better right to his own body than any other person within the limits of the universe. It would seem that the noble proviso of Wilmot must bring the mind of man to stand in front of the full blaze of the light of Nature and there behold man as he comes from his Creator, before he is ever injured by cruelty or appropriated by avarice. No legislative conscience-plasters are here spread over the question, to impair the natural sensibilities of the human mind.

. THE LAWS · MADE THE SCAPE-GOAT.

All legislation by which one man's liberty is taken from him and given to another, as a matter of advantage, is nothing but an attempt of the body politic to take the responsibility of the sin, which it is supposed could not be borne by the slaveholder, as an individual. Sad would have been the condition of the slaveholder, had he not converted his private iniquity into a law, and the slaveholding community aggregated and yoked together the most horrible and frightful of individual wrongs and outrages ever put forth by man against man, and then breathed into those atrocities the breath of law and called them legal and peculiar institutions. Thus the bold ruffians who laid the foundations of slavery in blood, by force of the pistol, the rifle, the bloodhound and the chain, instead of making the personal might of their own bloody arms the only tenure by which their supremacy was proclaimed over their man, came together in legislative assemblies, and asked the State to become their champion and wear their fearful honors, and under the idea of organic sin, to become the scape-goat to bear into the wilderness transgressions too heavy for men, as individuals, to bear. Thus when conscience cried against the crime, when the stones of the street unlocked their marble jaws and cried "shame" and "murder," the individual might point to the statute book and say, "*there* is the sinner; I am holy; a law-honoring man.   Let the wrath of the Eternal, and of all good men, be poured out on the session laws of South Carolina, but never, oh! never let them impute wrong to those who call in the aid of those statute laws."

Let this logic prevail, and the wicked men of a State may repeal every law of Heaven, and set the Eternal at defiance, and at the day of judgment plead in bar of God's law the session laws of South Carolina.   And if the plea is good for this world, as an organic sin-plea, it will be a perfect bar to accountability in the next.   For what is right and available in the eye of moral justice in this transitory world, will be so when the sun and moon shall set to rise no more. Yes, when the judgment day shall have come and gone.   Yes, and forever.   That which was right here, will never be wrong in the revolving circles of eternity. *Right* is a straight line running through time and eternity.   Man can never crook it. It is a line surveyed by the Almighty.

THE END.

REFERENCE TO PRINCIPAL TOPICS.

G.

H.

I.

L.

M.

N.

T.

U.

V.

W.

THE
IMPENDING CRISIS

OF

THE SOUTH:

HOW TO MEET IT.

BY H. R. HELPER,

OF NORTH CAROLINA.

A handsome 12mo. volume of 420 pages.   Price $1 00.

From Hon. William H. Seward.

"I have read 'The Impending Crisis of the South' with deep attention.   It seems to me a work of great merit, rich, yet accurate, in statistical information, and logical in analysis."

From Rev. Theodore Parker.

"It is an admirable work.   No man has hitherto made so complete a collection of the facts, and none put them in such 'magnificently stern array.'"

From Hon. Cassius M. Clay.

"It is just such a work as is needed in the present array of political antagonisms. The statistics are compact, lucid, and logically presented.   The tone of the author is manly, outspoken, and patriotic.   I regard it as the best compend of all the arguments against this our country's greatest woe, *Slavery*, yet published.   No intelligent citizen should fail to place it in his library.   The bookcraft of the work is of very fine style, and creditable to the publishers.

From Hon. Joshua R. Giddings, of Ohio.

"It is a manual for the times, calculated to meet the popular demand for informa tion upon the great question of the age."

Extracts from a review of 8 columns in the New York Tribune.

"Fortunate, indeed, are the non-slaveholding whites, that they have found such a spokesman ; one who utters no stammering, hesitating, nor uncertain sound, who possesses a perfect mastery of his mother tongue, who speaks as well from a long study and full knowledge of his subject as from profound convictions, and in whose vocabulary the words fear and doubt seem to have no place."

Extracts from the New York Evening Post.

"The author has collected in a volume of some four hundred pages, the most com pact and irresistible array of facts and arguments, to prove the impolicy of Slavery that we have encountered.

From the Jeffersonian (Ohio) Democrat.

"It is the greatest Anti-Slavery work ever issued from the American press."

Sixteen large editions of this masterly work have been sold.

We want competent Agents in every part of the country to engage at once in selling this work, to whom a liberal discount will be given.

Single copies in cloth, sent to any address post paid, on receipt of $ 1. Cheap edition, paper covers, 50 cents.

Address,
A. B. BURDICK,

New York